OPERA BIOGRAPHY SERIES, No. 10

Series Editors
Andrew Farkas
William R. Moran

I feel certain that there was a Golden Age of Singing, for I lived it.

—Frieda Hempel (1885–1955)

My Golden Age of Singing

by

FRIEDA HEMPEL

ANNOTATED BY

William R. Moran

WITH A PROLOGUE AND EPILOGUE BY

Elizabeth Johnston

AMADEUS PRESS
Reinhard G. Pauly, General Editor
Portland, Oregon

For Elizabeth Johnston
in appreciation of her courage and perseverance.
As she said, "I did know greatness when I encountered it
and took hold of the light it cast, come what may."

An autobiography in German by Frieda Hempel entitled *Mein Leben dem Gesang* was published in 1955 by Argon Verlag, GmbH, in Berlin. It was dedicated to Mr. and Mrs. George T. Keating. The present volume was prepared by Mme Hempel and Ms. Johnston in English.

Printed in Hong Kong

Library of Congress Cataloging-in-Publication Data

Hempel, Frieda, 1885–1955.
My golden age of singing / by Frieda Hempel; annotated by William R. Moran;
with a prologue and epilogue by Elizabeth Johnston.
p.   cm.—(Opera biography series; no. 10)
Includes bibliographical references (p.   ) and index.
ISBN 1-57467-036-0
1. Hempel, Frieda, 1885–1955. 2. Singers—Biography. I. Moran, William R.
II. Johnston, Elizabeth, 1913–   . III. Title. IV. Series.
ML420.H367A3   1998
782.1'092—dc21
[B]   97-35976
CIP
MN

AMADEUS PRESS
133 S.W. Second Avenue, Suite 450
Portland, Oregon 97204 U.S.A.

Contents

5

Foreword and Acknowledgments

by William R. Moran

Frieda Hempel's name rightfully belongs on any list of the most important and distinguished opera and concert artists whose public careers encompassed the first fifty years of the twentieth century. Attempting to establish artificial categories is always dangerous and subject to legitimate exceptions, but here our purpose is to introduce Frieda Hempel to the reader and define the context of a career to be examined in some detail. Artists emerging at the opening of this century had formidable competition from a previous generation who had created enviable artistic standards, many of whom remained before the public even when the ends of their careers were in sight. By 1900, Emma Albani, Lilli Lehmann, and Adelina Patti may have been looked upon as relics of the past, but many others, including Calvé, Eames, Melba, Nordica, and Sembrich, were very much in evidence on the operatic stage and concert platform for years, reminding audiences of their past and even present triumphs and maintaining high standards to which a new generation would be compared. Others who made their debuts late in the nineteenth century still had long careers before them, including Selma Kurz, Emmy Destinn, Louise Homer, Johanna Gadski, and among the men, Marcel Journet, Pasquale Amato, Giuseppe de Luca, Leo Slezak, and Enrico Caruso, to mention only a few.

But the turn of the century served as a threshold in several respects. Hempel's contemporaries were to be Farrar, Galli-Curci, Alda, Bori, Garden, Ivogün, Jeritza, Raisa, Matzenauer, Easton, Muzio, Onegin, and a little later, Rethberg, Ponselle, Flagstad, and others whose careers, like that of Frieda Hempel, would be profoundly shaped and modified by the First World War.

The new century brought another historically most important event: the perfection of the phonograph, which musicians and the public alike began to take seriously by about 1902. Hempel, her contemporaries, and those to follow could have their *entire* public careers documented by recordings. Hempel first stepped before the recording horn in Berlin in August 1906, while her last issued recordings were made from radio broadcasts of 1943. Geraldine Farrar made her debut in Berlin in 1901, her first recordings were made there in 1904, and she can be heard on private recordings made in 1942. These recording careers often included periodic remakes of popular numbers, sometimes because of the continuing advances in recording techniques, and we can often see the artistic growth of the singer as renewed study or exposure to different associates or conductors prompted reinterpretation. Such growth is evident in Hempel's recordings. Of course, we are immensely fortunate that the perfected phonograph captured at least approximations of a great many important voices of the previous generation, even if these singers were persuaded to record in years that were perhaps past those considered "prime." We cannot hear the voices of a Schumann-Heink, Nordica, Melba, Eames, Sembrich, Calvé, or Tamagno as they were at the start of their careers, but we have some idea how they sounded in their maturity, and can learn much about their vocal quality, musicianship, artistry, and singing style and techniques. Today most of these voices are instantly recognizable from their recorded legacy, even if their sound is preserved by primitive technology. How much better to have this, at least, than never to have any direct impression of voices, the sad truth about the famous singers of the pre-phonograph era.

Career in Brief

Born in Leipzig in 1885, Hempel made her operatic debut at the Berlin Royal Opera House in 1905 and later signed a five-year contract there. She was heard at Covent Garden in 1907 and made her Metropolitan Opera debut late in 1912, where she remained until 1919, singing 198 performances in eighteen roles. She created the Feldmarschallin in *Rosenkavalier* for Berlin in 1911 and at the Metropolitan in 1913. In New York she was acclaimed for her coloratura and lyric singing in Mozart roles, and was hailed as a successor to Marcella Sembrich in early Italian and Verdi roles. After leaving the Metropolitan in 1919, Hempel sang in a few operatic performances with the touring Chicago company, and appeared in occasional guest operatic performances in Europe, but she spent most of her time in extensive concert tours. In October 1920 she appeared in a Jenny Lind Centennial concert, complete with period costumes and props. This novelty proved such a success that she repeated variations of it in the United States and

Great Britain for years. During the 1930s and 1940s she made occasional radio broadcasts, and sang on the average about one New York concert each year until her last in November 1951. She died in Berlin on 7 October 1955.

The Annotated Memoir

In the introduction to a serious biographical memoir, famed theoretical physicist Freeman Dyson admitted, "I am well aware that memory is unreliable. It not only selects and rearranges the facts of our lives, but also embroiders and invents."[1] Mark Twain wrote, "An autobiography is the truest of all books, for while it inevitably consists mainly of extinctions of the truth, shirkings of the truth, partial revealments of the truth, with hardly an instance of plain straight truth, the remorseless truth *is* there, between the lines."[2] An author, by labeling a work *autobiography*, gives notice to the reader that what follows is not an unbiased recital of facts assembled by a computer, but a human account of those selected parts of a life by which the author wishes posterity to remember him or her. This is an author's privilege, which should be respected by any editor. If the author is a world-famous statesman or a giant of industry whose lifetime pronouncements and decisions affected the lives of many and perhaps the course of civilization, researchers will feel the necessity to supplement an autobiographical account with the viewpoints of less-biased observers for the benefit of the historical record, and systematic and investigative biographies will follow.

In the case of Frieda Hempel, this book may be the most detailed study we will ever have. For various reasons, Mme Hempel has given us access to a rather selected segment of her personal life. More than forty years after her death, some of these reasons no longer exist. During her active public career, she was the subject of much comment in the general as well as musical press, so that many facts about her life which she chose to omit in her personal account have been a matter of public record for years. If this book is destined to be the principal permanent record of this distinguished artist's career, it seems reasonable at least to sketch in some of the blanks in the story, to bridge the gaps for the general reader. In so doing, I have attempted to be circumspect in my approach and not to dwell on minute details. To tamper as little as possible with Mme Hempel's own words, I have appended occasional explanatory notes to her text. In addition, supplementary material has been gathered as a Postscript at the end of the volume.

An informal and abbreviated chronology compiled from press reports provides additional critical reviews and news items of interest so that excerpts which Mme Hempel quotes from her scrapbooks in bits and pieces, often with minimal if any attribution, can be read in their respective settings. A second section addresses a sampling of legal entanglements in which Mme Hempel seemed continually to be engaged. Particular attention is paid to one agreement entered into in 1925 which profoundly affected her private life and public career to the end of her days. The so-called Heckscher Affair was covered extensively by newspapers in New York and elsewhere during the 1930s and 1940s, and was the delight of those who had to provide copy for the Sunday supplements and the tabloid press of the day. Research has revealed the reason Mme Hempel could not discuss this matter even if she had wished to do so: her death removed this restriction. A third section deals in general terms with Hempel's long association with George T. Keating, a name well known to a generation of book and record collectors. The only mention of his name in the German edition of her book is in its Dedication. Even today, the editor's research efforts appeared distressing to some living persons, so this account intentionally omits many names and dates. The volume concludes with a listing of Frieda Hempel's operatic repertoire and a discography and review of her lifetime activities in the recording studios.

Acknowledgments

That this book has come to light reflects the courage, devotion, and patience of Ms. Elizabeth Johnston. Amadeus Press joins me in thanking her for bringing Frieda Hempel's original manuscript to us, for sharing her own memories, for lending photographs and other valued possessions, and for bravely encouraging our research.

We thank the Historic Singers Trust and Professor S. Henig, whose dedication to opera scholarship helped to make this book possible. Professor Henig recommended Amadeus Press to Ms. Johnston.

Robert Tuggle, director of the Metropolitan Opera Archives, generously supported this effort. The Archives' magnificent collection of Frieda Hempel photographs comprises a major part of the illustrations herein. We are also grateful for the correspondence between Gatti-Casazza and Hempel, and especially for an exhaustive collection of Hempel's press coverage compiled by the great Hempel fan Charles Stewart and given to the Archives by Vincent Spinelli. This collection served as the starting point for the chronology at the close of the present volume. The contributions of Mr. Tuggle and of the Metropolitan Opera Archives were critical to the creation of this annotated memoir.

Andrew Farkas, director of the University of North Florida libraries and my fellow opera biography series editor, reviewed drafts of the manuscript, located elusive references, lent photographs and programs, and provided unfailingly genial encouragement. Kathleen F. Cohen, assistant director at the University of North Florida Library, discovered the 1947 Prentice-Hall tax report, which proved most important.

James B. McPherson of Rexdale, Ontario, kept an eye open for references to Hempel's activities. His valuable contributions are also acknowledged in the discography.

Illustrations have been generously lent by other collectors as well, including Paul Jackson, Kenneth Lane, and Vivian Liff. Michael Aspinall's and Michael Henstock's encouragement and assistance are also gratefully acknowledged.

The late George T. Keating deserves appreciation here for his extensive correspondence with me over the years, and I would thank the members of his family as well. Research assistance has also been provided by Stanford University Libraries (Stanford Memorial Library of Music and Stanford Archive of Recorded Sound) and by Yale University Library. I want to thank the Pasadena Public Library as well.

Finally I thank Eve Goodman for her persistence in following up seemingly minor details and for her acute observations and questions, each directed to achieving clarity in an accurate and scholarly text. Thanks also to Karen Kirtley for her vision during the early stages of this endeavor, and Reinhard Pauly for his continued assistance.

Prologue

by Elizabeth Johnston

In 1951 I attended Frieda Hempel's last New York recital and then studied with her, soon becoming her secretary and ultimately her devoted companion. I accompanied her to Berlin in August 1955 and remained with her until her death in October of that year, a journey that I will recount in the closing pages of her story. For now I would remember her, and tell today's readers how her original autobiography has come to be published at last.

Frieda Hempel was always, as she says, "essentially a happy person." She writes, "My life was singularly free from illness, and severe trials and heartaches which have burdened me have not broken me in spirit nor in health." For this she thanks her religious convictions and her art. "Great music beautifully sung bears a message from heaven. Singing heals the spirit and lightens the heart." These beliefs always guided her and were in a deep sense her credo.

She tells us how fully she lived the present. "I am reminded that I am one of the very few singers living today whose career was at its height during the first years of this century. Time has passed so quickly and life has always been a very present thing to me, something so immediate that all yesterday is gone. Only yesterday I was singing with Caruso and Amato and Emmy Destinn. It seems so long ago!" Here she reveals the secret of her dynamic energy: her complete and intensive concentration on the task at hand. Only in this way could she master the many challenges of the opera stage and the concert hall, where the demands of the present are definitive.

Opera lovers will enjoy Frieda's account of her operatic appearances and delight in the stories of her friendships with famous colleagues in

Europe and America. Concertgoers will especially enjoy her vivid recounting of her performances as Jenny Lind. Her moving portrayal of her dog, Brownie, reveals even more of her love of life.

Frieda had great natural beauty. She was small of stature, with an exquisite figure, delicate features, famous "tiny" feet, and beautiful blond, wavy hair. Concert and opera reviews confirm this aspect of her captivating personality. Frieda comments that concert audiences seemed at times to be more interested in the "creation" she was wearing than in her singing. She dared to wear the latest Parisian styles, and in 1924 was the first stage celebrity to bob her hair, thus setting off a craze which no doubt dismayed many a husband, including her own. She was memorable in every way. As Peter Reed wrote in the August 1955 issue of *The Record Collector* dedicated to Frieda, "she was what a true singer should be, the true vocal messenger of the poet and the musician."

An autobiography by Frieda Hempel was published in German by the Berlin firm of Argon Verlag under the title *Mein Leben dem Gesang* in 1955. Frieda had signed a contract with Argon during her trip to Berlin in 1953, and when she returned to New York, she asked me to help her prepare the manuscript for German readers.

In June of 1952, Frieda had lost both her beloved Brownie and her longtime secretary, Miss Lilli, who had worked with Frieda every weekday. I had visited Frieda's apartment beginning in 1951 but had never known what she and Miss Lilli were doing in Lilli's office. I now realize that Frieda was dictating a manuscript. After Brownie's death, with new-found freedom from the care she had devoted to him, she again turned her thoughts toward her autobiography. She must have felt that she was more likely to find a publisher in Germany than in America, and in the summer of 1952 she flew to Berlin to ascertain Argon Verlag's interest. Just before her trip Miss Lilli had seriously injured herself in a fall, and Frieda sorely missed her daily presence. It was at this time that Frieda asked me to take over Miss Lilli's office responsibilities.

Neither Frieda nor Mr. George Keating, who paid for her trips during 1952 and 1953, told me why she was going to Berlin. I assumed that she was undergoing beauty treatments, but during her 1952 visit she could have shown her original manuscript to Argon. She returned to Berlin in the summer of 1953, having heard that Argon was interested and wanted to discuss translating and publishing her autobiography. In addition, they wanted Frieda to undertake a lecture tour under their auspices, using the book, her records, and a film as the focus. A contract was concluded.

When Frieda came back to New York in late 1953, she must have decided to write a new version geared to German readers. She dictated the text to me in English, chapter by chapter. I typed and corrected each portion and sent it to Dr. Fritz Engert, the translator, who returned the chapters promptly for Frieda's approval. She seldom suggested changes and was over-joyed that Dr. Engert knew so much about earlier days in Berlin. He was not only a skilled translator but also an excellent writer and researcher. To our efforts he was able to add much information on German cultural and social life during the first two decades of the twentieth century.

Frieda seemed to remember everything about her youth, and I was amazed at her fabulous memory. I was also astonished by her ability to recall numerous animal stories and many details of Brownie's saga. She never spoke of an English manuscript that she had already completed. Yet Frieda must have had it with her somewhere in the apartment when we were work-ing together and obviously turned to it without my knowledge. We may never know why she wanted me to believe that we were preparing an origi-nal version of her life story—though generous and sensitive, she was also a very private, even secretive, person. Perhaps she felt that this approach would be more likely to meet Argon's specific requirements, or perhaps she just wanted us to keep busy.

We completed our work late in 1954 during a time that would become increasingly difficult for Frieda. In December 1954 her dear companion Rosa Seidl, who had been with her since 1907, had a severe stroke, and Frieda took her back to Germany to spend the rest of her days. In late May of 1955 Frieda experienced the next rude intrusion into the customary pat-tern of her life. She was stricken with cancer and entered Manhattan Hos-pital for treatment. She decided to rent her apartment, fully furnished, for one year, beginning 1 July.

My first task in this new situation was to find a suitable tenant. I adver-tised and selected an impressive young man from the entertainment world who came highly recommended. I sent him to Frieda, who was satisfied and gave him the contract. I then set about the large task of getting Frieda's apartment ready to rent. The huge hall closet had always been locked, but now I had the key so that I could fill it with Frieda's things. There I placed the most exquisite linens, glassware, china, and silverware, as well as other valuable objects that had personal meaning for Frieda. The scrapbooks, reviews, numerous boxes of recordings, scores, letters, and special folders had already been stored there as objects of historical value.

One day as I was working among the boxes of records, what looked like a manuscript fell into my hands. I was so immersed in my task and under such pressure that I did not appreciate the long-term implication of this dis-covery. Since Frieda had never mentioned a manuscript to me, I looked at the title page and saw that it was Frieda's autobiography. The manuscript appeared to have been completed in 1952. Finding it was a shock, but I did not allow myself to get involved at the time.

Frieda was in the hospital, and my thoughts were constantly with her. I had taken a furnished room nearby so that I could be with her every day, along with her former husband, Will Kahn. We learned that she needed two operations, but she showed no fear or sadness. She remained cheerfully ready to accept her fate, still planning to fly to Berlin in August to share in the publication preparations for her autobiography in German. I never mentioned to Frieda that I had found her original manuscript, as I realized this would upset her, nor did she ask about it. Indeed it seemed far from her mind, knowing as she did that a German version would soon be on the market.

Frieda was dismissed from the hospital in early July. I had found her an apartment on Central Park West, just south of her own apartment, where she could feel at home for the summer, and in June had moved all my and Frieda's belongings there. Frieda had asked me to take a certain box of records and the film out of the closet and keep them with her personal belongings so that she could use them on her lecture tour in early August of 1955, but she did not mention the English manuscript.

Just before we left New York, I gave the manuscript to my dear friend Elaine Barbee for safekeeping. She had studied with Frieda in 1949 and 1950 and was thrilled to take care of it. She carefully carried it with her during all her professional changes of venue beginning in 1955, as singer, actress, and high-school teacher of instrumental music, moving from New York to Miami, back to New York, on to Long Island, to Hartford, Connecticut, and back to Miami.

Before Frieda died in Berlin on 7 October 1955, she named me her literary executor. I returned to New York early the next year, flying on to my home in Berkeley, then returned to Berlin in 1961 where I have lived ever since. Time passed, a difficult time—Berlin was being rebuilt; the public's memory of Frieda Hempel seemed to be fading. But fortunately we are now witnessing a resurgence of interest in the legendary singers: we want to hear their voices again and read their stories.

Over the years I attended performances of the noted countertenor Michael Aspinall, who is also a teacher, musicologist, and collector. At one point I told him that I had known Frieda Hempel well and had in safekeeping her original autobiography in English. He was extremely interested and spoke on my behalf to Professor Stanley Henig of Historic Masters, a British society of collectors of recorded vocal art.

I contacted Elaine Barbee in early 1990, and to my great relief and joy she still had the manuscript and mailed it to me immediately. I held it in my arms and kissed it when it arrived. I read Frieda's words, as fresh as the day she wrote them. She clearly had written the story with American and British readers in mind, and now her wish might be realized. I gradually checked the manuscript for structural coherence and arranged for Charlotte Schladitz to retype it, which she did beautifully. Professor Henig came to Berlin in 1991 to see the work in progress and suggested that we seek a publisher. He recommended Amadeus Press, which offers a series of books on the great singers.

The editors at Amadeus believed the manuscript a worthy discovery and over time were able to reassemble the larger picture of Frieda's life. From series editor and opera scholar William R. Moran came commentary and background, as well as the excellent discography, and Mr. Moran and Andrew Farkas reviewed the text in detail.

In this new, expanded volume, readers who may never have seen Frieda on the stage can enjoy the magnificent photographs, some from my collection and others from fond collectors in the United States and Great Britain. I wish to thank Professor Henig for his invaluable assistance, and Michael Aspinall for having smoothed the way for me in this important endeavor. I also thank Charlotte Schladitz of Berlin for her excellent work and Eddie Ruhl, who provided me with important information and contributed the handwritten Jenny Lind concert schedule. I would sincerely thank Elaine Barbee for having so faithfully guarded Frieda Hempel's original manuscript for thirty-five years. Finally I am exceedingly grateful to my dear friend Joan Beadling for her constant support and encouragement.

Although the German edition did not appear until two weeks after Frieda's death, she was at least able to hold its bright red dust jacket in her hands and surely realized then that the music world would soon enjoy the many wonderful moments in her exciting life. If she could have known that the original English manuscript would one day also appear in print, she would surely have been overjoyed and gratified.

My Golden Age of Singing

Preface

M *usic is a haven, a home for us all*—beyond time and hence beyond decades, beyond space and thus beyond localities into which fate thrusts us. It shares these attributes with all the fine arts, with science and research, and foremost with religion.

To have served music throughout my life and to have experienced the joy of giving music to thousands has been my great good fortune. Wherever I have found myself, whatever the situation confronting me, this home has never denied me spiritual sustenance and great comfort, never failed to give me contentment. To give testimony thereof is a prime purpose of this autobiography.

I enjoyed the great advantage of having launched my career as a singer during the Golden Age of Song and of arriving at the pinnacle of my chosen art at a very young age. My immediate predecessors were Patti, Melba, Tetrazzini, and Sembrich, whose great tradition I was able to carry forward. I sang with Caruso, and I sang under the batons of Toscanini, Blech, and Strauss, to mention only the greatest names.

Thus the obligation to prepare my autobiography became doubly pressing. There are few of us left who can report at first hand on the great era of the Royal Opera in Berlin and on the brilliant period of the Metropolitan. The almost forgotten past can come to life and, we hope, influence the future. Perhaps some of my experiences and suggestions will be of value to upcoming singers. For in spite of everything there are gifted young singers eager to learn, and music and song will always find young people to serve them.

I was already thinking about my autobiography when I learned from a young music lover that he was busy writing the story of my life. I realized that it was high time to really get busy on my own story of my life and career.

The tremendous work involved has proven fruitful: I am grateful for being able to shed light on the great epoch of music and song, and it has been a profound pleasure to relive everything. Many wonderful experiences have come to mind again, and I sincerely hope that my autobiography will also be a source of pleasure for my readers.

In the frequently difficult task of selecting and coordinating the extensive material involved, my dear friend and talented voice pupil Miss Eliza- · beth Johnston of Berkeley, California, assisted me with great intelligence and tireless effort. She has my enduring appreciation and gratitude for her dedicated assistance.

Frieda Hempel
Berlin 1955

Frieda wrote this preface in the hospital on 5 October 1955 at the request of her German translator, Dr. Engert. The translation into English has been provided by Elizabeth Johnston.

CHAPTER ONE

My Youth

And the days of my youth? Those happy days of dreaming were spent in my native town of Leipzig.

I had three sisters and two brothers. Mother had borne twelve children, but six had died in infancy. Emma was the oldest. She married very young in life and moved away from the family. Her marriage was a very unhappy one, but she never divorced her husband. In those days a German woman would rather suffer than break up a home. Helene, the next oldest, was tall, very beautiful, intelligent, and cheerful. We called her the general of the family, for her fine suggestions were always acted upon. My brother Emil was next. Then came Augusta. She, too, married early in life, but she died in childbirth when I was only twelve years old. Walter, the second son, three years older than I, was my constant companion. I was the last born of this great, happy family.

I was a Saxon child. I had long blond tresses, the reddest cheeks imaginable, an eternal smile, and greenish, wide-open eyes. My aunt was fond of saying, "Nothing ever escapes her eyes. Nothing ever escapes her ears!" All through life I have kept those eyes and ears open.

We lived in a rather spacious home on the fourth floor of a large apartment building. In those days traffic was not a problem, and we could play freely in the streets, scrambling out of the way of an occasional carriage. Often we would go near the banks of the river Pleisse, which was only a few minutes away. Here were great open spaces for us to explore.

I had poor health as a child, and so my parents enrolled me in a school outside the city. It was a beautiful half-hour walk from home, and I often took this walk four times a day. In this way I strengthened my body and filled my lungs with lots of fresh air. I passed the Gewandhaus, the Rathaus, and the Reichsgerichtsgebäude, and walked along the Stadtring, the old wall built centuries ago to protect the city.

The Gewandhaus, a very fine concert hall, always seemed like a monster to me when I passed with my schoolbooks under my arms, my hair flying, my bangs in my face, arms thin as matches, and legs even thinner. Never did I think that I would sing there some few years later with the famous Arthur Nikisch, that Gypsy, as they called him. He was a great friend of Elena Gerhardt in her youth. What a help it must have been to have such a genius at one's side! Surely she learned a great deal from him, for he was an extraordinary musician. When I later returned to Leipzig for that concert with Nikisch, the Gewandhaus had shrunk, and it seemed like any other building to me. But I walked around the building one morning before rehearsal and saw myself once more with schoolbooks under my arms and wonder in my face. Not too many years had slipped between us, but things had happened, so many things, so quickly!

We had two theaters in those days, Das Alte Theater and Das Neue Opernhaus. After school I would always detour past the opera house. A theater fascinated me, like magic, like a church, something I cannot even describe. It meant much more to me than the emperor's palace. I would walk around the opera house like Alice in Wonderland. I saw a fairy castle, and I saw dreamlike people gathered around the stage door, visiting or calling for their mail. For the artists, this was the place to be. They were gods and goddesses to me.

I had a special crush on a tall, blond coloratura named Miss Baumann. I had made the exciting discovery that she lived along my way, and I would follow her like a detective. In winter I would step in her footsteps in the snow, all the way to her house. This was enchantment; I might miss my meal, but I did not care. The theater was all I dreamed of, all I lived for, and she was part of it.

Even in those earliest days I could imitate and mimic people. I dearly loved to collect postcards of beautiful women and then to spend many hours trying to imitate what I thought would be their manner, their way of talking and moving about. I would mimic friends of the family, using red beets to paint my lips, making eyeglasses out of paper, and dressing up in whatever clothes I could find. Mother would even have special afternoon parties just to let me entertain her friends with imitations and singing, for of course I was always singing.

In winter, when the weather was bad, mother would give me money to buy a glass of milk at a tiny store near the school, and I would drink this milk and eat a sandwich she had given me for lunch. I would sit with my playmates and sing for them. I was rather popular, I think, for I was always full of play and sang prettily, as they said. I was not very good in school at first, and only later did I finish high in my class. In the first years of school I would rush home, throw down my coat and my books, and be off to play with my brothers. I was always climbing trees, sliding down hills with schoolbooks, and emulating my brothers in all their rough-and-tumble play. I believe that I had not yet acquired any vanity, for it was hard for me to understand that I was a girl and should not be stealing apples and cherries and romping about with those two active brothers.

And of course we were always playing with animals. We had white mice, rabbits, lizards, dogs, cats, and my special friend, the frog. He lived in a glasshouse, and he would tell me all about the weather and let me know in the nicest way whether I should take my lunch to school with me. For when he was up on his ladder, it meant sunshine, and when he came off the ladder, it meant rain! Mother had a pet cat whom she called Gretchen. One day Gretchen went out on the balcony to take a sun bath. The next thing we knew, she had fallen off, down four floors onto the street below. We all rushed down the stairs in great agony to pick up our poor little dead cat. When we opened the door, there was Gretchen, happily waiting to be let in. We never worried again about our cats.

Mother was a beautiful woman, with blue eyes, red cheeks, and white hair which made her all-the-more attractive. Her hair had turned white when she was thirty. She had a perfect disposition, and we all idolized her. She never scolded us and was so kind, no matter how many friends we brought home. Animals and pals she welcomed with equal kindness. She loved life, and she loved music and singing. She believed in God without going to church. Her faith was deep and sincere, and she inspired us to say our prayers every morning and every evening. Whenever there was a storm, and the thunder rang out and lightning crackled, she would say to us, "God is speaking. Listen to Him." And we would all sit still and listen. Even the progress of a meal was halted if He spoke. And to this day, I cannot do anything when it thunders. I am only aware of Him, as He says, "The one who sleeps, let sleep; the one who prays, let pray; the one who errs from my way, condemn." For this is what we learned as children. And what a simple, beautiful belief it was. I think that this is how God wants all children to believe.

We had all sung together since early childhood. Every afternoon, before turning on the lights, mother would gather us around her, and we would sing and hum sweet little tunes and listen to each other sing. How wonderful it was, especially to a child like me who loved music so much. If only mothers today would do this. It is a great heritage and tradition of European childhood; it familiarizes children early in life with song and with music. It is one of the greatest gifts a parent can bestow upon a child, this love of something beautiful, something upon which to fall back in time of sorrow and distress.

Father was a very fine woodcarver. He had a furniture store where he worked as cabinetmaker, but he had the temperament of an artist and could stand for hours in front of a beautiful piece of carved wood, caressing it as if it were a living thing. From him I received my feeling for form, and from mother came the joy of singing. Father was very quick-tempered, but mother always succeeded in calming him and smoothing things over, for she was a typical German *Hausfrau* and devoted her entire life to making father happy and keeping her big family in order. For while we were not exactly poor, from artistic woodcarving one cannot reap a fortune; it was quite a problem to feed and clothe us. But our parents were never discouraged. Mother would say, "When need is the greatest, God is the nearest." This simple, honest faith, this trust in God, helped them through all problems, and this is how we were raised.

Or should I say we raised ourselves? As I look back upon our happy, busy childhood days, I am convinced that nothing is more wonderful than a big family, especially a poor one. We wanted so many, many things that mother and father could not afford to buy for us, and so, what did we do? We became inventors, our minds and imagination were awakened; we became alert, observing, and resourceful. None of us was serious or heavy in character.

My aunt told me, in later years, that we Hempels had some Italian blood in our family. "Generations ago, our forebears were spice merchants," she said, "and they traveled around the country in wagons, selling spices." This story has always interested me. Our great love for music and for the theater must have come from them. I remember that when I was still a very small girl, my brothers and my sister Augusta and I joined a circus that came to town for a few days. Augusta rode a horse, my two brothers were Indians, and I was a kidnapped baby. My sister Helene had arranged for us to get into the troupe, and we all earned a little money for ourselves, which was exciting also. We went right on playing circus for weeks after the company had left Leipzig. It was probably my first public performance. I was brought in and tossed on a hay wagon and then covered up with hay. One day the man spilled water all over me, but I was already a little trouper, and I kept perfectly quiet there in the hay, soaked and shivering. Anyway, we had a happy time. Oh, what lovely days! None of us was interested in cards or games. We were always reciting, singing our heads off, or building miniature theaters. My brothers were very clever with their hands—this they had learned from father. Once they built a cardboard theater, replete with traps and scenery of every description. Here they loved to perform the Wolf's Glen scene from *Der Freischütz*. It was weird and ghostly, and I, the audience, was very, very frightened!

My smile, my constant, eternal smile, won me many friends. I recall one old lady who loved to chat with me. I passed her house on my way to and from school, and she often invited me in to visit. It was fun at first, but then of course it became a chore. But she was a wise woman, and so she asked me one day if I would thread needles for her for a small sum. Oh, then I could not go often enough, for when I had saved enough pennies, I would buy a ticket to the opera, high in the gallery but so close to the stage, I thought. When my brothers went with me, we would have a contest on the following day to see who could remember the most tunes.

I was already beginning to feel that somehow my mother had made one dreadful mistake when she singled out Emil as the special child. It had come about in this way. She was a woman of fantasy and imagination, and a friend had persuaded her to visit a fortuneteller, well-known in the city. This fortuneteller had told her that one of her children would become famous. Thinking it must surely be one of the boys, she suspected Emil, and he received all the special privileges that a good mother would bestow upon a child marked for future fame, privileges that would belong to me, as it turned out.

Among my best chums was the girl next door, whose father owned a fruit store. I would often call her over, and together we would sit in the courtyard, singing and harmonizing. Windows would open, heads would appear, and to a delighted, improvised audience we would give our concert. By and by my sister Helene began to realize that I had an irrepressible talent for music and for acting. She decided to do something about it, and one day when I came home, I found a piano in the living room, which she had paid for from her salary. I was to have piano lessons, to start with.

I went proudly to my first lesson, and I thought that the piano would sing for me. But when I began all the tiresome exercises I lost my first enthusiasm. There were many hours of diffident practice, until gradually I came to see how the piano could sing. Then I went to work and delighted my teacher with the sudden change in my playing. She often asked my parents to come and hear me, for I was developing a gift for phrasing and for interpretation, and she pointed out to them that my pianissimos and my crescendos were not written into the music.

Gradually I became her prize pupil, and I played in public at the age of ten. I can no longer remember the name of this teacher, but the last incident connected with her I shall never forget. I had gone for my lesson and did not find her in her rooms. I waited for some time, and finally went to the landlady to ask her whereabouts. The landlady was mystified, for she had not heard the teacher leave. We went back to the rooms, and she proceeded to throw open the several doors. As she opened the door to the closet, we both jumped! There was my teacher, standing upright, her back to us, and motionless as if dead! She was in a trance. Apparently she had overtaxed her strength, for in a state of semiconsciousness she had walked into this closet instead of going out the door. And there she stood. This was something I loved to perform for my friends.

"One, two, three, hurrah! One, two, three, hurrah!" Lora had come to live
with us. Helene had become engaged to a young doctor in the city, and on a
trip to Chile as ship's doctor, he had found Lora, a wonderful talking parrot.
Lora made herself at home immediately and took part in all the family scenes.
She could imitate many animals; strange bird calls, and sounds of dogs, cats,
frogs, and chickens filled the house. Her favorite line was, "One, two, three,
hurrah!" But she also made herself very useful. Mother had great trouble getting Walter out of bed in the morning. He was such a heavy sleeper that she
had to call him over and over again. Lora soon figured this out, and one
morning she took upon herself the task of waking Walter. "Walter! Walter!"
she screamed over and over again. Walter soon woke up, and every morning
after that it was Lora, and not mother, who called Walter.

Lora did not stay with us for long. Helene and the doctor were married,
and they moved to Berlin, taking Lora with them. Dr. Schaper soon established a fine practice, and then Helene invited me to live with them in Berlin. I had finished school and was now fourteen years old. It seemed wise to
have me busy at something, and of course I was delighted with the idea of
moving to the wonderful city of Berlin. Helene suggested that I become Dr.
Schaper's secretary and continue with my piano as well. This was agreeable
to all, and so off I went.

They had an elegant apartment on Königgrätzer Strasse. I had a lovely
room of my own, and I soon learned to help Dr. Schaper in his work. I
answered the mail, typed his letters, helped to mix medicines, and sometimes answered the door when the butler was out. I enjoyed this very much,
for I loved to greet his patients. He was a specialist in skin ailments, and
later became one of Berlin's foremost dermatologists.

My duties were not heavy, and after hours I was free to do as I pleased.
I would sit at the piano, memorizing and singing operatic bits and popular
tunes. I no longer cared so much for the piano; all I wanted to do was to sing
and be in the theater. Lora often sat on my shoulder, and she enjoyed these
concerts very much. But after a while these little evenings of music ceased to
satisfy me. I wanted to study voice, and encouraged by the obvious joy my
brother-in-law derived from my singing, I asked him if I could have singing
lessons. He refused, but a single refusal was not enough for me, and thereafter, every time he asked me to sing for him, I asked him again for singing
lessons. But he always said, "No, Friedel, that cannot be. You sing very well,
and I don't think you really need any lessons."

But I knew better and enlisted the aid of Lora. I taught her the words to
a popular tune, and when we were ready for our duet, I called my brother-
in-law in to hear us. Lora perched upon my shoulder as usual, but this time
she sang along with me. The words of the song went like this, "Ach Hedwig,
liebe Hedwig, was du verlangst, das geht nicht." (Hedwig, oh Hedwig, what
you ask of me, that cannot be.) Dr. Schaper was so entertained with this

mocking of his own words that he capitulated and agreed to do what he could for me.

The Stern Conservatory of Berlin was just a few blocks from our apartment, and Mr. Rothmühl, a close friend of Dr. Schaper, taught voice there, so we went to see him. He sent us to the director of the conservatory, Gustav Holländer, who then arranged for me to sing the following day for Frau Selma Nicklass-Kempner. I slept very little that night, and the following morning I was at the conservatory, carrying the music to my favorite arias and songs. Frau Kempner was delighted with my voice and accepted me at once. I signed a three-year contract which contained an option to change teachers if I were not satisfied with her at the end of the first year. My brother-in-law paid my tuition, and everything was arranged. I had only to wait for the beginning of the fall classes. Lora and I sang very happily together now, and I worked hard for my brother-in-law.

During the summer months my family moved to Berlin and rented a house in a suburb of Berlin called Wilmersdorf. I moved back home and commuted to my sister's every day to work. Helene had a lovely mezzo-soprano voice, and she took me with her to her singing lessons and to choir practice. I sang along just naturally, but I eagerly awaited the fall and my first singing lesson.

Inscribed in German: "My first concert gown worn at a student recital with Mischa Elman." PHOTO BY ALBERT MEYER. COURTESY METROPOLITAN OPERA ARCHIVES.

CHAPTER TWO

Student Years in Berlin

*F*rau Kempner, a woman of Jewish descent, was very tiny, hardly five feet tall. She was quite stout but light on her feet. She had grayish hair that was thinning, so she was more comfortable wearing a hairpiece across the front of her head. This I discovered very soon, for I attempted to impersonate her, but try as I might, my hair never looked like hers! She had an exceptionally large nose, and one could not have called her pretty. Often as I watched her cover her nose with the cup of her hand to show us where the focus of tone was, the hand seemed so small by comparison, but at other times I noticed only her eyes. Always beautifully groomed and enhanced with many jewels, she infused the classroom with an air of excitement. When she sang, tears came involuntarily to one's eyes. No other teacher could interpret Mozart as she did, with such finesse, such aristocratic taste, and such feeling.

The story of her life was as dramatic as she was. As a small child, an orphan, she would sit on the steps of the Stern Conservatory, listening to the singing that came through the windows. One day a lady stopped to ask her what she was doing. "Oh," she replied, "I'm listening. I can sing, too!" Now the lady said, "Come with me into the classroom; come and let me hear you." She sang for this woman, who immediately accepted her as a pupil and arranged for her adoption by a rich family. This lady who befriended her was none other than Marianne Brandt, the brilliant contralto,* and from her Frau Kempner learned what she was later to teach us.

---

*Marianne Brandt (Marie Bischof, 1842–1921) was among the great operatic figures of the last half of the nineteenth century. A pupil of Pauline Viardot-Garcia, she

Completing her studies at the conservatory, Frau Kempner went to Holland, where she became the idol of the country, singing there for ten years. Then she returned to Berlin, each day climbing the steps upon which her career had begun and teaching in the same classroom where Marianne Brandt had taught her.

I was well rested by the time summer was over, and mother had strengthened me with raw eggs, red wine, and often a thick sandwich between meals. I would work for my brother-in-law three days a week, and on Wednesdays and Saturdays would be free to spend all day at the conservatory. First-year students in voice received two lessons a week, with other optional classes in harmony, ear training, and similar subjects. Having already learned the fundamentals of music, I attended only the voice classes.

Each day Frau Kempner worked with from twenty to thirty pupils. Our classes began at ten o'clock in the morning and often lasted until late afternoon. No one was allowed to talk while she was teaching. We all sat quietly, listening to each lesson and awaiting our own time, for we never knew when our turn would come. By listening to the various corrections, we learned to distinguish between good and bad tones. What a marvelous idea, and what a help! Frau Kempner's main concept was "beauty of tone," no matter how loud or how soft. She was an excellent musician and had been a fine concert singer with exquisite taste and feeling. With her wonderful ear she knew when a tone was not placed precisely on pitch, and perfect intonation was demanded from all of us.

Seldom having time for a hot lunch, Frau Kempner would dismiss the class for a short while and content herself with a pick-me-up of caviar and champagne! This was extraordinary, I thought, and wonderful. Caviar and champagne were so expensive and so rich, but she really needed that energy-giving food, for she worked incessantly and with great concentration. She was very severe with us, and we were frightened to death when some student had not worked well at home and could not give Frau Kempner what she demanded. The pupil would be sent home without another word to learn her lesson before she returned.

Sustained tones and low scales were our daily work. For months we studied this way without ever singing a song. Most of the first year was devoted to voice placement. For hours I would practice: tone, tone, tone,

---

made her debut as Rachel in *La Juive* in 1867 and her Berlin debut as Azucena the following year, remaining with the Berlin company until 1882. She sang Fidelio at Covent Garden in 1873; at Bayreuth she created Waltraute in *Götterdämmerung* in 1876 and Kundry in 1882. She sang 189 performances in twenty-one roles at the Metropolitan during four seasons (1884–88). She was the first to sing Brangäne in Berlin, London, and New York. She retired from opera in 1890 and taught for many years in Vienna. She can be heard on three recordings made in 1905. *Ed.*

spinning the breath from *pianissimo* to *forte* and back again. When one can do this properly, the battle is won. Everything else is easy after this is achieved.

Yes, scales, hundreds of scales, in one key, in another key, on one vowel, on another vowel, *forte*, *piano*, crescendo—so we worked. Little pieces of paper lying around my room at home would have confused many people. For upon these slips of paper were marked, in a sort of code language, the number of scales, the vowel combinations, the rhythmic patterns, and the dynamic exercises practiced each day. In fact, I did my work so faithfully that one day my neighbor wrote on our front door, above the door bell, "You sing beautifully, but you are merciless!"

What did I care? I wanted to become a great singer, and so I went right on marking up pieces of paper and singing my scales. I usually practiced in the evening after dinner. During the day I worked for Dr. Schaper, returning home for the main noon meal and then commuting back to his offices for the afternoon. Father and my two brothers also came home to be with us, for in Europe it is customary for the family to dine together at noon, the main meal of the day. My brothers had gone into the business of orthotics, and they later became well-known for their artificial hands, noses, and legs. After they went to the front during the First World War, Emil told me that the Russian prisoners were afraid of anesthesia and asked only for a cigarette when amputation was necessary. Father had retired from business and had time now to carve many lovely delicate figures of wood. In the evenings he would read a newspaper and smoke his cigar, mother would sew, I would be in the next room practicing, and my brothers would go out to their club meetings or remain at home reading. They would often tease me, good naturedly, of course, singing my exercises with me, imitating my sounds, or calling out to me, "Ah, Frieda, you'll never make it!" Mother would soon hush them up. Movies, radio, television—these had not been invented so could not distract us. We had time to feel, to think, to concentrate upon simple things, and we found friendship and trust in each other. We shared family expenses, we shared joys and troubles, and we felt family pride. Whenever father would go out in the evening to play skat, the king of games, we would remind him to play in a manner worthy of his ancestor, a Mr. Hempel, who invented the game.

And so my days were filled with work as a secretary, voice practice, and study. To accomplish something was my main idea. I even became a little cocky and thought that I should leave my teacher at the end of the first year because my voice was not big enough to suit me. But during the summer months, another pupil and I worked together.

I would ask her, "How do you feel that tone? What do you do?" Then she would ask the same question of me. We worked with great concentration, and our voices changed considerably. She had a beautiful contralto voice and was extremely musical, and so we were of great help to each other. When we started the second year of classes, I astounded everybody with my voice. It was now as big and as lyric as any voice around. And how foolish I had been to think of leaving Frau Kempner. Obviously I had not quite understood something that she wanted from me, and during the summer months I had worked the problem out. Now I could give her exactly what she wished for, and we were both happy.

Frau Kempner began to train me in the role of Queen of the Night, in Mozart's *The Magic Flute*. How right she was to keep a young voice light and flexible. She stopped me from singing heavy tones and so preserved my natural coloratura timbre and flexibility. Staccatos, trills, and high tones came very naturally to me. But as a dramatic coloratura, I had a great deal of power as well.

It is the easiest thing to train a lyric singer, but you have to know a great deal about voice placement and bel canto singing to train a real coloratura, of which there are so very, very few. The coloratura will always be the queen of song on the stage and in the concert hall, for here is the most difficult study. One day during a performance of *Les Huguenots* in Berlin, Emmy Destinn and I stood together in the wings after the end of the second act. I had just been singing the difficult role of Queen Marguerite. "Oh, Hempelchen," she said, "I do hope that I never come back to this world as a coloratura. It means just too much hard, hard work!" She knew—that great and wonderful artist—she knew how one must always be on guard, working to keep the voice flexible and light.

I made many friends at the conservatory, and often on Sunday afternoons I would invite them to my sister's country home near Berlin. There we would go, singing, acting, playing, and eating cookies, cakes, and fruit. The boys were already very much taken with me, and I was never without a boyfriend. Joseph Plaut, especially, became my pal because he knew so many funny stories and told all his jokes in a dialect. He made me laugh to tears, and to this day I still love to laugh with him. I saw him again in Bad Tölz in 1952, and we laughed together until two in the morning. It all seemed like yesterday. He had become a famous comedian in Germany, always telling his wonderful jokes in dialect.

While studying, I kept my eyes and ears open, and when I heard that a Mr. Conried from America, from the Metropolitan Opera, was looking for singers, I decided that he should hear me. Without telling anybody where I was going, I rode on the trolley car to where Mr. Conried was auditioning singers. I went directly to him and asked if I might sing for him right then and there. He consented, and I sang the two arias from *The Magic Flute* in the original key with additional flourishes and high notes added, of course.

He then jumped up from his chair and said, "Marvelous! I want you for America. Of course, you are a lyric soprano." The size of my voice had surprised him, for it was a true dramatic coloratura, both in color and in power, and not the usual coloratura, light and without body. Well! Now I was to be a singer in America! I hurried back to Frau Kempner, with the greatest anticipation. I knew that she would be very pleased and proud of me. But what a reception I got! She said nothing but took me straight to Gustav Holländer, the director of the conservatory, and I was told, "You must finish your studies. You are not yet ready to go to America. You might earn fifty dollars a week now, but that is not for you. You shall one day earn fifteen hundred dollars a night, if you stay and really learn to sing. Now, go back to your class." But how right they were! And how grateful I am to them to this day for their honest and sound advice. What would our managers of today have said? "Sure, go ahead, fine. I'll draw up a contract." Where would I have been today, if I had not completed my studies carefully? And would I not have missed the greatest of all epochs in Berlin? Yes, I treasure the sensible schooling I received in Europe. We can say what we want, but there is no substitute for sound, thorough training, whatever the field of endeavor may be.

And so I stayed in the conservatory, working diligently and earnestly to complete my studies. Occasionally a manager from some theater would come to the conservatory to hear the advanced pupils. One day an agent, Madame Selar, after having heard me, arranged for me to sing for Mr. Löwe, manager of the municipal theater in Breslau, then considered the finest in Germany. He liked me very much and invited me to come to Breslau and audition for him on the theater stage. After assurances from Frau Kempner and Gustav Holländer that I was now ready to audition, I rushed home in great excitement and asked Walter to go with me. Together we took the milk train, and after a long, slow ride arrived in Breslau.

We went directly to the opera house and asked to see Mr. Löwe. Greeting me warmly, he took us into the auditorium and told me to sing as soon as I felt rested. I believe that I was too young to be frightened, for I was ready to sing immediately and eagerly gave the accompanist music to *Traviata*, *Magic Flute*, *Lucia*, and *Barber of Seville*. From these operas I sang all the main arias, one right after another.

When I had finally finished singing all that I wanted to sing, I sat down and waited for the verdict. Mr. Löwe came up onto the stage, smiling, and immediately offered me a contract for five years, starting at five hundred marks a month. I opened my eyes wide and looked down at my brother. We smiled at each other. Little sister Frieda is going to fool you, Walter, I thought. She is going to become a real opera singer, and sooner than you think. How quickly I signed that piece of paper, for so much joy was hidden there. Hardly taking time to say goodbye, Walter and I left the building and hurried to catch the next train home, where the excitement of telling everybody the good news awaited us. Walter was so proud of me!

How happy mother was. Such a contract—why, only experienced singers could expect to receive a salary like this, with a five-year guarantee besides! I was to start at Breslau upon completion of my studies, and so back to the conservatory I went. But now I was more, oh so much more, than a student. I was the envy of my class, for only I had such a contract in my pocket.

My brothers were now quite proud of me, but they still had to tease me. They would send me postcards of the opera house, the great Royal Opera House of Berlin, and over the top of the building they would write, "Frieda's Dream. Ha! Ha!" I sang for them at their singing society meetings and for their rowing club. Everything always went fine, and my first public appearances were crowned with success. I just sang my way into the hearts of my listeners. I would get paid a small sum, but the rowing club always rewarded me with something quite wonderful. They would take me with them in their long boats, and I would sit up in front and feel very important as we raced over the water of the Müggelsee.

I saw my teacher twice a week now for tone production and twice a week for coaching. In addition to this, I went on my free evenings to my Kapellmeister Gehrke to go over opera scores. Mr. Gehrke was a funny little man, skinny and pale, but very understanding and so patient in spite of his poverty. He had a great love for his work and for his pupils, and I am grateful to him for his excellent instruction.

Such disciplined study was of the utmost value to me. It would take a great deal of money to study and work with the same thoroughness here in America today. In Germany, Italy, France, almost anywhere in Europe, a musical education meant taking one's time and building from a solid foundation. It is so true that Art cannot be rushed.

Singers need time. The body must adjust to the demands of correct tone production while mind, soul, everything about which art flourishes must be cared for. We singers cannot live as others do, for too much talking, too much physical exertion, too much of anything is just disastrous. The voice must be guarded every minute, without being coddled, because as singers we must be ready to sing beautifully at all times. This we cannot do if we try to live like other people. We must awaken in the morning refreshed in mind and in body in order to practice, memorize, improve, and create.

I was never in smoky places, I was cautious about sudden changes of temperature, and I avoided exposure to the night air. My diet was well-balanced, and I ate well. I lived and thought as a singer. I went to all the concerts I could possibly afford and to many opera performances. My enthusiasm ran high, and I did not care where I sat. I simply had to hear all the great artists. When Caruso came in October 1904, I made myself a brand new blouse in his honor. Joseph Plaut called for me, and we went together on the trolley car to the Theater des Westens. Here we met all our colleagues in "musical heaven," as we called the gallery.

This was Caruso's first appearance in Berlin, and the house was quite empty. In a box sat a very beautiful, dark-haired woman in a midnight-blue paillette evening gown. The story went, for there were always stories in an opera house, that she was his sweetheart. I learned later that she was Ada Giachetti, the mother of his two sons.

Then he sang. Such sounds are never to be forgotten. I went home and told my parents that it was "just like gliding into a deep red velvet chair, so soft, so mellow, so perfect." Such phrasing and brilliancy, such elegant, wonderful acting, well, one just couldn't find anything wrong, just absolute perfection and the rarest beauty of tone that ever came from a human throat. Of course after the performance we all talked over the singing, and some of the boys criticized Caruso for this or for that. When you are young, you speak so freely and you know everything better than anyone else. For me it was a great and wonderful experience, and it inspired me to work even harder.

Geraldine Farrar came to Berlin as a beginner, and I became her great admirer. I went to every performance of hers and sat spellbound in the gallery. When I came home I would imitate her, trying all her gestures in front of the mirror. I even attempted to imitate her speaking voice as she used it in Auber's *Le Domino noir*. I bought every postcard I could find of her. She was so lovely!

Never again will we see or hear a Manon like her, so graceful and elegant. She was the first actress to bring the idea of public relations into Germany. Many stories were printed daily, and if any German singer had done the same thing, I am certain that she would have lost her position. But Farrar was a foreigner, and something foreign is always intriguing. Certainly the word *America* held great magic for the Germans.

It was our great privilege, as students, to hear inspiring artists such as Francesco d'Andrade, Ludwig Wüllner, Ferruccio Busoni, Eugen d'Albert, Joseph Joachim, Lilli Lehmann,* Julia Culp, Giovanni Lamperti, Marcella

---

*Lilli Lehmann (1848–1929) was a legendary figure of the operatic and concert stage during the second half of the nineteenth century. She was on the stage for forty-five years and sang some 170 roles from Philine (*Mignon*), Lucia, and Violetta to all three Brünnhildes. In the first Bayreuth *Ring* of 1876, she sang Woglinde, Helmwige, and the Forest Bird. In 1896 she returned there as Brünnhilde, roles she introduced to New York, together with Isolde. She was acclaimed for her participation in Mozart operas, for her Norma and Fidelio, and for such Verdi heroines as Amelia, Aida, and Leonora (*Trovatore*). In later years she turned to teaching; her pupils included Farrar, Fremstad, Kurt, Weed, and Telva. She made recordings in 1905 and again in 1907, and continued to give concerts until 1920. She was born in Würzburg, Germany, and died in Berlin. *Ed.*

Sembrich, Fritz Kreisler, Felix Weingartner, Karl Muck, Leo Blech, and Edmund Strauss. This last-named conductor had a special gift for understanding good voices, and he brought many good singers to the opera stage. This is a gift few people have; sometimes the greatest musicians have no foresight in this regard and cannot tell the potential of a young voice. Neither Richard Strauss nor Leo Blech had this gift, but Edmund Strauss did.

Hearing these great artists trained our ears. Great things were expected of us, for greatness was in the air all around. There was no amateurism; everything was done according to the highest possible standards. Our teachers knew this, and therefore demanded much of us.

Now I must tell you about one great experience of my student years. Max Reinhardt, the most modern of all stage directors in those days and the most artistic, was going to present *A Midsummer Night's Dream* in a fashion entirely new: no more painted trees, but real trees, real grass, real acting; no more old-fashioned gestures, just natural movements. And Moissi, Eysoldt, Eibenschütz, Höflich, Bassermann—all the great actors of the day were to be in his cast.

Reinhardt needed two elfins to sing from behind the trees, and so he came to the various conservatories in Berlin, looking for his two elfins. When he came to us, we were prepared for his visit. He listened to each of us and then left. The next day we learned that he wished to engage me and a mezzo-soprano of my class.

Our joy was unbounded! We reported to rehearsal and were fitted out with green tights to camouflage us as we stood behind the trees to sing our solos. Then we watched those great artists paint their lips green. With their uncombed wigs and their costumes, they looked just like creatures of the woods and caves as they danced and jumped about. It was a great experience to be on that stage with those artists and to feel the theater. The effect of the sunlight on those real birch trees, with all their natural shadows, will linger in my mind forever. The fairylike forest magic of Max Reinhardt's production is unforgettable and remains one of my most cherished memories.

My voice was immediately recognized as something unusual, and even the newspapers mentioned me most favorably. Max Reinhardt was very kind to me and paid me fine compliments. I was told that everyone was asking, "Who is she? Who is she?" when I sang. I was paid ten marks a night, a fortune to me. The following season, when Mr. Reinhardt asked me to return, I was very sorry to have to tell him that I held a contract for Breslau as leading coloratura. I could no longer sing from behind the trees for him; from now on I would sing in front of them!

Toward the close of my third year the public student recitals began. These concerts allowed the graduating students to perform in public, and they also advertised the Stern Conservatory and its work. On the fifth of

June 1905, I appeared at the Beethovensaal singing Schubert songs, the aria from *The Magic Flute*, and the Proch Variations.* I had prepared for this concert with great excitement. Mother had the seamstress make me a pink crêpe-de-Chine gown, my first evening dress, and I went for the first time to a hairdresser to have my hair done. I was eighteen but looked about twenty years older when they were finished with me, and I did not like it at all. As soon as I returned home, I dressed for the concert. I think that my parents and my brothers were far more nervous than I was; they wondered if I would come through it all without any stage fright. Mother gave me a sip of champagne for the occasion, and I think that this fortified me with a sort of daring. I wasn't excited; I sang my songs and then the Queen of the Night aria. I knew that my teacher was sitting there with fingers crossed for my high notes, but they came through fine. I was far too young to know what might really happen—I never stopped to think that the high notes might not be there! My assisting artist was a child prodigy by the name of Mischa Elman, and after the concert I asked him for his autograph. He wrote his name on the top of my *Magic Flute* score.

My fellow students showered me with little bouquets of flowers—three roses or a tiny bunch of violets, as much as they could afford. And how I cherished them: they came from the heart, and they were offered in real appreciation of my work. Mr. Heinemann, one of the famous teachers, brought me roses, and so did Mr. Seideman. They were all "feared" singers and teachers, these people who came to congratulate me, and they made me very happy, for then I knew that I had done well.

The whole family gathered at my sister's house, and everything was talked over: how I looked when I came out, how I made my bow, how I walked off the stage. My brothers kidded me again and gave me little bouquets of flowers, imitating my admirers. It was such fun!

My concert had created a sensation. For me this was heaven on earth. My teacher asked me to come to her house, and now she gave me free lessons. Everything seemed to center around me—such politeness and honor, suddenly!

Soon it was time for the presentation of the opera scenes by the graduating classes. We had been learning to act during this last year, 1905, and it had been great fun. We practiced gestures of all kinds: angry, joyous, positive, negative gestures, laughing, crying, walking, falling, all things that young artists of the stage had to learn. We had jolly laughs together after classes, imitating each other's actions. But Mr. Rothmühl had great patience, gained from years of experience with the likes of us, and he had finally succeeded in teaching us to move about the stage with some degree of freedom.

---

*Variations for coloraturo soprano with flute obbligato by Austrian composer and conductor Heinrich Proch (1809–1878). *Ed.*

Graduation exercises consisted of two series of scenes from the various operas. I was assigned the part of Mistress Ford in *The Merry Wives of Windsor*. It was quite a task for a beginner, for I was to be constantly on the stage, always in a gay, laughing, happy mood. But as I always loved to laugh and be happy, I had no trouble at all and felt very free in the part. It went well.

For my second scene I sang the part of Marguerite de Valois, in *Les Huguenots*, the role that later became so closely associated with my name. My costume for this performance was but a pale foreshadowing of the beautiful dress I would wear in Emperor Wilhelm's revival of this opera. But if I did not have a ruche to wear around my neck, I did manage to have a long train, a seemingly endless train, to maneuver. I swung it around with great abandon, as if I were quite accustomed to trains, and felt very professional. I sang the glorious cadenzas and the coloratura passages with great dexterity, and my success was tremendous.

With a contract for Breslau already arranged, I did not expect to be approached by any of the managers who came to these performances to select singers for their theaters. But Mr. Dröscher, the manager of the Royal Opera House, and Count Georg von Hülsen, the director, sent word that they wished to speak with me the following day at Frau Kempner's home. I had no idea why they wished to see me, but of course I went at the appointed time and stood before them. I learned that my performance had been extraordinary in many ways and that they desired to have me sing at the Royal Opera House for my debut.

This was something I had not even dared to dream about. My thoughts were on my Breslau contract; no other theater had entered my calculations. And certainly not the Royal Opera House of Berlin, the goal of all German singers. But that Breslau contract was not binding, for I was under age when I signed it, and my parents had not yet given their consent in legal form. Mr. Dröscher instructed my parents to inform Mr. Löwe that they wished me to remain in Berlin and therefore could not approve the contract. My career thus began with a breach of contract, in a sense. I do not believe that Mr. Löwe ever forgave me, although I know that he understood. For my part, I knew only that such an opportunity seldom came to a young singer, and I welcomed it with open arms.

I was to be offered a contract from the Court Theater of Schwerin. Following my debut in Berlin, I was to join that theater for three years, 1905–1907, and then return to the Berlin Royal Opera House as a regular member of the company. Before I really knew what was happening to me, I was in Schwerin, auditioning for the manager. Just as I was about to step onto the stage, a kindly old gentleman, General Music Director von Ledebur, called out to me, "Look out! Don't fall into the ocean!" The scenery to the *Flying Dutchman* was the setting for my audition.

And then everything was over. I had graduated, and my school days were gone, I was under contract at a court theater, and my debut was to take place, not in Breslau, but in Berlin, at the Royal Opera House. Those cards from my brothers, with the bold writing "Frieda's dream. Ha! Ha!" across the top, now stood in a place of honor. The unexpected had happened.

I enjoyed the hot summer days, swimming with my friends or going to Helene's country home for long walks and swims in the river. I was not very worried about my debut, for I was to sing *The Merry Wives of Windsor*, and I had sung the role of Mistress Ford long enough to be unconcerned about it. In all honesty, I do not think that I quite comprehended what was happening to my life. The step from the conservatory to the stage was taken rather as a matter of fact; I was busy with everyday things all summer, just like everybody else.

About a week before the first rehearsal at the opera house, I went to work with Frau Kempner again, and we went over the role several times. On rehearsal day I went to the theater just like a veteran, tried on my costume, sang the role with an accompanist, and came home again, attending to routine matters.

Then came the first orchestra rehearsal. At the end of the second act something happened. I did not know what it meant, but all the men of the orchestra stood up and clapped on their instruments. They told me on the stage that this was the greatest compliment a singer could receive. Now I could hardly wait for the performance. I watched everybody and everything, drinking in the "feel" of the theater and slowly realizing what it all meant. The eagerness and absolute satisfaction of soul and mind so filled me that I wanted to sleep in the theater and never leave.

I was sure of my voice, but I was never conceited. Rather, I was never satisfied and always felt that I could do better. Oh, it was wonderful to go out there and sing. And in the third act, when I had to come in on a horse, it was just like playing; I didn't realize that I might fall off and perhaps tear my dress or hurt myself. No, I had no fear, and instead it was all fun. Probably for this reason I did so well. From me the audience felt the joy of singing, the carefree feeling, the freedom, and the vitality, which I think have remained with me until this very day. I forget sorrows, life, age, problems; nothing matters—I walk on a cloud and just sing!

After the performance we all went to Kempinski, a fashionable restaurant, and there we ate, enjoyed the wine, and talked for hours. Criticism? What did I care? I was a beginner and couldn't be perfect, although I thought that I was. But that is youth, youth that knows no fear and no responsibility of a name to be lived up to. Yes, I was surprised at some of the criticisms I heard around the table about my performances, but I still expected to get good notices in the morning.

As it was unheard-of for an inexperienced conservatory graduate to make

As Mistress Ford in *The Merry Wives of Windsor*. PHOTO BY F. O. LUNDT.
COURTESY METROPOLITAN OPERA ARCHIVES.

a debut on the stage of Germany's foremost opera house, Count von Hülsen had sent special invitations to all the leading critics of the Berlin papers, the musical journals, and the musical correspondents of the leading foreign publications. Among the critics present were Leopold Schmidt of the *Tageblatt*, Oscar Bie of the *Börsen Courier*, Paul Ertel of the *Lokal Anzeiger*, E. E. Taubert of the *Poet*, Ludwig Bussler of the *Nationale Zeitung*, Otto Losman of the *Allgemeine Musik Zeitung*, Wilhelm Altmann of *Die Musik*, and Arthur Abell of New York's *Musical Courier*, among foreign correspondents.

The reviews were all magnificent. To my great sorrow all my copies of these reviews of an event that meant so much to me were lost during the turmoil of the war years. But I shall never forget the thrill of reading those glowing accounts of my debut. Arthur Abell kindly looked through his files at my request, and he sent me his review. Mr. Abell was highly respected by his profession, and to have my name appear in print for the first time in America in his column was an honor, for he also introduced the names of Mischa Elman, Jascha Heifetz, Julia Culp, and Bronislaw Huberman to America. His review reads:

> Frieda Hempel, the brilliant young coloratura, who created a sensation at the Public Concerts of the Stern Conservatory last June, made her debut at the Berlin Royal Opera House Tuesday evening, in Nicolai's opera *The Merry Wives of Windsor*. A few days later she sang the role of Queen Marguerite in Meyerbeer's opera *Les Huguenots*, and the second appearance only served to enhance the good impression made at her debut. It is an extraordinary event, when a young girl fresh from the Conservatory steps onto the stage of the Royal Opera House, and not only that, but wins an immediate and overwhelming success. Fräulein Hempel seems destined to make a great career as a prima donna. She has every requisite: a beautiful, fresh, flexible voice, an accurate ear, remarkable facility of execution, a brilliant trill and staccato—in fact, everything that goes to make up the perfect coloratura singer. At the same time, her interpretations of the roles essayed reveal a musical nature and an artistic temperament. Unless all signs fail, she will become a star of the first magnitude in the operatic firmament.

Inscribed in Hempel's handwriting: "This is Boy, who always puts an old potato in my luggage." PHOTO BY ATELIER ERNST SCHNEIDER. COURTESY JOAN BEADLING.

CHAPTER THREE

My First Year in Schwerin

*T*he *Magic Flute* I knew, but there were *Rigoletto, Armide,* and lots of parts that I had put down on the list of roles studied but that I did not know at all. Of course I was not worried. I knew that I could sing them technically because I had no vocal problems. But I did have to learn them and memorize them all. During the intermissions I could look at my score, and the prompter was always there in front of me, but even so, I had been a little bold. Such self-confidence is almost criminal, but at the age of eighteen anything goes. Mr. Gehrke got busy with me, and we had four weeks of strenuous study together. The typewriter, the letters, the doorbell, the packages to mail—all this was forgotten. I was now prima donna of the Court Theater of Schwerin, busy with my repertory and quite proud of myself.

I started in on my wardrobe. The theater supplied us with costumes, but they never fitted well, or so I thought, and I wanted to make a hit in every way. So I went to a theatrical dressmaker and had all my costumes made to order. I had no money, but I knew that soon there would be plenty. I would earn seventy-five dollars a month from the theater, and there would surely be many concerts for me. And so I arranged to pay for these costumes in installments. By the end of three months, I had earned three thousand dollars, and so the dressmaker was soon satisfied.

Mother and I prepared to move to Schwerin. We had little to pack, and soon all was ready. On the last day of August 1905, we bid the family farewell for a while, and within three hours the train brought us to Schwerin. It was raining heavily, and I confess I felt a little unhappy with these angry skies, but we immediately set out looking for suitable lodging. We found two nicely furnished rooms. The landladies were three elderly sisters, the youngest of whom was eighty-four years old. They were all very sweet and most willing that I should have a piano and sing whenever I wished. We had no bath and no running water, and we had to go quite some distance for other comforts, but it did not matter. The main thing was that here I could practice and learn those parts.

At first Schwerin seemed to me dreadfully small and uninteresting. I do not know how many inhabitants the town had. I only know that when you walked, you always met the same houses and the same people. There was no trolley and very little traffic; it was so unlike the big city of Berlin. Each window seemed to have a mirror in it, and by means of this mirror, everyone knew everybody's business. The old ladies would sit by the hour, watching the carriages go by, seeing who was in town and who was visiting.

The magnificent palace of the Grand Duke of Mecklenburg and his wife, one of Europe's most beautiful palaces, was situated at one end of the town in a beautiful park. In a corner of this park was the lovely court theater. I soon became well acquainted with my new colleagues. General Music Director Meissner was very helpful to me. Mr. Kpaze, the leading tenor; Florence Wickham, the stately contralto;* Frau Wiedke, the dramatic soprano; Mr. Lang, the fine tenor; Hermann Gura, the baritone; and also the stage manager and Mr. Karl Holy, the light tenor—all these warm, friendly people helped me to find my way about the stage and welcomed me into their midst.

I felt like a princess. I was on the stage, singing big parts, and it was all real. I especially enjoyed rehearsals for operas new to me. Mr. Holy, the tenor, began to show great interest in me. He was considerably older than I, and he had a good deal of stage experience. I was fortunate to have him at my side, for I learned much from him about acting. He would watch and criticize me in voice and in acting, and I often felt him to be "the power behind the throne." Every person on the stage needs someone like that; often it is the little sense of encouragement that molds a singer more than her own efforts. I shall always be grateful to Mr. Holy for his friendship and guidance.

I had left my two dogs, Max and Moritz, in Berlin with my sister, and so I was happy when Mr. Holy's dog, Terry, adopted mother and me. But

---

*American contralto and composer Florence Wickham was born in Beaver, Pennsylvania, in 1880. She studied in Philadelphia and Berlin, making her debut as Fidès in Wiesbaden. She was Kundry in the (U.S.) Henry Savage *Parsifal* tour of 1904–1905. After seasons in Munich and at Covent Garden, she joined the Metropolitan in 1909 where she sang twenty-two roles in 169 performances. In later years she composed ballet and operetta scores. She died in New York City in 1962. *Ed.*

we had our worries with Terry. Occasionally he would disappear for several days. Mother and I could not sleep, and we would try every means of locating him. Finally he would come home, all bloody and scarred. The doctor would stitch him up, and I would punish and scold. But his love for lady dogs was stronger than my words, and one day he would be off again.

He had a passion for the organ grinder. When we could not find him, we first listened for the sound of the barrel organ. For there Terry would be, howling to the music at the top of his lungs. He would follow the man through the streets, howling until evening came. The whole town knew Terry and laughed about his singing. A trained dog could not have done better. Terry was famous, and the organ grinder was grateful for an increase in business.

Some time later Mr. Holy gave me another dog, named Boy. Boy was a sentimentalist, and when we spoke to him, he answered back in a kind of depressed howl. He had a cute habit. He knew when I was packing to go on concert trips, for my trunks would lie open on the floor. This gave him his chance. When I arrived at my destination and opened my bags, I would find, among my delicate underthings, some old, precious bone that had been long hidden in the earth. Or I would find an old, brown potato when the bones were all gone. This discovery was always a touching moment for me. After a long, tiresome train ride, I would be refreshed by this lovely touch of home. Who says animals do not think? Wasn't it thoughtful of Boy to send a smile with me and make me feel happy until I returned home once more?

Mother took care of him, or better said, he took care of mother while I was gone. When I was back in town, the two dogs would follow me to the theater every day, and upon my telling them, "Go home, now, both of you," off they would go, faithfully returning home for a kind word and a dog biscuit from mother.

Occasionally I would go to Berlin for an overhauling of my voice by Frau Kempner and a visit to my family. Sometimes Frau Kempner would come to Schwerin and go over the roles with me, and she would give a concert herself at the same time. With such kind, helpful friends around, I had nothing to worry about. I had no struggles whatsoever.

The Duke of Mecklenburg was proud of his opera, with good reason. The best letter of introduction to any theater in Germany was a record of performance in Schwerin. Here many great artists were trained, and here one found the best conductors. Many rehearsals were held, and highly artistic, deeply musical presentations were demanded. Opera was presented twice a week and musical comedy once a week, with occasional matinee performances included in the week's schedule. Frequent concerts were also given in the smaller concert hall.

The atmosphere of a court theater differs greatly from that of a state theater. The state theater was always looked upon as somewhat commercial, while the court theater was more artistic and gave the singer a finer, more dignified education in music and in the arts. If you came from a court theater, every door was open to you as an educated, refined, gifted artist. Perhaps you would be paid far less than in a state theater, but you felt infinitely better paid. And if Schwerin happened to be the court theater of your apprenticeship, how fortunate you were! The sovereign of a court theater pays for all costs of management, and any deficit is his responsibility. In a state theater, all costs must be balanced by subscription. In a court theater you are supplied with costumes, and your vacations are still on salary. You are given a pension from the court theater after several years of singing, and for this very reason selection of singers is carefully made.

As a member of the Court Theater of Schwerin, I belonged, in a sense, to the family of the sovereign. With other members of the theater, I was often called upon to sing for the royal family in the palace. Crown Princess Cecilie, sister of the duke, would often come to the opera house with the royal couple, and with the Grand Duchess Marie, his mother, they would occupy the royal box, smiling and bowing to all their subjects. The Grand Duchess Marie had a palace in Rabenstein, a lovely, quiet place, and we loved to be summoned to sing for her there. She was very musical and appreciated our artistry in a way that flattered and pleased us.

Queen Wilhelmina of Holland came to Schwerin as a young girl to select her husband, Prince Heinrich of Mecklenburg. For this occasion we gave many gala performances and were all graciously complimented. There is something about royalty—not that they are different, but there is always a certain air of very charming manners about them. Their politeness, grace, and gentility were commanding, and we felt as though we were among a select few to be admitted to their presence. We strove to learn from them and to be deserving of their praise. Yes, the court theaters were the aristocrats, whether for opera or drama. The Hofburg in Vienna, or the Royal Schauspielhaus in Berlin or in Munich—there was nothing higher for an actor to strive for, just as the Royal Opera House in Berlin was the highest goal of a singer.

Now in Schwerin I created such a sensation that the house was sold out every time I appeared; people would come from Hamburg and Berlin just to hear me. As time passed and as I came to realize the responsibility that faced me every time I sang, I began to develop a little stage fright. Now I knew what it meant to have to do well.

As Schwerin was a small town with little entertainment, I spent most of my time at the theater. Mother would meet me for dinner after rehearsals, and then some colleagues and I would return to the theater and go to the box provided for artists. We did not need to dress up to go there but could come in our everyday clothes and sit there listening to our fellow singers. It was a great lesson to us all. Of course, often, instead of staying at the theater, I would leave with Mr. Holy, and we would go to a wine restaurant and visit and enjoy the people around us. Mother often seemed surprised at the long, long performances at the theater!

Occasionally I had dates with an officer of the duke's regiment stationed in Schwerin. These officers could sit in the first balcony at the opera and vie for my attention. They showered me with flowers and poems and soon discovered the restaurant where mother and I habitually dined. My lovely costumes had created quite a stir in Schwerin, and now stories went around that some great banker or even the emperor had paid for my gowns. Of course I kept them guessing and dazzled them with stage jewelry and new costumes as often as possible.

Often when mother and I were dining in the restaurant, these officers would come in, and soon I would begin to receive messages and gifts of flowers and wine. Mother enjoyed this show of affection and admiration as long as she was with me. Mr. Dabelstein, the owner, would show his appreciation of our patronage by showering us with large portions of food and excellent wines. He would often sit with us to make certain that everything was all right, and so of course I had to eat the large portions of food. I became rather roly-poly, I am afraid. Dear, good old Dabelstein, what a sweet soul! How his face would light up when we came in.

During this first year in Schwerin, I learned twenty new roles and gave fifty performances. Some parts were delicate, some more dramatic, all difficult for a girl of eighteen. I sang Gilda, Micaëla, Violetta, Leonora, Fiordiligi, Princess Eudora, the Forest Bird in *Siegfried*, a Rhine Maiden, and of course my famous role of the Queen of the Night.

When I was to sing the Queen of the Night, I never touched my lower tones. I stayed in the second octave to keep the extremely high position needed for that role. As I had been trained on Mozart, this part was easy for me. I even added higher notes, as one can hear in my records of that time. These additional notes I added were already present in the orchestral score and perfectly fitting musically. I am certain that they would have had Mozart's approval. Most of Mozart's concert arias were written for high coloratura, for they abound in high Fs, fast scales, trills, and staccato passages of great brilliance. Later Leo Blech wrote many extremely difficult cadenzas for me.

The weeks of the 1905–1906 season passed by as I studied and sang and gave my concerts in various towns nearby. Every single concert excited me. It was always a sort of debut. I never paid much attention to the money I was earning; I just brought the check with me and put it in the bank. Each month I sent money to Berlin to my father and brothers, and the rest I set aside. Expenses in Schwerin were very few.

I took long walks in the beautiful park, and in the evening I rode through the town streets over the cobblestones to the opera house. The elegant carriage of the theater would call for me on the evenings of my performances. After the performances we would be driven home again. Admirers would run alongside, getting a glimpse of us and thanking us. It was always a fresh experience, something sweet and rewarding.

People would stop me in the streets to pay me compliments or wait for me in front of my house. The young girls would approach me shyly and give me bouquets of flowers; they would follow me as I had followed Miss Baumann during my school days. I don't think that the grand duchess had more admiration and love than I. Everything was so warm, intimate, and personal. This is the charm of a small town. I had the most delightful spot for apprenticeship a girl could wish for.

CHAPTER FOUR

Bayreuth

*T*o *sing at Bayreuth* was to wear a special decoration; no greater compliment existed than to receive a call to participate in the summer festivals. Only the greatest artists from the finest theaters were engaged. Although we aspired to the Royal Opera House in Berlin and then to the Metropolitan Opera in New York, Bayreuth was something different.

One lovely day in late spring of 1906 I climbed off the train at the station in Schwerin. I had been in Berlin, singing a performance of *Les Huguenots* for the emperor, and I was quite tired from all the activities. Mr. Holy greeted me warmly and handed me a letter. His enthusiasm was catching, and forgetting my weariness, I eagerly took the letter and looked at the postmark. Bayreuth! Frau Cosima Wagner wished me to come to Bayreuth from 19 June to 20 August of this year to sing the role of the First Rhine Maiden in *Das Rheingold* and in *Götterdämmerung*, as well as the First Flower Maiden in *Parsifal*. I had been on the stage for only six months, and already the decoration was mine. I would meet the "big shots" and learn so much. It was very wonderful news to me, and it took me some time to settle down to work for the last few weeks of the season in Schwerin.

Bayreuth was a musical shrine, a mecca for all lovers of Wagner. The theater is situated on top of a hill, isolated and sacred, a temple of music. I remember the hill only too well, for the summer was hot, and the hill seemed to turn into a mountain as I climbed to rehearsals, yet for a young, healthy girl to take a carriage would have appeared foolish. The festival committee had arranged for our living quarters. We had two rooms in a three-story family dwelling, right in the middle of the town. The people living there did not usually rent out rooms, but during the festivals everybody helped to accommodate the artists and the tourists, as there were not enough hotels in this small town.

Mme Ernestine Schumann-Heink had rooms on the first floor, and we were on the second floor. She was a big, healthy woman, with red cheeks, tiny black eyes, and an enormous chest. Very, very outspoken, and diplomatic at the same time, she amused us all. "My great-grandfather was Italian," she would say when talking to an Italian count. "Oh, yes, my great-grandfather was a Frenchman," if her listener was a French marquis. And "Hurrah for the President, down with the Kaiser," if she happened to be in New York; in Germany, "Hurrah for the Kaiser, long live the Kaiser!" She was really a sort of happy clown, full of wonderfully quick wit and astounding energy, with a glorious, infectious laugh. She had just acquired a new husband, William Rapp, fine-looking, six feet tall, but without the slightest idea about music.

I seldom heard her practice, but she always seemed to hear me. One day she came to me and said, "Hempelchen, you must not sing those high notes so often. Be careful! You are young now, but you must save your voice!" She was kind to me and gave me wonderful advice. But I wanted to do everything just so, and I had to practice until I had it. She liked mother, and I often caught them chatting.

We had rehearsals three times a week, and on those days we rehearsed morning and afternoon. Mr. Müller was our coach, and I had the feeling that he wanted to out-Wagner Wagner. He was always stressing perfect pronunciation, and he would have me repeat the phrase, "Hei! wer ist dort?" in *Das Rheingold*, fifty times it seemed. Finally Frau Knüpfer, wife of the marvelous basso from the Berlin Opera House, interfered; she was the Second Rhine Maiden, and naturally she saw how this man tortured me. She went to Frau Wagner and complained, "How can Mr. Müller strain such a young voice in this manner?" Mr. Müller was advised to let the phrase alone. Frau Cosima, very conscious of her great name and of her responsibility, would come to the theater and show us all how Richard wanted the acting done. I can see her now on that stage telling the Isolde how to act the phrase, "vor König Marke zu stehen." She made a rather coquettish gesture with her right hand. This was how he wanted it. At times Frau Cosima disturbed us in our work, but we were of course devoted to her as a person. Siegfried, her son, was always in high humor, flitting from one artist to another, flirting and making jokes. Frau Beidler, her daughter, was well-liked.

Only the greatest conductors came to Bayreuth. Hans Richter was our conductor. He was a great man, and I stood in awe of him. It always upset me to see him going out with a shopping bag in his hand. I felt that he should only carry a baton, that he should not have to think of food. It did not enter my young head that he might enjoy this shopping. He paid me a great compliment by saying, "After Lilli Lehmann, I have never heard such a wonderful Rhine Maiden." Alfred von Bary was Tristan, Ellen Gulbranson was Isolde and Brünnhilde for many years, Paul Knüpfer sang Wotan, Schumann-Heink was Erda and Waltraute, and Emmy Destinn was Senta. Dr. Karl Muck was also at Bayreuth for many seasons.

Nowhere else were such performances given. The rehearsals ran from morning till night, and everything had to be exactly correct and in the great Wagnerian tradition. Here was a religious atmosphere; we were acutely conscious of the spirit of Wagner hovering over us and helping us. It did not seem to be a theater—it was real. During a performance one could scarcely hear a person breathe, and the audience sat motionless and silent, held spellbound with us in that artistic experience. We lived for those few hours and came away with a great sense of message and of strength through music.

When we were not rehearsing we would meet for picnics at a charming beer garden, the Eremitage, just outside the town. There we would rest in the clear, cool air of the forest. We would sit with a glass of beer and some rye bread, and Schumann-Heink with a big German knackwurst in her hand would tell us jokes in dialect. We would laugh our heads off and have a wonderful time in this simple fashion. Alois Burgstaller, the Parsifal; Fleischer-Edel, the Elsa; and Leffler-Burckhard—so many wonderful artists were there with us. When evening came, we would walk home together and then rest for the next morning's rehearsals.

After the performances we would all meet at a little restaurant called Eule, the owl, just across from the railroad station. We would have our dinner and visit. People would ask for our autographs and pay us lovely compliments. The restaurant was crowded then with visitors who wanted to see the artists and be with them. Many foreigners came to speak with us, and we always enjoyed these visits.

Sometimes we would take a room for ourselves, and there we would sit far into the night. Sometimes Rudi Berger would interrupt a conversation to say to me, "Hempelchen, I bet you a dinner you cannot sing a high F right now." I would stand right up and sing one, and then everybody would clap and tease Rudi. I held all those artists in sincere reverence and could never quite believe that I belonged to their group, that I was one of them. I felt so shy, and I was usually quiet. They all knew that I had an inferiority complex for I never knew if I had done well, and I would ask them for reassurance. Still quite young, I was often not aware of the fine things I did.

They knew that I needed encouragement. I need it still today. Mr. Bibb, Mr. Bos, in fact all my conductors and accompanists had to tell me, "Nobody does it like you; you are wonderful." With that in mind and nothing else, I would go on the stage and do my best. Count von Hülsen would say to me, "Hempelchen, remember that you are great. We have never had any-

1 Wieking, 2 Schumann-Heink, 3 Habich, 4 M. Bohnen, 5 Stassen
6 Siegfried Wagner, 7 Prof. Khnopff, 8 H. Breuer

A group portrait at Die Eule, the singers' restaurant of choice at Bayreuth, including Schumann-Heink (labeled as 2), Michael Bohnen (4), and Siegfried Wagner (6). PHOTO BY HANS MEYER. COURTESY ELIZABETH JOHNSTON.

one like you. Remember that!" In this manner he would build up my courage for a difficult role. Always, always feeling this inferiority, I would not even hesitate to ask the doorman, "How did I sing?" Although never sure of my work, I was always certain of my music and my words. But there are other artists who were that way, too. Caruso had many *encourageurs* around him all day. I believe that this uncertainty comes because we have such high ideals, we know how it should sound, our own artistic nature tells us. But because we aim at a perfection too high, we are extremely sensitive and shy. Certainly in Bayreuth I had reason to be timid, and so I sat quietly and listened and learned.

During the festival, the Wagners would "hold court," as the artists phrased it. To be asked to an evening at Wahnfried, the Wagner villa, was like being asked to meet the royal family. The most aristocratic people, the highest society of many nations came to Bayreuth and were entertained at Wahnfried.

But I was from Schwerin and Berlin, and quite accustomed to such gatherings. I enjoyed the evenings at Die Eule far more. There we enjoyed the warmth of each other's company, and at any moment someone would burst forth in song or in contagious laughter. To be an artist among such great artists was high court enough for me. I saw the twentieth of August arrive much too quickly, and when train time came, I wanted to turn the clock back and live through all these wonderful summer days once more.

A young Hempel as Violetta in *La traviata*. COURTESY STUART-LIFF COLLECTION.

CHAPTER FIVE

A Busy Year of Singing

M y second year in Schwerin began after a happy summer at Bayreuth. During this 1906–1907 season I gave many guest performances in the environs of Schwerin and in Berlin, and my fame was reverberating in ever-wider circles. My first year of singing had brought me about fifteen thousand dollars, and yet, if you will believe me, I was so busy learning my roles and caring for my voice that I was hardly aware that I had earned anything. I had made many guest appearances at the palace of the emperor in Berlin, and as he continued to call for me, my only thought was constantly to refine my acting and musicianship so that he might continue to favor me.

On 30 March 1907, my first engagement outside Germany took place. A call came from Ostende, near Antwerp, a famous resort where only the greatest artists were engaged. This exciting concert was so successful that I was asked to return for the summer season and give six concerts with orchestra.

I returned to Schwerin to be confronted again with astonishing news. The emperor had decided not to wait for me to finish my five-year contract at the Court Theater of Schwerin but had arranged for a release so that I could join the artists of the Royal Opera House in Berlin as a permanent member of that theater. I had become his favorite singer. A most touching farewell performance of *Traviata* finished my career in Schwerin. The title of Court Singer of the Grand Duke of Mecklenburg was conferred upon me, and I also received a high decoration, the Order of the Grand Duke of Mecklenburg. People had so taken me into their hearts and had followed my progress with such interest that I was sad indeed to leave my beloved

Schwerin. I had learned so much there and had gained such great musical knowledge that I was very spoiled. My colleagues had been so helpful, and there had been a lovely spirit of friendship between us, with no jealousy and no intrigue. My eyes were flooded with tears when I departed in April 1907.

London had sent me a contract, some weeks before, to sing in the famous May festival. I was to sing *Bastien and Bastienne* of Mozart, and *Hansel and Gretel* of Humperdinck. These were new roles for me, and I had worked on them a little during my free time. Now that the time had come to take the trip across the Channel in May of 1907, mother became worried. She just wouldn't cross the waters for anything on earth. So Mr. Holy agreed to come with me as my manager.

We arrived on the first of the month, after a horrible crossing. Those boats were small, and the odor of the sea, the fish, and the seaweed was enough to make me terribly sick. Mother never could have stood it. And then the constant rocking, rocking of the boat on the rough waters was frightful. My living quarters had been arranged by the London managers for Covent Garden. They were on Bloomsbury Street, not far from the opera house. I went to bed immediately in order to recover from my trip and had all my meals in bed. The next morning I went to rehearsal, and that same evening I sang Bastienne and Gretel in these two one-act operas. I made many mistakes in Gretel; singing the part of a child did not interest me much after all my queens and elegant, worldly women.

Nor could I get used to English cooking, and so I ate scrambled eggs and things that I could fix myself. The sharp and strong sauces they liked so well were just not good for my throat. A few days later Mr. Holy discovered Simpsons' and Lyons' Chophouse, and my eating problems were over.

But not my singing problems! I wanted to capture London with my *Traviata* and tried everything possible to get an audition. I pleaded with Mr. Higgins, the manager of Covent Garden, and Percy Pitt, the conductor, all to no avail. Instead of *Traviata*, I was to sing Eva in *Die Meistersinger* and Elsa in *Lohengrin*. Why these lyric-dramatic roles, why no coloratura?

The reason was Dame Melba. She dominated Covent Garden; her very word was law. She was unkind to me, just as she was unkind to my most intimate friend and colleague, Luisa Tetrazzini. Instead of giving me a chance, for she knew that I would have my usual success, she insisted that Pauline Donalda, a pupil of hers, be given the coloratura roles. This singer never made a name for herself,* and it must have been uncomfortable for Dame Melba to have me there in London.

---

*History has dealt more kindly with Pauline (Lightstone) Donalda, born in Montreal of Russian-Polish parentage 5 March 1882. Her debut, under the sponsorship of Massenet, 30 December 1904, was in Nice as Manon, where she also sang Marguerite, Mimì, and Micaëla, and Nedda and Jenny in the French premiere of *Chat-*

A gala performance of *Die Meistersinger* was presented, and my Eva was warmly applauded. For a Queen of the Night to sing an Eva and an Elsa was proof of great technical mastery, and perhaps the patrons who had heard of me as a coloratura were pleasantly surprised to learn of my versatility.

Caruso was also singing at this May festival, and now I met him for the first time as a fellow artist. When he learned that I was to sing in Ostende in Belgium in June, he was very pleased. He had sung there in the previous season and could not talk enough about the wonderful resort town. Madame Melba had never sung in Ostende, but Caruso had and I was going to, so I forgot all about her jealousy. Caruso told me not to gamble too much; he had gambled away most of his earnings. I did not know then that I would be singing *Rigoletto* with him in Berlin before many months had passed.

Mr. Holy and I took a few last rides in the wonderful London carriages. They amused us so; the driver, instead of sitting in front of us, sat above and behind us. We never became accustomed to this. There had been no time for seeing the sights of London. All during the festival, I don't believe that I noticed any difference between London and Schwerin. I only thought of singing, of the care and concentration that went with it. I knew that if I did not rest well and remain quietly at home, my singing would suffer.

Now it was time to return to the continent where the manager at Ostende awaited my arrival. We steeled ourselves for the crossing and embarked. I had gained much confidence in London, and I arrived at Ostende eager to follow in Caruso's footsteps. Here was my first view of high society with all its glitter and color. Ostende was famous for its gambling pavilion and for its great concerts. Guests came from all over the world to hear the

---

terton under the direction of Leoncavallo. Her London debut was 24 May 1905 at Covent Garden as Micaëla with Emmy Destinn and Charles Dalmorès. On 28 June she created Ah-Joe in the premiere of Franco Leoni's *L'Oracolo* with Dalmorès, Scotti, and Vanni-Marcoux. She often replaced Melba and sang Mimì with Caruso and Scotti and Marguerite with Dalmorès, Journet, and Paul Seveilhac, whom she married the following year. In the autumn of 1905 she sang Marguerite and Mimì in Brussels, where she later sang Manon, Elsa, and Eva. She broke her contract (and paid a fine) at the Monnaie in Brussels in order to become a member of Hammerstein's New York Manhattan Opera Company where her debut as Marguerite took place on 7 December 1906. She was also heard that season in *Carmen, Martha, Don Giovanni, Traviata, Lohengrin,* and *Pagliacci*. In 1907 she divided her time between Covent Garden and the Opéra-Comique in Paris and made concert tours in central Europe with Elman, Kreisler, Paderewski, Zimbalist, Kubelik, and Casals. She opened the season at Covent Garden in 1910, replacing Tetrazzini in *La traviata* with McCormack and Sammarco. The war restricted her activities to Canada, where she founded the Donalda Sunday Afternoon Concerts in Montreal in 1915. After an extended concert tour in 1921–22, she settled in Paris where she taught singing until 1937, returning to active singing in Montreal where she died 22 October 1934—a rather full career for a singer who "never made a name for herself"! *Ed.*

famous singers and to spend their money in hopes of winning more. Titta Ruffo, Jean Noté, Félia Litvinne, Lucien Muratore, Marcel Journet—all these singers had appeared in Ostende for the summer concerts.

On the beach were little cabins on wheels, which were rolled in and out according to the tide. Charming hotels and restaurants were crowded with elegant visitors, and the casino was the main attraction. It was my first visit to a gambling resort, and, as Mr. Holy had returned to Schwerin, I was alone and a little timid. The manager, Monsieur Marquet, met me and escorted me to the hotel where rooms had been reserved. I had been in Ostende in March, but at that time the summer season had not yet begun. Now everything was entirely different.

That evening Monsieur Marquet called for me. Arriving at the casino, I was fascinated with what I saw. It seemed that each woman was trying to outshine the others. I saw the most elegant women in deep décolleté, covered with brilliant jewels, and often a member of the demimonde sat casually next to a visiting queen, vying for attention. Everyone tried his or her luck at the wheel, and just as Caruso had done, so did I. We received handsome, fabulous amounts for our concerts, but at the end of the season the resort really had all of us for nothing, or even made money through our gambling. The temptation was too great, and besides, it was the thing to do in Ostende. In the afternoon everybody met on the pier in great style. In former days, people paid much attention to dress, which I liked, for it added a certain dignity to the place.

The concert hall, which sat twelve thousand people, had an orchestra of one hundred men, with Rinskopf as the conductor. These concerts were always very artistic and highly musical. I sang arias from the operas, the difficult Mozart concert arias, the Proch Variations, and other coloratura pieces. I quickly became the spoiled darling of Ostende, and the people were very good to me. By the time I left in August 1907, "La chanteuse légère," as they billed me, had seen and met the international world. I was invited to return the following summer, and in fact I sang there every summer until I left for America.

I returned to Germany and made my way to Munich, where I was engaged to sing at the Mozart festival in August. To sing in that charming, delightful little theater was just too lovely. I was to sing Susanna, and Fiordiligi in *Così fan tutte*. At that time the great coloratura Hermine Bosetti was in Munich, as fine an artist as one could hear. This made me wonder why I had been asked.

Maude Fay* told me a sweet story about my arrival there. They were

---

*Maude Fay was born in San Francisco on 18 April 1878. She studied with Aglaia Orgeni in Dresden and in 1906 made her debut as Marguerite in *Faust* in Munich. She created Ariadne for Munich shortly after the Stuttgart premiere, and Diemut rehearsing a Wagnerian opera in an upstairs room when Hermann Gura came running up to them and cried, "Come downstairs! Come and listen! Here is a girl who has everything!" They all came downstairs and stood listening in the back of the auditorium. "It was true, you were really unbelievable," she said. I had no idea that they had been listening. It was only my second season on the stage, and I was not confident musically about Fiordiligi, but I learned it, and my Munich debut was a great success. Felix Mottl conducted with spark and elegance. We sang it in the Possart version, with the excellent stage director Joseph Fuchs. It was the daintiest, liveliest performance imaginable, and in that theater the size of a matchbox, one could easily think Mozart was there.

in the British premiere of Strauss's *Feuersnot* under Beecham. She was heard at the Metropolitan in 1916 as Sieglinde and Elsa but found her activities greatly restricted by her German training and repertoire at the time of the First World War. She married Powers Symington and spent her later years in San Francisco where she could be seen frequently as a patron of the San Francisco Opera. She died 6 October 1964. Her memoirs, *Living in Awe*, were edited by her nephew, Marshall Dill, Jr., and privately printed in 1968. *Ed.*

Hempel as Gilda in *Rigoletto*. COURTESY STUART-LIFF COLLECTION.

CHAPTER SIX

The Royal Opera in Berlin

*I*n *Berlin once more,* this time for the 1907–1908 season, and indeed this time to stay, I began the search for a suitable place to live, for of course Wilmersdorf was too far away from the opera house. Before long I found a sweet apartment at 68 Augsburger Strasse. Mother returned home to be with father and the boys, and so I went to an employment office to engage a maid. At home I needed to work over my scores and sing my scales and exercises: there was little time left for cooking and housecleaning, and I needed someone to travel with me and care for my gowns and costumes. At the agency I met Frau Rosa Seidl, a Bavarian, born in Regensburg. I liked her and engaged her immediately.

Rosa Seidl, such a faithful soul. She has been my maid, cook, nurse, secretary, and banker for more than forty-five years. Without her help I would have been in desperate situations several times. To her I confide, and from her I take advice. She has seen kings, emperors, presidents, and artists; she has cooked for the greatest, the wealthiest, and the poorest. She has had great patience with me, often sitting up through the night, waiting for trains, packing, unpacking, attending to my wardrobe and costumes, waiting on people, and nursing me through illnesses. Most of all, she has been kind to my many stray animals. No matter what I would bring home—cat, dog, pigeon, abandoned or sick, with broken wing, lost, hungry, whatever it might be—after a little argument Rosa would accept it and care for it. When I met her in Berlin, her husband had just left her, and, having given her small son to a foster mother, she was looking for work so that she might support him. Later, friends took care of the boy, and Rosa saved every penny she made so that one day she might live with her son again. She sent money to Germany from America and had a beautiful house built near Berlin for her son. He married and became well-established as a mechanic. Pictures of the grandchild arrived for Rosa and photographs of her son, six feet tall, handsome, and good. She lived for letters from him and sent many packages of food and clothing from America during the war years while her son fought with the Germans on the Russian front.

After the Second World War, her son returned to his home in East Berlin, in what was designated as the Russian zone. Rosa planned to return to Germany and live with her little family, but fate decided differently. One day two Russians came to her son's house and asked him to come with them. He soon returned, and there seemed to be no trouble. But those same men paid him a second visit, and this time he never came back.

My family, my friends, and I tried to locate him for Rosa. We contacted the Red Cross to no avail, and we asked help of the police; no one could find any trace of him. The agony of the young wife with her small daughter and the great sorrow of Rosa were terrible and pitiful. Finally, after the family had waited for years and years, a stranger came to the wife and told her that her husband had died of tuberculosis in a prison camp. This news gave Rosa sorely needed consolation, for she knew then that her son was no longer suffering in some unknown place away from his family. I do hope that this was the truth, but who knows?

My Berlin apartment was soon furnished and arranged to my liking. I had four large rooms on the top floor and a wide balcony off the parlor. This room I decorated in French style, with antique white furniture and a large red carpet covering the floor. A handsome mirror was hung over the mantelpiece, and in one corner was my new Blüthner grand piano bought from the firm in installments. I paid it off quickly, for I was making plenty of money by then. The other three rooms were furnished with equal care, and there was no one prouder than I when the last chair was put in place.

Soon I had visitors on the balcony. Being on the top floor, I thought that I was alone with my sparrows. I had of course begun to feed the few birds that rested there, and the news traveled rapidly throughout the bird kingdom. In no time I had a regiment, and they made so much noise that I often had to wait until their argument was over before I could hear my own voice again. What's more, my sparrows and I were not unobserved.

Twenty years later someone confessed that he had watched us. Charming Mrs. Andrew Carnegie had invited me to her Tuesday evening musicales here in New York. They were lovely, simple affairs. Mr. Carnegie had installed a magnificent organ in his home, and we always heard delightful organ music at these concerts. Gustav Haug was the splendid organist engaged by Mr. Carnegie, and one evening when buffet supper was being served, he came over to me and introduced himself, adding "Oh, no, we are by no means strangers. You did not know it, but I lived opposite you in Augsburger Strasse in Berlin. I watched you feed that ever-growing flock of sparrows each day, and I sometimes saw a mass of golden hair hanging over that balcony. You had washed your beautiful hair, and you were drying it in the sun." How foolish I had been to think that nobody ever saw me! And how delightful that I should meet that man twenty years later in New York.

I loved my little apartment. It was mine. Mother came in almost every day to listen to me or to go to the opera with me. Sometimes she would sit in the audience; at other times she would stay in my dressing room to be with me and to help me dress. She loved the theater, and it flattered her when people came with compliments for me. She became an important person in this theater.

Father bragged about me wherever he went, and just by accident he would have a picture postcard of me in his pocket. The truth was, he stuffed his clothes with my pictures, so that he looked ever-so-much larger than he really was. Whenever I met him, I would say, "Now father!" and take out dozens of cards from each pocket of his suit. He loved the ladies, and when one of my girlfriends would meet him, she would surely be invited to have coffee and cake in a coffeeshop. There he would talk about nothing else but Frieda, and in this way my friends would find out how I practiced, who my boyfriends were, and what new gowns I had.

My debut as a regular member of the Royal Opera in September 1907 was a great disappointment to me. I quite naturally expected to sing a leading role for my first performance. When Count von Hülsen informed me that I was to sing the part of a Rhine Maiden, I felt like quitting. I told him that it was unfair to ask me to start in such a role and that he should have given me the Queen of the Night. He answered that I was too young for the part. The Queen was much older and had a child. So I asked him, "Must I get a child before I can sing the Queen here in Berlin?"

He laughed and told me not to worry. In a way he was right—the role should be sung by a mature woman. Anyway, my pleading had its effect, and my next role on 11 September 1907 was Lucia. This was what I had dreamed of, and the morning after the performance I awoke to find my name on the front pages of the newspapers. I was established as the leading coloratura soprano of Germany. From then on I had only leading roles in the most outstanding productions. Today I understand Hülsen's motives. He was such a gentleman that he had to consider the other coloratura soprano Emilie Herzog, an excellent artist, who planned to retire shortly.

Caruso was to come to the opera house to sing one performance each of *Rigoletto* (on 23 October 1907) and *Lucia di Lammermoor* (on 27 October). I had been informed that I would sing Gilda and Lucia with him, and this knowledge haunted me. For weeks I carried my little notebook of Italian

As Juliette in *Roméo et Juliette.* PHOTO BY F. O. LUNDT. COURTESY MICHAEL ASPINALL.

words with me, memorizing the text of the duets. I wished to compliment Caruso by singing with him in his own language, although I would sing the rest of my roles in German on those two evenings as usual. I did not speak Italian, and so in my little book were three lines, the German words to a duet, the Italian words, and the literal German translation of these words. Like a parrot I learned this Italian and then memorized the meaning of these words so that I could sing them freely and with understanding. On the trolley, at the opera house, wherever I was, I clutched this notebook in my hands.

Then came the rehearsals. I just stood in awe and watched him. He never sang at a piano rehearsal but would only hum and give his tempos. He talked very little, and one could see that he took care of his voice. Even at full stage rehearsal he sang full voice only when others were singing with him; his own parts he just hummed. He came on stage with a hat and a cane, going over scenes in which he had a partner.

Therefore not until the night of the performance did I know what it meant to sing with Caruso. I followed his intentions almost unconsciously—they were so right and so natural, so warm and so human. In October 1909, when we sang *La bohème* together, I really felt that he was in love with me and meant everything he sang, and I cried with him and gladly gave in to his wooing. This was no acting, no theater—this was just honest, sincere feeling and expression: this was real life. Only a great artist or a great conductor can achieve this, and such performances always reach the audience and "bring the house down."

With the brilliant coloratura arias in *Rigoletto* and in *Lucia di Lammermoor,* one always gets an ovation, and so the public was as kind to me as it was to Caruso. He had the greatest respect for the Berlin audience, and Berlin adored him. He knew that in Berlin music and art were deeply understood and appreciated, and this knowledge gave him stage fright each time he appeared. He also knew that publicity hindered rather than helped the singer in Berlin, and so he refrained from using any.

Other roles assigned to me were Mistress Ford, Marguerite de Valois, Gilda, Lucia, Violetta, Micaëla, Juliette, Susanna, Constanze, Woglinde, Angela in *Le Domino noir*, Margiana in *Der Barbier von Bagdad,* and the princess in Boieldieu's *Jean de Paris*. This last-named opera was staged as a special favor to the emperor. The charming coloratura soubrette Francillo-Kaufmann* was the page, and I shall always remember her warmly. She died

---

*Hedwig Francillo-Kaufmann was born in Vienna in 1878 and died in Rio de Janeiro in 1948. She studied with Aglaia Orgeni in Dresden, making her debut in Stettin in 1898. She was at Wiesbaden 1899–1902, Munich 1902–1903, Berlin 1903–1905 and 1907–1908, Vienna 1908–12, and Hamburg 1912–17. She taught in Berlin, then Vienna. After World War II, she married a Brazilian and taught in Rio. *Ed.*

in South America, and a pupil of hers brought me a picture taken just after this performance in Berlin, which Francillo-Kaufmann wished me to have, with her love and admiration. I was deeply moved to realize that colleagues do not forget one another over the years, and saddened by her death.

When I was not performing, I would sit with the chief electrician in his box in the first wing of the stage. This was a rare favor that I won from him, for actually no one was allowed there while he was working. But I had made him my friend and took care not to disturb him.

CHAPTER SEVEN

The Emperor's Skylark

*T*he *great revival performance* of Meyerbeer's *Les Hugue-nots* took place on 23 March 1908, an evening my colleagues and I would never forget. Unter den Linden was more beautiful than ever. The entire avenue was a mass of color, with garlands of flowers hung from tree to tree, flags of many nations fluttering in the breeze of twilight, thousands of tiny lights shining from the palace windows and from the many government buildings, and magnificent wreaths adorning the pillars of the Brandenburg Gate.

It was the emperor's evening, a gala evening of entertainment for the royal guests who had been invited to Berlin. And Berlin was the emperor's city. As I rode along Unter den Linden on my way to the Royal Opera House for my performance, I felt it pulsate with warmth and love for the emperor; each citizen of this proud city knew that no one was as great as he. The children would walk for miles to get a glimpse of him; they would climb the high trees just to see his face, and when he waved his hand, they were certain that he was waving just to them. The hearts of the men and women would jump a beat as he passed, still waving just to them.

In a short time now the royal party would drive down Unter den Linden toward the beautiful opera house as the Berliners waited to see the emperor and to honor the guests. They lined the avenue and stood in festive mood, adding gaiety and laughter to the sounds of evening. This was a night long awaited, for on this festive occasion the magnificent performance of the completely revised *Les Huguenots* was to take place. For weeks the newspapers had carried stories of this production: the emperor himself had conceived the idea of such a revival in which the stylization and the melodic freshness of this old opera would be blended with the naturalness and the realism of a modern operatic production.

Day after day His Majesty had attended rehearsals. Seated in the front row of the orchestra, he had supervised the stage action, checked the costumes in detail for the slightest error in style, verified the authenticity of each piece of newly designed stage scenery, and molded in his singers the characters of the opera as he conceived them. The responsibility of the performance was his alone, and to him would belong the achievement. Everything was now in readiness, and the emperor's guests were in Berlin to share with him the fruits of his labor. The opera house looked like a dream. The royal box was flooded with cut blossoms, and roses hung in festoons from the balconies in a blaze of color. The auditorium was sprayed with heliotrope, the favorite perfume of the emperor, and nothing had been overlooked in preparation for this gala evening.

I was the leading coloratura of the Royal Opera House, and so the role of Marguerite de Valois, Queen of France, had been given to me. As I hurried to my dressing room to prepare for the performance, the excitement of the evening flooded through me with renewed intensity. Although I was still in my early twenties, I had sung many times for the emperor, and I knew that he expected a perfect performance. This responsibility rested heavily upon me, for I desired above all to justify his faith in me.

As curtain time approached, a dazzling audience began to assemble. Looking through the curtains, we saw beautiful women dressed in the latest French creations, tastefully displaying their exquisite jewelry. Attending them were field marshals and admirals resplendent in red or white uniform with decorations on their chests, and elegant gentlemen in full dress. Everyone stood waiting for the entrance of the royal party. The director Count von Hülsen stepped in front of the curtain and with three taps of his large black cane announced the arrival of the emperor.

The national anthem of the time, "Heil dir im Siegerkranz," was played as the party entered the royal box. The emperor and the empress with their guests—the czar and the czarina of Russia, the king of Bulgaria, the king of Belgium, Prince Heinrich, and others—greeted the audience, and then everyone sat down and the performance began.

That unequaled opera conductor Leo Blech conducted with a fire, a *souplesse*, a grandeur that only he could command. Paul Knüpfer was a true Marcel, even in his looks, with soft brown eyes so trustworthy and consoling and a bass voice as deep as the ocean, soft and rich. Karl Jörn was Raoul, a very handsome tenor with a fresh natural voice. Emmy Destinn was Valentine. She tossed off high Cs with a softnesss that was ever so magnificent. Francillo-Kaufmann was the page. As Marguerite de Valois, I had to wear a Mary Stuart ruche, which went around my neck like a lampshade. It was terribly uncomfortable to sing in, but nothing could be done about that. The ruche was authentic.

Although I did not appear in the first act, I was dressed and standing in the wings as the opera commenced. This foresight allowed me to play a major role in a scene backstage that was certainly unrehearsed. In this act, Emmy Destinn, as Valentine, was to be carried onto the stage in a sedan chair drawn by two mules. The two mules chosen for this task had behaved beautifully at the rehearsals, but now for some reason one mule decided not to move. The other mule accepted the situation and stood patiently still. It was time for Valentine to make her entrance, and as I realized what was occurring I rushed over to the mule and began to plead with him. Impeccably gowned and adorned with jewels, ready to make my entrance as the Queen of France, here I was coaxing that mule and pushing his rear!

I spoke low, I spoke high, I spoke softly, I spoke harshly to him, and still he wouldn't budge. Was it stubbornness or stage fright? I shall never know. But I have always had a way with animals, and I told him again that he should, he must, he had to move. He finally understood my feelings, and just in time he did move. The audience surely would have been amused if they had seen what was going on behind the curtains.

Everything else went smoothly, and at the close of the second act came the long intermission and the great moment. For we had been invited to come to the private loge of the emperor, just off-stage, to be received by him. We gathered there and stood, trembling with anxiety and curious to know if our efforts had pleased, when suddenly the door opened and the emperor stood before us. He was dressed in one of his favorite uniforms, that of the Hussar regiment. He wore a white coat with a contrasting broad red ribbon crossed from his shoulder to his hips, golden epaulets and cuffs, diamond-studded decorations of all shapes, medals encrusted with rubies and sapphires, and a saber at his left hip. He carried his helmet under his arm. Behind him was a shorter man dressed in a dazzling white uniform. He was the czar of all Russia. These two rulers looked like fairy princes to me in their magnificent, imposing uniforms of state, and my knees shook in wonder and admiration. I thought of all the people they commanded and was almost stupefied by that thought.

There was a moment of silence in which we made our devoted bows, and then the emperor addressed me in a manner as simple as that of any ordinary gentleman.

"Fräulein Hempel, how did you ever become such a fantastic singer? I shall always call you my skylark, for you soar into the heavens with those high tones. How do you achieve this? When you sing with a flute, I often wonder which is you and which is the flute. It is fantastic!"

Bowing again, I replied, "Your Majesty, I have always loved to sing, and it has been the dream of my life to become a great singer. I have never failed to pray day and night: 'Dear Lord, let me become a great singer.'"

"Well, He has certainly answered your prayers," he said. And then, lifting his finger like a warning sign, he added, "Take care of that heavenly voice. It should be wrapped in cotton, and you must never sing a note of Wagner."

As he moved away to speak with my colleagues, the czar of Russia approached me. He showered me with compliments and insisted that I come to Russia to sing for him. He was such a shy little man with a soft warm voice, and he spoke German fluently. I kept thinking how much he looked like the emperor. The only difference was that the emperor had his famous wax mustache, and the czar wore a goatee. I thanked him for his kindness and curtsied.

Such a moment, such great men, and such an honor! For a young German girl who had just worked long and diligently at her scales and her trills, the experience was overwhelming. I felt that the earth might give way beneath me. I walked back to the stage in a daze, envisioning for the remainder of the evening the picture of those two monarchs and the great people whom they ruled. The performance was an enormous success, and the audience called us back many times for applause even after the royal party had left.

The next day I received news that made me extremely happy. Count von Hülsen informed me that the emperor had decided, on the evening of this performance, to make me a Königlich Preussische Kammersängerin, a Royal Court Singer. I was the youngest singer ever to receive this honor. It was usually given after twenty-five years in the service of the court theater, and a handsome pension was granted with it. It represented the realization of a life-long ambition. And often in later years I was referred to as His Majesty's youngest Court Singer.

I went immediately to the printers to have new calling cards made up with the words "Frieda Hempel—Königlich Preussische Kammersängerin" on them. What a thrill it was. I handed them out to all my friends, to the shopkeepers, and even to passersby. For days I could not rest. My thoughts always returned to that evening when the emperor addressed me as his skylark and placed his blessing upon my voice.

We gave this opera eleven more times in the remainder of the season. I would stand in the wings listening to Emmy Destinn mold those big tones down to the finest *pianissimo*, and she, in turn, would listen to my highest head tones. We studied and learned from each other.

During this first year in Berlin, the demands for my appearance on the concert stage became increasingly heavy, and I frequently asked Mr. Holy to come down from Schwerin and help me with the business details. When his theater would not allow him to leave, we would talk by long-distance telephone. He was such an understanding person, and he had a fine sense of humor. We enjoyed each other's company very much and grew fond of one another. When he was away from Berlin I missed him, and he was lonesome in Schwerin. After the closing performance of the season in Berlin, a presentation of *Les Huguenots,* we celebrated the event by announcing our engagement.

In June 1908 mother and I returned to Bayreuth. Mr. Holy came with us to be with me and to hear the festival. In August I returned to Ostende for a series of concerts, and he acted as my manager and arranged all the travel and business details. I had not the slightest talent for this sort of thing, and besides, I was busy with practice and rehearsals.

One evening Mr. Holy called my attention to the fact that Andreas Dippel and Alfred Hertz of the Metropolitan Opera in New York were in the audience. I sang well and was showered with flowers and attention. They came to compliment me and spoke very highly of my work, but they made me no offer. Still, I was happy that they had heard me. My Berlin contract had four more years to run, but perhaps they were looking ahead. We could only guess.

From Ostende we went to Spain for the first time, and there I gave several concerts before returning to Berlin for the opening of the 1908–1909 season in September. Back in my own little apartment, I soon returned to the established routine of practicing, feeding the sparrows, rehearsing, and performing. Rosa was glad to have me back so that she could cook the things I liked to eat. She had stayed by herself in the apartment all summer, and I guess she had been a little lonely.

Soon I was busy again with Italian. Caruso and I were to sing *Bohème* together on 29 October,* and this was to be my first appearance as Mimì. I studied the role in German and then learned all the duets with Caruso in Italian as I had done the previous year.

On the night of the performance I did not even realize that he was Caruso, the greatest tenor in the world. He was Rodolfo, and I was Mimì. We inspired each other and truly captivated the audience. Friends recently showed me two reviews of this performance, and I was overjoyed to read them again after all these years. Wilhelm Kleefeld wrote:

> *Bohème*—in the first act the public listened only to Caruso. But gradually another personality began to make itself felt, not cleverly, not sensationally, no, rather in the most tasteful, artistic, modest way. She came

---

*According to the chronology in Caruso and Farkas (1990, 674 and 676), Caruso only sang two performances of *Bohème* in Berlin: that on 24 October 1908 with Farrar and that on 21 October 1909 with Hempel. *Ed.*

more and more into the foreground, rose higher and higher, until— one could believe neither his eyes nor his ears—there she stood, together with Caruso, on the same supreme level of achievement, his equal, in a masterful creativeness of striking validity. Was it possible? Was this Fräulein Hempel, who with such giant strides had risen to the sacred heights of art? True, she has been recognized as a Queen of Song since her first appearance. With an incomparable voice, she danced effort- lessly up and down the grand scale and became leading high-soprano, the star of bravura technique. One marveled, but one remained cool. Now, all of a sudden one recognized an error in judgment. Out of the technical master, the coloratura virtuoso, appeared the great interpreter, full of warmth and brilliance, full of true, natural, human feelings which spoke not to the intellect, but to the heart. And all hearts opened to her, and sang praise to the new princess of song.

The other review is by the great and gifted critic Oscar Bie. He writes:

Caruso and Hempel in "Bohème." This time the drama of a wonderful guiding voice and a devotedly submissive voice. He all strength and manliness, mature, proud, self-confident, strong and courageous, she all woman, awakened, springlike sweet and delicate, blossom and color and butterfly, filled with heartfelt devotion, and with the joy of one who would die for love. These two voices enter into the realm of love at the end of the first act. The duet is a phenomenon of nature. His heroic manliness combines with her sweetness. He directs her voice as a dancer directs his partner. He fills the phrases with breath and sound and light, and she follows him with touching tenderness, as though she would interpret his feelings with trembling desire and with untold grace responding to his wooing. Her voice is the essence of natural, tender simplicity. What opportunity they had who were present on this eve- ning, to study and to enjoy the blending of these two instruments, not to be distracted by roles, notes or technique, but to observe the one thing that was there to be observed: the power of a man and the sweet devotion of a woman, clothed in the two voices best suited to portray them, voices that so blended, in rare moments, as to achieve a miracle.

One afternoon in November I was waiting in my apartment for Leo Blech to arrive. We were to go over his charming little comic opera in one act, *Versiegelt*, a work he had just finished composing. The phone rang, and I received the thrilling news from his secretary that the great American impre- sario Signor Giulio Gatti-Casazza wished to speak with me. I arranged for him to come up immediately, and in a few minutes there he was, a very handsome man indeed. For a few seconds we found ourselves in a strange situation, for he spoke little or no German, and I knew very little Italian in those days. I quickly searched my mind for appropriate phrases from my operatic Italian and managed to piece together a flowery greeting which brought a smile to his face. Using the few phrases that came to mind, repeating them in different order, using my hands for gestures of explanation, and deciphering his gestures, I gradually eased the tension, and we got along splendidly in a sort of sign language. When he offered the most excellent contract for the Metropolitan, to begin in 1912, I knew exactly what he meant, and it took no knowledge of Italian to sign that contract.

It was an exciting moment for me, yet all during the interview I was somehow disturbed. It was not until he was ready to leave that I became conscious of what was upsetting me. He was smoking constantly, and the ashes were falling all over my beautiful red carpet. I could not find any phrases in my repertory to deal with these problems, and he did not seem to see any of the ashtrays placed around the room. My poor, beautiful carpet! Just as he was leaving Leo Blech arrived, and together we brushed up all the ashes, laughing and rejoicing over the good news at the same time.

Then he played his opera for me. He wished me to create the leading role, and I was of course very happy to do so. It was written more for a mezzo-soprano, but I would have sung the part even if it had been written for bass. Leo Blech had always been so very helpful to me, and he was such a wonderful man. His opera is full of gay and sparkling music, and the plot is quite delightful. The mayor of a city gets locked in a clothes closet, and after many complications, the doors to the closet are opened, revealing a young couple instead of the mayor. It was presented first in December and was repeated twelve times during the season and given often in later years.

To my mind, Leo Blech was the greatest of all opera conductors. I have sung with only the great conductors, but there was none so sincere, so artistic, so fiery, so very elegant, so wonderful to sing with as Leo Blech.

True, he was often harsh and despotic, but one had to forgive him—he gave so much of himself. I remember that I once sang in a performance of *Carmen* with him. I was Micaëla. I must have forgotten to dot an eighth note for I received a letter from him, folded four times. I opened it, and in the middle, written in large letters, was the word *PFUI!* I was a little hurt for I had done my best, but I was amused also. In the next act I sang the aria as correctly as possible, and then another note came, folded four times. In the middle of this sheet of paper was the word *BRAVO!* Oh, he was strict. One had to become a fine musician under such careful guidance. He was sincerity itself, and he would never dream of having a publicity man at his right hand, as we see done today.

He was industrous from morning till evening, living only for his art. Such things as coming late to rehearsals, rehearsing with hat in hand, or smoking were out of the question. Sometimes, after rehearsal, I would beg

In Berlin as Queen of the Night in
The Magic Flute (facing page), in
an unidentified role (left), and as
Susanna in *The Marriage of Figaro*
(below). COURTESY STUART-LIFF
COLLECTION.

Frieda Hempel
a. Königin der Nacht
i. „Die Zauberflöte."

him to compose and arrange some new cadenzas for me, and I would have them the next day. He must have worked late into the night on them. He arranged all my cadenzas, and they were all very difficult.

One could not imagine a better interpretation of *Carmen* or a finer *Aida*. You were lifted out of your seat. When he conducted Mozart the strings were like one violin playing. Such elegant phrasing and such temperament—Leo Blech had no equal.

It is human nature that we cannot learn to appreciate what we have when we have it. Today I am sad that I did not realize at the time what great men I had the good fortune to be with. There was Karl Muck, the finest Beethoven interpreter of our time. To hear him conduct the Ninth Symphony was to hear perfection. The elegant Arthur Nikisch in Leipzig cast a fascinating spell over the audience. Felix Weingartner conducted my *Traviata* performance like a symphony. Felix Mottl in *Così fan tutte* made one feel the sparkle of champagne. Hans Richter, in Bayreuth performances, made one live in a different world with his interpretations of Wagner. Yes, few living today can begin to approach the standards set by these men.

News of my contract with the Metropolitan spread rapidly through the opera world, and I was a very proud and happy person. On the other hand, 1912 was a long way off, and I was also content to be Königlich Preussische Kammersängerin in Berlin, and the favorite of my emperor.

In January of 1909 I was called to Leipzig for a concert at the Gewandhaus with Arthur Nikisch. How many rich memories that visit kindled in my heart, memories of happy days not too long ago. In February I went to Monte Carlo with Mr. Holy, who always acted as my manager for these trips to foreign countries. I sang three performances of *Rigoletto* in a delightful tiny theater.

Back in Berlin once more, I sang fourteen performances at the opera house in March and ten in April 1909. During these two months I sang many new roles, including Benjamin from *Joseph in Egypt*, Rosalinde in *Die Fledermaus*, Marguerite in *Faust*, and my first Queen of the Night in *The Magic Flute* for Berlin. Fiordiligi, Eva, the Forest Bird, Gertrude in *Versiegelt*, and Mimì were all assigned to me, keeping me quite busy and out of mischief.

In May I had the great fun of going to Schwerin, where I sang all three roles in *Tales of Hoffmann*. I went to visit my three sweet old landladies and sat in my old room once more. And Terry, Mr. Holy's dog, was so glad to see me. I had taken Boy to Berlin, but Terry had stayed in Schwerin. He still sang with the organ grinder and seemed very contented. Mr. Dabelstein greeted me with his usual magnificent cooking, and we spoke about the officers and the flowers, the wine, and the messages, chatting on for hours.

The 1908–1909 season ended in Berlin with a performance of *The Marriage of Figaro* on 10 June, and on 14 June I was in Cologne for the festivals, singing Susanna again. Now I had a whole month in which to rest. The year had been an important one and a tiring one. I had received two new medals, one from the grand duke of Altenburg, and one from the grand duke of Anhalt, and I had a Metropolitan contract. I had also earned a great deal of money for a young girl, and so I felt quite contented as I took the train for Wolkenstein, a little village in the Dolomites.

Here I intended to spend three weeks quite alone and away from singing, music, admirers, and friends. I wanted to take long walks in the mountains and drink in the fresh, cool air. But on my very first walk through the "long valley," the mountains were so overpowering that I had to run back, frightened by the way the mountains were closing in on me. The valley got smaller and smaller, and I felt crushed by the giants above me. I reached my hotel completely exhausted. I shall never forget that feeling.

As Rosina in *The Barber of Seville*. PHOTO BY REMBRANDT STUDIO. COURTESY
METROPOLITAN OPERA ARCHIVES.

CHAPTER EIGHT

King Leopold of Belgium

M y *beloved Ostende* called me again, this time for a long stay. The people had taken me into their hearts, and I sang four concerts in succession in the sold-out Kursaal, followed by a concert in Antwerp. Returning to Ostende, I sang seven more concerts, always with the wonderful orchestra under the direction of Monsieur Rinskopf.

The king of Belgium visited Ostende every summer, and he had heard of my *succès fou,* as the Belgians called it, a crazy, fantastic, insane success. One night in 1909 he sent word that he would like me to sing for him at his palace in Läken, near Brussels. Monsieur Rinskopf arranged a little "at home" concert. The concertmaster, the flutist, the first cellist, the pianist, Monsieur Rinskopf, Monsieur Marquet, and I left immediately for Brussels. Here the king had made arrangements for us to stay at a hotel. I took a room where I could practice, and I dressed for dinner in a jade-green, princess-style evening gown which looked lovely with my blond hair.

After dinner a royal carriage was sent for us, and we were driven to the palace. There we were shown into a parlor tastefully decorated in true French style, as intimate and warm as any private parlor. We waited a short while, and then the doors were thrown open wide, and the king and his companion, the Baroness Vaughan, made their entrance. He was a very handsome man, tall and aristocratic with an imposing, long white beard, and he walked with a cane. The baroness wore a black dress with deep décolleté. Around her neck were sapphires as I had never seen them before. I would never have thought such sapphires could exist: they were as large as walnuts and so stunning. She had a beautiful, tawny complexion, and a rather big nose, I thought. But then most French women have pronounced noses, I have observed.

We were formally introduced, and the concert began. We had prepared a regular program with each artist appearing as soloist. I sang some arias and songs and closed the program with Mozart's "Lullaby,"* a piece that had become a favorite request wherever I appeared.

After begging us to be seated, the king and the baroness conversed with us. As he had been born in Coburg-Gotha, King Leopold naturally spoke German fluently, and so he talked a great deal to me, complimenting me on my good looks and of course on my singing as well. Baroness Vaughan became a little irritated with him for talking with me for so long. Perhaps she was somewhat jealous, for I was young, pretty, and talented, and he was fond of the ladies. I enjoyed him immensely. I did not speak French, but I could carry on a simple conversation with the baroness, who was very gracious to us. After being served French pastries and champagne, we visited a little longer and then returned to Brussels in the royal carriage. The next morning we took the train back to Ostende, and that evening I gave another concert in the Kursaal.

A few days later I received a royal message that His Majesty's courier would call on me. To my great surprise, the king had bestowed upon me the highest order a woman can receive in Belgium, the Officer's Cross of Leopold II. I was the only woman living who wore that decoration, and my only concern was that I had to wait until I returned to Berlin to show it to my family and to Mr. Holy, who had remained in Schwerin.

Monsieur Marquet, the owner of the casino and one of my admirers, was delighted. He was proud of me and showed me off whenever he could. It was a shame that I did not know French well enough to understand his endless compliments. The floral arrangements he sent to me after each concert were tremendous—they had to be carried to my hotel by two men. He did not spoil the other artists like this, but I was a beginner and a pretty young girl as well.

Monsieur Marquet owned two other casinos, one in Coburg and one in Spain at San Sebastian, where roulette and baccarat were played. He invited me to sing four concerts in Coburg and four concerts in Spain, and I accepted.

Coburg was a sweet little resort and I enjoyed it, but I am sorry that I went to Spain. The public at San Sebastian was wonderful to me, and after each concert I was obliged to give many encores. I was happy about that, but I made the mistake of going to a bullfight. This sport is barbaric; such cruelty is unbelievable in a civilized world. The real heroes are the horses of the

---

*Although popular, the piece (K. App. 284^f) is not by Mozart. *Ed.*

picadors and the bulls themselves. In later years I met the famous baritone Emilio de Gogorza* and told him of my disgust and indignation. "We Spaniards must see blood. It is in our very nature," he answered.

I was in despair and only too happy to return to Ostende, even though it meant taking one of those horrid little boats from Calais again. We were all so seasick, and so crowded together! It was almost as bad as crossing the channel. From Ostende I soon returned to Berlin, where there was a love of animals and culture, and an emperor.

The 1909–10 season was scheduled to begin for me on the seventh of October, with a performance of *La traviata*. I had very little time to visit with my family and tell them all about Ostende, Spain, and the king of Belgium. They were delighted with my decoration. It is a Maltese cross set upon a wreath, and above it is a replica of the royal crown. In the center of the cross, in tiny gold letters on a background of black, are the words "L'Union fait la force." On the reverse side is a gold replica of the ensigns of King Leopold. It hangs on a wide ribbon of royal blue with a center stripe of black. We all studied it and admired it.

Soon the season was in full swing, and before I knew it, the time had come to go to Paris for the March festivals. The emperor was proud to have me go; I was to be the only German singer there. Paris had just had a small flood, and so he said to me as I left the opera house the evening before my departure, "Take a boat with you—they have just had a flood there."

The festival, running from the seventh to the eleventh of March 1910, opened with a wonderful performance by Mounet Sully, the great French actor, and Sarah Bernhardt. Then we gave *Rigoletto* and *Les Huguenots*, the first opera in Italian and the second in French. They raved about my singing, but they found me pretty "Dutchy"-looking. We laughed over this in Berlin, for I had worn the costumes of the Berlin opera house, and I suppose they just did not look chic enough for the Parisians!

Paris is the most beautiful city in the world. They call it Paradise for dogs and Hell for horses. There certainly is truth in this. How often I had to call a policeman to keep a cruel driver from hitting his poor horse on the heel, already bandaged from numerous whippings, to make the horse pull faster. And often the policeman would just shrug his shoulders. Every time

---

*The distinguished concert baritone Emilio de Gogorza was born of Spanish parents in Brooklyn, New York, 29 May 1874. He was educated in Spain, France, and England, and studied singing in New York with Moderati and Agramonte. His debut was in concert with Marcella Sembrich in 1897. A pioneer in the recording industry, he acted as direcor of recording activities for the Victor Talking Machine Company for 1902 to 1908 and was personally responsible for engaging prominent artists for that company's Red Seal Records. These, among many others, included Caruso and Emma Eames, whom he married in 1911. He taught singing for many years in New York, where he died 10 May 1949. *Ed.*

I came to Paris I suffered, and I was not alone in this. I am so glad that the automobile came and saved these poor animals from such treatment, such bestial cruelty. The dogs were allowed to sit on chairs in restaurants, but the horses? All the Latin countries are cruel to animals, and for this reason alone I have seldom sung in France or Spain or Italy. Their cruelty to animals would drive me mad.

The opera house is beautiful, and their ballet is lovely, but it was funny to see a Brünnhilde appearing in high French heels. Félia Litvinne was the only French singer who understood Wagner.* In general, the voice of a French woman is not well placed for Wagner, although their baritones and basses are excellent. The French woodwind players are all excellent, and the flutists are extraordinary.

From Paris I went immediately to Budapest for two concerts, and then I returned to Berlin to sing the soprano part of Beethoven's Ninth Symphony, with Dr. Karl Muck conducting, on 15 March 1910. On 17 May I left for Brussels to sing in the Théâtre de la Monnaie for Leopold of Belgium. I sang *Traviata* with the Russian tenor Dmitri Smirnov and *The Barber of Seville* with Chaliapin.

Chaliapin was fantastic as Don Basilio. In the first act he had such wonderful makeup that I could hardly keep my eyes off his face. And his long-brimmed hat was used to provide a delightful bit of unexpected humor, for upon entering the stage, he bowed slowly and deeply, and rainwater poured from this brimmed hat to the great amusement of the audience. The next time he appeared with me on stage, I seemed to have to raise my eyes a little to look into his face. This went on, and each time I sang to him in a new scene I had to keep raising my head. I wondered if something had happened to my body or to my posture. Finally, in the big scene I found myself looking way up at him, with my head tilted back. The audience roared with laughter, for he looked like the tallest man in the circus! He had just put stilts on, each pair a little higher, until he looked like a giant. He played many such tricks on his colleagues and on the audience.

In later years, when I heard him in concert in London, I was surprised to find that no printed programs were issued. Instead, little booklets were given out, and he would announce the page numbers of his songs. I found it very irritating to hear the rattle of pages all over the hall, but his singing

---

*In fact Félia Litvinne (1860–1936) was not French. She was born in St. Petersburg of a Russian father and a mother of Canadian extraction, so she may have had some French blood. She studied with Victor Maurel and Pauline Viardot-Garcia, and made her first public appearance in Paris in 1880. Her first American tour was in 1885; she was in Brussels from 1886 to 1888 and first appeared at the Paris Opera as Valentine in *Les Huguenots* in 1889. In 1896–97 she was at the Metropolitan (forty-three performances), where she was heard as the *Siegfried* Brünnhilde, Isolde, Elsa, Donna Anna, Sélika, Aida, and Chimène in *Le Cid. Ed.*

quickly dispelled this reaction. He was impressive on the stage, and his voice was magnificent. Another time we made the trip to Budapest together. I found him very intelligent, quiet, and not a bit "stagy." What a great eater he was!

During the intermission of the performance of *The Barber of Seville*, the king called me to his box, and I was introduced to his daughter, the Princess Clementine, and her husband, Prince Napoleon. This visit to the box started the wildest rumors. He is going to marry her, he buys all her clothes, he is crazy about her—so the stories went. Of course not a word was true. I always bought my own gowns in Paris from my own hard-earned money. I had received jewels and high decorations from kings and emperors, but only as a reward for my talent, the result of hard work and sacrifice. The gossipers knew that very well, but my being in the box of the king was fuel for their fire.

King Leopold fell ill shortly after that performance, and I was never to see him again. I admired him, as did the Belgians, and his death saddened me. After his death the Baroness Vaughan had a sad time, and, if I am not mistaken, she later drowned herself in the lake in the Bois de Boulogne in Paris. Her four children were taken away from her at the time of Leopold's death. How beastly the world can be, to make a woman suffer as she did! What had she done, other than to ease a lonely man's life and give him comfort and happiness? Her reward was heartbreak and disgrace.

People always connected the dancer Cléo de Mérode with him in some kind of romance, but it was the work of gossipers. He loved pretty women, and why not? It is the most normal thing in the world. That is what we are made for, to attract and to be loved and admired. It is only the meanness of the mind that connects evil with it. If a king should talk to any woman, "there must be something behind it." Strange—such conversations are usually dignified and irreproachable. King Leopold was a gentleman of the old school, but people just loved to see it differently.

After these two appearances in Brussels, I returned to Berlin and finished the 1909–10 season. I had been singing an average of fifteen times a month throughout the year, and I had traveled constantly, so that my plan for the summer was just to rest at Bad Kissingen. Yet as soon as I arrived there in July I received a telegram from Lilli Lehmann to come immediately to Salzburg. She begged me to sing the role of Queen of the Night in her performance of *The Magic Flute*. It meant practicing again, travel, and no rest, but as a favor to her, I accepted.

The old Salzburg Theater was a tiny place. Lilli Lehmann sat in the wings and sang every note with us. The entire production was in her care. And she said to me, "Hempelchen, if you had not come, I would have sung the Queen of the Night myself." I am certain that she would have done so. She was an extraordinary woman, with great will power, enormous energy,

Hempel as Euridice in Gluck's *Orfeo ed Euridice*. COURTESY ELIZABETH JOHNSTON.

and supreme musicianship. Her very life was singing, and I think that she and I had that in common, along with our great and sincere love for animals. I just could not imagine living without an animal, being kind to it, and sharing life with it, for we are created by the same force. And Lilli Lehmann felt the same way.

Back in Bad Kissingen, I spent a wonderful summer and returned to Berlin to have my thoughts forcibly drawn back to King Leopold. One morning on my way to the opera house for the first rehearsals of the 1910–11 season, I arrived at Friedrichstrasse to hear my name being repeated in the streets. The newsboys were all shouting, "Frieda Hempel in wild orgies at palace of King Leopold of Belgium!" I was frightened to death and hurried on to the opera house, knowing full well that such publicity could cost me my position there. I had no idea what it was all about, even though I had bought a newspaper and read the article. Count von Hülsen was waiting for me, angry and upset. He immediately questioned me about the whole affair, for he could not allow any member of the staff to be involved in scandal. If I could not clear my name completely, he would have to dismiss me at once. I was frantic. I explained to him that the only time I had ever been to the palace of the king was on the occasion of the concert. According to the story in the newspaper, I had been carried out drunk from one of the king's wild parties, along with several other women. This was such an absurd accusation that I really had no need to defend myself. Count von Hülsen set about immediately to get at the truth of the matter and started suit at once against the author of the offensive article.

Here is what happened. A valet of the king, having been dismissed from service, decided to get his revenge by writing his memoirs. After the king's death, the book was published. It contained many spicy stories, most of them pure fiction. He wrote, "At one of the king's parties, the ladies were all carried out drunk, and among them was Frieda Hempel."

As a result of the court action taken, the reporter was given a year in prison. I tried to get the sentence reduced, but the judge was firm. He said, "It is so difficult to achieve a good reputation and a fine name. It is too easy for others to besmear that name. We must have protection from such action as this."

The young singer in Berlin. PHOTO BY GERLACH. COURTESY STUART-LIFF COLLECTION.

CHAPTER NINE

The Great Epoch in Berlin

When Emperor Wilhelm rode along Unter den Linden, a fine big military band in front of him and his five handsome sons at his side, the children went wild, the gentlemen lifted their hats, the women waved. Sometimes when he came unannounced for his daily ride, he would see me in a carriage driving to rehearsal. He would salute me with, "Guten Morgen, Fräulein Hempel, wie geht's?" Heavens, I felt flattered and would tell everybody at the theater what had happened. There was no question about it: I was his favorite.

The music I sang was just to his liking, and he admired my "fireworks" so much that I sang at his palace every time one of the family had a birthday. The birthday of the empress was celebrated with as much glamour as possible. A concert with orchestra, cold-buffet supper, and a ball in her honor would be arranged at Potsdam. When I sang for the family in a more intimate setting, the emperor would always ask me to sing the "Il Bacio" waltz by Luigi Arditi. After I had sung it with great swing and a Viennese touch, he would slap his hand on his knee, smile at me, and say enthusiastically, "Hempelchen, das haben Sie wieder fein gemacht!" (Little Hempel, you have done that wonderfully again!) He just loved that simple piece.

He was a very handsome man. As he stood or walked, his left arm rested on his sword. He was born with that arm shorter than normal, and when he carried it in this manner, the discrepancy was not noticeable. His speech was free and easy, and his manners were unaffected. He had many friends among the aristocracy of Berlin, and his carriage was often seen in Tiergartenstrasse, or in Rauchstrasse, in that section of Berlin where the splendid mansions of renowned Berlin families were located.

To call him an antisemite, as Emil Ludwig did, was perfectly absurd. His greatest friends, Eric and Eduard Simon, were Jews; they enjoyed his confidence and were often entertained at the palace. He admired the wit of Heinrich Grünfeld, the cellist, also a Jew. He bestowed many titles on gifted Jews of Germany and entertained them at court. His great hospitality to other sovereigns brought a great deal of money to Berlin. He did everything in the grand manner, and these celebrations were always unusual and outstanding. The visitors flocked to the city, which had a face like no other city in the world in those days.

Large sums of money were spent on cultural projects, and it was the ambition of every artist, writer, and scholar to serve his emperor. A title meant more than money. A decoration was coveted. I call it the greatest blessing of my life to have lived and to have participated in an active way in that period of greatness. No other city had such a large number of outstanding resident musicians living and working together. Those of us who remember that era can never forget its fascination and its glamour.

As a student I had become aware of the very high standard for performance in Berlin, and now, as an artist, I was responsible to uphold that standard. My colleagues in the musical field included Leo Blech, Richard Strauss, Karl Muck, Felix Weingartner, Eugen d'Albert, Leopold Godowsky, Fritz Kreisler, Willy Burmeister, Xaver Scharwenka, Paul Ertel, Rudolph Ganz, Artur Schnabel, Serge Koussevitzky, Teresa Carreño, Franz von Vecsey, Carl Flesch, Christian Sinding, Ferruccio Busoni, Joseph Joachim, Julia Culp, Lilli Lehmann, Giovanni Lamperti, Mischa Elman, and many others. These musicians lived in Berlin and performed there. The public knew how to judge and how to listen, and was not easy to please. There was neither favoritism nor publicity; we simply filled the hall with our sincerity and our art.

Every year a great ball was held in the Philharmonie Saal, a big concert hall. This ball was arranged by the press for charity. Outstanding men and women in every line of endeavor would gather here; the greatest people of our time laughed, danced, and exchanged ideas, sparkling with wit and knowledge.

A lottery table was set up, and prominent writers and painters donated something of their work as prizes. We artists gave of our services. At little tables you could find Conrad Ansorge, that great Beethoven interpreter; Eugen d'Albert; Francesco d'Andrade, the great Don Giovanni; Leo Blech; von Hülsen; Max von Schillings; and Heinrich Grünfeld, the famous cellist and humorist. At another table, Hermann Sundermann, Ludwig Fulda, Arno Holz, Herbert Eulenburg, Alfred Kerr, Fritz Klimsch, and Georg Kolbe would be talking together.

Good music and art were also supported privately, at the wonderful "at home" evenings given by our wealthy, distinguished families. The Mendelssohns, von Bleichröders, von Oppenheims, von Simons, Dr. Hans Bie, Frau von Staub, Dr. Mamroth, and other great families added their luster to the brilliance of Berlin. They gathered great talent in their homes and frequently received the emperor on these evenings.

I sang at one of these gatherings, and years later I heard an interesting story told by a gentleman who had been present. He recounted, "We had a stag party just before leaving for the front and every officer was asked to express his final wish. A great variety of wishes were expressed, and one officer said that he just wanted to hear the 'Rosen Arie' in *Figaro* sung by Frieda Hempel." He concluded, "I was that officer." His name was Walther Rathenau.

The emperor entertained many of these people at the palace. One evening a small group gathered to celebrate the birthday of the empress. I was on the program, and an American singer was also asked to sing. I suppose she had gone to Paris to buy a dress for the occasion, and Parisian it was—so much so that the emperor was compelled to send von Hülsen over to tell her to cover up her Parisian décolleté, which was, I must admit, very extreme. She sang her numbers holding a large fan gracefully across her bosom, and she fanned herself busily for the remainder of the evening.

Having successfully defended my name against the yellow journalist, I was still the emperor's skylark and his youngest Court Singer. My first role of the 1910–11 season was Marie in *La Fille du régiment*, or *Daughter of the Regiment*. *Jean de Paris, Le Postillion de Longjumeau, Joseph, L'elisir d'amore,* and *Daughter of the Regiment* were all popular in Berlin, and I loved to sing them. The emperor always attended when I sang Marie, for he loved to hear my drum solo. I had practiced daily with the drummer of the orchestra, for a drum is a difficult instrument. My drum solo in this opera brought me almost as much applause as my singing.

During these winter months I traveled a great deal, and I became a little careless about my health. When I came down with a severe cold, the doctor found my tonsils in bad shape. To be certain that the cold would not develop into diphtheria, he gave me serum immediately. I had to stay in bed, and that made me very unhappy. It was December 1910, and we had just started to rehearse Humperdinck's new opera *Die Königskinder*, in which I was to create the leading role. The emperor soon heard of my illness and sent me a picture of himself, with all good wishes for my speedy recovery. Lola Artôt de Padilla sang the role for me, and she was a fine artist. She had a lovely voice and was a highly cultured woman. We became close friends. Her mother had been the famous singer Désirée Artôt de Padilla.

As soon as I had recovered enough to go outdoors, I began to ride every morning in the wonderful Tiergarten. I had had little time to go horseback riding, and now for a few weeks I rode a great deal in this wonderful forest, where sometimes in the early morning one could see a deer crossing the

Hempel with Enrico Caruso in Donizetti's *L'elisir d'amore,* with baritone Rafe and bass Ludwig Mantler, Royal Opera House, Berlin, 1910. COURTESY ELIZABETH JOHNSTON.

Hempel as the Goose Girl in Humperdinck's *Die Königskinder* (The Royal Children), Berlin. PHOTO BY REMBRANDT STUDIO. COURTESY STUART-LIFF COLLECTION.

paths. The empress had planted a beautiful rose garden which attracted hundreds of people on Sundays.

After World War II the Carriage of Triumph was gone from the top of the Brandenburg Gate and all the beautiful buildings were in ruin. Only a bit of the burned-out Adlon Hotel was still there. There is nothing sadder to see than the ghost of a building. What would Berlin have been without the Adlon? This famous hotel helped to make Berlin an international city. With its warm, friendly atmosphere, it was not a hotel but a home. You were not room number so and so; you were a member of the family. Mr. and Mrs. Adlon would do everything in their power to help you. They would show you around Berlin, point out the celebrities in the dining room, help you with your travel plans, inquire after your health, and take such a personal interest in you that you never wanted to leave the city. Maharajas and simple tourists would be treated with equal consideration and esteem. The Adlons even used money from their own pockets to pay the bills of many guests. As a young American girl, Mrs. Adlon had come to Berlin to study voice. She married Mr. Adlon, and their marriage was one of the happiest in the world. Louis Adlon, the father, had started the hotel, and in his son's hands the hotel became an institution.

After six weeks of rest at home, I returned to the opera house. I soon began to travel again, singing in Budapest, Vienna, Frankfurt, Mannheim, Leipzig, and many other cities. The requests for me were constantly increasing, and I worked hard. But I was strong, I lived very simply, and now I watched my health carefully and avoided all unnecessary fatigue. The year flew by, and soon it was summer again. This time I did not allow my vacation to be interrupted, and I had a complete rest.

On 5 September 1911 I appeared in concert in Baden-Baden. After the concert Count Hugo von Eckener, captain of the sensational new zeppelin, invited me to make the very first long-distance flight with him. I was quite frightened at the prospect, but I accepted, and Karl Holy also came along. We boarded the ship and made the trip from Baden-Baden to Berlin.

I met a young couple on board, Mr. and Mrs. von Isenburg, and they told us that two passengers had been asked to relinquish their tickets so that we could come along. Mr. von Isenburg then said to me, "Oh, Miss Hempel, when you sing again in Bremen, you must look up my mother. She is a great admirer of yours." I sang in Bremen soon, and I kept my promise and called his mother. We had dinner together in their elegant patrician home. Her daughter later married Mr. Sielcken of New York, and their estate Maria Halden in Baden-Baden was known to everyone. After his death, she married Josef Schwarz, the famous baritone of the Vienna Opera and Berlin Royal Opera.

That zeppelin trip took nine hours, which was record time in those days. I could hardly wait to put my feet on solid ground again. I enjoyed the publicity the trip had given me, but it had been very nerve-racking.

Josef Schwarz was one of those singers who was always looking for resonance in the voice. One day in 1924 in Carlsbad at the promenade where one took the spring waters, he greeted me with, "Mi—mi—mi—Hempelchen, how are you—mi—mi—mi—it certainly is a fine day—mi—mi—mi—you look wonderful—mi—mi—mi." He had his coat collar up around his ears, a scarf around his neck, and a handkerchief in front of his mouth.

"What is the matter with you, Sepperl, are you sick?" I asked. "No," he replied, "but I have a concert in October." This was July! He was known to be very eccentric about the care of his voice and with good reason, I now thought. Poor Sepperl, he died much too young, just two years later. He was so good to his family, and so handsome and kind. The ladies in Berlin were all smitten with him, for he had great charm.

The news had spread that this was to be my last year in Germany before leaving for America to sing at the Metropolitan Opera House. I was showered with letters of admiration, presents, and flowers. Waltzes and songs were written for me, and dishes were named after me.

At the Berlin opera house, after every one of my performances I would receive a large floral arrangement with a card in it reading "From a sincere admirer." This had been going on for many months, and I still had no notion who the sender was. Now I began to notice something strange about the box just opposite the royal box. It could seat ten people, but every time I sang, only one gentleman sat there. He always left the box immediately after the curtain went down, and so it was impossible for me to recognize him.

One evening I went out on the stage just before the performance and looked through the little peephole which is in every theater curtain. But he was not yet in his box. He did not take his seat until after the performance began. I kept wondering if perhaps he was sending me the lovely flowers. And then one evening the floral arrangement arrived with a note instead of a card. The sender requested permission to call. I was having some friends in a few days later, so I answered him and asked him to call at that time.

I was terribly curious and very pleased indeed when a handsome, well-dressed gentleman, young and blond, arrived at my apartment. He soon had the opportunity to confess to me that for a long time he had admired my small feet and hands, and of course my art as well. He always had a box near the stage, he told me, and he had come to every one of my performances. The "sincere admirer" and the mystery man in the box were one and the same! He begged me for another visit, and after that we saw a great deal of each other whenever I was not traveling. Finally one day he asked me to marry him, but he also asked me to give up America and stay in Berlin. He could give me all the comforts and luxuries of life, for he was a rich baron, the owner of several coal mines. But I could not make such a decision so quickly, and so I begged Baron von Z. to give me a little time.

Hempel as Baroness Freimann in Lortzing's *Der Wildschütz*, Berlin,
1907–12. COURTESY ANDREW FARKAS AND WILLIAM R. MORAN.

CHAPTER TEN

Richard Strauss

*T*he *most important production* of the 1911–12 season was
the new opera by Richard Strauss, *Der Rosenkavalier.*
During 1911 Richard Strauss conducted frequently at the opera house
in Berlin. He conducted *The Barber of Seville, The Magic Flute, Les Huguenots,* and other coloratura-type works for me. In operas like these, if there is
a singer with a special gift for trills, high notes, and staccatos, she "trims" the
vocal part. Working with such a singer requires a gifted conductor.

The great Richard Strauss was very uneasy with the liberties I took, for
he thought coloratura work rather silly. He would come to my dressing
room at the beginning of a performance and say, "I don't know how long
you will trill, or what else you will do, but go ahead and sing—I will follow
you." Only a great man could be so humble. He was very kind to the men
of the orchestra, and he once apologized to a trumpeter to whom he had
given a wrong cue. He was understanding with the singers.

One evening when we gave *The Barber of Seville,* he came running to my
dressing room, all excited, and said, "Jesus, Jesus, you just sang a high F-
sharp!" I had sung the Proch Variations with a high F-sharp and had added
other high notes, and he just could not get over it. This inspired him to
write the part of Zerbinetta for me, in *Ariadne auf Naxos,* with its tremen-
dously difficult passages, almost impossible to sing. I have the original manuscript as well as the first printing, with all his corrections.

One morning his new opera *Der Rosenkavalier* was given to us. We
looked through the score, and we were not enthusiastic about it. It was very
modern, more speaking than singing, and there seemed to be little melody.

We were accustomed to the bel canto style of *La traviata* and *Rigoletto,* where a flutelike tone is employed with legato technique and balanced phrasing. This was more declamatory.

We could not quite understand this music. But the separation of voice and orchestra, the new orchestral color, the fresh harmonies with all their dissonances, and the wonderful sweep of the music soon overpowered us. The instruments of the orchestra were the real actors. And the more we worked, learning and memorizing our parts, the more we came to realize the beauty, the greatness, and the originality of this opera. It was grand, powerful, yet gentle. It captivated us all and has since captivated the musical world.

Because of my good figure and good legs, Strauss asked me to study the role of Octavian. He had seen me in *Der Wildschütz,* where I had impersonated a young student. I must say that the role of Octavian was quite different! I was glad when Strauss came back to me a few weeks later and asked me to study Sophie. This part suited my high voice much better. After I was again ready with the part, he came once more and said, "Hempelchen, I have no Marschallin—you must be my Marschallin."

I studied these parts with a young man by the name of Alwin Pinkus, a very talented musician, but so skinny that my mother, who often sat in on our rehearsals in my apartment, kept him there for meals in order to fatten him up. He later became the husband of Elisabeth Schumann under the name of Karl Alwin. We had endless rehearsals, for the intervals were new and strange, and difficult at first. And of course learning three roles instead of one just added to the difficulties.

I find that the warmth that is so magnificent in the songs of Strauss is found in few of his operas. One has more the feeling of ecstasy, of expectation, of enthusiasm. Only his opera *Der Rosenkavalier,* at the end of the first act and at the close of the third act, contains something poetic, wise, and heavenly sweet. In everything Strauss wrote for orchestra, with or without voice, there is something so strong, so German, so straight, so gigantic in rhythm, technique, and temperament that one is swept away as if by elemental forces.

Our performance took place on 14 November 1911. Richard Strauss never conducted the first performances of his work, and so Dr. Karl Muck was the conductor. Our cast included Lola Artôt as Octavian, Claire Dux as Sophie, Paul Knüpfer as Baron Ochs von Lerchenau, and me as Marschallin, the field marshal's wife.

Strauss explained to us that the opera was to be played in the manner of *Figaro,* light, gay, full of French-Viennese atmosphere, intrigue, and resignation. Octavian, he said, is really like Cherubino, a little more cultured and riper, perhaps, and with good taste in his love affairs. The Marschallin, he explained, is a woman of the world, a little religious, a little demimonde, flirtatious, elegant, understanding, and resigned to any situation in life. She

Lola Artôt de Padilla as Octavian, Richard Strauss, and Hempel in her dressing room during rehearsals for *Der Rosenkavalier* in Berlin, 14 November 1911.

Hempel with Paul Knüpfer (left) as Baron Ochs and Baptist Hoffmann (right) in the Berlin premiere of *Der Rosenkavalier*, 1911. PHOTO BY ZANDER & LABISCH. COURTESY STUART-LIFF COLLECTION.

is full of grace and charm. Baron Ochs is a dumb, bold fortune hunter, who, in his love affairs, prefers to stoop low and mingle with servants. Sophie is pure, innocent, and very young.

Today we seem to have gone far astray from these concepts. The part of the Marschallin is performed by a large woman with a big, dramatic voice. Octavian is sung by a husky contralto, and the figure of Baron Ochs is reduced to a comical, slapstick character. As Strauss said to me years later, "If I had wanted a strong, husky person for Octavian I would have written the part for a tenor. The young boy Octavian should have a soprano-like sweetness. And I did not write heavy notes for the Marschallin. I composed the part for graceful, easy, parlando singing."

At the performance, we had to make one change in the first act. The opening scene should show the Marschallin in bed, resting and relaxing, with Octavian on the floor, kissing her and caressing her. But the emperor and his empress would never have permitted themselves to attend such a performance, being responsible, as they were, for the good conduct of their subjects. And they did not like the music of Wagner and Strauss in any event. They were faithful to the old classics in which the music was easier to understand and to enjoy.

As we certainly wanted the emperor and the empress to appear on the night of the performance, von Hülsen and Strauss agreed to substitute a chaise longue for the bed. This chaise longue was crowded with lace pillows. As the Marschallin, I was dressed very beguilingly in a simple negligee. Everything was so correct, so sweet, and so exquisitely conceived that I can say it was perhaps my greatest success.

I do not criticize, but I often wonder how it is possible to so disfigure this role. It is wonderful when properly understood. The Marschallin is not a crying, lamenting old woman. She is an ageless woman of the world who knows the true nature of men. She takes a change of heart very philosophically and encourages Octavian to ride with her in the Prater, still flirting with him and loving him in her light and elegant way. Her philosophy? "Light one has to be, with a light heart and hand to hold and to let go. If one is not so, life will punish, and God will show no mercy." So true, Hofmannstahl's words for her at the end of the first act are marvelous; Shakespeare could have written them.

Richard Strauss was an easygoing man. He was never arrogant at rehearsals but worked calmly with us. He listened to our suggestions and even considered our opinions about his music. For instance, we singers suggested that in his song "Ständchen," the last note be held two bars instead of one. He took this suggestion and thanked us for it.

He was an excellent storyteller and often entertained us with tales of the theater and of the various artists. He also loved to play cards and often sat with Paul Knüpfer and Councillor Levin, his great friend. He was extremely tidy about money matters. One day we were rehearsing *Der Rosenkavalier* when the librarian of the orchestra interrupted Strauss to report that he had returned a certain orchestral score to Fürstner, the publishers of Strauss's music. Strauss had given this man money to pay the small rental bill, and evidently there were three pennies due back in change. The orchestra librarian stood there, confidently expecting a tip for his services, and Strauss stood waiting for his three pennies in change. When the man realized what was expected of him, he began to search through all of his pockets for the missing pennies. "Well!" said Strauss, angrily, "Don't you have a stamp for it?"

The wife of Richard Strauss often gave us cause to wonder and to laugh. She thought very little of his family background and often remarked, "He is only a peasant, but I am a de Ahna," a well-known name. She seldom spoke well of him—quite the opposite—and when we rehearsed one of his works she would often say, "Oh, I am going back to the mountains. He can listen to his own music!" Or she would say, "Nobody can sing that!" He seemed to get a thrill out of such treatment, something we could not understand. I suppose there are two characters in each of us. I often wondered whom he admired and visualized in his heavenly songs. It could not have been his wife! It must have been just a vision, an ideal conceived in his own mind.

In September 1947 I saw him frequently; a photo from this time appears in this chapter. I was staying in St. Moritz, and nearly every day I would buy some cakes in the famous Hanselmann Bakery and then walk over to Pontresina where the Strausses lived. It was a walk of about an hour. There, in Pontresina, we would sit in front of the Hotel Saratz in the little garden and have our coffee and cake. There was a little orchestra of three men—a violinist, a cellist, and a pianist. They played all kinds of music, and nobody paid much attention to them. But when they started to play excerpts from *Tosca*, Mrs. Strauss leaned back in her chair, listened for a while, and then exclaimed, "Listen, Richard, *that* is music!" And this remark to the greatest composer of that time!

Shortly after our premiere of *Der Rosenkavalier*, I went to Nuremberg with Strauss to sing the Marschallin for the first time under his baton. It was a tremendous revelation to me to hear this work as he heard it. His personality towered above orchestra and soloists. He inspired, he hypnotized us with his whole being, and we felt his every intention. There was such spark and freshness in the opening, and the famous waltzes had a genuine Viennese lift. We left immediately after the performance for Berlin, and on the train Richard Strauss and I talked a great deal about *Ariadne*. I had impressed him so much with my coloratura technique of trills, staccatos, and high notes that, as I have mentioned, he had written the part of Zerbinetta for me. It is a demanding role, and singers must not sing it too often in the original version. I am glad to see that in current productions this part has been considerably simplified and cut. I promised Strauss that I would study it during the summer.

In Berlin we were soon ready with a performance of a delightful little *singspiel* that we had prepared for the emperor. Called *Der Grosse König* (The Great King), it was written by Frederick the Great,* an accomplished flutist and excellent amateur musician. The score contained numerous flute solos, which had been played by Frederick the Great at his own performances. I was the only singer in the cast, and as Barbarina, the king's mistress, I had several solos. The other members of the cast were actors. The emperor loved this little work, for it was gracious, simple, and historically significant.

Back in September, at the beginning of this 1911–12 season, I had worked strenuously on *Rosenkavalier*, and the endless rehearsals with the coach, the ensemble, the orchestra, and the full cast had tired my voice. Now, in Feb-

---

*While the emperor wrote some librettos and was also a composer, it seems more likely that his admirers created this singspiel based on melodies he performed and may have written. *Ed.*

ruary, I found that the constant change from the Marschallin to my lighter, coloratura roles had overtaxed my voice, and so I rested for a full month.

In March I returned to the opera house and entered into a final four-month schedule of opera and concert appearances, often twelve times a month. Whenever I sang with orchestra, in Budapest, Hamburg, Bremen, Nuremberg, Bad Oeynhausen, Wiesbaden, or wherever I happened to be, the members of the orchestra always saluted me by standing and clapping on the backs of their instruments in respect for my art and my musicianship. I needed no lengthy rehearsals, and I understood the intentions of the conductors. All over Europe I received this unusual compliment, and it meant a great deal to me.

In Warsaw I gave a concert with piano. There was a ban on singing in the German language, and so my program was sung in Italian and French. But when they asked for Mozart's "Lullaby," I insisted on singing it in German, for I could not stand any translation. Thus I became the first woman to sing in the German language in Warsaw, and the ban was broken. The audience loved it and applauded me tumultuously.

I had also been invited several times to sing in St. Petersburg, with orchestra, but I never found an open date. I was sorry about this, because Sembrich and Tetrazzini both told me how enthusiastic the Russians were, and how, in their excitement, they threw diamond bracelets and jewels onto the stage and showered the artists with presents.

My contract with the Royal Opera House of Berlin ended on 27 June 1912 with a performance of the *The Marriage of Figaro.* I did not say good-bye to any friends because I was not planning to leave for America before October, if indeed I would leave at all. My head was pounding with questions waiting to be answered. Should I go to America, should I marry the baron, should I remain in Berlin and marry Mr. Holy? I had the summer in which to decide.

I went to Riffler Alp for my vacation but soon traveled on to Venice. I registered at the Hotel Excelsior on the Lido. Here was a fine beach, and life was easygoing and pleasant. Many artists preferred to go there rather than to the Mediterranean. I spent many evenings with Fritz Kreisler, his wife, and other mutual friends. We would sit in those delightful, tiny restaurants in Venice, after having crossed to the island, and exchange stories and gossip. Once in a while I thought about and studied the part of Zerbinetta, which I had promised to look at.

One day I received a letter from Strauss, inviting me to his home in Garmisch, where he wished to work on the role of Zerbinetta with me. I replied that I should be delighted to come, and a few days later he greeted me on the doorstep of his charming home. We worked together every day. He explained the role to me, describing his idea of the character of Zerbinetta and how she should be portrayed. Over and over again we worked on those extremely high passages, which were much more difficult than anything I had ever done. My recreation was a long walk in the mountains with Mrs. Strauss. The Bavarian mountains are sweeter and more restful than the gigantic, stony Dolomites with their overpowering loneliness. The quiet valleys and the summer-green hills refreshed me as nothing else could; in my memories the genius of Strauss is wedded to this summer in the Bavarian countryside. The date of the first performance of *Ariadne* was not yet fixed, and so I returned to Berlin, having agreed to sing the role of Zerbinetta at the first performance if I could arrange my schedule.

I had received an extension of time from the Metropolitan Opera because I had been unable to come to any final decision. I gave a concert in Budapest in early October and then realized that I was not well. My voice was tired, my mind was tired, my body was tired. The strain of constant tension showed suddenly, and I was ordered to stay in bed and to receive no visitors. As I rested there, I tried to sing a little. My soft voice would not respond. A shock of great fear ran through me. So often, during the preceding months, I had felt uneasy about my *piano* tones, and now I had to face the fact that I had overtaxed my voice.

Singing ten to twelve times a month in public and changing constantly from heavy to light singing, from Strauss to Mozart and from Wagner to Meyerbeer, had been very difficult. The constant rehearsals, the travel, and the changes of climate had all affected my voice and had caused fatigue. We singers keep on working, thinking stupidly that the show must go on. I disliked canceling engagements, and I thought that I could keep on singing because I was young and strong. Why did I think that I could do it? Nobody can do it!

The difficulty with my soft voice worried and haunted me. This was the danger signal, the red light. If the soft voice does not respond, the singer must stop and consider nothing but the voice. Many careers might have been saved if singers had heeded that warning. Even my esteemed colleague Caruso at times failed to heed that warning. We all want to please the managers and cause them no trouble, and so we continue with a tired instrument. Managers are the last ones to appreciate this fact, however. They just let you go when you are no longer in good voice. I hope that my colleagues will take this advice and think first of their voices. They will sing better after sensible rest, and then the managers will be only too happy to have them back.

As soon as I was able to leave my bed, I went to see a throat doctor. The first thing he said was, "Et tu, Brute?" And he was right. I, too, had failed the singing voice. He told me that I had a little swelling on one of the vocal cords, and that it would only go away with rest. But then he did something that I now consider criminal: he taught me to see my own vocal cords. I bought a regular doctor's outfit—lamp, mirror, and everything else—and I sat for hours trying to see the condition of my own vocal cords. Something that an experienced doctor would recognize immediately as phlegm would be a nodule to me. This looking at my vocal cords became an obsession, and my mother and father pitied me and cried for me. I saw myself sitting in front of a typewriter, just typing—the honor, the earnings, the glory gone with the voice, no marriage after such heart-rending failure, nothing! If I had known about Christian Science in those days, I would have been able to deny this silly, imaginary condition, because nothing was really wrong, nothing that rest would not cure. I had no nodules.

As the small voice began to respond again, the hope became stronger than the fear. I began to think of the Metropolitan Opera and of my contract which meant so much to me. I knew that I would soon sing again as beautifully as ever, and I continued to rest. The baron and Mr. Holy were waiting for my decision. Mr. Holy begged me not to go to America but to stay in Berlin where I had a secure and honored position and a public that adored me. I received desperate letters and phone calls from the baron, asking me to stay with him, to be his wife, to travel with him, and to enjoy the luxuries that he could give me. And mother was crying her eyes out as she pictured me crossing the ocean, never to return. I tried to console her with the knowledge that I would only be gone a few months, but for her America was at the other end of the earth.

I grew weaker and weaker in my decision to sail, and I had just about decided to ask Gatti for a year's postponement when I received a cable from Otto Goritz, advising me that the Metropolitan had started negotiations with Selma Kurz of Vienna. I cabled back that I would sail for America on 14 December 1912, and I booked passage on the *George Washington*. I told Mr. Holy and Baron von Z. of my decision and then prepared for a farewell concert at the Philharmonic Hall.

When I went onto the stage the night of the concert, I felt as though I were saying goodbye to my own family. The house was packed. After each of my song groups, wreaths of all sizes were handed up over the footlights, tied with ribbons of blue, red, or white, bearing the most flattering, tender inscriptions: "To the German Patti," "To the Saxon Nightingale," "To the Incomparable Artist," and "Auf Wiedersehen!" The applause seemed never to end, and after the concert, when I came out to get into the automobile, the music lovers just carried me into the seat and then ran along the side of the car, cheering me and calling out "Auf Wiedersehen!" My family, a few friends, and I went to the famous restaurant Kempinski and celebrated.

The next day was a sad one. I felt terribly lonely. I had said goodbye to all my Berlin friends who had been so appreciative of my art. I had worked hard to earn their love, and I had received it to the fullest amount. Now it was all over. No more silly notes from Leo Blech, scolding or praising me, no more fatherly advice from Count von Hülsen, no more admiration from

Hempel saying goodbye to her parents upon her departure for the United States, December 1912. FROM *Mein Leben dem Gesang* (BERLIN, 1955).

the emperor. And no more singing in that cozy opera house where I had started and in which I had become the greatest coloratura singer in Germany. The three-year contract from the Metropolitan did not seem so wonderful, and I was almost sorry that I had signed it.

Luggage of private wardrobe and theatrical costumes had been taken care of, and now I said a last goodbye to all my lovely things in the apartment. Mother and father were going to stay there while I was gone, and Boy would remain with them. Rosa was coming with me. Closing the door behind me, I joined mother and father and Rosa, and off we went to Bremerhaven.

I just could not be in that city again without singing for Mr. Albert and his fine amateur orchestra. I had often sung with him, and the proceeds from my concerts paid for new instruments. Again I was showered with flowers and best wishes. The people of Bremerhaven had decorated my cabin beautifully, and their love and admiration filled the room.

Sailing time came closer and closer, and finally there we were, Rosa and I, standing at the rail and waving farewell to mother, father, and friends.

Disappearing from my sight was the land that had been so kind to me, so generous, and so helpful, the land in which I had lived through a most heavenly period of my career.

This broad, heavy liner, the *George Washington,* was a magnificent ship. It was equipped with all the modern comforts, which impressed me. Even the rough December weather failed to dismay me in my great enthusiasm. I had a wonderful cabin, beautifully decorated with floral tributes from the people of Bremerhaven, and Rosa had a cabin nearby.

I was the only artist on board, and so the other passengers made a great deal of fuss over me. Each night I was invited to join a different group of people, and each time I would appear in a different evening gown, elegant and sparkling. I had a marvelous time talking, dancing, and dining, and I was carefree and happy with my fellow passengers. I forgot all about my voice and just enjoyed everything.

But nothing so wonderful could last. On the fifth day out the weather changed, and we began to plough through extremely heavy seas. I became dreadfully seasick, and the "anti-seasick" pills made me even sicker. All I could do was to stay in my cabin and open all the portholes. This upset the steward no end, because of course the seawater rolled into my cabin with every lurch of the boat. He came in constantly and very politely closed the portholes. As soon as he had left, I would get up and throw them wide open again, taking the seawater full in the face as I did so. Of course I caught a severe cold from all of this, but at the time my only thought was for fresh air, which kept me from being deathly ill.

The captain himself was worried about the dangerously high seas, and we were all relieved when the ten-day voyage was over. We arrived safely in New York harbor on 24 December 1912.

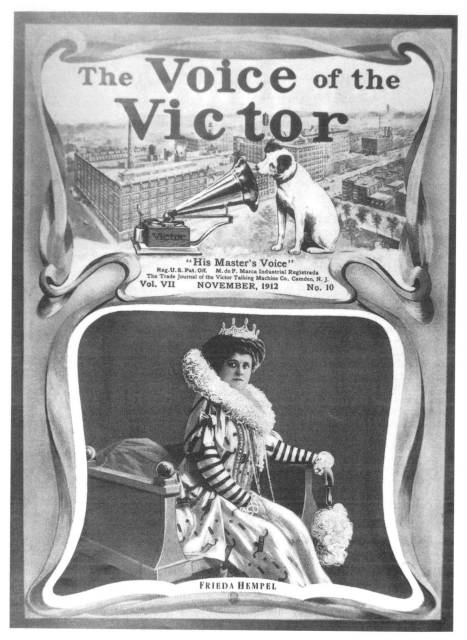

Hempel presides as the queen, Marguerite de Valois, in Meyerbeer's *Les Huguenots*, on front cover of *The Voice of the Victor*, the trade journal of the Victor Talking Machine Co., Camden, New Jersey, November 1912, before her Met debut in this role. COURTESY WILLIAM R. MORAN.

CHAPTER ELEVEN

America

I was met at the pier by the very clever press agent for the
Metropolitan Opera Company, Billy Guard. He took me
immediately to the huge hall where baggage was checked by customs officials, and then he introduced me to the newspaper reporters. I had caught a
glimpse of the Statue of Liberty and the famous New York skyline as we
entered the harbor, and I was thrilled to realize that I was in America at last.
But I had little time for impressions of any sort now, for my attention was
on these men who began to address me all at the same time. I could not
speak a word of English, nor could I understand what they were saying to
me, and so I just stood there, looking quizzically back at them. Rosa stood
behind me, no doubt wondering what was wrong and what these people
wanted of me.

I was frightened, for I had never seen this system of publicity at work.
We had nothing like it in Europe. And in addition to being frightened, I was
still very ill and wished only to go directly to the Knickerbocker Hotel,
where the Metropolitan Opera Company management had reserved rooms
for me. But I knew that in America this publicity was important, and I hesitated to leave. I asked Mr. Guard what to do, and he said not to worry, that
it would not take long. "Just say, 'Sure, Mike' to whatever they ask you, and
they'll understand." I followed his instructions, not knowing at all what
these words meant. "Sure, Mike," I said several times, and the men began to
laugh heartily. I laughed, too. Then Mr. Guard spoke to them and told
them what they wanted to know, I suppose. I had no idea what he was saying, and I couldn't even read the English-language newspapers the next day.

Finally the interview was over, and we left for the Hotel Knickerbocker on 42nd Street and Broadway.

It was a big, busy hotel, with a nice dining room and a homelike atmosphere. I was very pleased with my rooms. They were elegantly furnished, with red damask-covered chairs and deep rugs. The walls were very thick, and I was relieved to know that I could practice undisturbed.

Gatti-Casazza and Maestro Giorgio Polacco, the gentleman who was to conduct my debut performance of *Les Huguenots,* came to see me immediately. They were quite dismayed to learn that I was suffering from a severe cold. I could hardly talk above a whisper, and I begged Gatti to postpone my debut. I could not shake off such a cold in three days, and that was all the time I had. But he replied that the house was completely sold out and that he could not make any changes. It would not matter a bit if I sang with a cold, he said, because the audience knew of my reputation in Europe, and many people had already heard me and knew of my capabilities. They would understand if I did not sing perfectly. And so I agreed to appear.

The next day I stayed in my room. I was anxious to see the famous city, but I knew that I must rest if I was to sing at all. Gatti invited me to attend a performance of *Faust* that evening, and when I entered his box at curtain time I stood unable to speak. The enormous house was the open mouth of a lion, ready to devour me. The biggest houses in Europe had not prepared me for this! The singers seemed so tiny and so far away, and the acoustics bothered me. I had to leave before the performance was over because I had an early-morning rehearsal ahead of me. That night I saw nothing but the huge open jaws of a lion in my dreams, and I awoke unrefreshed.

The rehearsal went well enough, and my voice responded satisfactorily. The orchestra members stood up and applauded me enthusiastically, and I began to feel a little bit more secure. But the next day, the day of the performance, I was tired and frightfully nervous. I rested all day, and when I arrived at the opera house that evening, I was overjoyed to find Gatti waiting for me in my dressing room. He comforted me and told me again that the people in the audience were my friends, and that I should not worry. But it was only natural that I should have terrific stage fright because everything was so new, so big, and so very different.

As I entered the stage, I felt lost in that enormous house. The audience was so far away from me that it seemed impossible for them to hear me at all. When I finished my big scene, I stood and listened, not daring to believe my own ears. They had certainly heard me, and now they flooded me with applause and bravas. I was certainly grateful.

It was so wonderful, and it gave me such a warm, secure feeling to have Caruso as my partner in the duet. My much-adored Emmy Destinn was Valentine, and Antonio Scotti and Bella Alten were also in the cast. I was overjoyed to make my debut in America with such magnificent colleagues.

Gatti had copied the Berlin stage settings of *Les Huguenots* exactly, and this colorful opera, which had introduced me to Berlin, now introduced me to New York. I had twelve curtain calls, and I was "deluged" with flowers, as the papers put it the next day. The reviews were wonderful, and I was relieved that everything had gone so well.

A young American girl, Ilka von Horn, had studied voice with me in Berlin, and now she had followed me to New York and continued to work with me. Whenever I had a little spare time she would take Rosa and me about New York. Everything in the city seemed so big, so busy, and still so calm and controlled. In Europe if so many people were together in one place, they would be flustered and confused. The suspicion and distrust that we Europeans knew as members of small countries whose boundaries were guarded were contrasted here by broad-mindedness, kindness, trust, and naturalness. I loved it all, what little I saw of it in those first weeks. I began to feel at home among these friendly people.

Performances came in quick succession at the Metropolitan. I sang the Queen of the Night in *The Magic Flute*, then Olympia in *Les Contes d'Hoffmann* (The Tales of Hoffmann), and then again the queen in *Les Huguenots*. By the middle of January 1913, I was well over my cold and secure with my voice, but it took me the whole season to overcome the nervousness that followed my having been required to make my debut while still indisposed.

On 14 January Mrs. Cornelius Vanderbilt invited me to sing for her at a musicale and dinner in her Fifth Avenue mansion. It was a very cosmopolitan gathering, and I immediately felt the presence of elegant, cultured, interesting people. After dinner everyone gathered in the large music room, and Mr. Eugène Ysaÿe, the great concert violinist, and I presented our several solos. We closed the concert with Gounod's *Ave Maria,* with violin obbligato played by Mr. Ysaÿe. Many people came up and complimented me, and one very plain-looking, tiny, shy man shook hands with me and spoke to me in German. Then he left the house immediately. I never forgot him. His name was Andrew Carnegie.

Another type of concert certainly astonished me. Where in the world would one expect to see a packed house at eleven o'clock in the morning? My first Bagby Musical Morning concert, on 27 January 1913, was a strange experience for me. Only in America was such a thing possible. I don't believe that anyone in Europe would ever have had such an idea. Mr. Albert Morris Bagby was a musician himself and very popular around New York, especially with the high society. He was a most tactful man, and he knew how to tell his friends exactly what they wanted to hear. He flattered the ladies right and left, and when he began these morning concerts he had their complete support.

It was his intention to give these society women the pleasure of hearing world-famous artists, and then serve them a delightful luncheon in the mag-

nificent dining room of the old Waldorf Astoria where the concerts were
held. He asked only the most renowned artists to appear, and I do not believe that any artist ever refused his offer. Of course, we singers hated to get
up so early in the morning, for we had to be up by seven in order to awaken
our voices and be ready for a concert at eleven. Caruso expressed himself to
me very drastically about this, saying, "Eleven o'clock is just the time for me
to spit and gargle, not the time for me to sing a concert!" But we were handsomely paid, and we all enjoyed singing for Mr. Bagby's audience of elegant society women. I admit that they clapped gloved hands with great gentility and often left me wondering if they had really enjoyed my singing!

It was considered quite a social achievement to be counted as a regular
member of this concert audience, and the unfortunate general public could
not obtain tickets. It was amazing to realize this, but then the ladies of society adored Mr. Bagby, and trusted him to such an extent that some of them
even allowed him to handle their estates. This gentleman really deserved
the highest praise and admiration for his achievement. He put his heart and
soul into these concerts and luncheons, and they were always most successful. He would select his own artists, usually combining a singer from the
Metropolitan with one or two great instrumentalists. He would supervise
the choice of selections, and he reviewed the gowns the prima donnas had
chosen to wear. He took no chances, for he wanted everything to be as perfect as possible.

We presented good but rather light music, entertaining and pleasant.
"On Wings of Song" by Mendelssohn and "Oh Had I Jubal's Lyre" by Handel were two favorites of Mr. Bagby, and I sang them every year for him,
along with some Schumann and Schubert. He often came to my home to go
over the program with me, and I would hum the songs for him. He was
politeness and tact personified, a gentleman in the true meaning of the word.
He would accompany an artist to the stage and advise her as to just which
encores were suitable, and after the concert was over, he would invite her
most politely to attend the luncheon.

At the luncheons Mr. Bagby displayed another gift, the gift of gathering
interesting people together. I always met someone exciting at these affairs, a
prince or an ambassador or a famous writer from some place on the globe.
These concerts and luncheons made Mr. Bagby a rich man, and he deserved
his fine success. When the old Waldorf Astoria was torn down to make way
for the Empire State Building, he moved the concerts to the Plaza and then
to the new Waldorf Astoria on Park Avenue. But to my mind the unique
atmosphere was no longer present. The ballroom where the concerts were
given seemed too large. We artists were too far away from the audience for
the successful projection of intimate songs. The energy that should flow
between artist and listener never crossed the footlights, and the meaning of
the songs was lost.

When Mr. Bagby died, this singular form of concert died with him. No one else had the peculiar genius needed to make such an undertaking successful. There was only one Mr. Bagby, and his death meant a great loss to the artistic world.

The Knickerbocker Hotel was a convenient place for singers from the Metropolitan because it was only a short walk to the opera house. For this reason many members of the company lived there. Caruso had the whole ninth floor for his use later on, but this first year of my stay he had a suite next to mine. I seldom heard him practice, but his accompanist played constantly. If Caruso was to sing Canio in the evening, I heard the score of *Pagliacci* being played all day long. Scotti also lived at the hotel, and he and Caruso were inseparable friends. I think that Caruso profited a great deal from this friendship, because Scotti was such a perfect actor and helped Caruso in many ways. The attractive dining room was popular with visitors who wished to get a glimpse of us, and they seemed to be delighted to see Toscanini, Farrar, Scotti, Caruso, me, and other artists, dining with friends.

Every Friday night a long bread line formed at the Broadway kitchen door, and poor men in tattered clothing lined up to receive the leftovers from the kitchen. One cold February evening, after a performance at the Metropolitan, Caruso and a few others and I decided to walk back to the hotel together. As we passed the Broadway side of the Knickerbocker, we saw all these hungry men waiting for food. In the line stood a very old, thin man, clad only in a threadbare suit. Caruso stood there for a few seconds, looking at him, and shaking his head. He spoke with the old man and then took off his fur-lined winter coat, put it across the shoulders of the man, and walked into the hotel with us without saying a word. Such was his great heart!

During January we rehearsed intensively for the performance of *La traviata* which was to take place on 29 January. Maestro Gennaro Papi worked a great deal with me on my Italian pronunciation, which was naturally a little imperfect. He called me "La donna con le belle pelle," the lady with the beautiful skin, but in spite of this lovely compliment, I did not like him. He loved to repeat everything one said to Gatti-Casazza, and no one admires such a person. Both Umberto Macnez, the tenor, and I were new in the cast, and I must say that he was far more consumptive than I, the Violetta. He tried his best, but his voice was just too small for the Metropolitan auditorium.

During this performance on 29 January, one incident amused me a great deal. It was my first real introduction into the secret arts of publicity. At the last moment, just before I was scheduled to appear on the stage, I wound some cheap piece of jewelry around my ankle, because I knew that my legs would show quite a bit under my modern dress. We had always given *La traviata* in modern dress in Berlin, and I followed the same custom in New York this first year. Well, having fastened the bracelet to my ankle, I came out onstage and sang my role. The next morning I saw my picture on the front page of a newspaper, with the ankle bracelet clearly visible. The news reporter had discovered that this bracelet was "a gift from the Kaiser," the sense of drama and the clever twist of fact which is the tool of the American newspaperman. And of course no one believed my protestations: they all preferred to believe the story in the newspaper.

I had great success with *La traviata,* and Toscanini became a great admirer of mine. One day he came backstage just before a performance of *Tales of Hoffmann* which Giorgio Polacco was to conduct and said to me, "You just sing—let him follow you!" Toscanini, knowing that my natural instincts for phrasing and coloring were right, did not wish to see my interpretation hindered. I was proud of this compliment. In fact, throughout my operatic and concert career I always had the true respect of the conductors, and so I must have had a natural instinct for the "right" way within me from the beginning.

Toscanini selected me to sing the role of Eva in *Die Meistersinger von Nürnberg.* Before my arrival Emmy Destinn, Bella Alten, and Johanna Gadski had all sung this role, but a dramatic voice is not the right voice for Eva. Toscanini realized this, and when I joined the Metropolitan he chose me to sing this role for him. It was a great disappointment to me not to be able to sing my Italian roles under his baton, but the heavier operas and the Wagnerian works were entrusted to him and to Alfred Hertz. I must pay Toscanini the great compliment of saying that for an Italian he understood the German spirit and feeling extraordinarily well, especially in *Die Meistersinger* which is so typically German. I was greatly surprised to find this out, for it is not easy for an Italian to capture the rather sentimental, poetic German atmosphere in the second act, nor the greatness of the last act.

A singer or a conductor who can acclimate himself to different styles and different languages reveals great artistry. And, in general, this talent is rather rare with Italians. Caruso himself had some difficulty in adjusting his voice to different languages, and he was perfectly at ease only when singing in his native language. The Italian singer is a natural singer. He probably sings operatic arias in the streets of his hometown at the age of six, and he grows up still singing just this typical Italian repertory in the same beautiful way. And this is all his countrymen ask of him.

The German singer, on the other hand, is much more capable of adjustment. As a German artist, he is required by his public to know the literature of several different languages. And even though he may be primarily an operatic singer, he must sing German lieder with musicianship and art. Tetrazzini once said to me, "Friedolina, if I could sing songs the way you do, I would sing them all the time, and let the coloratura fireworks go." We all know that she had a very childlike middle range, and because she had not developed these notes, she could not sing songs with any degree of artistry. I was also a coloratura soprano, but I was expected to have an extensive song repertory, and so I cultivated my middle range as well as my high range. And such cultivation implies extensive study and long, hard work.

During my first months at the Metropolitan, everything seemed many times bigger to me than at home. I noticed this more at rehearsals when the houselights were on. The rows of seats stretched on and on, and the balconies climbed higher and higher. In the evening, when the houselights were dimmed, I felt more comfortable. It was new to me to see so many boxes empty at the start of a performance, and the bright lights from these empty loges disturbed me. But by the end of the first act most of the occupants had arrived, and when the houselights went on the sight was breathtaking. The elegance of the gowns and the glitter of jewels were fabulous.

Singing for the Metropolitan Opera Club was also a different sort of experience. What a wonderful sight that was! Nothing but men, sitting in three rows, and all of them focusing their opera glasses on me as I sang. I met quite a number of charming gentlemen at this club, among them James Cutting, a handsome man who became my good friend, Richard Schuster, a New York banker, and Adolph Pavenstedt, head of a great export-import firm, who later ran into difficulty in the Bolo Pacha* affair.

At the end of February 1913 I was called to Boston to sing in *The Barber of Seville.* And so for the first time I entered Grand Central Station, which looked more like a palace than a railroad station to me, with its marble floors and its great lights. The trains themselves were elegant, and I remember the dining cars only too well. I always tried to empty my glass of water, for I had been taught to eat and drink everything that was served to me, this being considered only polite. But the waiter no sooner saw my glass empty than he filled it again. I never drank so much water in all my life. Finally I complained in desperation to a companion, and I learned that the waiters were also trained, and that they were required to keep the water glasses constantly filled. This information settled my stomach a little and gave the waiter a little rest, I imagine.

The opera house in Boston was much more European in style, smaller and more intimate than the Metropolitan, and the acoustics were heavenly. It was pointed out to me that my partner was none other than the famous tenor John McCormack. I had never heard of him, but I listened in rehearsal to some beautiful singing and phrasing. However, my personal taste has always been for the darker quality of voice color, as Caruso had.

Back in New York, I sang once more in *Tales of Hoffmann.* In the cast

---

*Paul Bolo Pacha, accused of spying for Germany, was tried and executed in 1918. *Ed.*

was Dinh Gilly, who made a great hit singing the aria "Scintille, diamant." I have no doubt that he learned everything he knew about singing from Emmy Destinn. They were great friends, and they spent much time together. I seldom saw Emmy Destinn by this time, although in Berlin we had spent pleasant evenings chatting about her hobbies. She was a great lover of the occult sciences—she had an extensive library on the subject and held séances in her home. She also collected rare books and owned many extraordinary volumes. Napoleon, the great Frenchman, was her idol. She knew all there was to know about him. I admired her greatly for her many interests and enthusiastic pursuit of information about her hobbies.

Toscanini selected me to sing the soprano solos in a performance of Beethoven's Ninth Symphony in New York in April 1913. Following this performance, I left for Europe for the summer. I had fallen in love with America, and I made plans to find a permanent home in New York upon my return in the fall.

CHAPTER TWELVE

Der Rosenkavalier

C *aruso and I sailed for Europe* in May of 1913 on the same boat, and we enjoyed many games of shuffleboard together. It was spring, and the weather was lovely. In Berlin I was happy to see my family again, and I sang a few performances at the Royal Opera House for my beloved Berlin public.

After a short vacation in the Black Forest, in August I went to Italy to study Italian. Ilka von Horn was my traveling companion, and we had with us my two fox terriers, Boy and Struppi. We stopped at Montecatini for a short visit and then went on to Florence. In this beautiful city I spent most of my time at the Palazzo Pitti. The beauty and great strength of that building appealed to me, and the wealth of art which it contained held my attention for days. I sat for a long time in front of a Madonna by Raphael. She was so natural and so full of life that I wanted to talk to her.

One day in front of the Palazzo Pitti, I saw an Italian woman leading a little dog on a long leash. He was no bigger than the palm of my hand and was clipped like a lion. He was a little Pomeranian, and of course I had to have him. I purchased him from the woman for thirty lire, a trivial sum, and immediately named him Pitti. A few years later, after he had become a member of the Metropolitan Opera and had appeared in *Der Rosenkavalier,* some people offered me five hundred dollars for glamorous Pitti. But I have never sold a friend yet, and I did not sell Pitti.

From Florence Ilka and I went to Parma where I planned to study Italian with Professor Rasi, the manager of Eleonora Duse, the great Italian tragedienne. We loved the city, but after a few days there we both developed a most annoying rash. We could not imagine what the cause might be. One night we stayed up and turned the lights systematically on and off, expecting the worst. When we found nothing we took heart, a little, and the next day we sprayed the rooms and bought some menthol powder. That night before going to bed, I covered myself with this powder, and of course I shivered all night long from the cooling effect. Even this did not help, and it was most embarrassing, for I was covered with tiny red spots and my skin itched dreadfully. Fortunately, Gatti-Casazza arrived in Parma to attend the big centennial festival of Verdi's birth. When I complained to him of being unable to find the culprits responsible for my rash, he laughed heartily and told us that our diet of Chianti red wine and fruit was responsible for the rash. We immediately changed diet, and the trouble disappeared, thank goodness!

Ilka and I returned to Berlin after enjoying the music of the festival and learning a good deal of Italian. My three dogs were with me, but Pitti was so tiny that he traveled in one of my hats and gave me no trouble at all. After appearing again at the Berlin Royal Opera House, I prepared to leave my family and friends once more, and in October I was back in New York for the 1913–14 season. I left Boy with my parents, who were living in my Berlin apartment, and I brought Struppi and Pitti with me to New York.

On 19 November I sang my first Queen of the Night at the Metropolitan Opera under the baton of Alfred Hertz. We began final rehearsals for *Der Rosenkavalier,* which was to have its premiere performance on 9 December.

Meanwhile, on 22 November 1913, we gave a performance of *Un ballo in maschera* by Verdi, with a magnificent cast and a great conductor. Caruso, Destinn, Amato, Matzenauer, Rothier, de Segurola, and I sang together under the baton of Toscanini. When Gatti-Casazza was asked, upon the occasion of his retirement, which performance under his management had been the greatest, he replied, "*Un ballo in maschera*—such a cast will never again be brought together."

Most of the *Der Rosenkavalier* cast had been working on their roles during the summer. The members of the cast who did not speak German had a great deal of work to do. As the opera was to be sung in German, I needed little preparation. Madame Ober had sung the role of Octavian many times with me in Berlin, but the other principal singers, Anna Case as Sophie, Otto Goritz as Baron Ochs, Hermann Weil as von Faninal, and Karl Jörn as the Italian singer were all going to sing their roles for the first time.

Mr. Hertz caught the spirit of the opera admirably, and the performance went well. The work created much discussion. Most of the critics did not know what to make of it, and the public found it long and boring at first hearing. It has taken a long time for the public to become familiar with this score, and of course in time the *Rosenkavalier* waltzes have become extremely popular.

As Princess von Werdenberg, the Marschallin, before the U.S. premiere of *Der Rosenkavalier*, Metropolitan Opera, 9 December 1913. PHOTO BY MISHKIN. COURTESY WILLIAM R. MORAN.

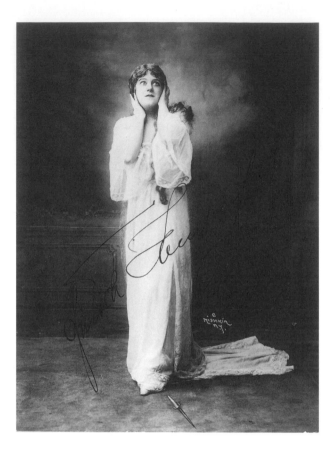

As Lucia (photo by
Mishkin at left) and
Oscar in *Ballo* (below).
COURTESY METROPOLITAN
OPERA ARCHIVES.

W. J. Henderson wrote that the score was "commonplace," and he thought that the ending was a "lamentable piece of bungling." He concluded his review, after praising me for my style and my diction, by saying that "the thing has no standing as a work of art. It is not even a good piece of workmanship." So poorly did an esteemed critic judge this wonderful opera!

As I have said, I had created the role of the Marschallin in Berlin under the close supervision of Richard Strauss, and I sang it subsequently many times under his baton. He often told me that in his estimation I was the ideal Marschallin. And in 1947 I received a postcard from him, upon which was written, "Meiner bezaubernden Marschallin" (To my bewitching Marschallin). In view of these facts, I hope that a few comments about *Der Rosenkavalier* and about the Marschallin, in particular, will be appreciated. As I mentioned earlier, Richard Strauss and Count von Hülsen discussed this opera at length with us in Berlin. No details were overlooked in that production, and many things not indicated in the score became traditional in performance.

This is the pattern that I set for the Marschallin in Berlin and New York. When the curtain rises, I have left the bed and I am reclining on a couch, clad only in a low-cut nightgown and a very light robe. My hair is held together with a dainty lace cap, as was customary in the times of Maria Theresa. My shoulders are very much exposed. Octavian and I continue to kiss and embrace one another. The boy is reclining at my feet, worshipping and adoring me, and very much in love. I tell him to hide as breakfast is brought in, and I change from the light robe to an elegant dressing gown, so that I may receive the tradespeople and the hairdresser. Suddenly Baron Ochs is announced, and Octavian quickly changes into women's clothes, so as not to be discovered in my boudoir. Then, as the tradespeople enter, I seat myself at the dressing table, which has been moved to the center of the stage. The hairdresser removes the little cap that I am wearing, covers my shoulders with a short cape to protect my gown, and starts to dress my hair for the day. After he has finished, he examines my head from all sides and then powders my hair, as was the custom in Maria Theresa's time. Looking into the mirror, I find that not only has he dressed my hair poorly, but he has overpowdered it. Disturbed by this unflattering image, I say to him, "Heut haben Sie ein altes Weib aus mir gemacht!" (Today you have made an old woman out of me.)

This thought takes hold of me, and I become pensive. I send Baron Ochs away after the tradespeople have left, and I seat myself at the dressing table again. I begin to think about the passage of time and how mysterious it is. I am not frightened, but I realize what life and time really mean. Octavian returns, and as I look at him, I realize that I shall not be able to hold him for long. He will surely fall in love with a younger woman. He notices a slight shadow of sadness in my face, but I say that it is just a mood. I cannot help showing a little of what I am thinking, and Octavian denies that he will ever lose his love for me. I am not sad but I understand, through this new awareness of life, that I cannot expect to hold him. Still, I do not intend for this moment to come just yet, and I invite him to keep me company in the Prater if I ride in the afternoon. I remain as desirable and as charming to him as ever.

Today this concept of the Marschallin has been weakened a great deal. The role is frequently given to a dramatic soprano. Margarethe Siems, who created the role in Dresden in 1911, and I, who sang it in Berlin under Richard Strauss and in New York, were lyric coloraturas. If Strauss had wished to cast a dramatic soprano as the Marschallin, there were several excellent ones available in Dresden and in Berlin. But he definitely wanted a light, lyric soprano for this role, and although I was already studying the role of Sophie, he asked me to be his Marschallin. How can the gaiety, lightness, and elegance of this dainty woman be portrayed by a large woman who habitually sings Isolde? Is not the example set by Strauss himself authentic enough?

And I have seen a highly praised Marschallin appear in the first act, as the curtain rises, in a poison-green taffeta gown! What elegant, dainty woman would wear that and expect to be beguiling to her lover? Chiffon, tulle, and lace: those are the materials she should have chosen from, delicate materials in dainty pastel shades. Just look at some of the famous paintings and prints of the times. The ladies are in soft morning gowns with little caps on their heads. The paintings of Jean-Marc Nattier, of François Boucher, and of William Hogarth show this clearly. In fact the levée of Hogarth was used as a model for the first-act scene with the tradespeople and the hairdresser. And remember another thing: the Marschallin and Octavian have just awakened from a night of love, and it is not likely that the Marschallin would be beautifully gowned for the day. On the contrary, she has not yet put on her morning gown.

And what has happened to the hair of the Marschallin? Perhaps this seems unimportant, but actually it is of the utmost importance. In the time of Maria Theresa around 1770, a lady of gentle birth was coiffured by a hairdresser each morning. Her hair was set in curls and then powdered. In performances of *Der Rosenkavalier* today, the Marschallin appears at the very beginning of the first act with her hair already beautifully combed and curled. It makes no sense, therefore, to have the hairdresser enter her boudoir and prepare to dress her hair. He can make no changes in the already perfect coiffure, and in current productions he no longer even powders her hair. Why, then, does she say to him that he has made an old woman out of her? This key statement, upon which the development of the whole opera depends, no longer has any meaning for the public, and it certainly can have little meaning for the Marschallin herself. It is exactly the handiwork of this hairdresser, who, having removed the little lace cap that holds the disheveled hair in place, arranges the hair in unbecoming curls and overpowders it, which upsets the Marschallin. It is the white hair that shocks her, for she sees herself as the old woman she will one day be. If Strauss saw the dramatic value of this and therefore directed the hairdresser to overpowder the Marschallin's hair, why have the stage managers of today eliminated this action? They err in allowing the Marschallin to appear with perfect coiffure, and they err again in failing to direct the hairdresser to overpowder her hair. Consequently, they destroy the validity of the key sentence of this act.

Strauss himself had great fear that the monologue, into which the Marschallin's thoughts lead her, would be tragically sung and overdramatized. He stressed to me the fact that the philosophy of the Marschallin is not a tragic one. It is rather a philosophy of smiling resignation, an understanding of the fact that one need not fear growing old. The Marschallin must not become a lamenting old woman; she must not cry and pity herself. The monologue must move along in a flowing tempo—it must not drag and grow heavy with tragedy as it so often does today. This is a point of utmost importance also, because if the Marschallin does not properly understand the monologue, the beautiful sense of understanding with which she accepts Octavian's love for Sophie cannot be communicated.

Now I should like to make one comment about the last act. As you know, the Marschallin goes to a shabby inn. She surely does not want to be recognized by the class of people whom she will encounter, and the whole visit is very painful to her. As the Marschallin, I dressed very inconspicuously for this act. I wore a gown of dark-green brocade, with simple lace trimmings, and a light chiffon scarf over my shoulders. On my head was a simple white wig. In current productions the Marschallin appears at the inn dressed as though she were going to a Beaux Arts ball. She wears a towering high wig, a muff, a cape, and an enormous gown of loud, showy material and color. Such tasteless overdressing is not in keeping with the refined sensibilities of the Marschallin.

I am concerned with these deviations because they seriously affect the character of the Marschallin. I realize that the desire to retain traditions is somewhat old-fashioned these days, but in the instance of the Marschallin, I am certain that my few suggestions will not disconcert the modernists.

Octavian is a dainty seventeen-year-old boy. No woman of tall, stately figure can successfully portray this young lover. And certainly no contralto who has the slightest difficulty with her upper notes should sing Octavian. Lola Artôt de Padilla, who created the role of Octavian in Berlin, was ideally cast. Of the several singers who have essayed this role more recently, perhaps Risë Stevens most closely approximates the true Octavian as Strauss conceived him. Sophie is described by Baron Ochs as having shoulders "like a young chicken." In other words, she is a slim, undeveloped young girl, and no mature, buxom woman can achieve such an illusion.

If what I have just written about *Der Rosenkavalier* can be of help to young singers and young stage managers, then I shall be happy. The role of the Marschallin is dear to me, and I am certain that she will continue to live as the admirable, elegant, and charming woman Strauss intended her to be.

During the final rehearsals of this opera at the Metropolitan, my beloved dog Struppi fell ill, and one morning he died. I came to rehearsals that day with swollen eyes and a sad face. When Gatti learned of my sorrow, he laughed heartily, and teased me for taking the incident so tragically. I believe that Gatti never had a dog, and so he could not have known how much comfort and happiness left me when Struppi died. Only a person as devoted to animals as I could understand the sense of loss that encompassed me.

But I still had Pitti to console me, my little five-pound Pomeranian from sunny Florence. He was always with me in my dressing room, and the darling of everybody. One evening, without preparation and with no rehearsals at all, he became a member of the cast of *Der Rosenkavalier.* I was on stage for the first act, as usual, but this time my maid Rosa wanted to hear the opera, and so she left Pitti alone in the dressing room and stood in the wings, listening and watching. A little while later Pitti succeeded in opening the door to my dressing room. He bounced along backstage, crossed in front of the footlights, and leapt up into my lap with a great show of affection. By delightful coincidence, we were performing the scene in which I receive the tradespeople, and so I immediately indicated to the tradesman who was trying to sell me a parrot that I would buy this dog. In this manner a perfectly natural bit of stage action was created out of what might have been seen as carelessness. Because his entrance was so beautifully timed, we were all able to laugh heartily about it afterwards. And since that night, Pitti always performed with me in *Der Rosenkavalier.* This was certainly not an idea of Richard Strauss, but rather Pitti's idea. Never paid for his work, he performed for the sake of art.

One day, during the time of those busy final rehearsals for the premiere of *Der Rosenkavalier,* I received a nosegay, a charming little bouquet, from a Mr. William B. Kahn, along with a letter of introduction from Emmy, the daughter of my teacher in Berlin Frau Nicklass-Kempner. Mr. Kahn was an American of course, but he had met Emmy in Munich, and she had suggested that he call on me. I was happy to receive the bouquet and the note, but unfortunately I neglected to answer him because I was extremely busy, and my mind was still with Struppi.

Three weeks later I received a second note, asking if I had enjoyed the flowers. I was terribly embarrassed at my oversight, and with profuse apologies I invited him to tea. I was now living on West 88th Street near Riverside Drive, and Ilka von Horn was staying with me. Mr. Kahn arrived punctually, and to my delight I found him to be a very handsome young man. He spoke German fluently, a talent decidedly to his advantage for I still found English difficult. He had a great sense of humor, and we three spent a delightful afternoon together. I grew to like his company very much. He showed me around New York City and entertained me with his delightful and intelligent conversation. He was a great music lover and seemed to know every German song by heart. He knew the great works of music equally well, was very well read in literature, and had excellent judgment in painting and sculpture. It is little wonder that he became my favorite escort.

By now I had become deeply impressed with America, and I could not help thinking that I would stay. All my problems with my admirers in Berlin were whisked away as I made new friends here, and their flowers and gifts made me very happy. And now Mr. Kahn spent a great deal of time with me, and soon I began to see less and less of my other admirers. We were very happy together, and we secretly became engaged to be married.

Meanwhile my professional appearances with the Metropolitan kept me busy indeed. In addition to the performances at the Metropolitan Opera House, weekly performances were presented by the management in Brooklyn and in Philadelphia. And if I happened to be a member of the cast I went along on those weekly trips to Philadelphia each Tuesday.

There I loved to sing in the beautiful theater of the Academy of Music. Behind stage a true European atmosphere prevailed, because everything was smaller than at the Metropolitan and we were all closer together. The tenor in the room next to mine would warm up his voice, singing hundreds of mi–mi–mis, the baritone across from me would snarl his lo–lo–los, and I would sing trills and staccatos. It might have seemed like a madhouse to many people, but we all loved it, and nobody objected to anything.

The Philadelphians welcomed us warmly and enjoyed these evenings immensely. After the performance we all boarded the midnight train in a great spirit of happiness and relaxation. The trip to Philadelphia was always quiet, for we singers rested and relaxed our voices for the evening. We were all conscious of our responsibility to the public. But on the return trip we acted like grownup children, laughing, telling stories, playing cards, eating sandwiches purchased from a lunch wagon, and drinking coffee from paper cups. Instead of sleeping, we all sat up until the train arrived in New York about two o'clock in the morning, and even then we were having such a good time that we did not want to leave one another.

The critics from the New York papers often went with us to review the performances for the Philadelphians, and James Huneker was a great favorite with us. This jolly Falstaff of a man, with his magnificent sense of humor, kept us all entertained with his wonderful tales. I seemed to be a pet of his, for he always landed in my drawing room to my great delight. Those were wonderful evenings.

All too soon the season ended, and my second wonderful year in America was over. I had sung fifty-one times for the Metropolitan, and I had given many concerts in various cities. Mr. Kahn was unable to come to Europe for the summer because of business commitments, but I had several professional engagements to fulfill and I wished to go to Italy for a while to study Italian. So I sailed early in May with the promise to return as soon as possible.

CHAPTER THIRTEEN

Giulio Gatti-Casazza and the Years 1914–16

*D*uring that summer of 1914, I spent some happy days in Berlin with my family and my many friends, and I sang a few performances at the Royal Opera House, which remained forever dear to me.

Then I went up into the Swiss Alps, to a tiny hamlet in the Engadin called Sils-Maria. High snow-covered mountains, sweet valleys filled with mountain flowers, quiet blue lakes, music from a simple Swiss chalet, yodels ringing from the mountain ranges, and the fresh innocent laughter of the village maidens all helped me to be grateful again for the gift of life itself. Here one was so close to nature, to God; here one realized how beautiful the world was. How unimportant we humans became, how useless the rushing and the striving, when we could all be crushed in a second by the great power that created such beauty and such grandeur.

Here in Sils-Maria is surely the perfect setting for poets and dreamers. The great German poet and philosopher Nietzsche wrote *Also sprach Zarathustra* on one of those little islands in the lake of Sils-Maria, and it was here that he died, calling out to his God.

I went out to that little island every day and sat and sat, and thought, and drank in all the beauty around me. But all too soon I was disturbed by ugly noises. The peace was broken, and I was frightened. I heard cannons roaring and became aware of the Swiss soldiers and their maneuvers. This was not a good omen, and I realized that I must return to Berlin immediately. I arrived there on the first of August, the very day that war was declared.

During the 1914–15 season. PHOTO BY MISHKIN. COURTESY ROBERT TUGGLE.

I stayed in my apartment with mother and father to await news from Gatti-Casazza. I had intended to return to America, of course, but at this point it looked as though the Metropolitan Opera Company would have to abandon its 1914–15 season. The European artists of the company had come to Europe for the summer, as usual, to vacation and to fulfill professional engagements. Now they were scattered all over the continent, in Belgium, France, Italy, Germany, and elsewhere, and many of the men would have to go to the front to fight. Everything was in great turmoil, and none of us knew what steps to take.

I remained at home, making only one short trip to Schwerin. Like so many of the other artists I thought that with the new, modern weapons the war would surely be over in a matter of weeks, and like them I did not want to sacrifice my hard-earned Metropolitan contract for the comfort of being with my family during these trying days. And so I waited anxiously for news from Gatti.

Then one day the joyful message arrived that the 1914–15 season would begin as usual in November, and that the Metropolitan management would aid us in obtaining visas and passports. We were instructed to meet Gatti-Casazza in Naples in October, where we would then board the *Canopic,* an English ship hired by Gatti for the express purpose of bringing us all back to America safely. For of course the northern waters were no longer safe, and the usual route was closed to us.

Every person sailing on the *Canopic* had to be registered as a member of the Metropolitan Opera Company, and as I had invited the youngest daughter of my teacher, Frau Nicklass-Kempner, to come to America with me, I registered her as a chorus member. Rosa, my maid, was young and pretty, and so her papers stated that she was a ballerina!

It was raining heavily when we arrived in Rome on our way to Naples. We had left Berlin with mixed feelings of apprehension and happiness, and the gloom of Rome did not help us to turn our thoughts toward the joyful days ahead. The principal hotel in which I wished to stay was filled, and only the royal suite was available. But Emmy Nicklass turned to me and said, "Well, that is just the place for the Queen of Song!" and so we decided to stay. The royal suite was sumptuous, and after we had unpacked our things, we became fascinated by the crystal light fixtures. They glittered from every corner of the room, and our curiosity impelled us to count the light bulbs. There were 158 of them! In this stagelike atmosphere our high spirits returned, and the next morning we left for Naples in a happier frame of mind.

In Naples I greeted my good colleagues Emmy Destinn, Geraldine Farrar, Caruso, Amato, Toscanini, Gatti-Casazza, and others. We were all taken on a tour of Naples by the most famous Neapolitan of them all, Enrico Caruso. I had never been in southern Italy, and I was unprepared for the impression I received from Naples. The clear, shimmering atmosphere was like the essence of sound, and the unique beauty of this city flowed through every fiber of Caruso's being. I could understand now how such glorious tones had come to be, how such a voice belonged to such a city.

When the entire company was assembled, the *Canopic* received her precious cargo and raised anchor for the high seas and distant America. She stopped only at Almería, on the Mediterranean coast of Spain, to load a shipment of grapes. And it was here that I witnessed my second bullfight. A group of us went ashore in a tiny fishing boat while cargo was taken on. Walking a short distance, we arrived at an arena, empty and dusty on this warm afternoon. Caruso, who had been our guide, sent us into the bleachers and disappeared with Scognamillo, his secretary. We were no sooner seated than a furious fight began. Scognamillo was the matador and Caruso was the raging bull. We fell into the spirit of the ancient sport and filled the arena with our cheers and bravos. When the bull and the matador were exhausted, we let them go and returned to the fishing boat that was waiting for us.

We had been warned to stay by ourselves, for a disease of the eyes was rampant in Almería, and the poor victims were walking around blinded and stumbling, their faces puffed up, enormously swollen. This sight recalled to many of us the plagues of the Middle Ages, and it was difficult to realize that New York was only ten days away. Caruso and Scognamillo husbanded us safely through the streets to the waterfront, and with mixed feelings of depression and relief, we embarked for the *Canopic,* which stood at anchor.

When we arrived on board we were greeted by the shouting of three Italian stowaways, "Vogliamo andare in America!" (We want to go to America!) They cried, "Non abbiamo soldi!" (We have no money!) Caruso began to talk to them, and after giving them each one thousand lire persuaded them to leave the ship quietly and return to Italy. As the fishing boat moved away with its new cargo, we heard singing and cheering from the throats of these three travelers, and we called back wishing them bon voyage.

In a short time we, too, left the city of Almería and headed for Gibraltar and the Atlantic Ocean. We were a little uneasy at the thought of floating mines, and we knew that the crew had been alerted. The ship's lights were not turned on, and the decks were darkened with canvas coverings. We were asked to use candlelight in our cabins. In addition to this worry, I had another problem. My cabin was infested with bedbugs, and I kept candles burning all night long in an attempt to protect myself. When I discovered that Maestro Polacco, in the cabin adjacent to mine, had the same troubles, I felt better.

Nobody discussed the war. There were too many nations represented on board, too many emotions involved, and too much happening that we knew nothing about. I took long walks with Pitti or sat in a deck chair and visited with my colleagues.

Emmy Destinn was the only person among the group of artists aboard who remained in her cabin all day long. And so we decided to serenade her, and Toscanini volunteered to conduct us. But when we had all assembled in the lounge, Caruso was missing. We could not find him, and Toscanini suggested that we go on without him. Without being detected by Emmy Destinn, we gathered outside of her cabin window, which opened out onto the deck, and Toscanini raised his hands to give us the cue. Suddenly the cabin window opened wide, and there was the round face of Caruso, framed in Emmy Destinn's night cap! He stole the show.

The voyage was without incident. When we reached safer waters the lights were turned on, and life on board ship returned to normal. Upon our arrival in New York we were besieged by newsmen, and papers all over the country carried the story of our crossing. The news stories all attributed our arrival to the untiring efforts of Manager Gatti-Casazza, who had to get the consent of the highest authorities of Germany, France, England, and Italy to arrange for all these artists to leave Europe.

Will Kahn and many friends met me to celebrate this happy return. The 1914–15 season was to open with a performance of Verdi's *Un ballo in maschera* with the same outstanding cast of the previous season, and so we went right into rehearsals.

De Segurola, the well-known bass, came in for special attention at one rehearsal. He was always impeccably dressed, with hat, cane, and monocle. This picture of the elegant man of the world was disturbed by his nervous habit of stamping his right foot vehemently with each bar of the music as he sang. His voice had already acquired an annoying tremolo, and now with each stamp of his foot, the impact jarred his whole body, disturbed his vocal production, and dislodged his monocle, which was fortunately attached to a cord on his lapel. Finally Toscanini could stand it no longer. He cried out angrily, "For heaven's sake, stop singing with your foot and sing with your throat!" and poor de Segurola was left without his crutch.

People have often asked me if singers at the Metropolitan were ever tempted to outsing one another. This seldom happens, but during a performance of *La Gioconda*, Caruso and Amato staged an impromptu rivalry in the great duet. Their voices, Caruso's baritonal tenor and Amato's high baritone, blended so perfectly that one could tell them apart only with difficulty. Toward the end, they held on to the long, sustained high notes beyond their written value, their powerful voices echoing through the auditorium. The audience, sensing what was happening, gave them a tremendous ovation.

During this winter season there were a great many repetitions of *Rosenkavalier, La traviata, The Magic Flute,* and *Les Huguenots,* and other Italian roles in my repertory, and so I spent much time at the Metropolitan Opera House. Every time I entered my dressing room I had the same reaction of amazement. These rooms were unattractively painted in an ugly dark green. They were very poorly ventilated, because a piano stood in front of the single window which we dared not open because then the people on 40th Street would have heard our practicing. Gadski always had yards and yards of chintz draped around the walls of her room to add some cheer. These rooms were certainly not befitting the great artists who used them.

The men were housed on one side of the Metropolitan Opera House, and the women had their rooms on the opposite side. We had no Green Room, no central meeting room where we could come together for visits and discussion, and I missed the warmth between artists which I had known so well in Europe. Here everything was too big and too impersonal.

As my repertory was to a large extent Italian, I had to work with the Italian singers and the Italian conductors. The men came to rehearsal with hat and coat on and cane in hand. I confess that I never became accustomed to this informality, because it seemed to me that hats, coats, and canes belonged in a dressing room and not on the stage. My partners gave me the impression that they were just about to leave at any moment! They smoked a great deal, and Mr. Papi, the head coach, thought nothing of blowing his cigarette smoke right into my face as he talked to me. I did not like him anyway, and in my opinion he did not belong at the Metropolitan.

Mr. Bodanzky was another member of the staff at the Metropolitan who did not command my respect. With conductors such as Leo Blech, Wilhelm Furtwängler, and Felix Weingartner doing such magnificent work in Europe, it was a mystery to me why Mr. Bodanzky, from a little theater in Mannheim, should have been selected to join the staff of conductors here. To my way of thinking, Bodanzky was always in too much of a hurry. He rushed his tempos to such a degree that when I sang with him I could hardly get my words out. I think that he was probably rushing to get back to his card game, for he was a passionate poker player.

During a rehearsal of *The Marriage of Figaro,* as I stood in front of the mirror preparing to put on my bridal wreath, he suddenly yelled up at me, "Why don't you do something different?" "What do you suggest?" I called back, keeping my temper as best I could. He had no answer. I would not dare to change Mozart, but Mr. Bodanzky thought that he could. He was rushing through the score at breakneck speed in an effort to bring youth and sparkle into the performance. But in my opinion it is the alertness of one's inner self that creates youth—not hysterical tempos.

It was my great fortune to have been a member of the Metropolitan Opera Company under the management of Gatti-Casazza. It is not an easy task to manage an opera house, and certainly the problems of the greatest opera house in the world are manifold. A manager must have great authority, shrewd business sense, the ability to judge voices, and the rare gift of vision. He must be tolerant but firm, he must keep himself in the background, and he must build careers for his artists. Gatti-Casazza was just such a manager.

He lived entirely for his work, sitting in his office from morning till evening, seldom appearing at public functions, and making few speeches, even in his native language. He was present at every rehearsal, and at every performance he was backstage, making certain that everything went well. In fact, his presence in my dressing room was sometimes embarrassing. I would have to change costume, and I could not seem to make him understand that it was time for him to leave. The maid would often save the situation by coming in to tell me that it was time to change, and then of course he would leave.

I considered him a wonderful friend. His suggestions were always so kindly given and so helpful. If a singer was nervous for some reason, Gatti would pat him on the shoulder and tell him not to worry. Or if someone had a cold, he would say, "Just take it easy. Leave out the high notes if you wish." And when praise was well-deserved, he never failed to compliment a singer.

Although occasionally Gatti-Casazza was quite stubborn and not open to suggestion, he was right most of the time and equal to any challenge that might confront a man in his position. After all, he had a little army under him, an army of colorful, warm-blooded, temperamental people, full of pride and ambition. And we obeyed him as soldiers obey their general. When he appeared on stage during a rehearsal, discipline tightened up, and nobody counted but Gatti.

One day the great Russian Chaliapin let his temper get out of hand. He criticized everything and everybody, nothing suited him, and he refused to continue the rehearsal. Someone called for Gatti, who came immediately to the stage from his office. He stood there, his hands in his pockets as usual, his face immobile, and his head hanging. He said nothing for quite some time but just stood there like a sphinx, as we described him among ourselves when he took that attitude. Then he burst out in anger and said, "If you do not like it here at the Metropolitan, you may leave whenever you wish." The proud Chaliapin became as meek as a mouse, and rehearsal continued.

Gatti had great respect for the German singers in his company because, as he once remarked, "They always know their parts, and they are all very sincere." And of course he loved to be with his countrymen, the Italian singers, who kept him laughing with their wonderful stories. Gatti came to my home often, and I regret that my Italian was not fluent enough to enable me to cope with his rapid-fire, staccato conversation. We had many interests in common, and I enjoyed his true admiration. I was never the prima donna with him, and I know that this fact was appreciated.

No artist under Gatti's management was allowed to concertize extensively before the opening of a season. He did not want the singers to tire themselves, because, in his mind, the first responsibility of an artist under his management was to the Metropolitan itself. Unlike singers of today who divide their allegiance between opera, television, radio, and concert stage, we devoted all our attention to the Metropolitan, we concentrated great love and devotion here, and our performances were proof of this.

For his part, Gatti displayed great vision in his choice of casts. His primary objective was to let the artists shine and to give the public an opportunity to hear great voices, beautiful interpretations, and authoritative musical conceptions. The more perfect the blend of voices and the more beautiful the singing, so much more successful the performance. Every other consideration was of lesser importance to him.

Today the scenery seems to have taken precedence over the poor singer. The stage has become bigger and is cluttered with new and elaborate scenery to such an extent that the singer looks completely insignificant. Voice projection is hampered by the sound-absorbing trappings of the set, and the very self-assurance with which singers should portray their role is taken from them as a consequence.

I attended a performance of *Aida* at the Metropolitan long after my time there, and I remember only the huge oversize columns and a naked dancer. Certainly I came away from that performance with no treasured memory of beautiful singing, and yet Zinka Milanov, one of the finest singers today, was the Aida! She was unable to project her art, she was unable to capture her audience because she was literally swallowed up by the scenery and hindered by distracting stage action.

Scenery in an opera house should be lovely, fitting, and expressive, but it should not overshadow the action for which it exists. I would rather listen to a magnificent voice on a bare stage than see a movie-script setting that denies that voice its mission, which is above all to move deeper. For the drapes, the columns, the walls, and the various "visions" of the modern stage absorb all the beautiful overtones of a voice before those overtones can cross the footlights to expand in the depth of the auditorium. It is those overtones that give to each voice its peculiar quality. The ability to produce a voice rich in overtones is a gift given only to the greatest artists; they should not be deprived of this hard-earned, personal quality and beauty of voice.

I feel sorry for the singers of today who must hurdle such an obstacle. Certainly Gatti placed us at no such disadvantage. Scenery was definitely of secondary importance, and if one reads the various reviews of opera in former days, one finds very little mention of scenery. And why should they discuss stage settings when they were privileged to hear the free, unhampered voices of Patti, Melba, Jean de Reszke, and other great artists?

Gatti had such faith in the Metropolitan as an institution that shortly after Toscanini left in 1915, he said to me, "Everybody can be replaced. I am getting along without Toscanini, and, if need be, I can get along without Caruso." I did not agree with him in this. When Toscanini left us, a certain spirit of greatness and inspiration was lost, and when Caruso, the second of those two peerless artists, passed away, the gala atmosphere of a performance and the stimulation of a truly irreplaceable personality were forfeited.

Mr. Otto H. Kahn, the great financier and music lover who became chairman of the Board of Directors of the Metropolitan Opera Company and who had the main say in its policies, came backstage quite frequently to chat with us and to discuss various problems. He heard me often in *Der Rosenkavalier,* and one evening after a performance he came up to me and said, "Miss Hempel, no matter how often I hear you in *Der Rosenkavalier,* I never fail to get chills down my spine when you sing, 'Ich weiss auch nichts—gar nichts.' You fill that pause with so much meaning." Otto Kahn was a great modern tycoon, and he was held in the highest esteem by every great artist. I was honored by the compliment he paid me and happy to know that my portrayal of the Marschallin had moved him.

Another visitor backstage gave me great pleasure when she complimented me on my acting in this role, describing it as a performance "marvelous and magnificent." She was a beautiful woman with a glorious, deep voice, and I soon learned that she was Ethel Barrymore, the great American actress.

I had five appearances at the Metropolitan Opera House in November of 1914, and in December I appeared there six times. The company also presented operas of my repertory in Brooklyn. This busy schedule kept me in New York for the winter, and the rather long trip by taxi from my apartment on West 88th Street to the opera house on Broadway was taken very frequently.

This apartment, which Ilka von Horn's mother had located for us in November 1913 and which I had kept for this season as well, was a large, gloomy place on the mezzanine floor. The six rooms, with their high ceilings and lack of sunlight, were perhaps not as cheerful and comfortable as I would have liked. The rent was very high, too, I realize now. But Riverside Drive was two doors away, and the advantage of being near the river probably accounted for the high rents.

I was not content, but with me the question of utmost importance was, "Can I practice without disturbing anybody and without being disturbed myself?" This necessity for undisturbed study has robbed me of a great deal of comfort in my life, but I believe that I really could live in a stable if I had to, in order to be free to work and practice. It is agonizing to have to perform without having been able to limber up. And this is true of all performers, be they musicians, athletes, actors, or dancers. This limbering up is far more important than the performance itself. I find that I must be free to sing at any time of the day, and all day long if necessary. I cannot go somewhere and practice for just an hour. I must live with my piano and with my music.

And so at least the problem of practicing was solved on 88th Street, even if the living quarters left much to be desired. We tried to make the rooms as attractive as possible, and my good Rosa prepared wonderful meals for us in her sunless kitchen. The apartment was sparsely furnished, certainly not to my liking, but as I did not intend to remain there for another season, I did not bother to make many changes.

I made excellent use of the sloping hills that led from Riverside Drive down to the Hudson River. At that time, the riverfront was undeveloped, and instead of the beautifully landscaped parks and highways which now lie between Riverside Drive and the river, there were only uncultivated slopes leading down to the old railroad tracks that skirted the Hudson.

But in a sense this was to our liking, for within a few seconds after leaving our apartment, we would find ourselves in what would pass for open country. Whenever there was good, fresh snow on the ground, a penetrating bite to the morning air, no early rehearsal for me, and no performance in the evening, we would bring out from the back room a large red sled and carry it over across the drive. Down the hills we would slide, over and over again, having the time of our lives. We seldom met people as foolish and as carefree as ourselves, but this in no way deterred us from this wonderful sport. Unfortunately, this handsome sled was stolen from our apartment shortly before the winter snows were over. Instead of replacing it, we took to walking.

In those days it was not always easy to find a taxi, and often Ilka would have to go down to Broadway and fetch one for me. There were subways, of course, but I did not want to risk catching an infection or a cold from breathing the stale, drafty air of the subway train. My responsibility to the Metropolitan was too great, and any indisposition would cause disturbance to the management.

For the evening performances I usually hired a private car with driver. This was quite customary, as few people owned their own cars. I also shall never forget an electric car which a Mr. Kenworthy placed at my disposal early in 1914 as publicity for his firm. I was scheduled to appear at Aeolian Hall with the New York Symphony Orchestra on the afternoon of 1 March. He called for me at the appointed time, planning to drive me himself to the hall. I stepped in and seated myself, carefully arranging my lovely concert gown so as not to crumple it.

On this particular day there were several inches of snow on the ground, and we had to move slowly and cautiously through the streets. Suddenly the car stopped moving. Mr. Kenworthy had gotten stuck in a drift near the curb. The electric engine was not strong enough to force the wheels free. Time passed and I became worried. There was no other car in sight; nobody came our way. The hour of the concert arrived and I knew that I would never make it in time. I was in despair, for I had never before disappointed an audience, and certainly Walter Damrosch would never, never forgive me.

Suddenly, before I had even realized what had happened, Mr. Kenworthy jumped out of the car. A large touring car had turned into the street, and he stopped the driver and begged him to speak with me. I informed the gentleman of my predicament and asked him to help me. He willingly consented and, calling out to a friend who was seated in his car to come and help, opened the door of our car and asked me to allow him to lift me into their car. No sooner said than done, and we were driving hastily to the Aeolian Hall.

By now the concert was well under way, but Damrosch had cleverly altered the program and was just finishing the last of his orchestral selections when I entered. I cannot tell you how perfectly furious he was when he saw me. I felt that he would never forgive me for that tardiness, even though I was not guilty of carelessness; rather the weather was responsible. At that moment, however, there was no time for explanations. I rushed onto the stage, greeted the orchestra members, who smiled back at me with looks of relief, and began my numbers. The balance of the program was ruined, naturally. But when I explained to the audience the cause of my tardiness, they were very kind to me.

After subsequent concerts with Damrosch, I redeemed myself in his eyes, and he singled me out as being the most punctual of artists at rehearsals, arriving well in advance of the time announced. Perhaps Luisa Tetrazzini could be called my direct opposite in this respect, for she often failed to show up at all for rehearsals, sending her accompanist instead to represent her.

For evening performances at the Metropolitan, I would arrive at the stage door in my hired car. I never became quite accustomed to the colorless approach to this opera house. It contrasted so drastically with the grounds of the theater in Schwerin, the grandeur of the Royal Opera House in Berlin, and the splendor of the setting of the Prinzregent Opera House in Munich. In driving to the Metropolitan I simply came down Broadway and stopped at 39th Street. The building stood there among other buildings, quite without distinction, on one of the busiest streets in the center of the business district with no opportunity for architectural display.

The foyer is likewise very simple and functional, and only when one enters the auditorium itself does one feel the rich beauty of the golden damask curtains, the red velvet seats, the rising tiers of boxes, and the carvings above the stage. When I entered the stage door, a Miss Morton would greet me cheerfully, as she greeted all of us. If, in the morning after a performance, a singer came raging with anger at some critic, she knew exactly how to console him and before long his anger would subside. Or if for any reason we arrived late to rehearsal, she would know how to minimize this problem. We all relied a great deal upon her for setting our spirits aright, for she had that peculiar gift of enabling us to see these things as something essentially unimportant. Yes, we all were very fond of her.

The mistress of the wardrobe, Mme Musaeus, was a person for whom we had affection of quite another sort. For her we all felt a helpless anger, even though we loved her dearly. It was she who gave us our costumes, and she made us furious with her last-minute deliveries. How many outbursts of anger that poor, dear person must have had to endure! If a critic remarked that "she was not in good voice at the start of the opera," he would often be pointing to the results of Mme Musaeus's handiwork, for she made us all dreadfully nervous by her habit of delivering costumes at the very last minute. The first signal would sound, the second would ring, and still we had no dress. At the third signal she would hurry down, slip the dress on us, and trail behind us fastening the hooks as we rushed onto the stage for our cue. She never disappointed us, I must admit, but the nervous tension of that waiting, combined with the nervousness that precedes every appearance, brought out such streams of anger that one by one we began to have our dresses made by a private dressmaker.

Reflections of the war in Europe reached the stage of the Metropolitan, and for the opening performance of *Un ballo in maschera* on 16 November, a notice was posted: "Flowers or other gifts will no longer be presented on the stage, but hereafter will be brought to the dressing rooms." We were to be kept neutral by strict discipline, and the efforts of the management to keep tranquil relations prevailing among the artists of many nationalities never relaxed.

One review of the performance pleased me a great deal:

> Caruso's suave phrasing and his masterful tonal manipulation were a greater vocal lesson than any mere teacher could give. Amato's contribution revealed all its former warmth and power. Destinn sang conscientiously, if not thrillingly. Matzenauer missed the key at times, and looked terrifying in her Santa Claus makeup, but her temperament remained at the boiling point. Hempel's coloratura has gained in technical finish and charm of delivery. In timbre her voice sounds the most youthful of any at the Metropolitan.

Youth in a voice means purity of tone, and this is the source of all beauty in a voice.

On 20 November we presented *Rosenkavalier*. We had only a few rehearsals, for whenever there was no change of cast, few were needed. We all merely hummed our parts through once and became familiar with the tempos and with the conductor's ideas.

By now the New York critics had become better acquainted with this opera and they spoke more favorably. The critic of the *New York Sun* wrote:

> Miss Hempel repeated her exquisite impersonation of the Countess, one of the most artistically finished creations at present before the opera-

going public. All the young students of vocal art in this town ought to be sent to hear what can be done by the employment of repose, dignity and quiet style in singing.

Another reviewer said of me:

> Her histrionism reflected a touch as deft as it was charming, and her singing has never sounded more pure in timbre or more ravishing in quality. She may truthfully be said to have surpassed her best previous efforts here, and the Metropolitan is to be congratulated upon the acquisition of such an artist in its personnel.

Still another critic wrote in the *New York Sun*, "Praise has frequently been given to Miss Hempel's finely wrought impersonation of the Countess, which continues to be one of the most symmetrical and artistic contributions to the gallery of portraits in contemporaneous opera." I must confess that as I sit here looking through the scrapbooks that were kept for me by Will Kahn, I am delighted to learn that the standard of performance toward which I was constantly reaching was being recognized by the critics.

Our performance of *The Magic Flute* on 23 November was successful, and again I received good reviews. I was grateful for commendation of this role, for it is a most difficult one. I am standing on a little platform, strapped around my waist to a post, and after I have been elevated up into the heights of the scenery, they tilt me gently forward, and there I sing! Singing anything would be difficult in such a position, but to sing a dramatic recitative and a lyrical aria like "O zittre nicht" is to accept an enormous challenge. My early Mozart training proved my mainstay, and because of this security I loved to sing the role, but surely no other heavenly queen is subjected to similar tribulations! Is it any wonder that Queens of the Night do this famous operatic character injustice at times?

"Miss Hempel, as Queen of the Night, is at her best now in this role, which is so trying from a vocal standpoint. Her two arias were superbly sung," reads one review. Another critic had this to say:

> Frieda Hempel, in her favorite role of the Queen of the Night, was radiant. It is in few operas that the vari-colored voice of the soprano is given such splendid freedom as in this musical drama from the pen of Mozart. With the majesty that is her second self, with the triumvirate of beauty of voice, personality and feature that is hers, she rose to the heights that her very lofty role required of her. It is easily one of the best characters in opera for Hempel, and holds a beauty for her that it denies others.

After a performance of *La traviata* on 28 November, I prepared for a concert at the Metropolitan. It was to be my second appearance in one of these famous Sunday Evening Concerts. They were most delightful. The audience came in casual dress, and the whole atmosphere was light and charming. The programs were always popular in character, with several artists participating. Usually one or two big stars were presented, along with lesser singers of the company.

We sang on the open stage, arranged for concert, and the orchestra accompanied us from the pit. It always interested the public to see us in person, for they knew us only when we were costumed and made up. I wore my prettiest gowns for these concerts, and enjoyed the experience of being myself on that stage. At this particular concert I sang the orchestral arrangement of the "Blue Danube Waltz," which Leo Blech had written for me, much to the delight of the audience. The brilliant cadenzas that Blech had added so successfully for me came as a surprise to the audience, who responded so warmly that I had to sing an encore.

In December came the revival of *Euryanthe* by Carl Maria von Weber. This opera had last been presented in 1887, with Lilli Lehmann as Euryanthe and Marianne Brandt as Eglantine. After only a few performances it was dropped from the repertory. Now, under the direction of Arturo Toscanini, this work was once more presented to the public.

Henry Krehbiel said, "Toscanini . . . wished to supply the missing link between operas of the old type and Wagner's lyric dramas, and knew that *Euryanthe* was that missing link." I was proud to have been assigned the role once allotted to Lilli Lehmann and to have this opportunity to work with Toscanini. Under the system prevalent at the Metropolitan, there was no chance for a singer to perform more than a small part of her repertory, and therefore the complete gamut of her voice could not be revealed. My roles at the Metropolitan, with the one exception of *Der Rosenkavalier*, were coloratura or lyric roles, and parts such as Mimì, Elsa, or Bertha in *Le Prophète*,* which I had sung in Europe, were not assigned to me here.

---

*For most of Hempel's Metropolitan career, she was only available during the fall season. For operas like *La bohème*, which ran throughout the entire season with many performances, Gatti had a standard team some of whose members were always available. For Mimì, he used Alda, Farrar, and Bori, with the odd performance by Muzio and Peterson. During Hempel's time at the Metropolitan, Elsa had been sung by Gadski, Fremstad, and Destinn, with the odd performance by Fay, Rappold, and Zarska. A note in *Musical America* for 25 December 1915 certainly suggests that the role had been offered to Hempel: "Just as Signor Gatti-Casazza was trying to induce Frieda Hempel to sing Elsa in *Lohengrin*, a role, by the bye, which she sang abroad, the contract with Emmy Destinn was signed." *Le Prophète* had been missing from the Metropolitan stage since 1902. When it was revived with a new production on 7 February 1918, Hempel was in Edison's recording studio and then was off on a transcontinental concert tour. The role of Bertha was given to the Met's new star, Claudia Muzio, with whom it remained until after Hempel had departed the Metropolitan. *Ed.*

Hempel with Johannes Sembach in *Euryanthe* by Weber. Metropolitan Opera, 1914–15. PHOTO BY WHITE. COURTESY METROPOLITAN OPERA ARCHIVES.

My performance therefore drew attention from the critics, one of whom wrote: "Miss Hempel was the first and last big surprise. She sang no mincing coloratura, but a broad style, of which only the *Rosenkavalier* had given a hint before. There was a clear understanding of the fact that Euryanthe, with all her silly troubles, was a princess born and bred." In the *New York Times* I read:

> Miss Hempel made a remarkably fine Euryanthe, and her impersonation deserves to be put down among the very best she has offered to New York. She alone commanded in sufficient measures not only the dramatic but the florid element in Weber's music, the union of which makes much of it so difficult. In beauty of voice and in the ingenious and pathetic significance of her acting she was wholly admirable.

And on this same day a story appeared by the veteran critic W. J. Henderson. Although he dealt primarily with subjects other than opera, he closed his essay with this:

> There is such a small amount of real singing on the stage of the Metropolitan Opera House that the less said the better. Opera is the happy hunting ground of the bad singer with a big voice and an immense amount of physical energy commonly called "temperament." To sing with repose, finish and exquisite balance is to prove to the majority of operagoers that you have no temperament. Run all over the stage, brandish your arms, shout and declaim and storm like a vocal fury, and these same listeners will rise to you. Nevertheless there are some artistic singers in the Metropolitan Opera House Company. Just at the moment of this writing the one who gives the connoisseur of singing the most pleasure is Mme Hempel, because she tries all the time to sing lyrically and to attain her effects by absolutely legitimate means.

When I was shown this article, I felt honored, quite naturally. My colleagues at this time included Caruso, Destinn, Pasquale Amato, Otto Goritz, Leon Rothier, Elisabeth Schumann, Frances Alda, Geraldine Farrar, Johanna Gadski, and Margarete Ober. But just imagine my surprise when I continued reading, "She sings out of tune much too often, and sometimes does curious things to her phrases, but since most of those associated with her sing out of tune more often than she does, and rip phrases to tatters oftener, there is a preponderance of merit in her favor."

Now, is it possible that we artists were such poor technicians, such tasteless musicians, that we would all err so dreadfully in this manner? Where, then, were the great singers who could sing in tune? This reminds me of the morning Enrico Caruso came into the entrance hall at the stage door where Miss Morton happened to have the morning papers with their inevitable criticisms. Reading that he had sung out of tune, Caruso scribbled furiously across the page "Liar!" I am afraid that Mr. Henderson just did not hear correctly, and in fact I understand that he later became quite deaf. This story finds its perfect analogy in the story of the soldier who remarked that the whole army was out of step with him.

Now came two opera performances in Brooklyn, *La traviata* and *The Magic Flute*. Most of us traveled by subway to the Academy of Music where the operas were given. In those days the automobile industry was in its infancy, and such complications as a flat tire or engine trouble were not quickly and easily solved. Consequently we found it simpler and more prudent for that distance to bundle up carefully and enter a subway train, which then carried us directly and quickly to the door of the Academy. We arrived singly, as a rule, but often a group of us would return to New York City together after the performance.

The Academy of Music was more like a European theater. The auditorium was smaller, and as we sang on the little stage, we felt closer to the audience and responded easily to its warmth and its enthusiasm. The scenery was from the Metropolitan, of course, and it was shipped to Brooklyn and adjusted to the smaller stage. The whole format was different, therefore, and everything seemed cozy and intimate, as I had known it in Europe. The Brooklynites gave us wonderful welcomes, and they were very appreciative.

Now began preparations for Christmas. The very first day I had ever spent in America was Christmas day of 1912, when I was homesick with memories of the family tree with its tinsel and presents. The quiet New York streets with their closed shops and my intense concern about my impending debut had saddened Christmas for me. Many more Christmas days had to pass before I was able to forget. I recall this Christmas, spent in my 88th Street apartment. We decorated a large tree for ourselves and a little tree for the dog. Will Kahn, Emmy Nicklass, and a friend of Ilka's joined us for a wonderful Christmas dinner cooked as only Rosa could cook it.

Christmas has always meant a great deal to Germans, and I am no exception. I have celebrated this holiday every year. I usually spent a great deal of time and money on my trees, and I was very proud of them. I kept them all in white, with silver tinsel and artificial snow sparkling in the light of the simple candles. I used delicately blown glass figures of birds in white and silver for ornaments, and at the top I placed nothing but myriad strands of silver tinsel. And the dog's tree was a duplicate in miniature.

Only my closest friends were with me, never more than two or three, to keep a cozy feeling of home. Later on, having no children of my own, I tried to make this day a happy one for a few youngsters who were poor or orphaned. I would bring them to the house and entertain them with presents and good food.

One Christmas day when living in my apartment at 271 Central Park

West, I was hostess to the children of the policemen of the City of New York who had lost their lives in action. Mayor Walker of New York and his wife were also my guests that day, and we staged a lovely party. We placed gifts under the tree for the children, and after opening these presents, and looking to see what everybody else had received, they began to sing for us. One little tyke, just three years old, was the life of the party. After having sung a little song for him, I asked him, "Who sings better, you or I?" "I," came the forthright answer.

As was inevitable, the newspapers heard of the party, and one paper announced: "Frieda Hempel entertains at 271 Central Park West the children of the policemen of New York City who lost their lives in action." I never heard the end of that!

It seldom happened that I had to sing on Christmas day, and only once [in 1916] did I have an operatic appearance on 25 December, in *Martha* at the Metropolitan with Caruso and De Luca: "Enough people were willing to cut short their Christmas dinners yesterday to fill the Metropolitan House twice over, in the afternoon for Humperdinck's *Hänsel und Gretel,* and in the evening for the time-honored *Martha* of Flotow."

Two late-December opera performances brought the year 1914 to a close for me. The spring season 1915 was fully booked by now. I had at least nine performances every month, some opera and some concert. I was under the Wolfson Management, the firm that handled all the major stars of the time. Concerts in Cleveland and Boston in January, a concert in Providence, Washington, and Rye in February, and an appearance with the Mozart Society of New York were all scheduled for me.

At this time Mr. Frank Bibb was my very gifted accompanist. And I must say that he was a most handsome, red-headed young man who captured the hearts of the young ladies in the audiences. He was a wonderful companion and full to the brim with energy and enthusiasm. He helped me immensely, for he knew all there was to know about the song literature of America.

His greatest achievement was his fudge. He made the most delicious candy I have ever tasted, and he kept me constantly supplied with this fattening food. One hobby of his I never understood. He had an obsession for electric trains and locomotives. He was actually able to construct whole trains, and set them up with tracks, signals, switches, and all the accessories a trainman needs. But I have since learned that many successful businessmen also indulge in this hobby, to the great consternation of their wives.

At one of these concerts an amusing incident occurred. Shortly after Mr. Bibb had started a number, one of the piano legs suddenly toppled down. Bibb jumped up from the piano, rushed around and propped it in place again before the balance of the piano was upset. Returning to his seat while I smiled graciously at the audience, who did not know how to react at this point, he played the introduction and off we went again. Once more the leg began to give way. Now, as Mr. Bibb rose again, the audience began to cheer him on in his work. Again he wedged the leg back in and returned to his seat. When the leg fell off again, for the third time, the audience literally howled with delight. And I must say here that such a friendly reaction from an audience was typical. The American people love to dramatize the unexpected, and they are not hindered by reverence to manners. They are wonderful in this respect. Now, of course, a gentleman came out from backstage and securely fixed the leg so that we could continue our concert for a very happy audience.

Early in March 1915, Will Kahn and Emmy Nicklass finally succeeded in locating an apartment for me at 271 Central Park West, near 86th Street. It did not face the park, but a ten-room apartment on the same floor, which did overlook this beautiful park, would soon be vacant, and it was promised to me. And so I decided to take the smaller one on the west side of the building for the time being.

This move was made without much effort, for I still had no furniture of my own and the apartment into which I moved was already furnished. I leased it immediately, and 271 Central Park West was my home from that time onward. I believe that I was then the only foreign artist to establish my permanent home in America. At the same time I took my first steps toward becoming an American citizen.

During March and April I was kept busy, as usual, singing at the Metropolitan and fulfilling concert contracts. On 9 April I sang another Biltmore Concert, with Fritz Kreisler and Giovanni Martinelli as co-artists. These concerts were, in a sense, an imitation of the Bagby concerts, but they were never quite the same. Something was missing, some elusive quality, and I believe that this quality was Mr. Bagby himself. The 1914–15 season at the Metropolitan ended for me on 31 April with a performance of *The Magic Flute*. I also sang two more concerts, one at the Ann Arbor Festival Series, and one in Evanston, Illinois.

Just before sailing from New York for Switzerland and my Sils Maria, I received the cable that told me of my mother's sudden death. I was unable to be with my father and my sisters and brothers for the burial services, and I was desolate. In Sils-Maria I found some measure of comfort, but there is no denying of the fact that when the mother dies, the child is lost. With mother still around, one feels secure and nothing can happen. One can always turn to mother for help, and she will know what to say and what to do. How true is the saying, "Wenn du noch eine Mutter hast, so danke Gott und sei zufrieden; nicht allen auf dem Erdengrund ist dieses hohe Glück beschieden." (If you still have your mother, thank the Lord and be content; not everyone on earth is granted this great fortune.) Suddenly the family and the friends are there, but the dearest one of all is gone. And in that realization I was now lost. Only in the beauty of the mountains could I find solace for her death. Upon my arrival in Berlin, late in August, my family took me to my mother's grave in a small cemetery in the city.

On 13 September 1915 I gave a concert in the big Philharmonic Hall. My manager for this concert was Mr. Sachs of the important firm of Wolff and Sachs, concert managers. The concert went well, and my Berlin followers were not disappointed.* The critics here, as in America, appreciated the simplicity and the honesty of my efforts.

I sailed for America on a Dutch boat, the SS *Noordam,* and traveling the high northern route, we arrived safely in New York early in October 1915. I had only a few days there, just long enough to reopen my apartment on Central Park West and to visit with my close friends. By 14 October I was in Lindsborg, Kansas, for the first of a series of eight concerts which Wolfson Management had arranged for me.

This pre-season tour took me to Lynchburg, Topeka, Kansas City, St. Paul, Minneapolis, Pittsburgh, Chicago, and Columbus, and so in this two-week period I traversed a good deal of territory. But I saw absolutely nothing of these towns, and my only recollection is that they all looked alike: first the railroad depot, then the colored section, then the town hall and the post office. Everywhere the type of building was the same, or so it seemed to me. For I was accustomed to travel in Europe where the change of nationality automatically invoked a change of character in the architecture, and where a trip the length of this would have carried me across boundary lines more than once.

And if there was variety to be seen, I had no time to look for it. Upon arrival in a city, I would go directly to the hotel and rest from the long train trip. Then my concert gown had to be freshened up by Rosa, while I limbered up my voice and went to the hall to acquaint myself with its acoustics, or submitted to an interview by the local newspapers.

Lindsborg, Kansas, had a large Swedish population, and these people had great love for fine music, so I enjoyed singing for them. In Kansas City I met Madame Schumann-Heink again, and as we chatted, she asked where my next concert would be. "St. Paul," I replied, "and I am looking forward so to this concert, for I understand that in St. Paul there are a great many Germans." "Yes," said Schumann-Heink, "many Germans, but not many will come to the concert. They would rather stay home and drink beer!"

---

*Musical America for 23 October 1915 (p. 29) reported: "The proceeds [of this concert] will be devoted to the founding of Miss Hempel's projected national orthopedic institution for the benefit of crippled soldiers." Some segments of the German press, expressing contempt for native artists who had flown from the war to a safe haven in "Dollarland," labeled Hempel's project as an "egotistical publicity stunt." See Postscript, "An Informal and Selected Chronology." *Ed.*

Unfortunately, I am afraid she was correct in her statement. And if it had not been for the warmth of the non-German-speaking audience that did hear me, I would have been very disappointed. The German music lovers here in America still do not support the artists of German descent, although just the opposite is true of the Italian, the French, or the Spanish music lovers, who fill the halls for their artists. Otherwise, how could it happen that an outstanding German artist, who fills the halls in Germany, cannot even attract enough people in New York City to present a concert in Town Hall?

In Minneapolis I opened the season's Orchestral Concert Series on 22 October. "It is a rare treat," wrote the critic, "to listen to such a voice as Mme Hempel's. Beautiful in quality throughout, well-rounded in tone, its flexible coloratura effects are produced without apparent effort." My friend was correct: there was no apparent effort in the singing. But the necessity of keeping oneself in condition to perform without apparent effort in spite of the constant changes of climate, diet, and sleeping accommodations exacts its toll on the artist. One of the cruelest things a woman had to do at that time, when travel facilities were not what they are now, was the ordeal of facing an interviewer early in the morning after a long ride through the night on a train.

Conscious of the saying, "It is the first impression that counts," we knew that we had to look like a prima donna as we stepped off the train to face the welcoming committee. There must be no sign of fatigue, no rumpled clothing, no limp hairdo; rather cut short our dubious rest than not leave enough time for the inevitable grooming of hair and the making-up of the face. Yes, indeed, we had to look glamorous at all cost, and only hope that before the impending concert we would find time to rest a little.

In Chicago I appeared in a Sunday afternoon concert at Orchestra Hall. This time I shared the program with Pasquale Amato, the famous baritone from the Metropolitan. We sang no duets in such joint recitals. Rather, each of us presented groups of songs or arias in alternation. Samuel Chotzinoff was our accompanist. We were both very well received and called upon for encores.

I see by the clippings in my scrapbook that my encores in English were especially appreciated: "Her English enunciation was so clear that it would have been an excellent lesson to many American singers." I had been making every effort to master the English language, and although I was not "faultless" in my choice of words, as one interviewer claimed, I was nevertheless able to converse freely and colorfully. But this increasing knowledge of the language did not account for the clearness of my diction in singing by any means. In singing, the complete control of vowels and consonants, in all their various combinations, will enable a singer to enunciate perfectly in any language. And conversely, a singer who does not have this control cannot sing well even in her own tongue.

By Tuesday I was in Columbus, Ohio, for my last concert. Here my colleague was Antonio Scotti. It was election night, and a "fearful night for such affairs" as concerts. Nevertheless we sang to an audience of 3500 people. This concert was the first of a series arranged for the city by the Women's Music Club, an organization typical of those fine civic groups in America which devote much effort to cultural projects. The stage was beautifully set with colorful floral arrangements, and the morning papers described it as a "bower of beauty." In this concert Scotti and I sang the duet from *Don Giovanni,* "Là ci darem la mano," and we were asked to repeat it. Scotti was such an elegant actor and his operatic selections were presented with such color that one forgot the fact that he was standing on a concert stage and not upon the operatic stage.

The reviews were most flattering:

> Radiantly young and beautiful, and gowned in exquisite taste, she made an ingratiating concert figure to begin with. Then her singing left nothing to be desired. Some of the chief joys were the Handelian air, "O Sleep, Why Dost Thou Leave Me?" which she sang in practically flawless English, and Strauss's "Blue Danube Waltz," in which her pure and even trill and her splendid sense of rhythm were both evident.

Further, "The fascinating personality of Miss Hempel, her facile diction in three or four languages, with their dialects, and her genuine interpretative power give her almost the same place in the soprano department that Schumann-Heink still maintains in the contralto." I was becoming increasingly interested in concert performance, and in fact I had already scheduled my first Carnegie Hall concert for the coming spring. I was gaining more confidence in my efforts to reach the American audience, which so challenged me with its enthusiasm and its eagerness.

Samuel Chotzinoff, who was my accompanist for this tour of concerts, was one man who could sleep anywhere at any time. No matter where we were or when I needed him, I seemed always to find him asleep. No doubt he was storing up energy for the climb that has since carried him so high in the managerial field of music. And if he was not sleeping, he was copying music for me or for some other artist—he copied so much music that I believe he could have continued to sleep and do that, too. He was complimented by the newspapers for his exquisite artistry in the playing of a Schubert accompaniment for me, and this compliment was well warranted. After this concert in Columbus I returned immediately to New York to attend rehearsals for my appearances with the New York Symphony Orchestra and Walter Damrosch on 5 and 7 November.

I must digress to tell a little story. When people complimented me upon my colorful English, as they often did, I never failed to give Walter Damrosch the credit. For one of the first English books I read was George Ade's

Fables in Slang, which, Mr. Damrosch had assured me, was the purest English extant. And if I sometimes shocked my friends, I nevertheless got my point across with emphasis, thanks to Mr. Damrosch.

Damrosch had selected a light, brilliant program, including a first performance of "Adventures in a Perambulator" by John Alden Carpenter. Mr. Krehbiel tells me that I "charmed the auditors into a delightful state of receptivity with the air from Mozart's *Il rè pastore*" with violin obbligato. Some objections were raised as to the appropriateness of a number such as the "Blue Danube Waltz" on this program, but again Mr. Krehbiel came to my aid, writing, "'The Beautiful Blue Danube' was made to be sung by a chorus of men before it became one of the most fascinating of all instrumental waltzes. So there was no harm in making it once again into a showpiece for a florid soprano voice. Miss Hempel sang it brilliantly." And he added, "But it was in the Mozart air that her exquisite voice and style were heard to the best advantage, for there they went to the heart."

My first appearance at the Metropolitan this season was in *Der Rosenkavalier* on 28 November. But I was most concerned about the coming performance of the *Barber of Seville,* a revival in which I was to sing Rosina for the first time from the repertory of the Metropolitan, and much interest centered around this effort to reinstate the work. Giuseppe de Luca made his Metropolitan debut in this performance, and he received high praise and a warm ovation for his interpretation of Figaro.

The noted New York critic Richard Aldrich wrote of my performance:

> The chief point of distinction in the performance was Mme Frieda Hempel's brilliant and accomplished singing as Rosina. The archness and mischievous vivacity of that young woman do not sit at all times easily and securely upon her; but not for a good while has so pure and vibrant a soprano voice delivered the florid measures with such great ease and certainty. In the lesson scene she sang Arditi's waltz "Parla." Her listeners were almost willing to believe that the restoration of the opera to an active place in the season was sufficiently justified by her participation in it.

There was much controversy among the critics as to just how Rosina should be portrayed, and Mr. Krehbiel expressed himself in these precise terms, "All the great exemplars of the part of Rosina in the past and the nature of the part itself, especially as illustrated by Rossini's music, seem to indicate that it should be enacted with greater lightness and verve, more vivacity and archness than Miss Hempel put into it." I did not agree with him, very probably because my concept of the role had been developed in Berlin under the guidance of Leo Blech. Rosina, a lady of gentle breeding and the ward of Dr. Bartolo, was a young woman of feeling and sensitivity, not necessarily seri-

As Rosina in *The Barber of Seville*.
PHOTO BY MISHKIN. COURTESY ROBERT
TUGGLE.

ous-minded, but certainly not light and carefree. Mr. Krehbiel describes Rosina as a "mischievous, arch, vivacious, and generally lively person, but in a very delicate and graceful way." To my mind, this is an excellent description of her, and exactly this concept was what I tried to portray. But to emphasize the mischievousness and the liveliness at the expense of the delicacy and the grace would have been wrong, I felt.

A critic for the *New York Evening World* wrote: "Frieda Hempel was Rosina. She was a pretty picture, arch and piquant, and she sang with charm and grace. More and more Miss Hempel justifies her European reputation, the worth of which some of us failed to recognize." This article indicates to me that the qualities responsible for that European reputation were beginning to impress the ear of the American listener as well.

December was filled with engagements at the Metropolitan. The revival performance of *Martha* was of paramount interest to the public, for this opera had long been neglected. Now Caruso and I were to recreate the roles of Lionel and Lady Harriet.

Sembrich and Bonci had last sung this opera seven years previously, and it was exciting for me to follow in the footsteps of Marcella Sembrich, who was now my very good friend. She had an extensive knowledge of the concert literature in America, and she gave me a great deal of assistance with the planning of my concert programs. She was an excellent musician, as is well known, and she had distinguished taste. Working together, we became

Caruso and Hempel, Ober and De Luca in *Martha* in the Met premiere on
11 December 1915. PHOTO BY WHITE. COURTESY METROPOLITAN OPERA ARCHIVES.

devoted to one another. Some time later she said to me, "I always advise my pupils to attend your concerts, because I know that they will get an excellent lesson in the art of singing."

One day she and her husband, Mr. Stengel, came to my home for dinner. As we chatted together, I admired her beautiful pink taffeta evening gown, a new creation in the very latest style. The butler announced dinner, and we entered the dining room and sat down. Noodle soup was served to each in turn. As the butler leaned over to serve Madame Sembrich, she turned to her dinner partner, and with a magnificent sweep of her arm, swept the soup into her lap. Fortunately she was not burned, but her lovely pink gown was ruined by this onslaught of noodles. She was an excellent sport about it all, and the dinner soon continued with all of us in high spirits.

She and I worked together to put Italian words to the "Blue Danube Waltz." I first sang the "Blue Danube Waltz" of Strauss in the Leo Blech arrangement with German words. But I realized that here in America where German was not understood, I might as well fit Italian words to the vocal line. Marcella Sembrich agreed with me in this, for the coloratura waltzes that we sang were in Italian, and this language is more suitable for such music. The nonsense might just as well be Italian as German for the text was unimportant and without poetic value, in any event. Italian, being more limpid, seemed to be less in the way.

Martha, an old-fashioned opera, pleased public and critic alike. One writer, after carefully explaining that he was an avowed Wagnerite, went on to say, "Justice compels me to say that when Frieda Hempel trilled out the final notes of 'The Last Rose of Summer,' I joined in the vulgar acclaim of those who don't know anything about art but are dead certain as to what they like. And I was glad to hear her sing it again, even though she did it in English." Referring to Caruso, he said, "For a time it seemed as if Mr. Caruso would be forced to sing 'M'Appari' a second time. But they finally let him go with eight or nine bows of acknowledgments of their approval. He was in excellent voice." This reviewer also wished me well in one important respect. After complimenting me by saying that my voice was always lovely, and that my costumes were in excellent taste, he added, "Not the least among her many assets is her physical attractiveness. May she never grow fat!"

We gave this opera only four times during the season, and then once again at the end of 1916. Each time, the song "The Last Rose of Summer" was repeated, and when Caruso joined me for the last bars of the repetition, we blended our voices as we had blended them in the Berlin performances years before. As the critic wrote, "Either Hempel or Caruso would have marked the evening with red letters in operatic annals—the combination was irresistible and at times electrifying."

We all had great fun in this opera. As Lady Harriet pretending to be a peasant girl I had a wonderful time. And how funny it was to see Caruso and De Luca showing us how to spin. Caruso enjoyed this scene so much that some critics accused him of too much clowning. But he was wonderful as a peasant, I thought, and I truly felt sorry for him when he fell in love with me in the opera.

Superstition plays a great part in the life of many an artist. And habits, which soon acquire the power of superstition, are often dangerous. It was my habit always to step upon the stage with my left foot first, and if for any reason I failed to do this, I would be miserable throughout the performance and in constant fear of some mishap. Remember the left foot, I would say. And to drop a comb on the day of a performance would be to announce impending doom, disaster, and destruction! Foolish as these fears were, they possessed me in this overdramatic fashion. Don't drop that comb, I would always say to myself—do you want to spoil the performance?

Of course these superstitions in no way affected my performance, other than to make me nervous if I invoked them. But when a habit such as that of singing with the hand to the ear took possession of a singer, she would become a slave to it, even when on the stage, as was a soprano at the Metropolitan Opera. For if the hand was not there, behind the ear, this singer would fear for her tone.

Caruso was in like manner a slave to the atomizer. There in the wings, with a white towel over his arms, was the valet. I noticed this particularly in *Martha,* for during our duet he would sing his lines and then disappear in the wings to have his throat sprayed, while I sang my lines to him. He was clever enough to camouflage this by clowning, but I felt sorry for him for I knew that he had really become a slave to the atomizer.

One day, when he was singing a solo and the valet was not watching, I picked up the atomizer and sprayed my own throat. I suppose I was thinking that if it helped him, it would help me also. But to my horror, I discovered that my throat felt completely numb. Caruso was having his throat sprayed with a mixture containing cocaine, well-known to throat doctors, who use it to artificially tighten the vocal cords. I am convinced that Caruso did not need this artificial stimulant for his voice but had rather become a slave to the thought of needing it. For my part, I never touched his atomizer again.

On 15 December we sang *Der Rosenkavalier* in Philadelphia, and I was unfortunate to catch a cold on the train. I was to appear in *Martha* on 17 December, but I found that I could not talk above a whisper. I called Mr. Gatti-Casazza to tell him that I could not appear in *Martha.* Here is what the papers say: "Gatti-Casazza, being an impresario with years of experience, would not take 'no' for an answer, and Miss Hempel sang the title role of

Martha last night, and sang it without any plea for indulgences on the part of the management. She sang admirably, and her 'Last Rose of Summer' was exquisite."

It was because of a throat doctor that I was able to sing at all, and if I had injured my voice in any way by artificially stimulating it, the managers would have been the first to let me know of my impaired powers. I have never approved of this submission to the will of the management against one's better judgment, even though, as you see, I was myself guilty of so doing. Fortunately I suffered no lingering aftereffects, but such a thing can happen, and that is wrong.

My appearances at the Metropolitan continued throughout January, and in February 1916 I gave my first Carnegie Hall recital. Preparations for this debut recital in New York were extensive. The customary hour for such concerts was afternoon, and because of this fact many singers appeared in afternoon dress and wore hats. But the stage meant evening to me, and the darkened auditorium and stage lights certainly canceled all remembrance of the hour. Consequently, I dressed in evening gown instead of in afternoon attire.

It had been impossible for me to enter Paris during the summer months that I had spent in Europe, and so early in the season I had begun to visit the New York dress salons, looking for a dressmaker whose taste coincided with mine. I selected Lady Duff-Gordon, who, under the trade name of Lucille, maintained a shop on West 57th Street.

We began to discuss possible designs for my concert gown. The style of evening dress, at the moment, was a tight-fitting, clinging one. But Lady Duff-Gordon had another idea for me which I liked very much. She suggested that I wear a pale blue tulle and satin dress with a barrel skirt—a hoop skirt. This was the vogue in Paris but still well in advance of the American styles. It would take a good deal of courage on my part to introduce it on a concert stage, but I knew that it would nevertheless be quite correct and stunning. The dress was ordered then and there.

Carnegie Hall is a large concert hall, situated some twenty blocks north of the Metropolitan Opera House. In 1916 this section of the city had few business establishments. The surrounding buildings were smaller, and the shops were quite exclusive. The hall itself was essentially unadorned, and yet through the years it has acquired a dignity that is compelling. In the building that rises above the hall are many floors of rented studios for teachers of music, dancing, and acting. The young students moving constantly in and out of Carnegie Hall enhance the peculiar charm of this building.

The concert audience of 1916 was a very critical one. As the principal concert hall in the city, Carnegie Hall was the meeting place of those musically educated persons who demanded the utmost from the top-ranking artists of the day. I was very excited by the thought of singing for such an audience, and I knew, certainly, that a Carnegie Hall success would enhance my reputation as a concert artist.

On the afternoon of the concert I was driven to the hall in my hired Packard automobile and arrived in good time. Mr. Coenraad Bos, the foremost accompanist of the day who later toured with me for many seasons, was there to greet me. The stage was filled with beautiful flowers from my many friends, and it was all so lovely that I felt only happiness.

I do not know what the women in the audience expected me to wear, but apparently nobody expected to see a hoop skirt, for when I walked out on the stage, an audible gasp ran through the hall, which gave a tremendous thrill. In the reviews the next day, many compliments were paid to this daring and beautiful creation of Lady Duff-Gordon, and I was told that I gave many women members of the audience quite a shock. When I wore this same dress for a concert later in the season in Syracuse, one critic wrote a charming story of this dress:

> The great audience, which numbered between 3500 and 4000 people, sat in the calm of good breeding, and clapped its white-gloved hands when Leopold Stokowski scored a veritable triumph with his magnificent orchestra. But when Miss Hempel appeared, it forgot its good breeding, forgot everything, almost forgot to applaud. It just gasped. And that gasp was an unmistakable, articulate sound. It was "whoops!" For there appeared upon the stage a life-size reproduction of what many women possess, and all have seen in the shop windows, a hoop-skirted doily, to be put over the telephone. Be that as it may, it was some gown. The women raved inwardly, although whispering with a shrug to the next-door neighbor, "I would never wear a hoop skirt, would you?" And the men, well the men just exclaimed under their breath in various gradations of expletives. Frieda was a dream. Her hair was done charmingly, and the top part of the frock was exquisite, as indeed was the entire outfit when one became accustomed to the outlines, and examined the texture and design. But Frieda was there to sing as well as to be seen, and sing she did, into the hearts of all.

I had come to Carnegie Hall to sing, and the concert was the success I had hoped it would be. Perhaps what Mr. Aldrich wrote of it pleased me the most:

> Frieda Hempel, who is now and has been for several years the chief reliance of the Metropolitan Opera House in coloratura singing, gave a song recital in Carnegie Hall yesterday afternoon, February 15th. Miss Hempel gave a delightful exhibition of an art that she has unquestionably made finer and more finished since she first came to this country. Miss Hempel is one who takes thought about her art, and has raised herself to a higher artistic stature thereby.

Speaking of the German lieder which I sang (Schumann's "Widmung" and "Nussbaum," Schubert's "Die Forelle," Brahms's "Vergebliches Ständchen," and Mozart's "Warnung") he said:

> It would not be too much to say that she struck quite the right note of expression and found an infinity of exquisite detail. . . . Nor could there be wished a greater perfection of diction than she showed in these German songs—a diction whose finish is allied with the beauty and freedom of her production of tone.

A *New York Times* review of considered opinion is well worth quoting:

> Even Frieda Hempel's most enthusiastic admirer hardly has suspected that Giulio Gatti-Casazza's German soprano would develop into as accomplished and as interesting an interpreter as she proved herself to be. Prima donnas rarely have the intellectual concentration, the penetration and the imagination to move their listeners in the confines of the concert room where they are bound to curtail their usual means of expression, and light sopranos, like Miss Hempel, whose emotional scope is naturally restricted, have special difficulties to contend with in holding the attention of their auditors. Frieda Hempel's programme was not nearly so voluminous and varied as the typical programme of Marcella Sembrich. The range of her art, therefore, may yet be questioned. But it is hard to think of any light soprano besides the famous Polish woman who has so much artistic intelligence, temperament, warmth, and emotional intensity.

The review closes with a tribute to Mr. Bos: "Needless to say, the valiant Coenraad 'the Fifth' played the accompaniments with great skill. But why did he not offer to assist Miss Hempel in receiving the mass of floral tributes brought down the aisle by the ushers?" I would answer this question by saying that Mr. Bos, out of a sense of modesty and because of his respect for me and for the dignity of the podium, felt that I should personally receive the flowers and embrace them. He was indeed a true gentleman at this moment, a fact that the critic should have recognized.

My comments on this recital close with a quotation from the *New York Sun*: "The singer was dressed in a Dresden china effect of blue flounces, wonderful hoops and rising skirt to the ankles, which made a sensation when she walked into view."

I had planned to dine with friends at the Ritz after the concert, but during the course of the afternoon I was informed that Johanna Gadski, who was scheduled to appear as Eva in *Die Meistersinger* in Brooklyn, had become ill. She would be unable to appear, and Mr. Gatti-Casazza begged me to sing the role of Eva in her place. The concert did not tire me in voice, and although I was quite exhausted from the tension and the excitement, I agreed to appear in Brooklyn that evening in view of the emergency. And so the public was treated to a performance of *Die Meistersinger* as scheduled, with only one change of cast.

Following the Carnegie Hall concert, I made several appearances out of town with the New York Symphony Orchestra. We appeared in Washington, Baltimore, St. Louis, Cincinnati, Detroit, and Cleveland, with Walter Damrosch as conductor. A Baltimore critic must have had some unpleasant experiences with coloratura sopranos, for he wrote, "Her voice is clear and smooth, her style good, and her technique ample. This made trills of her trills and scale passages of her scale passages, and not wails of unpitched sounds." In St. Louis I learned that as a coloratura I was "reasonably emotional." This was good to know. This same writer went on to say, "All in all she is a finished artist, and should have been heard by every pupil, and also by every vocal teacher in St. Louis, not so much for her sake as for their own, for they could have profited greatly."

In Philadelphia I received a wonderful welcome:

> Frieda Hempel took the house by storm. She is even more captivating as a concert singer than in opera, appearing in her own natural and altogether delightful personality. Miss Hempel's lovely, limpid voice, polished delivery and elegance of style are too well known and recognized to require extended treatment. Her loveliness was enhanced by the quaint style of her dress. The distended skirt and the general air of old-fashioned garb suited her perfectly. She made an attractive picture, and could not fail to delight everyone, even were her voice less lovely.

Another critic commented that "in tonal beauty and ease and fluency of execution her singing is so sympathetic and so entirely worthy from an artistic standpoint that the most showy coloratura music seems worthwhile as she sings it." For this concert I sang the aria from *Ernani* of Verdi, the "Slumber Song" from Meyerbeer's *Dinorah,* and "Serenade" of Richard Strauss, and of course the "Blue Danube Waltz" of Johann Strauss. I suppose the epithet "most showy coloratura" could apply to any of these, if one dislikes coloratura.

After 15 February I was no longer with the Metropolitan. Having signed only a half-year contract with the management, I was free in the spring months of 1916 to concertize extensively. With the single exception of an appearance in Boston in *Der Rosenkavalier* on 6 April, I sang only in concert.

On 6 March I gave a recital in Detroit at the Arcadia Auditorium. For this concert I again engaged Mr. Chotzinoff, and we presented a difficult program that kept both of us awake. The Detroit critic raved:

> With difficulty one refrains from almost constant reiteration of the superlative in writing of Mme Hempel's voice and her employment of

it. Since the time of Sembrich no such art of the coloratura school had been heard in this part of the world. It is even doubtful whether in artistic finish, the older singer was greater than her successor. There is an unfailing ability to create variety of mood, and a really astonishing facility in dramatic expression.

Such wonderful reception was being accorded me in all these cities that I no longer wondered about my ability to reach the American audience, in spite of the language barrier. In May my concerts took me into the south again, to Norfolk, Virginia; Raleigh, North Carolina; and then back to Ann Arbor, Michigan.

In Norfolk I appeared for the second of three concerts presented in the first Spring Music Festival of that city. Pasquale Amato had preceded me, and Sophie Braslau and Mischa Elman in joint concert followed me. For these concerts an old building, the Second Regiment Armory, had been fixed up, its ugliness camouflaged with flowers and greens. On the night of Mr. Amato's concert, a terrific thunderstorm arose, and the clattering sound of the rain on the iron roof all but stopped the concert. The next night the skies were clear, and I did not have to match my tones against the thunder. I was fully aware that many of the listeners had never been to a concert before, and as I sang my German lieder I felt inadequate. But somehow the beauty of these songs carried its own message, even if the text was not understood, and the listeners rewarded me with long applause. As the reviewer wrote, "There has appeared no woman singer in Norfolk for many years past who met with such genuinely enthusiastic applause, or who gave such entire satisfaction."

On 4 June I joined Mme Schumann-Heink, Marie Sundelius, and Clarence Whitehill in Boston for an open-air performance of *Elijah* by Mendelssohn. Mr. Damrosch was our conductor. The orchestra was enlarged, and a chorus of one thousand voices was brought together for this tremendous production in Braves Field. The audience was frightening in size, for more than ten thousand people came to hear the oratorio. The weather was excellent, and the only disturbing element was the constant whistling and shrieking of the locomotives traveling on the tracks immediately adjacent to the field.

A rather clever cartoon appeared in the newspaper, showing me standing in the middle of the huge field where baseball games were played. I was gowned as for the performance, but in my hand was a baseball mit, and close by me ran a baseball player, chasing the ball I had just thrown! This difficult undertaking scored a great success, nevertheless. The Bostonians were surprised to hear my excellent English. The *Boston Transcript* review stated, "'Hear Ye Israel' was given so beautifully by Miss Hempel that it seemed as if the audience would demand its repetition."

Mammoth Production of

"ELIJAH"
(IN ENGLISH)

BRAVES FIELD
Sunday, May 28, 1916, at 3 o'clock
In case of rain next pleasant Sunday

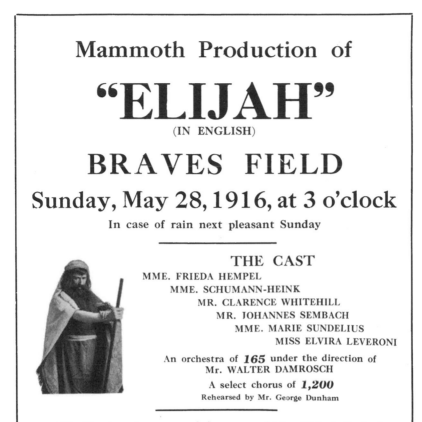

THE CAST
MME. FRIEDA HEMPEL
MME. SCHUMANN-HEINK
MR. CLARENCE WHITEHILL
MR. JOHANNES SEMBACH
MME. MARIE SUNDELIUS
MISS ELVIRA LEVERONI

An orchestra of **165** under the direction of
Mr. WALTER DAMROSCH

A select chorus of **1,200**
Rehearsed by Mr. George Dunham

Mr. Kronberg has arranged the stage, which will be built in four raised tiers, with a sounding board top, at a distance of about 100 feet from the center of the grandstands.

Only the Grandstands Will Be Used

The price of seats to subscribers will be $1.00, $1.50, $2.00, $2.50. Boxes, seating six, $20.00 to $25.00. Single seats in boxes, $4.00 and $5.00 from now until May first. After May first, the balance of seats unsubscribed for will be put on sale at an advanced price.

Orders and checks to be made out to S. Kronberg, 177 Tremont St., Boston, care of Eastern Talking Machine Co.

S. KRONBERG, General Manager.

Tel. Oxford 4680

Advertisement for the mammoth production of *Elijah* at Braves Field in Boston, 28 May 1916. Metropolitan Opera Company program for the Boston Opera House, spring season, 1916. The performance was postponed to 4 June. COURTESY PAUL JACKSON.

Directly after the performance Mme Schumann-Heink and I left to join a company which was to begin a tour of several large cities with a production of *Siegfried*. In the company with us were Clarence Whitehill, Johanna Gadski, Otto Goritz, and Johannes Sembach. Mr. Bodanzky was our conductor. The orchestra was from the Metropolitan Opera Company, under whose management the production was staged.

Four of the principal cities visited were Cincinnati, Indianapolis, St. Louis, and Pittsburgh. In each city the opera was staged in the baseball field, and the novelty of outdoor opera attracted huge crowds. During the first moments the restlessness of the vast audience and the cries of vendors of cushions, peanuts, candy, and soft drinks marred the effects of the orchestra. Problems such as these confronted Mr. Bodanzky as he conducted the orchestra and singers on a makeshift stage. Horns, train whistles, and outdoor noises in general also had to be endured.

Perhaps the most amazing incident occurred at St. Louis. The portable stage had been erected at too great a distance from the seats, and when Mr. Bodanzky commenced, hardly a sound was heard by the audience. There came a sudden rush of people laden with wraps, chairs, and other articles, hastening down the aisles and over the ball grounds to a place of advantage immediately in front of the orchestra and stage. Great noise and excitement accompanied this rush, and it was fully forty minutes before some six thousand people had settled themselves immediately in front of the stage on the precious baseball diamond which was the bone of contention in erecting the stage. It is doubtful whether such action has ever before been taken by an audience in the United States. As for the performance, it was a triumph.

Our appearance at Forbes Field in Pittsburgh had to be postponed one night. The freight train carrying the stage equipment broke down just outside the city, making it impossible for us to present the opera. The unavoidable delay in arrival of the *Siegfried* train disappointed thousands of persons who had arranged to attend the performance, and many persons from nearby towns had to find overnight accommodations.

It seems that Siegfried's visit to the baseball fields of America was not without mishap. As the Forest Bird, I had warned him about Fasolt and Fafner, about the Tarnhelm, and the most wonderful Brünnhilde. I should have warned him about baseball!

In Indianapolis things went comparatively well. According to a review:

> Of the feminine roles, honors must go to Frieda Hempel, who took the part of the Bird of the Forest. Miss Hempel did not appear on the stage, but her brilliant and clear birdlike notes proved as refreshing as a summer shower. Her coloratura soprano amounted to almost a revelation, and one regretted that in the brief visit to this city she could not be heard in a more general role.

The tour closed by the end of June, and I returned to New York. During the late spring, the front apartment had become vacant at 271 Central Park West, and I had moved into the spacious ten rooms, which were temporarily furnished. Now I engaged Elsie de Wolfe to decorate and furnish the apartment for me during the summer months. I would be in Lake Placid and then in Germany, and the decorators would be free to work while I was gone.

Elsie de Wolfe had at one time been on the stage, as one of Charles Frohman's stars. Known as the best-dressed woman on the American stage, she had nevertheless deserted this profession to embark upon a new career as an interior decorator. As Lloyd Morris expressed it in his fine book *Incredible New York*, "Millionaires were finding her notions of elegance far more costly than their own untutored, wistful dreams of splendor." When I met her in 1916 she so impressed me with her vivacious, charming personality and exquisite taste that I knew she would be just the person to entrust with the task of planning my apartment for me. I gave her a carte-blanche contract, and left for Lake Placid with a light heart.

CHAPTER FOURTEEN

A Summer During the War

I *was able to book passage for Germany* in 1916 by way of
Copenhagen, but with a sailing date not until 16 July, I
decided to go to Lake Placid in the meantime. Marcella Sembrich had told
me so much about the Lake Placid Club and had asked me so often to join
her there that I was most eager to see it. Bidding Will Kahn adieu for a little while only, for he had promised to sail to Europe with me to assuage my
terrible fear of floating mines, I left for Lake Placid in a Packard that I purchased for the trip. The chauffeur was a delightful Irishman named Mr.
Mulnane, and Rosa and I enjoyed his company very much.

The Lake Placid Club was one of several similar clubs on the lake front.
Surrounding the central club house were many rustic cottages which were
rented out to guests. These cottages as well as the excellent golf course and
swimming area were available to club members only. Through the recom-
mendation of Marcella Sembrich, I was given a cottage next to hers, called
The Larches.

We were overwhelmed by the beauty of the country. The thick, dense
woods were quite different from anything I had seen in Germany where
nearly every inch of ground was cultivated. I had no fear of the German
woods, for I could always find my way out, but here there seemed to be
miles and miles of wilderness. I would never risk walking through the
Adirondacks even with a guide, but I enjoyed driving up the roads and
encountering the wildcats, bears, and porcupines that crossed our path. I had
never seen anything like this.

Often we drove for the whole day, stopping at little inns for meals, seeking the most unsophisticated places and enjoying their simplicity and their quietness. My companion was Mrs. Wilcox, whom I had met upon my arrival. She had seen me dining in the club and had been introduced to me by mutual friends. She was most charming and attentive, and the individuality of her manner of thinking and talking made her a most challenging companion. She had long had deep admiration for me and would often amaze me by climbing over a fence to pick a flower from the swamps at the lake's edge. She was determined to give me this flower, even at the cost of soiling her elegant white shoes in the mud! Nana Wilcox and I were to become longtime friends.

It was not long before I fell under the spell of the game of golf. I began to take lessons every day, and soon I was on the golf course all day. This sport is excellent for singers, far better than tennis which can strain the breathing muscles and dry the throat. After walking over the entire course once and sometimes twice a day, I would go down to the lake shore for a swim, and all this exercise was wonderful.

Many artists and musicians came to Lake Placid, and among the group this year was Victor Herbert, with his wife* and his daughter Ella. This wonderful composer of musical comedy and songs was delightful to be with, and I spent many afternoons listening to him playing his tuneful melodies. Then his family would join us, Mrs. Herbert, Ella, and a proud Boston bull terrier who romped all over the room in his excitement at seeing his master again. We would all have tea and then go out for an evening stroll.

One evening, just at dusk when everybody was gathering at the club for dinner, I stood on my balcony for a moment before leaving my cottage. Looking out across the lawn, I spied a most beautiful animal, the likes of which I had never seen before. It had the most beautiful white stripe adorning its black body, and it stared at me with great pride. When I arrived in the dining room I told everybody about my strange and wonderful discovery, but instead of impressing them, I afforded them great laughter. I had seen my first skunk! Now what should I know about a skunk? We do not have them in Germany. Had I met him on the road, I am certain that in my innocence I would have spoken to him and tried to pick him up. Now, of course, I know better.

When the time came to return to New York I did not want to leave at all. It seemed quite unbelievable that in just a day's driving I would be back in the biggest city of the world, threading my way through crowded streets and breathing the dust-filled air. But if I was to sail as planned, I must leave. I knew that I would return the following summer, and so I finally told Mr. Mulnane to pack the car, and we left the next morning for New York City.

---

*Victor Herbert was married to the Viennese opera singer Therese Förster (1861–1927), who was engaged by the Met in 1886. *Ed.*

Mr. Kahn and I sailed on the SS *Christiania Fjord*, which took a very northern route to avoid floating mines and enemy ships. The captain was very kind to us, and he often invited Mr. Kahn and me to his cabin. He even let me steer the boat for a little while. When we arrived in the northern fjords, we crept through them slowly. Often when it seemed that we were again in open waters, we would come upon another fjord. It was exciting, and I soon forgot the fact that we had subjected ourselves to the perils of ocean travel in wartime.

We arrived in Bergen and were introduced to our first smorgasbord, where the enticing varieties of food were spread out on a long table. Another surprise awaited me, for I had never before been able to read a newspaper at midnight without a light. At this time of year the sky was bright throughout the night, something I had never seen before. The captain then took us to Kristiania, now called Oslo, which had a Parisian quality of charm, gaiety, and lightness complemented by the clear atmosphere and delightful climate. I would have stayed longer, but I had to get to Berlin, and Mr. Kahn had business to attend to in America.

In Berlin I stayed in my own apartment, which my father had kept for me. My chief purpose in coming to Berlin was to give a concert for blinded soldiers at the Hospital Charité. This was a very moving experience for me. I had two brothers at the front, and although I was living and singing in America, I still felt very deeply the plight of the German soldier.

In October 1916 I sailed again for America, on the SS *Bergensfjord*, following the same northern route. Mr. Gatti-Casazza remarked in a newspaper interview that it had been impossible to bring over any new artists for the coming season at the Metropolitan: "The women absolutely refuse to come over here. They are afraid of submarines." Well, I was one artist who was not afraid to travel.

I enjoyed the company of Mr. Bodanzky and Mr. Otto Weill on the boat, and we played cards every day. When we stopped at Kirkwall in the Orkney Islands of Scotland,* the British officers asked to see me in my stateroom. I was still a German citizen, and therefore my belongings had to be searched for contraband material. The officer-in-charge went carefully through my trunks and checked my papers. One young officer who was looking through my suitcases gave up his search when he came across a photograph. He hesitated for a moment and then boldly asked me if he could have it. So I autographed it for him. As he took it, he shut up the suitcase and

---

*This was Scapa Flow, the chief naval base of the British fleet during World War I. Two years after the visit Hempel describes, in November 1918, the German fleet was interned here, only to be scuttled by the German crews in June 1919. The base played an important part in World War II, and Scapa Flow witnessed the sinking of H.M.S. *Royal Oak* by a German U-boat on 14 October 1939. *Ed.*

discontinued his search entirely. He was much more interested in the picture, I guess. Nothing was found, and so all was well.

I sang for the British officers at the ship's concert that night, pleasing them with my "Annie Laurie" and "The Last Rose of Summer" to such an extent that they gave me freedom of the port until sailing time. In a few days we cleared port, and as we sailed away I thought to myself, "How unbelievable! These wonderful English officers and my brothers are being asked to fight one another."

Mr. Bodanzky then confided to me that he had been dreadfully worried for my sake, and that he was greatly relieved when he learned that I had been given permission to sail. I suppose that a man was better able to visualize the danger I could have been in. My prominent position in Berlin and my previous connections with the royal family had made me suspect, and he realized this. For my part, I had not even thought of such dangers. I innocently assumed myself to be just an artist, returning to fulfill my contracts.

Hempel as Leila, De Luca as Zurga, Caruso as Nadir, and Rothier as Nourabad in the Met premiere of *The Pearl Fishers,* 13 November 1916. PHOTO BY WHITE. COURTESY METROPOLITAN OPERA ARCHIVES.

CHAPTER FIFTEEN

New York in War Time

As I entered the door to my apartment at 271 Central Park West, I wondered what vision would greet my eyes, but I had not even imagined such loveliness. Elsie de Wolfe had created a fairyland for me. The hallways were covered with mirrors, the floors hidden by deep wall-to-wall rugs. Exquisite pieces of furniture were set carefully in place, and the colors were delicate and marvelous. I cannot describe in words the charm and elegance of those beautiful rooms, bathed in sunlight and looking out over the broad expanse of upper Central Park. The photographs of my apartment which appeared soon in *Vogue* and *Harper's Bazaar* give only a slight indication of how beautiful it was. I was overjoyed to be in my own home at last, a home so beautiful and so livable at the same time.

Before the opening performance at the Metropolitan, which was to be a revival of Bizet's *Les Pêcheurs de perles* in which I sang the role of Leila, I gave several concerts out of town.

In Pittsburgh, where I sang on 3 November 1916, I had the pleasure of meeting Mr. and Mrs. Emil Winters. Mr. Winters owned steel mills in Pittsburgh and other companies in Europe. Following the concert, they gave a reception for me in their mansion. We became friends, and when Mr. Winters came to New York after the death of his wife, he stayed at the Plaza and entertained a great deal. He loved music, and his parties were attended by many prominent artists as well as by important business personalities. On one evening Mr. Winters introduced the Watsons and the Kondolfs. Mr. Watson and Mr. Kondolf were at that moment being considered for the presidency of the International Business Machine Company, and the deci-

Hempel as Leila, by Caruso.

sion had not yet been announced. I can imagine that the evening was a difficult one for both gentlemen, and we all shared the anxiety and the anticipation. The next day Mr. Winters informed me that Mr. Watson had been given the position.

The *Pearl Fishers* revival at the Metropolitan created great interest. It was virtually a novelty, for it had last been heard in 1896 with Emma Calvé as Leila. Only two acts had been given at that time. We were singing in French, with a cast including Caruso, Giuseppe de Luca, Leon Rothier, and me. Sigmund Spaeth wrote of this work:

> The chief fault of the opera is that it is too lyrical. One florid melodious number follows another, with so little variety that the effect soon becomes monotonous. If the leading parts were not taken by great singers and artists, the interest of the audience would soon give out. But as it happens, practically every number in the score is adapted to vocal display, and therefore "The Pearl Fishers" may well turn out to be a success.

Speaking of my performance, he continued, "Frieda Hempel achieved some moments of unqualified beauty. The Broadway musical comedy star who proudly sings variations over a melody in the chorus will find Miss Hempel doing the same trick vastly better in Bizet's comparatively ancient work." There is indeed a great deal of florid writing in the score and difficult ensemble work. The duet which Caruso and I sang is particularly appealing, and as one writer put it, "It is a lovely song to remember with gratitude and desire."

The pageantry and colorfulness of this opera, and the beauty of the music despite its florid style, should have secured a permanent place for it in the repertory. But it was given only three times during the season. The weakness of the libretto was to blame in part, and perhaps, as Mr. Spaeth remarks, there is too much of the old-fashioned florid piece. Nevertheless, the opening performance was a success in every way. As the critic wrote in the *New York Times* on 14 November:

> Two of the chief favorites of the company were in the cast, Mr. Caruso and Miss Hempel, the performance was one that challenged warm admiration, and there was naturally an outpouring of enthusiasm. There was the realization that if the opera itself was not a masterpiece of the first rank, it at least supplied a part admirably fitted for Mr. Caruso, in which his voice, and his long phrasing were to be heard to excellent advantage; and another for Mme Hempel's beautiful singing, including a certain amount of coloratura. The singing of Mr. Caruso and Mme Hempel as Nadir and Leila was of the highest beauty.

It was at this time that Sigmund Spaeth requested an interview. He was curious to know how it happened that although I had come to America with the reputation as an outstanding coloratura soprano, capable of performing the trills, staccatos, and florid passages which are the joy of the "trick voice" as he called it, I nevertheless had achieved my greatest successes in lyric roles such as the Feldmarschallin, Eva, and Euryanthe. I answered him by saying that a gifted singer should be able to interpret every type of vocal music. I assured him that I considered florid singing quite as artistic as lyric, dramatic, or any other kind of singing. All correct singing requires technique, study, and practice, and one kind of singing, when perfect, is on just as high a plane as any other kind. However, I admitted, I would rather stir the hearts of an audience with one simple song than provoke gasps of astonishment by the most difficult feat of technique.

The newspapers were making much of some remarks I made concerning German women. I had noticed in Berlin that the German women were noticeably thinner and consequently more elegant than I had remembered them. The wear and tear of anxiety and privation were removing the superfluous fat, and the women were reaping the reward of sleepless nights, bleak days, and awful suspense. So *Musical America* of 28 October 1916 quoted me, "Elephantiasis of the ankle, like typhus, is conquered by the rigorous treatment of war. There is a new cure for plural chin, as well as for gangrene. Mme Hempel has somehow made the world seem brighter." But it was true. The women in Berlin had looked quite elegant in their new slim styles. And in a sense I was envious, for the luxuries of living in America were conducive to added weight, and I had to tell my good Rosa more than once not to cook so abundantly for me.

I did not care for the very modern Isadora Duncan style of flowing garment, but preferred rather close-fitting clothes, and so I had to watch my figure. I never designed my own dresses, but I did have them designed for me by the greatest dressmakers. In Paris, my favorite houses were Schiaparelli, Molyneuse, Callot Soeurs, and Chanel. From these houses I bought my concert gowns and my stage costumes as well as my personal gowns.

This might sound like a pleasant task, but on the contrary it was very tiring and nerve-racking. First I would consider the stage gowns. Selecting the material involved a great deal of time. I would always visit several establishments before deciding on a particular weave and color. Sometimes I would return to the place where I had chosen a certain material and would find it gone. This meant adjusting myself to the loss and beginning all over again. Finally the material would be purchased and the pattern selected. Then I had to attend numerous fittings, agree or not agree to suggested changes, and subject myself and the dressmaker to the annoyances of the trade. Then as I planned my opera costumes while the fittings were proceeding for the stage gowns, untold complications would arise. At the same time I would be planning my own winter wardrobe, which included coats, dresses, suits, house-gowns, shoes, golf clothes, and beach costumes. I was never in Paris for any length of time, and so all this was usually done in a great hurry. Fortunately, I had a figure that was easy to fit, and a pocketbook that was filled. I could afford the very best. It was not difficult to find shoes for me in Paris, for I had very small feet, and the most delicate Parisian shoe can be worn to advantage on a tiny foot. And so it went, buying this, searching for that, ordering this, rejecting that, being fitted, asking advice of my dear friend Nana Wilcox, who was often in Paris with me and who had excellent taste, and packing my trunks with all the new acquisitions when the ordeal was over.

Because of this great care in the selection of my gowns, I earned the distinction of being the best-dressed woman on the concert stage. And although it may seem strange, it is nevertheless true that many persons, speaking to me of a concert of long ago, will refer not to what I sang but to what color gown I wore. They will tell me how it was cut and how beautiful it was, and how lovely I looked on the stage.

For a concert in Albert Hall in London, I once wore a beautiful red velvet gown. After the concert, a prominent, elegant gentleman said to me, "This red velvet gown is so beautiful! When you are through with it, will you give me one of the sleeves so that I can make a pillow out of it?" People greeted me with a comment about some gown, saying, "I hear you wore an exquisite pink satin gown in Chicago. Will you wear it here?" I wondered, sometimes, if anybody ever listened to my singing.

Hempel's gowns attracted compliments throughout her career. COURTESY METROPOLITAN OPERA ARCHIVES.

I have spent a fortune on my gowns, for I believe that an artist should be attractive to the eye as well as to the ear. A concert is a festive occasion, a time of beauty and loveliness. Every detail should be perfect, from the impeccable tailoring of the suit of the accompanist to the smallest element of design in the gown of the soloist. After all, the eyes of the listening audience are upon the stage for a full hour and a half, and no ugliness, no shabbiness, should distract. Each appearance in a city is a new experience for me, and must also be a new experience for the audience. So I never wear the same gown twice in the same city.

Lady Duff-Gordon made many of my operatic costumes during the war years. I always received compliments on these gowns from the gentlemen of the press. The costumes for *Martha, The Pearl Fishers, La traviata, Rosenkavalier,* and others were created by her. Only once did she err badly in her judgment, a lapse not lost on the newspapers, who asked, "What was that creation from Lucille?" This was in *La traviata,* when she put some ridiculous dresses on me, I must admit. But I wore them only once. The costumes for *The Pearl Fishers* cost me more than one thousand dollars and brought down upon me the consternation and the wrath of my close friends, who wondered how I could be so foolish as to spend all that money on costumes. But at that time I was perhaps a little careless with money when it came to clothes, for I felt that the public deserved the best of everything.

I must also say that a beautiful gown will make no impression if the posture and the stage deportment of the singer are defective. There is an art to walking out upon a stage. The audience must sense in your very walk and in your face an assurance and an authority. Arthur Hopkins, the great theatrical producer, once said to me, "I would engage you just for your walk onto the stage." My singing, my gown, and my manners were all part of my profession.

The winter season 1916 moved on apace, with performances of *Rosenkavalier, Traviata,* repetitions of *The Pearl Fishers,* and finally, on 30 December, a revival performance of *L'elisir d'amore* of Donizetti. This work had been off the boards for six long years, and now Caruso, Scotti, and I were singing it again. The score reveals Donizetti's gift for comedy and humor, as well as his melodic genius. It was a perfect vehicle for Caruso, and he completely captured the audience with his singing of "Una furtiva lagrima."

Each time we sang *L'elisir d'amore,* I was conscious of Caruso's extreme nervousness. We would be in our places on the stage, and as the moment arrived for the curtain to rise, a great change would come over him. Up to that time he would be standing in such an utterly relaxed position that he seemed close to falling on the floor—his arms hung limp, his back bent double, and his legs relaxed. Then his legs would begin to tremble from fear. Just as the curtain rose he would stamp his right leg, straighten his body like a

Hempel as Lady Harriet in *Martha,* in costume by Lady Duff-Gordon. PHOTO BY HILL. COURTESY ROBERT TUGGLE.

bullet shooting up into the air, and raise his head high. There stood the great Caruso whom the audience knew and asked so much of.

Madame Sembrich told me that she became seasick before every performance as a result of extreme nervousness. I, too, was frightened before each appearance, and I often wondered in those moments why I chose such a difficult, nerve-racking profession. Every artist, conscious of the standard of performance required by the audience and by the critics, is fearful that she or he will fail to meet that standard this time. And so every performance, every appearance is a new challenge. And quite naturally, the higher the standard, the greater the fear.

The role of Adina suited me well. "Miss Hempel made a vivacious and piquant Adina and contributed some of the most effective and brilliant singing of the day," wrote the reviewer for *Musical America* in January of 1917. And in the *New York American* of New Year's Eve 1916 I read this amusing report, "Miss Hempel, in excellent condition, gave a charming portrayal of Adina." It was practically a doctor's certificate of health, I would say. On the same day Mr. Henderson wrote in the *New York Sun* that my general impersonation of the role was a charming one. He added, "She sang with lovely voice, much florid facility and with sparkle and grace of style."

Hempel as Adina and Caruso as Nemorino in *L'elisir d'amore* for the Met premiere on 30 December 1916. PHOTO BY WHITE. COURTESY METROPOLITAN OPERA ARCHIVES.

Caruso's singing of "Una furtiva lagrima" was so magnificent that the audience would not let us continue until he consented to repeat this aria. But Caruso stepped to the footlights and said in mumbled English, "To repeat is not allowed," much to the delight of the audience. What he actually said has never been decided, but he was quoted in the papers as having said, "I would sing, but I am disbarred," or "I would like but I am prevent," or "It is not permit," and other similar versions, which the creative mind of the journalist was capable of concocting. Caruso's English was poor but certainly not that garbled!

On 24 January 1917, I sang the role of Susanna in a revival of *The Marriage of Figaro*. This opera had last been given at the Metropolitan 13 January 1909, with Marcella Sembrich, Emma Eames, Geraldine Farrar, and Antonio Scotti. Our cast consisted of Mme Matzenauer, Giuseppe de Luca, Farrar, and myself. Richard Aldrich of the *New York Times* on 25 January of 1917 summed up the performance in these words:

> It could not be said that there was a general understanding of the style of singing demanded by Mozart's music, either in the airs or in the recitative; the delivery of such recitative being now almost a lost art among dramatic singers. The most acceptable compensation for the loss of the great singers who have sung this music in the past was offered by Mme Hempel, who has the voice, the art, and much of the beauty of style it demands.

On the same day, the *Tribune* noted that the attempt to keep this score within its original scope of delicate balance in the large auditorium failed. The orchestral shadings of Mozart, which Mr. Bodanzky sought, were lost in the back rows. The writer added:

> It seems a thousand pities that the deterioration of singers, coupled with the lack of a lyric theatre adapted to operas of the old school, is threatening to banish Mozart and Rossini from the local repertory. All that can be called a survival of the Mozart style in last night's performance was summed up in the performance of Miss Hempel; she alone knew equally well how to act her part, sing her airs, and speak her recitatives.

Mme Matzenauer's voice was considered too heavy for the role of the Countess, and there was some criticism of her high tones. Nevertheless she received a long ovation for her splendid singing of "Dove sono." We were discussing the review the next day as we gathered in the dressing rooms of the Metropolitan, and Mme Matzenauer made the classic comment, "Oh, my high notes are all right—they just have to get used to them!"

A performance of *Martha* on 26 January was reviewed by the critic at the *Philadelphia Public Ledger* in a manner that pleased me a good deal. He referred to my "Last Rose of Summer": "The only way to sing that song was the way taken by last evening's prima donna—the way of art divested of any apparent artifice, returning to first principles and making the direct appeal of the music unadorned, with no simpering graces and no elaborate pretense." My constant efforts to reach listeners' hearts by the simplest, most direct means, through the beauty of the music itself, were here confirmed once more.

On 17 January and again on 9 February, we presented Richard Wagner's *Die Meistersinger*. In spite of the war abroad, there was as yet no anti-German sentiment at the Metropolitan. Speaking of the opera itself, the reviewer for the *New York Journal* wrote:

> At times it is more satisfying than at others. Last evening was one of these occasions, chiefly because Miss Hempel was involved in the performance, and also because Mr. Bodanzky appeared to be a little more alive than he has been for some time. Miss Hempel has sung Eva here only some two or three times. Last evening this was once more so apt an Eva, so excellent a piece of intelligent, human histrionism, so creative of the rare aura of charm, and moreover, so delicately yet firmly and clearly sung an Eva that one felt a most lively curiosity concerning her Elsa.

I had sung Elsa in Europe, but I was not likely ever to sing this role at the Metropolitan because of the system of division of roles. And it would have been difficult for the New York audience to accept me in that role, accustomed as they were to my singing of Queen of the Night and my other coloratura roles. Perhaps they would not even be willing to believe that I could sing Elsa. [See note, page 140.]

Mr. Henderson of the *New York Sun* wrote of my Eva, "Mme Hempel's impersonation of Eva afforded sheer delight to both eye and ear. It combined beauty of voice and vocal style, excellence of diction and charm and dramatic intelligence in acting." I was always proud of Mr. Henderson's comments, for he was the dean of critics in New York.

During the matinee performance of *The Marriage of Figaro* on 3 February I had learned of the severance of relations between Germany and America. I was immediately questioned by reporters, who came to my dressing room. I remember saying to them, "I feel awfully sorry, because I love America so much. But, as art is international—as is evident from the fact that even today Russian artists are singing in Germany—so I hope to continue singing in America and in Germany for many years to come." Mr. Bodanzky, who was an Austrian, said, "Music must speak for us." Those of us who were of German or Austrian extraction were now beginning to feel the effects of the international dispute, for we now found ourselves in an ambiguous position. And for me, it was the beginning of a difficult period, because both Germany and America wanted to claim me, and yet in each country I faced great antagonism.

I did not wish to think of such things, for I had a very busy schedule. On 12 February 1917 I gave my second New York recital. This took place in the afternoon, and in the evening I sang the role of Susanna in *The Marriage of Figaro,* marking my last appearance there for the season. For my recital I was unable to have the support of that definitive accompanist Coenraad Bos, for he was away on tour. Instead, Richard Hageman* played for me.

The next day Henry Krehbiel commented in the *Tribune:*

> Perhaps the most obvious thing about Miss Hempel's concert was its sincere, altogether amiable and quite successful effort to perpetuate the tradition of both operatic and song singing which Mme Sembrich has represented almost alone for a generation. Miss Hempel chose a good model and did honor to her exemplar, not only in her selections, but in her manner of singing. Never has her voice sounded more fresh and beautiful, never has it come forth more spontaneously, more fluently, and with greater limpidity and equality of register.

Going on to discuss *The Marriage of Figaro,* he said of me:

> She was the one singer in the opera who showed full knowledge of the technical requirements of Mozart's singing and who disclosed complete familiarity with the musical text as it was read in Mozart's time. There are conventions in the airs as well as the recitatives, which are to be learned from tradition and study of the art of song.

The critic for the *Globe* commented on my schedule:

> It is extremely unusual for an artist of Miss Hempel's professional eminence to be willing to sing twice the same day. Miss Hempel's programme in the afternoon was long and exacting, and the role of Susanna is also long and has its exactions. It is worth of special note, and to some persons of special study, that Miss Hempel finished the double ordeal with her voice fresh, and no weariness that was apparent.

Mr. Henderson wrote in the *New York Sun:*

> The conclusion of the engagement of Frieda Hempel has removed from the Metropolitan stage one of the best singers this public has heard in several seasons. She is set down in the catalogues as a coloratura soprano,

---

*Richard Hageman, conductor, composer, and pianist, was born in Leeuwarden, Netherlands, 2 July 1882. He studied at the Brussels and Antwerp conservatories, becoming conductor at the Royal Opera, Amsterdam, and accompanist to Mathilde Marchesi in Paris. He came to the United States as accompanist at the Sunday Evening Concerts. He later headed the opera department at the Curtis Institute. His opera, *Caponsacchi,* was first produced in Germany in 1935 and at the Metropolitan in 1937. He died in Beverly Hills, California, 6 March 1966. *Ed.*

probably because she is one of the very few who can and do sing florid music. But her loveliest art is that of pure lyric type. She has done nothing more beautiful than her impersonation of the heroine of *Der Rosenkavalier,* while her Eva in *Die Meistersinger* is of such exquisite charm that it commands the heartiest admiration of all lovers of finished operatic interpretation. Let us hope that nothing may occur to interfere with her return next season. We are bound to consider that in the event of hostilities with Germany, the positions of the German singers at the Metropolitan may become untenable.

I wondered, also, whether I would return to the stage of the Metropolitan for another season, and when the audience gave me a long farewell ovation, I felt deeply moved. The future was so uncertain, and I had already begun to feel the undertow of war hysteria. But the public at the Metropolitan, as well as the music critics whose comments reflected the thoughts of the people, wished me well. The *New York Evening Post* critic said, "In the evening Miss Hempel sang for the last time at the Metropolitan. How can the Metropolitan get along without her? Hers is one of the very few great voices now to be heard there."*

Instead of resting after so strenuous a day, I boarded a train at midnight and set out for Lorain, Ohio. Here I gave the first of a series of concerts booked very closely together. Then I was driven by car to Cleveland for my next appearance. We had to drive through snowdrifts, and combat strong, icy winds, but we made the thirty-mile trip in good time. And on 16 February 1917, I was in St. Louis, appearing as soloist with the St. Louis Symphony Orchestra.

Being known to the St. Louis public as the Forest Bird because of my invisible appearance of the previous season in the baseball-field *Siegfried,* I succeeded in reinforcing that birdlike reputation. The critic wrote, "Madame Hempel sustained a trill calculated to cause a canary to die of yellow envy. It was brilliant beyond words." Even the headline read, "Hempel sings like a bird."

My concert in Detroit on 20 February had its comical aspects, I am afraid. Paul Eisler was my accompanist for this recital, and I had entrusted him with the care of the music. The first part of the program went along beautifully, and the audience of more than three thousand people enjoyed our work and applauded us generously. After the intermission, I returned to the platform and began the second part of the program. Mr. Eisler followed me with the music and sat down confidently at the piano.

All went well until we arrived at the song "Deep River" in the arrange-

---

*Hempel did return the following year. Her last Met performance was 10 February 1919. *Ed.*

ment by Harry T. Burleigh. I put myself in the mood of the song, took a deep breath, and sang the opening phrase "Deep River." I thought to myself, as I sang, how strange the piano sounded. Then I realized that Mr. Eisler was playing the music to another song about a river! We just couldn't get together. The papers remarked the next day that I had been wading in the Burleigh river, and Skipper Eisler tried to take me down another river. They say I turned to him and smiled, singing, "You're playing the wrong music, you're playing the wrong music," to phrases of "Deep River." In any event, he finally stopped playing, got up, and went out to see if he could find the right music. It was not there, and so we never did finish the river songs. "Frieda Hempel smiled in her broad German way through it all, and took the enforced interruption in such evident good humor that she converted it into a real asset so far as the audience was concerned," commented the reviewer for the *Detroit Free Press*.

After concerts in Rochester, New York, and Providence, Rhode Island, I traveled to Chicago for a concert on 4 March. Remarks were made that the printed text of the songs was superfluous because of the remarkable purity of my diction. Nevertheless, I always saw to it that the listeners had a copy of the text to each number, with English translation. It was so much easier for me to sing to a public that understood me. Of course this was an added expense to me, because in America the programs are not sold to the public, as they are in Europe. They are given away, and the little profit that the European singer enjoys from these sales becomes instead an expense to the singer in America.

I had given concerts without preparing an English text for the public, and I found that the response was a good deal less enthusiastic. To a person who did not understand German it was of no help that my German diction was clear. And although the critics had said that when I sang Italian, it was impossible to believe that I was not an Italian by birth, this did not help a listener who knew no Italian. I wanted the public to grasp the sense and the mood of the song as I sang it, and I wanted them to let me know that I had conveyed that meaning to them. For this reason, then, I supplied English translations at every concert.

Remember, also, that in those days entertainment was not specialized. The public was not divided into movie, television, and concert fans. The concert audience was by no means as select as it is today, and in a small city or town it generally contained all those people who wished to be entertained for the evening. Now I wanted to reach each person as directly as possible. This meant helping those who knew no language other than English, and they constituted the largest portion of every audience. There would occasionally be a small minority of listeners who, having recently come to America, would still speak their mother tongue. But certainly the vast majority of those in an audience spoke only English.

Leaving Denver, Colorado, on 22 March following a concert there, I journeyed back to Boston by train for a concert of songs at Symphony Hall. Mr. Bos met me there and played for me. I had not taken an accompanist with me on the concert tour just ended, and I had had the problem of adjusting to the local accompanist in each town. It was a great relief to sing once more with the wonderful artist, Mr. Bos, at the piano.

My Boston review was heartening: "It was a tribute to the popularity and the ability of Miss Frieda Hempel that Mr. Mudgett ventured to give her the entire program in her Sunday afternoon concert. His confidence was not misplaced, for the size and the enthusiasm of the audience showed that it appreciated the excellent singing which rewarded it." The Boston audience was a most distinctive, selective one, and I considered a success in that city to mean much. I was a favorite in Boston, but Boston was indeed a favorite with me as well.

Back again to Grand Rapids, Michigan, and then Toledo, Ohio. I loved the caption in the *Toledo Blade:* "German, wonderful singer, captures Toledo audience." The story read, "The Germans captured Toledo last night, at least one of them did. Frieda Hempel made a complete conquest of her great audience at the Valentine. Great things had been heard of her, expectation was on tiptoe, and all anticipations were fulfilled." As had now become customary in public gatherings, the audience sang the "Star-Spangled Banner" at the close of the evening.

A few more concerts, and then it was summer and time to go to the Adirondacks for a vacation.

CHAPTER SIXTEEN

A Question of Loyalty

*I*n the early fall of 1917, I began a long tour of the South-
west. Paul Eisler traveled with me as my accompanist. I
had been reengaged by the Metropolitan Opera Company for the 1917–18
season, and I was scheduled to sing *L'elisir d'amore* on 15 November. This
meant that the tour had to be closely booked so that I could appear in eight
cities within one month.

Just before leaving for Oklahoma City where my first concert was to
take place on 10 October, I announced to the papers my engagement to
William B. Kahn and stated that we would be married on 8 June 1918 at St.
James Church in New York City. This news seemed to quiet fears in many
quarters that I was pro-German, for these narrow-minded people now rea-
soned that because I was about to become an American citizen through marriage, I would no longer feel any allegiance to the country of my birth. I
shall speak about this later.

If I had any illusions about seeing the proverbial Wild West, with its
cowboys and its dashing pageant of frontier life, I was soon awakened. Oklahoma City, although it was only some thirty-odd years old, was already a
thriving, modern city. Automobiles, Fifth Avenue styles, smart shops, and
cosmopolitan restaurants were all in evidence and testified to the amazing
capacity of the land for growth and expansion.

I opened my concert with a group of German songs, for I could find no
valid reason for omitting them as so many singers had done. They were
received with attention and with appreciation. Then I sang some Mozart
and closed with French and English songs.

From Oklahoma City we went to Waco, Texas, and then to San Antonio. Hotel reservations had been made in advance by the Wolfson Agency,
who managed my concerts, and immediately upon my arrival, the inevitable
interview would begin. "What do you think about the war?" I would be
asked. "Why should I talk about it?" I replied. "I am no politician: I am a
singer and an artist. An artist has nothing to do with wars." In this city I sang
"Dixie" for an encore. This is a favorite of the south, and I even had to repeat
it. (In 1919 I recorded it for Edison.)

My next stop was in Houston, Texas. I learned that a local organization
had just concluded a Hempel concert, using Victor Records, and had thus
introduced me to the Houston music lovers by proxy. "People no longer
have any excuse for not being acquainted with the voice and style of great
singers before their personal appearance," read the advance announcement
of this recital. Still, it gave me a strange feeling of competition. The audience
here numbered more than three thousand, and they were delightful. The
Houston review noted, "It was one of the most wonderful concerts ever
heard in this city, and every music lover in the city today is praising Miss
Hempel's glorious voice and the splendid program she gave." I gathered
from this that the contest had not been won by my host.

At each concert on this tour I presented a group of German songs, and
not once was any objection raised. And I generally included such sweet,
simple songs in English as "Annie Laurie," "My Curly Headed Baby,"
"Long, Long Ago," and "Sweet Suffolk Owl." Invariably "Last Rose of Summer" was requested. "The Blue Danube Waltz" was by then synonymous
with my name, and it always appeared on the printed program. I built my
programs carefully, with much attention to their balance.

Next, in Dallas, I sang in the Dallas Opera House as a guest of the Schubert Choral Club. This was not an opera house at all, but just an auditorium.
The city was attempting to launch plans to erect a municipal opera house,
and I placed my support strongly behind this project. The Schubert Choral
Club was another of those civic groups that voluntarily arranged for city
concerts, the city government itself lacking concern for cultural projects.

After a concert in St. Joseph, Ohio, I joined Giuseppe de Luca for a
joint recital in Detroit, Michigan, on 30 October. Here, for the first time, I
was obliged to omit German works at the request of the management, the
Central Concert Company. They did another strange thing. At intermission
they announced, with a provincial sense of pride, that the audience was the
largest ever in attendance at a Detroit concert, numbering some four thousand persons. Commenting on my singing of "Dixie," a critic said, "Miss
Hempel sang 'Dixie' delightfully with a rapid tempo that would be quite
impossible for most people because of the difficulties of articulation." I
found it to be very effective indeed at this rapid tempo, and I loved to sing
it. Perhaps my happy mood also added something to the rendition.

There was much talk in the papers concerning offers to appear in motion pictures, but I was not interested in this medium. I had realized that it would take me completely away from the concert and opera stage, and that would be impossible. My whole life was bound up in singing, and the acting talents I had were useful to me only on the stage.

On 9 November I was informed that a concert scheduled for me in April of 1918 in Youngstown, Ohio, had been canceled by the mayor; the reason given was that I was anti-American. At the same time, a concert by Fritz Kreisler was canceled.

It so happened that in my concert at Providence, Rhode Island, on 4 November, I had opened the program by singing "The Star-Spangled Banner." This had been requested of me, and I saw no reason for not complying. In no sense did I become anti-German, or pro-American, by so doing. As an artist, I served my audience. The audience was American, and so the American anthem was sung. For the duration of hostilities, this song was obligatory at all public gatherings.

I answered the Youngstown accusation in the following words:

> The allegation that I ever uttered anywhere, at any time, any anti-American sentiments is a malicious and unqualified falsehood. As a woman alone in this country, observing to the letter every obligation and custom which is due the American public—which has been so kind to me, and which feeling I deeply reciprocate—I think the attack is most unwarranted and cowardly.

On 12 November the objection was withdrawn, and the concert contract was honored.

On 15 November 1918 I was once again on the stage of the Metropolitan Opera House, singing with Caruso in *L'elisir d'amore.* Because of the pressure of public opinion, the Metropolitan management had dropped the contracts of Johannes Sembach, Hermann Weil, and Carl Braun as well as that of the contralto Margarete Ober. The newspapers were informed of the decision of the management to retire all German singers and to ban German works. Madame Matzenauer and I had both been retained. Her husband was an Italian, and I was presently to become an American citizen through marriage.

Yet in spite of this favorable decision in my behalf, I was a German by birth, and I was grateful for the continued warmth and friendship of my colleagues in the Metropolitan. Margarete Ober sued the Metropolitan for fifty thousand dollars, claiming that her contract had been annulled without her consent.

One reviewer of *L'elisir d'amore* said, "It may be only fancy to think that an artist so good as Miss Hempel always has improved over the summer, but certainly her singing seemed more fully developed than ever before."

The wonderful success of my southern tour and the feeling of confidence I now had before the massive American audiences probably gave added assurance to my operatic performance.

For my *Traviata* appearance on 17 November, I wore new gowns which provoked much comment: "In gorgeous new costumes, Frieda Hempel again demonstrated vocal powers that were as astonishing as they were admirable." One reviewer ventured to ask whether Verdi would have approved of my wig and gowns, but he concluded by saying that no doubt Verdi would have enjoyed them.

On 20 November I traveled to Boston to sing the soprano solos of the Ninth Symphony of Beethoven, under Karl Muck. It was a great honor to sing with this magnificent conductor of Beethoven scores, and the performance was a most memorable one.

The Daughter of the Regiment received its long-awaited revival on 11 December in Philadelphia and 17 December in New York:

> Friendly relations were established in the operatic world between France and Germany, when Frieda Hempel, one of the few remaining Teutonic singers in Giulio Gatti-Casazza's company, kissed the flag of the country now at war with her fatherland, and raised her voice fervently in the cry of "Vive la France." The occasion for this artistic armistice was furnished by a revival of Donizetti's innocently militaristic and delectably melodious *La Fille du régiment*.

Madame Sembrich and Luisa Tetrazzini had sung the role before me, and although of course I had sung it many times in Europe, I had not yet had the chance to sing it in New York. I had practiced the drum diligently for many days, and having already learned to play it in Europe, I was able to freshen up my technique quickly.

Sigmund Spaeth commented that I "set all doubts at rest" regarding my drumming technique and that I "did enough drumming in full footlight to qualify as a siren of the snare!" I must give Mr. Nickel, the drummer at the Metropolitan, all due credit for helping me. The role requires a great deal of a singer. Although it is written for a coloratura-lyric voice, there is much dramatic singing to be done. And as Marie, she must be full of temperament, light and vivacious, and winsome. I loved to sing this role and to carry the audience along with me in the wonderful rhythmic, marching melodies.

I scored a success in every way. The critic at the *New York Evening Telegram* wrote, "Miss Frieda Hempel, a worthy successor of Madame Sembrich as the Daughter of the Regiment—a role beloved of all coloratura sopranos since the days of Jenny Lind—sparkles through the play, singing and acting to the manifest delight of her audience." I sang the Proch Variations in the third act and provoked one reviewer to remark, "These variations are so difficult, fortunately, that they are now seldom heard!" Yet the

Hempel as Marie in *La Fille du régiment*, in a Metropolitan Opera photo
inscribed "To the Camp Lewis Boys—With all good wishes, Frieda Hempel."

New York Sun writer didn't mind the coloratura fireworks. In his review of 18 December of 1917 he said, "Miss Hempel decorated the music with what the Italians call 'fioritura' until it shimmered throughout its entire length. She even introduced Proch's everlasting 'Variations' in the third act in order to put even more twinkles in the starry firmament."

The Daughter of the Regiment offers a challenge to singers with flexible voices and furnishes valid, musical entertainment whenever the singers in the cast are thoroughly capable of undertaking the old florid music. Fernando Carpi, Antonio Scotti, and I were entrusted with the responsibility of securing a success for the Metropolitan management, and we did not fail. "The Metropolitan still possesses artists of the first rank, capable of contending with the difficulties of a style of music which has long ago gone out of vogue," wrote the reviewer for the *Musical Courier*, adding:

> Frieda Hempel, as Marie, was the bright particular star in the galaxy of artists on the stage, first because she is such an accomplished singer, with a beautiful natural voice, and second, because Donizetti has so written his music that no artist but a star of the first brilliancy can do justice to it. No higher compliment can be paid to Miss Hempel than to say—what is perfectly true—that she lived up to the high traditions of a role in which she has had many famous predecessors, including no less a mistress of the art than Marcella Sembrich. Her success with the audience was instantaneous.

Another aspect of the performance was noted: "An interesting incident of the evening and one which roused the audience to much enthusiasm was Madame Hempel's kissing of the French flag and her cry of 'Viva la Francia', both of which the action of the piece calls for." This incident caused loud repercussions in Germany.

The hysteria of war affords a wonderful opportunity for lesser talents to shine by virtue of denunciation of the great artists for one reason or another. The tools of slander, insinuation, and intrigue can be employed to influence public opinion and to call into question the integrity of an artist. Only the greatest of artists suffer in this way, for it is the greatest whom the lesser will dethrone. As a result of the hysteria of the Second World War, it was Kirsten Flagstad, Wilhelm Furtwängler, Walter Gieseking, and Felix Weingartner,* who were called upon to defend their good names. And even Richard Strauss complained to me of feeling the pressure of resentment. During the First World War, Schumann-Heink, Matzenauer, Kreisler, and I had to combat accusations and lies concerning our loyalty to one country or another. Although I had been retained by the Metropolitan for the 1917–18

---

*Weingartner stopped conducting in 1938, before war broke out. *Ed.*

season, Margarete Ober had been dismissed and her contract annulled. Her subsequent legal suit against the Metropolitan Opera Company was answered in these words, according to the *New York American* of 27 April 1918: "The plaintiff injured the discipline and orderly conduct of the defendant's business by her acts and speeches of hatred against the United States, its President and Government." In the meantime, Miss Ober had returned to Germany, and there she began to speak against me.

I learned from Otto Goritz that she was spreading rumors concerning my performance of *The Daughter of the Regiment*. She was jealous that I had been retained, and although she could find no example of any expressly anti-German action on my part, she managed to construct a transgression against Germany from this bit of stage action.

According to the story of this opera, all the soldiers of the regiment are my fathers because they have found me on the road and have raised me as their child. Relatives finally find me and take me off to marry a nobleman. I must say goodbye to my regiment and to the beloved flag of my regiment.

I cry bitterly after singing my farewell aria, and with my last high note I cry into the flag and kiss it. In the last act my soldier sweetheart, who has become a high-ranking officer, comes to claim me, and we all sing for joy, "Viva la Francia." I say "Viva la Francia" because we sang the opera in Italian and not in French.

I was Marie, the daughter of the soldiers, and not Frieda Hempel. I do not even know what flag was used in our Berlin performances when I sang the role, but I presume that it must have been the French flag. The fact that a performance of this opera at this time produced a patriotic reaction among the listeners was coincidental, as far as I was concerned. When I spoke to Gatti-Casazza about the rumors that were being spread in Germany, he replied, making light of the incident, "I engaged you as a singer, not as a person who is engaged in politics."

I did not follow the progress of these rumors in Germany, for I was unable to return there until some time after the war. As soon as the blockade was lifted, I went to Berlin to see my father, who was ill with cancer. A shock awaited me.

My good maid, Rosa, went out one morning to buy some food for us. She returned crying bitterly. The storekeeper had said to her, "How did they let Miss Hempel in, after all she has done?" The story had been embroidered upon, and now the people heard that I had wrapped myself in the French flag, and had walked down Fifth Avenue, supposedly singing the "Marseillaise"! I had also allegedly sung this in the opera, as an interpolation. They said I had sung the opera in French and had kissed the French flag in ecstasy.

Now, the "Marseillaise" is not in the score of *The Daughter of the Regiment*; therefore I could not have sung it. The Metropolitan was a distinguished institution, and Gatti-Casazza would certainly not have allowed the interpolation of the French anthem. No such demonstration took place. And if I had walked down Fifth Avenue singing that song and draped in the French flag, I would have been arrested, I am certain.

I had invested more than 413,000 Reichsmark in German war bonds, I had sung for wounded soldiers whenever possible, I had donated large amounts to charity, and I had carried in my heart concern for my brothers, who were at the front. It did not seem possible that I could be considered unpatriotic. True, I had married an American, and I had pursued my career in the United States in spite of the war, but did that make me unpatriotic?

I read stories about my supposed actions in the newspapers until I could stand it no longer. So I went to Arthur Wolff, a well-known lawyer in Berlin, and asked him to take action to stop this false propaganda. I told him that I would like to face the person responsible for spreading these lies.

August Püringer, writing later in the *Deutsche Zeitung* of 14 September 1923, said, "Among the real German people, Schumann-Heink has no place anymore." It is well known that Mme Schumann-Heink had sons fighting for America and sons fighting for Germany. It was this same man who was attacking me in 1920.

Mr. Wolff made an appointment with him, and I faced him. He was a well-fed, red-faced man who seemed unable to look me straight in the eye. I asked him if he had fought for his country. I asked him if he felt right in sitting comfortably behind his desk, writing such accusations about a woman who is in a foreign land, unable to defend herself.

For he had started these stories before I was able to return to Berlin. I asked him if he had seen me do all these things. He blushed violently and turned and left the room. But Mr. Wolff followed him down the corridor and drew the truth out of him. Putzi Hanfstängel* had written him this gossip from New York, and he had repeated it. From pure hearsay Mr. Püringer had fabricated this propaganda from news sent him by the foreign office in Berlin. I never knew Putzi Hanfstängel, but I had heard many unfavorable reports about him. I could have sued him for slander, but it did not seem worth the bother. These men should have been proud of the German artists who enhanced the good name of the nation by their achievements.

As Frieda Hempel I engaged in no politics. As the singer and artist I

---

*German-born, Harvard-educated Ernst "Putzi" Hanfstängel (1887–1975) was at this time Adolf Hitler's foreign press chief. One of the future Führer's earliest supporters and the only academy-educated man in his closest circle, Dr. Hanfstängel tried to influence Hitler away from the incipient excesses and cruelties of the Nazi regime. When he saw his efforts had failed, he broke with Hitler soon after the Roehm Putsch in 1934. Fearing for his life, he escaped to Switzerland, exile, and internment in 1937. *Ed.*

complied with what was required of me, and I would have kissed a row of flags if that had been in the script. Yet through the malicious gossip of a Putzi Hanfstängel and because of the intrigue of a jealous woman, I was insulted in Germany.

I wept oceans of tears. I recalled one concert in America that had been canceled because, said the management, my beauty and my art would give the audience a picture of German culture so in opposition to the image of Germany's infamous militarism that I would lull to rest the spirit of antagonism.

I faced some anti-German propaganda in America, but in general I had little trouble. I sang "The Star-Spangled Banner," I did not object when Liberty Bonds were solicited during the intermission of a concert, and I agreed to omit German songs when asked to do so. But the charge that I married an American just to become a citizen of the United States is easily disproved by the fact that Will Kahn and I had been friends since 1913, and our marriage in 1918 was the natural fruition of this friendship. Indeed, it was Will who helped me in 1916 to secure a return visa to the United States. I was detained in Germany, and he went to Washington, D.C., and enlisted the aid of Wilbur Carr of the State Department. Mr. Carr succeeded in getting me cleared with the immigration authorities, so that I could return to the United States to fulfill my many contracts. My marriage was not entered into for political reasons, and my subsequent American citizenship in no way infringed upon the deep love I had for my native land.

America had been kind to me, and so had Germany. What reason have I to hate? I sang for German soldiers, and I sang for wounded American soldiers. I was not a man who could carry a gun; I was an artist who could ease suffering wherever I found it.

And so it is with artists in time of war. I have in my scrapbook a cartoon, showing Emmy Destinn, Enrico Caruso, and me singing together on a stage. The cartoon is from a German paper and accuses us of having sold our souls for money and glory. The title of Emmy Destinn's song, which she holds in her hand, is, "Down with Germany, long live Czecho-Slovakia." Caruso is singing, "Down with Germany, long live Italy," and I am singing, "Down with Germany, long live the dollar." The cartoon is titled "The Ungratefuls." Apparently the creator of this drawing would have any artist who had ever sung in Germany now declare his allegiance to Germany.

But artists function in a world that is outside of war and all its implications. Artists strive to heal the wounds that are caused by war, wounds individuals of every nation would never inflict upon one another willingly. And always, after the hysteria of war has died away, the artist is again welcomed for his gift of beauty. I was "forgiven" by the German press in 1926. The spirit of reconciliation, of which the 1925 Locarno Pact was a political manifestation, was also at work in artistic circles.

Since the 1914–15 season, Gatti-Casazza had offered us half-season contracts only, and since then I had sung in the winter seasons and in the spring season Maria Barrientos had sung the coloratura roles. This had left me free to give concerts in the spring. In addition, in January of 1918, I left the Victor Talking Machine Company and joined the artists recording for Edison. Now, under the Wolfson management, I sang twenty-five concerts in three months. This brought me much more money than I could have earned at the Metropolitan, and I enjoyed giving the concerts.

The Edison Company gave me excellent publicity, including a very clever experiment. They invited a group of experts to listen to an Edison recording of my voice. At the same time, I stood beside the machine and sang whenever the machine stopped. A song without any accompaniment was used, and the judges were all blindfolded. It was claimed that no difference could be detected between the tone of the voice on the record, and the tone of the voice in the studio. This claim was never disputed, nor was the integrity of the judges questioned, for the Edison records are indeed exceptional in quality and in faithful reproduction of sound. Edison was a sweet man with a great sense of humor. He attended my concerts regularly, and after his death his charming wife and their son continued to come to my New York recitals.

My February concerts were all in the East. Following appearances in Washington, D.C., Boston, and other principal cities, I gave my Carnegie Hall recital on 26 February. This time I scheduled an excerpt from Rossini's *Otello* which drew this remark from Mr. Henderson in the *New York Sun* the next day: "The local operatic stage should be proud of Miss Hempel. Her delivery of the excerpt from Rossini's *Otello* was a piece of exquisite art, finished and polished to the last degree. Such singing is rarely heard at the Metropolitan except when Miss Hempel does it." I also sang "Der Nussbaum" in German, without evoking any criticism. On the contrary, I was commended for my courage.

At the close of my season with the Metropolitan in late February 1918, I left for an extensive tour of the far West. I began in San Francisco on 10 March. Paul Eisler was my accompanist for this trip, and Mr. Copley of the Wolfson firm traveled with us as manager. It was a success in every way, and in both San Francisco and Los Angeles I was asked to return for a second concert, which I did. The public and the critics were most generous in their enthusiasm. I sang in all the major cities of California, and then traveled to Portland, Oregon; Seattle, Washington; and Omaha, Nebraska, for concerts.

The *Los Angeles Times* critic wrote:

San Francisco would not let Frieda Hempel leave the auditorium, when she sang there last week, until all the lights were put out. It was a landslide for the great soprano. Los Angeles, more conservative, only de-

In a novel publicity "experiment," Hempel was "photographed while singing in direct comparison with the New Edison's Re-Creation of her exquisite voice," shown in a Metropolitan Opera program for the 1917–18 season. In a Met program for her debut season, 1912–13, Hempel endorsed Hardman pianos.
COURTESY PAUL JACKSON.

manded of her an unusual number of encores—more, actually, than any other Philharmonic artist has given this season. More than any other coloratura soprano, Hempel recalls Sembrich, especially in her interpretation and exquisite phrasing. And there is no other trill so wonderful, unless it is the famous natural trill of Melba.

As we traveled through the rich California valleys, I was amazed to see the miles and miles of land covered with thousands of orange trees, and to see the vast stretches of farmland containing endless numbers of green vegetable plants. I learned that these orchards and these farms were not worked by the owners alone. Hired labor came in for the harvest, and the produce was picked, packed, and sent to market by organizations employed by the owners. The tremendous scope of this undertaking seemed quite unbelievable to me.

And as if to challenge the magnitude of these efforts of man, the giant redwood trees, many of them over a thousand years old, towered above the valleys on the Coast Range. We drove through one of them in a car, during a short trip to Yosemite near San Francisco. They are so large that one was hollowed out to allow a car to pass through. This was an experience that every visitor to the West Coast of the United States should have. The trees stand straight and tall, and their branches combine to keep the sunlight filtering through to the ground as if through stained glass windows of a cathedral. Their majesty and their beauty are breathtaking.

I returned to New York in May of 1918, and on 8 June Will Kahn and I were married at St. James Church in New York City as I had announced. We had a very small, private wedding in this Lutheran church, and immediately following the wedding we left for Lake Placid.

We spent a wonderful three months there, swimming, playing golf together, hiking along the trails of the Adirondacks, and visiting with friends at the club in the evenings. My little dog Pitti, shorn of his winter coat and clipped like a lion, was the delight of everyone. He galloped along the trails, cheering us on with his happy barks and his prancing manner.

I closed the piano and gave no thought to my voice. I knew what lay ahead of me in the coming year, and I rested now. I gave one concert for the Lake Placid Chapter of the Red Cross, which brought in $2500 for that worthy cause. We returned to my New York apartment in November. On the eleventh of the month, we were at a party given by musical comedy star Mitzi Hayos when we heard the news of the armistice. There was great excitement in the streets, and we joined the throngs in celebration.

On 14 November I sang again at the Metropolitan in *The Daughter of the Regiment.* I indulged in a little prank at this performance. As Marie, I was to utter an exclamation of surprise upon learning that I had an aunt. The Italian "Porco di bacco!" meant nothing to the audience, and so I decided to

Frieda Hempel and William B. Kahn (far left) were married on 8 June 1918 at St. James Church at Madison Avenue and 73rd Street in New York. According to press reports, the bride's physician, Dr. E. J. Sarlabous, gave her in marriage. The pastor was the Rev. Dr. J. B. Remensnyder. COURTESY METROPOLITAN OPERA ARCHIVES.

use an English expression. I said, "Gee whiz!" and delighted the audience, although not all the critics approved, I must admit.

A performance of *Martha* with Caruso on 7 December 1918 was enthusiastically received, even though von Flotow, who wrote the opera, was a German. Henry Krehbiel wrote in the *Tribune*:

> The performance came near to being a concert of nations. It was written by a German who had formed his style on the French. Its original German text was sung in Italian, and the principal singers were: Frau Hempel, a German; Signore Caruso, an Italian; Mrs. Homer, an American; and Pan Didur, a Pole. It was conducted by Herr Bodanzky, an Austrian. The "Star-Spangled Banner" was sung during one intermis-

sion, and "God Save The King" during another, for the management was not forgetful of the fact that it was Britain's day.

My reviews continued to be excellent; my performance in *La traviata* earned this praise on 9 January 1919 from James Gibbons Huneker, the well-known critic for the *New York Times:*

> *La traviata* took on new life because of the beautiful singing and acting of Frieda Hempel. She has seldom sung with such fervor and delicacy, acted so unaffectedly and with such pathos, or looked so charming. What a singer, what an artist, what a personality! Pity it is that Miss Hempel nears the end of her present season at the Opera House. Her art is rare nowadays.

On 18 January I sang in a revival of *Crispino e la comare* of Luigi and Federico Ricci. In the opinion of Mr. Henderson the next day in the *Sun,* the revival of this opera "was demanded by the need of giving Mme Hempel's floridities a field of activity," and he added, "One cannot die of pulmonary adagio in the final scene of *Traviata* forever." He continued, "Since there are no new operas for florid singers, let us away to the dead past and cull flowers from the cemetery."

This opera had been given in New York for Patti in 1884 and for Tetrazzini in 1909, at the Academy of Music and at the Manhattan Opera House, but this was the first Metropolitan Opera Company production of it. The libretto is delightfully humorous, mingling the natural and the supernatural; the music is filled with the buoyancy, the sparkle, and the gaiety of Italy's humor. Antonio Scotti and I were supported by Sophie Braslau and Andrès de Segurola. Scotti was a magnificent actor and singer, and it was great fun to do this opera with him.

On 6 February 1919 I announced the formation of my own organization for concert management which I maintained for many years, with my office on Madison Avenue. My husband gave a great deal of his time to this organization, and his aid was indispensable. I had not yet decided to leave the Metropolitan and devote all my time to concerts, but on 10 February I made what was to be my last appearance at the Metropolitan Opera House, in a performance of *Crispino e la comare.* At the time I did not realize that this would be my last time on the stage of the Metropolitan—nor did the public know this—but I was moved by their tribute after the performance.

On 18 February I sang again in Carnegie Hall and then left for an extended tour of the Northeast, closing with my annual recital in Boston on 8 March. The Boston audience is notably difficult to please, and because Boston was known in the early days as America's most cultured city, the selectivity of taste was rightly come by. I had learned this about Boston and

Scotti and Hempel in *Crispino e la comare*, 18 January 1919, this opera's premiere performance at the Met. COURTESY METROPOLITAN OPERA ARCHIVES.

this year gave great care and consideration to my program. I was well rewarded. Every critic commended my choice of selections, which included Mozart, a modern French group, four Shakespeare songs set by various composers, and a closing group of selected folk songs. "Altogether the program was a delight both to musicians and nonmusicians, and was executed with all the brilliancy which has been characteristic of Mme Hempel's previous appearances in Boston," wrote the reviewer in the *Boston Advertiser* the next day.

H. T. Parker, the famous critic for the Boston *Evening Transcript,* was always very kind to me, and he devoted long columns to my work. I read them with appreciation and after every Boston concert looked forward to considering their skillful analyses. He closed his review of this concert of 8 March by saying, "As a singer of songs, Miss Hempel's prime begins to run full, deep, wide, and warm."

While in Boston, I was taken to the magnificent Mother Church of the Christian Science church. I was astonished to learn that this elegant, architecturally pure building was erected through the efforts of one woman, Mary Baker Eddy, founder of the Christian Science movement. The original church now functions as the small chapel of the Mother Church, as the combined edifice is called. The beauty of detail—from the mosaic of the floors to the carvings on the rosewood pews and pulpit—makes of the smaller chapel a perfect expression of Mrs. Eddy's harmonious concept of life. And the main church, constructed later, is extraordinary in its unique, widespread architectural plan as well as in its tasteful detail.

This building is famous in America for its beauty, and it is one of Boston's great landmarks. I had long been interested in Christian Science, and this visit to the Mother Church more completely persuaded me of the strength to be found in its teachings. I began to read the literature and found a refreshing sense of the joy of living within the pages. I only wish I could be a good Scientist, but this is very difficult to accomplish. Yet I am grateful for the shedding of great fears and the ability to accept disappointment which this way of thinking has prompted in me.

On 12 March I sang with the New York Philharmonic Orchestra at Carnegie Hall, for the Save-A-Home Fund. This organization arranged for a series of concerts throughout the season to raise funds for philanthropic work, such as paying the rent for people in trouble, tiding them over illnesses and periods of unemployment, keeping families together, and saving children from the streets. Carnegie Hall was filled for each concert, and credit for the enterprise went deservedly to the newspaper, *Evening Mail.*

In Washington, D.C., on 14 March, I sang at the National Theater, with Frank Bibb as my accompanist. Mr. Bibb was now Lieutenant Bibb, having just returned from France. He and I went to Walter Reed Hospital after the concert and repeated part of the program for the soldiers there.

They were wonderfully inspiring and so brave and uncomplaining that it was a privilege to appear before them. Afterward I was able to speak with a few of them. Many were in wheelchairs and on crutches, and yet as they spoke with me they showed no concern about their handicaps but chatted easily about the songs they had liked and thanked me for coming.

On I went to Atlanta, Georgia, and towns in South Carolina. While I was there, a friend sent me an article by James Huneker, entitled "Caruso on Wheels." Mr. Huneker often traveled with members of the Metropolitan Opera Company and wrote about us:

> Another time I talked with Frieda Hempel, who is one of the rapidly dwindling race of artists who know Mozart as well as Donizetti. What a Marguerite she would be! On the train she is like her contemporaries. She sits. She chats. For all I know, she may doze. Singers are very human. To fancy them "grand, gloomy and peculiar" is to imagine a vain thing. If they have one weakness in common, it is to read newspaper criticisms of their performances. This is very discouraging to the music critics.

No, Mr. Huneker, many of the reviews that I am now quoting, and the hundreds more that I find in the scrapbooks that my managers kept for me, I am reading now for the first time. And if I were not writing this book, I would never have known what wonderful things were said about me. If I had known that I was so often so highly praised, I might have been a more egotistical person. Wouldn't I have been proud! But study, travel, and constant performance kept me isolated, and the black piano absorbed all that was in me. I thought only of the next concert, the next concert, not how was the last concert. I believe this attitude is typical of all sincere artists, and such artists have no "weakness for the press."

My husband was with me on this trip, and he was the classic Yankee in the south. As he sat in the audience at each concert he enjoyed watching the reactions to my singing of "Dixie." I never sang it in straight tempo. Rather, when I came to the phrase, "Oh I wish I were in Dixie," I sang the first two words with a decided elongation of beat, a broadening of expression into almost a cry of joyful anticipation. With the word *wish* I returned to a very rapid tempo. This swept the listeners along with me quite in spite of themselves, and a unity of feeling filled the hall so powerfully that only the beloved "Home, Sweet Home" could follow.

I was reengaged in each of these cities, as I had been in Boston and in Washington. In fact, my schedule promised to be so full that I realized a renewed contract with the Metropolitan would result in great financial loss to me, unless some arrangements could be made. On 3 April the *Musical Courier* carried this notice, "Frieda Hempel is having difficulties in her negotiations with the Metropolitan Opera management for the renewal of her contract. There is, of course, no question of her art involved. It is purely a matter of business."

I want to say here that my relations with Mr. Gatti-Casazza were most friendly at all times. He admired my artistry and my reliability. Under any other circumstances he would not have wanted to see me go. He said, "It is impossible for me to pay you the fees you receive for concerts." The highest fee he ever paid to an artist was $2500, which he paid to Caruso for one evening. My concert fees were rising steadily, and soon for the Jenny Lind concerts I made $3000 a concert. I often gave four of these in a week, if the distances were not too great between cities.

It was not only financial gain that prompted me in my decision. As a concert singer, I had far greater outlet for my artistry. I had greater freedom in interpretation and in expression. There were so many nationalities represented in the various audiences, and as a concert singer I could please French, Italians, Germans, and Americans by properly constructing my programs. I made these programs very cosmopolitan, and therefore I became popular with the public.

I did not set out to educate the public but to entertain them with music that was appealing. In this manner I attracted their attention: they were interested in every note I sang, because I did not sing music beyond their understanding. This, in turn, inspired me, and the more I sang, the freer and more relaxed I became with the public.

It would have been monotonous for me to sing a *Traviata* or a *Martha* only once a week. And this was all Gatti-Casazza could offer me, at the time. I wanted a wider range for expression, and I had found it in the concert field. For this reason and for financial reasons, therefore, I did not renew my contract with the Metropolitan. Gatti-Casazza and I parted the very best of friends.

Mr. W. J. Henderson wrote on 28 September 1919:

> In looking over the list of singers (of the Metropolitan Opera House prospectus), this writer finds the fulfillment of one prophecy made to him with no small vigor two years ago by a prominent member of the company that Miss Hempel "must go." Well, she is gone and the art of singing is so much the poorer at the Metropolitan. Frieda Hempel was one of the best woman singers in the company.

I never found out who had made this prophecy, but no doubt it had anti-German sources.

After a series of eight concerts in May, I felt that I had sung enough for the season, and I headed north for Loon Lake in the Adirondacks. My husband joined me a short while later, and we motored into Canada to stay at Lake Louise, where we were joined by Nana Wilcox and her husband.

The four of us turned into mountain goats, climbing over the rugged trails day-in and day-out, until at last I had to rest in bed for some time, because I suffered from a fallen arch. As soon as I was well again, we donned our knapsacks once more and wandered aimlessly over the beautiful mountains. We ate our picnic lunches by the banks of a wandering creek or on a hilltop. At one point I sat down to rest, during the early hours of a long hike, when Nana shouted to me, "Be careful, Diva, you are practically sitting in a bear trap!" I jumped back as quickly as if I had been stung by a tarantula and saw before me the yawning hole, covered with branches. How frightening!

The country is wild, and because we were often away from the customary trails, we encountered many animals. But of course we carried no guns, and we had no need to fear these creatures. It was a wonderful place to be, and when we returned to New York after spending another few weeks in Long Beach on the way back, we were ready for a strenuous year of work.

My 1919–20 season was completely booked, and I was scheduled to sing more than eighty concerts throughout the country. I had as my accompanist, for this season and for some eight years to come, Coenraad V. Bos. August Rodeman, the superb flutist, also traveled with us for the first time, and he, too, remained with me for many years.

In 1914 I had spoken to Mr. Bos at a dinner party which we were both attending. He was sitting with Julia Culp, for whom he played exclusively at that time. I told him that if he was ever free, I would like to engage him as my accompanist. Now at Long Beach, while at the Lido Hotel, I received a telegram from him stating that Julia Culp had retired from the concert stage and that he would be most happy to join me. He was in Berlin at the time. I wired him back immediately, telling him to come at once to America.

Mr. Bos went to Holland and there applied for a visa from the United States consulate. He was a Dutch citizen, but he had married a German woman and had been active in Berlin. These two factors were against him, and he was refused entry. When he finally arrived, he told me that he had been very upset because he had wanted to come to America very much. He had asked the consulate if it would help to write to President Wilson's daughter, Margaret, whom he knew well. They said to write if he cared to but they assured him that it would be of no avail. Nevertheless he did write to her. She was a singer, aware of his standing in the musical world. She replied, saying that if he, the magician of accompanists, could not come to America, something must be wrong, and that she would do all she could for him. In two weeks the consulate gave him his visa, advising him to keep his views to himself if he had any that might harm him in the eyes of the American public. And so, thanks to President Wilson's daughter, I had the wonderful assistance of Mr. Bos.

Our tour started on 4 October, and during that month we appeared twelve times up and down the coast, with great success. In November we again had a full schedule. In Washington, on the seventh, my concert was wonderfully received. As the reviewer for the *Washington Times* wrote:

> Pure vocal art is a rare achievement today. The singers whose art may be gauged for its technique in the same manner that one estimates the execution of a pianist, may be counted on one hand. Such a singer is Frieda Hempel, whose concert yesterday called for seats on the stage. The singer, too, was quite the most attractive concert figure to come to us, with her peacock velvet gown and the flowing ostrich feather sash of the same lovely hue.

Margaret Wilson attended this Washington concert, and I replied to her compliments on my singing by thanking her for giving me Mr. Bos.

My dog Pitti, who always traveled with me, was so tiny that he still slept in his muff, which was an indispensable part of my traveling equipment. By this time he was so well known that in each city he had to be photographed with me. Rosa, who was with me also, took good care of him during the concerts, and so I never had to worry.

December passed quickly, with its many obligations, and on New Year's Eve we were back in New York with our close friends. Will and I always looked forward to returning to 271 Central Park West after such a tour as this. The beautiful, snow-covered park stretched out below our windows, and we watched the children with their sleds playing on the slopes and calling to one another. We often put on winter clothing and walked through the snowdrifts in the park, forgetting that we were in the middle of New York.

My annual Carnegie Hall concert, which took place on 3 February 1920, brought an encouraging review in the New York *Sun*:

> Since leaving the opera, Mme Hempel has abandoned her insistence on appearing as a coloratura soprano, and has been satisfied in being what she has always been to a surpassing degree, a lyric soprano of beautiful voice, and equally beautiful art. Last night she was in her true element, and all that she did, she did with exquisite effect.

It seemed that my decision to concentrate on concert work was a right one. As one writer noted, my voice was fresh and not worn from the usual half season of operatic appearances and rehearsals.

Now we left for Florida, Alabama, and Texas: Mr. Bos, Mr. Rodeman, Will Kahn, Rosa, Pitti, and I. Everywhere we appeared before filled houses, and the people were wonderful to us. Will had to return to New York by the middle of the month, and we went on to Texas. Texas was a wonderful, expansive state. The people were all so healthy-looking and cheerful. And the men were so handsome that I could have fallen for one of them.

After my concert in Fort Worth, two young men came into the artist's room behind the stage and showered me with compliments. Then they

Hempel and her Pomeranian. COURTESY ANDREW FARKAS.

asked me where I would be singing next, as they wanted to hear me again. "I have to sing in Austin tomorrow night," I told them. "Oh, Miss Hempel," they exclaimed, "The trains are not at all reliable and they never arrive on time. You might not get there on time. Won't you let us fly you over?" I thought they were joking, and being very spontaneous by nature, I quickly replied, "Oh yes, I'd love to fly!" I was still in high spirits from the concert and flying seemed just the sort of thing I would like to do, something new, something exhilarating and daring. But I didn't mean it at all.

They took me at my word, however, and they promised to call me at midnight after they had completed the arrangements. I do not think that they believed I would really go through with it, but they were eager to try and persuade me, and they gave me time to think it over.

When they called at midnight, I thought to myself, "Don't be a coward," and very brazenly I said, "Yes, I will fly with you in the morning, but my accompanist has to fly with me." They replied that they had two planes, each carrying one passenger, and that I would ride in one and Mr. Bos in the other. "But I have no clothes for flying," I said meekly, feeling myself caught in the trap of my exuberance. They answered, "Don't worry about that. We will have warm caps and leather jackets for you both, and you will be fine."

Mr. Bos seemed quite willing to fly with me, and so there was nothing else to do but to wait for the morning. I could not sleep at all, thinking of the silly promise I had made and imagining all the things that could happen to me. After all, I did not know these men from Adam, and I did not have the slightest idea if they could even handle a plane. But I had said yes, and there was no getting out of it now.

Rosa and Mr. Rodeman left by train around three o'clock in the morning, and Mr. Bos and I were called for at six by the two flyers. Mr. Rodeman had made it quite clear that he did not envy us, saying, "I would not risk my life like that for a carefree promise." But by now Mr. Bos and I were quite excited and looking forward to the novel experience.

The charming woman who had engaged me for the local series concert in Fort Worth drove with us to the airport, and as we approached it she said casually, "This is the field where Vernon Castle's plane crashed a little while ago, killing him instantly." I looked at her in a defenseless way and said nothing. Mr. Bos grinned.

Soon things began to happen. We were given caps and jackets, and of course our luggage had gone on with Mr. Rodeman, so all we had to do was climb in the planes. I shook hands with the woman, thanking her for her interest in our welfare, and I shook hands with Mr. Bos. Then I climbed into the cockpit. We took off, and for the first minutes my hands were almost cramped from praying. Then I saw Mr. Bos's plane coming alongside, and when he waved to me, I was able to wave back and laugh.

I thought, as I saw him appearing and disappearing from my side as the planes jockeyed in the wind, "Well, Mr. Bos is with me. Nothing can happen now!" It was such a silly thought but it gave me courage, and soon I was enjoying the sight of the early morning sun on the lands below.

Mr. Bos told me later that he kept thinking, "Now, if Frieda crashes, I must notify her husband right away," forgetting that he, too, was in a plane. For we had not had time to let either Mr. Bos's wife or my husband know what we were going to do. We landed in Waco for lunch, and by then our fears were gone. Actually, we were quite proud of our adventurous exploit. We took off again after dining and arrived safely in Austin, more rested than our companions who had traveled the whole distance by train.

I was a little deaf and somewhat dizzy at first, but these disturbances soon passed away, and the evening concert was a success, as always. When my husband learned of this trip, he was very angry, and he said, "This is one time I am glad you did not make the front pages of the newspapers." For it was true that flying in 1920 was not the safest thing to do.

Among the concerts given in March was one in Wichita, Kansas. Will had joined us in New Orleans, where I had sung on 1 March, and it was very fortunate that he was along with us in Wichita, because when we arrived at the station of the city, around eleven o'clock in the evening, there were no porters to be seen. The station was deserted. We had numerous suitcases, and the three men could not carry them. So my husband reconnoitered around the sheds until he found a huge truck used for loading baggage. He pulled it up, and we all loaded the bags on, one by one. Then came the question of finding an exit to the platform. As I stood watch with Rosa and Pitti, the men went forth to search. Mr. Bos finally located a sleepy man who agreed to work the freight elevator for us, and so the truck was pulled onto the elevator, and we all descended to the street. Here all was quiet. No taxi to be seen. Nobody on the street. No one concerned for our welfare. I sat down on a suitcase to wait, while the others debated as to the next move. I thought to myself, "If the life of a prima donna were only the bed of roses people think it to be!" After what seemed to be hours of waiting, a car was located by my resourceful husband, and soon we were in the hotel I assu m

A Wichita newspaper printed this statement, "Conceded to be the most beautiful prima donna of the day, she was radiant in a peach-colored baronet satin gown, with a startling purple sash." They should have seen me the night before, sitting on the suitcase containing that gown, waiting with aching bones and tired thoughts for a vehicle to take me to a place where I could rest.

By April I was in New York for a performance of Mendelssohn's *Elijah*, with Walter Damrosch and the Philharmonic Orchestra of New York and the Oratorio Society. There had been bitter discussion about whether I should be allowed to appear, because of my German birth. The fact that

Mendelssohn was a German did not seem to concern anyone. I was allowed to sing, as it turned out. Mr. Henderson wrote of this performance:

> For at least one listener a joy of the evening was the sound of Mme Hempel's mellow, limpid tones. One does not hear such fluent singing often; fluent not in the sense of agility, but of clear, smooth, sustained and musical treatment of the melodic phrase. The ultimate object of all technic is the production of beautiful tone. Mme Hempel's technic accomplished this and her intelligence enables her to employ her technical skill artistically.

Concerts continued, requiring me to travel a great deal by train. We headed out to the midwestern states, and there were many hours to fill. Madame Lucrezia Bori had given me a delightful idea, and now I had time to develop it. She had suggested that I embroider the signatures of my colleagues at the Metropolitan on fabric, for it had become known that I was quite expert with the needle. So I had taken pieces of linen and stretched them on oval frames the size of doilies. In the center of each I had my friends sign their names. Now I had an ample collection of names, including Gatti-Casazza, Enrico Caruso, Geraldine Farrar, Scotti, Amato, Emmy Destinn, and all the favorites of operagoers. I began to embroider the names in white, on the white linen, and they were very elegant indeed. This is an idea that I can recommend to women today who still enjoy the art of needlework. They should use these doilies decorated with the names of their personal friends, for luncheons and get-togethers. I still have the ones I made, and I use them upon occasion. These signatures can start off a fine discussion.

We also found another way to pass the time. On these trips Coenraad Bos and I became great card players. Our favorite game was gin rummy, which we would play by the hour, absorbed in the game and very serious about our winnings or our losses. We were well-matched and generally came out even. Mr. Rodeman could never be persuaded to play with us. It distressed us to arrive somewhere on a Sunday, because the Blue Laws had resulted in the closing of all places of amusement. The streets would be deserted, except for the men standing around wondering what to do to pass the day. Once Mr. Bos and I sat in a railroad station on a Sunday morning, waiting for a change of engines to be completed. When we decided to play a game of cards, Mr. Bos set up a table, using my hat box which was near. The cards were considered tools of the devil, and on a Sunday the devil must away! So the next thing we knew, the stationmaster was sweeping up the cards in one hand and picking up the box with the other, saying, "Don't you folks know that there's no card playing 'round here on Sunday?" We laughed and agreed that we had sinned, according to the clock.

We had our troubles with other things, too. Occasionally we would arrive in a town at a time when all the better restaurants were closed. This

Hempel displays a footstool covered with her own needlepoint in her apartment at 271 Central Park West, probably in the 1930s; in 1916 *Harper's* and *Vogue* had featured her apartment, decorated by the well-known designer Elsie de Wolfe. PHOTO BY UNDERWOOD & UNDERWOOD. COURTESY ELIZABETH JOHNSTON.

meant that I would have to go to bed hungry. If I slept through the noon hours after having arrived early in the morning, I would likewise frequently miss my lunch. All these little problems had to be solved as they occurred, but we never failed to find an answer.

The constant interviews in each new city were tiresome. In one city the reporter came to see me late in the afternoon, and he proceeded to sit down on top of my freshly ironed concert gown, which was draped over the chair. I was so angry I could have cried because Rosa had worked so hard to get all the folds fresh and in place. I gasped and pulled him from the chair, but it was too late. Rosa had to iron the delicate dress all over again, and she was not happy about it.

But there was compensation for all these annoyances, even in addition to the joy of the concerts themselves. I found the people so warm and so sincere in their appreciation, so unspoiled by notions of what culture should be, so eager to be part of something beautiful, that to the joy of singing was added the joy of giving.

True, I once arrived in a little town where the hotel accommodations were impossible. There was no place to hang my clothes, no light except for that of a single candle, and no running water. I insisted upon leaving, and at a nearby college I was given the room of a student for the night. The people at the concert, all dressed in their finery of years ago, loved my singing of the many popular home songs and begged me to sing "Home, Sweet Home" for them. This was compensation enough.

Often the door to my hotel room would not lock at all, and all through the day, in the corridor outside, I would hear the voices of people as they passed by and wonder who would turn the knob and come in. I might be on the ground floor, where the curtain was torn, and Rosa would tack up some newspaper in front of the window so that I could change my dress. But the concert would be a new challenge to me in this kind of little town where all the folks had gotten together to bring a "real artist" to their city. It just seemed that sometimes they forgot to make certain that the living accommodations were in order. Probably most of them had never even been inside the hotel of the city. I am speaking now of the little towns in the Midwest and the Northwest.

Often, when in the southern states, Will and I would walk down to the negro quarters, which in the smaller towns were usually very primitive, one-room huts near the railroad tracks. In front of one of these we spoke to a mother of eight children, who was soon expecting her ninth child. She was coughing frightfully and she seemed quite ill. The little children looked up at us with big, round eyes full of hunger. We left and soon returned with a large basket of food for these poor little souls.

Another time we were able to see happy, singing children, healthy and contented children who belonged to the "family" of a large plantation.

These negroes, unlike those of the cities, were part of a group, cared for by a white family. In Wilmington, North Carolina, on 19 April 1920, I sang a concert and then enjoyed the pleasure of being a guest of Mrs. Caesar Cone in Greensboro for a few days. She had a large plantation, and several negro families lived on her property and worked for her. One afternoon she said to me, "Come, Frieda, let's go out to the plantation. I want you to hear the singing." We drove out to the negro quarters of the plantation, climbed out of the car, and walked to a little one-room wooden cabin where workers and their children always gathered for prayer services. The leader rang a bell and all the workers and their children appeared. We followed them into the cabin. The leader of the group stood up in front of them and sang a pitch with upraised hand. Soon the room was flooded with the sound of sweet voices. The harmony was perfectly balanced, and the purity of their voices moved me deeply. They sang their spirituals for me, with their sense of rhythm betrayed in the movement of their bodies as they sang. They are born dancers, and they are magnificent in their elastic, graceful movements. I expressed my appreciation by singing for them "The Last Rose of Summer," at Mrs. Cone's bidding. It was a wonderful experience for me.

One afternoon Mr. Rodeman came and awakened me from my important afternoon rest. I never allowed anybody to disturb me at this time, for this period belonged to my public. I needed this relaxation and rest to prepare myself in mind and in body for the evening's concert. But this time Mr. Rodeman dared to disturb me because his distress was caused by the discomfort of an animal, and he knew that I would wish to help. "There's a donkey lying in the middle of the road, and he seems starved to death, almost! Nobody pays any attention to him. I know that you will be able to do something for him." I hurried with him to where the poor neglected animal was lying. He had worn the surface of the road to a bright shine with the constant movement of his legs as he tried to raise himself. He was breathing heavily, and the bones in his body stood out in fearful relief. There were many houses in the neighborhood but nobody paid the slightest attention to the beast.

We went immediately to get food for him, which he devoured. Then I called the police, and asked for the address of an animal doctor. "Oh, he's in jail. He got caught selling dope!" said the policeman, in a sleepy, lazy voice. "Well, where is the animal hospital?" I asked. "Huh! We don't have any of those things here!" was the reply. "I am Frieda Hempel," I said, with anger in my voice. "There is a sick donkey lying here in the street. If you don't come and take care of him, I will not sing the concert tonight. I shall wait here for you, and mind you come quickly." In a few minutes a doctor arrived, to whom it was quite plain, even though he was not a veterinarian, that the donkey was very old and very ill. He assured me that it would be the most humane thing to do, if I would agree, to let him put the animal out of its misery. This was done, and the concert took place as planned. But I did not feel very friendly toward the people in that neighborhood.

Mr. Bos always played a group of piano solos at each of these concerts, and generally he selected his compositions from the standard classical repertory. Occasionally, however, he would put on the program a work called, perhaps, Theme and Variations by Rachmaninoff. And at this concert, before going out to present his piano solos, he would ask my husband or me for a little melodic theme. This he would carry in his head until it was time to play the Rachmaninoff. Of course there would be no such work by this composer; rather it would be an intricate, well-constructed fugal composition upon our theme that Mr. Bos would improvise for the audience. We delighted once to see an irritated critic come around backstage afterward and say to Mr. Bos, "That piece by Rachmaninoff, it was beautifully played. But I confess I have never heard it before. Where did you find it?" Such knowledgeable critics were seldom encountered, however. Usually the ruse was not discovered, for Mr. Bos was quite capable of spontaneously creating fine music, idiomatically correct and melodically moving. Even the most outlandish combinations of notes given him by Will would not dismay him. The more complicated, the better, he thought.

Mr. Bos would sense those evenings when I would be willing to go along with his impish moods, and he would suddenly elongate the introduction to a song. I would have taken the deep breath and practically have sung the first note when I would hear him wandering off into some pattern. I would have to camouflage the breath, and smile and wait for him to resolve his figurations, but it was great fun. In this harmless way we relieved the monotony of the long tours, and the public lost nothing. I had my revenge upon Mr. Bos, at these times, by elongating my cadenzas. He would wait for me to resolve my melodic line to the dominant chord, and I would avoid doing so until I felt that I had exhausted all the pertinent melodic material. Only then would I allow him to enter with the piano, and together we would close the piece in the manner written. This, too, was not taking too much license, for the art of coloratura cadenzas is based on such free improvisation.

Fortunately, we were both good musicians, and so we never ran into complications that we could not solve. And the delight at having given free reign to our imagination freshened the entire program for us.

Mr. Bos once entertained us in quite another manner. We were in a small town with nothing to do for the afternoon, and so Will suggested that we go to a movie. In those days of silent film, the music was supplied by a pianist. Shortly after we had taken our seats in this little, boxy movie house, the young woman who sat at the square piano got up and left the hall. Seeing her leave was cue enough for Mr. Bos. He slipped into the chair and began to improvise the most wonderful background music to whatever action appeared on the screen. The only parallel to this art today may be the running commentary in the presentations of Victor Borge.

From his store of musical memory, Mr. Bos would fish up some classical figure that would exactly comment on the action seen. And often the selection of material would be so utterly humorous that Mr. Rodeman, Will, and I were soon upsetting the stolid customers with our uncontrollable mirth. It is a shame that there is no outlet today for the wonderful gift of improvisation which so many of the master musicians command. Mr. Bos was marvelous, and when the young lady returned and saw him sitting there and heard him play as she could never play, her face was the picture of dejection. She had lost her job, she thought! But no, Mr. Bos relinquished his chair to her once again, and we left the movie house in high spirits.

In May of 1920 we were in Red Cloud, Nebraska. This little village was like a real western town that one sees pictured in the movies. The hotel, if one could call it that, was a one-story wooden building, very simply furnished with the customary pieces. The main street was lined with Fords of the farmers who had come into town for Saturday purchases and to hear the long-awaited concert.

This town had just completed its first combined auditorium and movie house. Donations from townspeople and well-to-do farmers of the district had resulted in the erection of a fine building, and my concert was to be the gala opening affair. A big artist from the east was the only proper person to do justice to this fine civic enterprise, and the committee had selected me for that honor. I was quite surprised when I received this offer from such a small town, but the generous check was in the bank before the concert even started, and so I knew that the size of a town did not necessarily betray the size of the pocketbooks of its inhabitants.

When I entered the new auditorium, I found it to be very handsome indeed. The walls were still damp with paint; the newness permeated the air. The audience was an unusual mixture. Some of the townsfolk were dressed in their finery, others were casually attired, and the farmers sat there in their clean overalls with their wives sitting by side them and in simple things. It was a big day for them all, and they were hearing their first real concert in their new $100,000 hall.

We gave them a lovely concert, and then I sang many popular songs for them as encores. Each ticket had cost five dollars to cover the expenses of the evening and to pay off the last costs of the building. Yet even at this high price the hall was crowded to overflowing with enthusiastic citizens of this proud little town. Judging from their applause and from the number of encores they demanded, they must all have loved the concert. Certainly I enjoyed every moment of it.

In June my husband and I sailed once more for Europe, transoceanic travel having been resumed. We went to Paris first, and then to Sils-Maria in Switzerland. Just before sailing, I made public my decision to appear with the Chicago Opera Association for six performances in October 1920. I was a little homesick for the operatic stage by now, and the chance to sing roles with such stars as Alessandro Bonci, Titta Ruffo, and Rosa Raisa was inviting. This operatic commitment in no way interfered with my concert tours because all my appearances were scheduled within the period of one month, leaving me free for the rest of the season. It was also at this time that I agreed to participate in the great Jenny Lind centennial celebration of 6 October 1920 in Carnegie Hall, but I will tell that story a little later.

CHAPTER SEVENTEEN

With the Chicago Opera Association

I returned to America aboard the *Mauritania*, arriving on 20 September 1920 with my new Parisian wardrobe. I set to work immediately on the Jenny Lind concert that was to take place the next month.

A concert in Toledo, Ohio, on 11 October opened the musical series in that city. The *Toledo Times* commented upon my new concert gown, "The singer's marvelous gown, ornamented with life-sized grapes, a distinctly Parisian creation, and her wonderful jewels were almost as much of a sensation as her singing." In Springfield, Ohio, three nights later, again to open the year's musical series, I was interviewed about clothes. Says the journalist:

> One would have known she had just come from Paris. She was wearing a little street suit which nothing outside of Paris could have produced. It was a stunning shade of light brown, and there was a wonderful little terra-cotta hat. The coat had all the style that lines and perfect tailoring can give, and the skirt? Short! Very short, of course. There were silk hose of just the right shade, and adorable strap slippers in patent leather. "What do you think of the round-toed slippers so stylish now in Paris?" she was asked. "I don't like them," Miss Hempel replied. "They make one's feet look so big. Why should a woman make her feet look big? I am surprised at this. The Parisians are usually so dainty and so petite."

Paris had been very gay and colorful that summer, and one would never have known that there had been a war.

Ever at the forefront of fashion. COURTESY ANDREW FARKAS.

When we arrived in Springfield, Mr. Rodeman came in to see me at the
Hotel Shawnee with a look of great concern on his face. "Miss Hempel, I
found the tiniest little kitten on the street, and he is all skin and bones and
covered with fleas. Can I bring him to you?" Mr. Rodeman had long since
learned that I could never say no when animals were in need of help. "Yes,"
I replied, "bring him to my room."

The poor little kitten was a sight to behold. He was sick and cold and
skinny. "Now, the only thing to do is for you to go to the drugstore and get
me some flea powder at once," I told Mr. Rodeman, as I wrapped the animal up in a big towel. When he returned with this powder, I soaked the kitten's fur with it and then brushed him, combed him, and cleaned him. Soon
he was ready to feed. We got milk and meat for him, and he devoured every
scrap of food and then curled up and went to sleep.

When he awoke, he started to play, scampering all around the room
and investigating my suitcases. Mr. Rodeman and I wondered what to do
with him now. We would be leaving the city in another two days, and so we
decided to give him away. To find him a good home, I announced in the
papers that I had a kitten to give away and suggested that whoever wanted

him should bring me a beautiful basket for him to sleep in. I promised that I would give him to the woman who had the prettiest basket.

Next day the women began arriving, each with a basket decorated with ribbons, silks, and bows. One woman had a particularly magnificent basket, all bound in blue silk, with a little blue silk lining and tiny pillows of pink rosebuds. She was so happy to meet me. I knew that she would love the kitten, with its soft fur and its own pink ribbon, and so I gave it to her. She promised to call it Frieda, which made me happy. I thanked all the other ladies for having shown such interest in my kitten, and all were glad that he had found a good home. Thus you see that although in the evening I was the prima donna, I didn't concentrate on singing alone during my travels. My love for animals knows no limits, and nothing was then, nor is now, too menial for me to do if the comfort and the health of an innocent animal is concerned. The gaze of an animal, as it looks up into my eyes, is something so sweet and so tender that it melts my heart with its helplessness.

My first engagement with the Chicago Opera Association took place in Milwaukee. This organization toured the United States each year, appearing for a limited engagement in each city. This October tour was limited to the presentation of three operas: on the first night in each city *Cavalleria rusticana* and *Pagliacci* were presented in a double bill, and on the second night *La traviata* was given. Immediately after the performance of the first two operas in Milwaukee on 18 October, the scenery would be loaded on the train and taken to the next town, Springfield, to be set up for a performance on 20 October. In the meantime we would give *Traviata* on 19 October in Milwaukee, and then our scenery would be shipped to Springfield for 21 October. Thus the entire two-week tour was handled, giving me six performances.

My colleague for this opera was Alessandro Bonci, the great lyric tenor. I would have lunch with him, and he would tell me of his childhood days. He was so weak as a child that he never dared to dream that he might one day become a great singer. When he began to study voice, his mother fed him a great deal of cod-liver oil, and he said that this had made him well and strong. He was a graceful person with lovely manners, and one heard that very plainly in his singing. He was very small in stature, and he had to wear high-heeled shoes to add a little height to his five feet, two inches. He was a beautiful legato singer of the utmost refinement. His voice itself was not as outstanding as Caruso's, but he sang in a more cultured way, and his exquisite artistry made him a close competitor to Caruso.

The other members of the company at that time who sang in the *Cavalleria rusticana* and *Pagliacci* performances were the great baritone Titta Ruffo and Rosa Raisa, an outstanding dramatic soprano. But because of our schedule I had little chance to be with these artists. Only once, when a Sunday intervened in Sioux City, Iowa, did we all get together.

Because of this extra day, I was able to hear the two operas on a Monday, 25 October. For some reason I arrived a little late in the box and was cornered by a newspaper journalist in the lobby just before I entered. He wrote:

> Miss Hempel explained, a little breathlessly, about thinking she had more time than she had, fumbling the while for the lacy handkerchief, scented delicately with something from Paris. Miss Hempel wore an evening frock of black lace and satin, a fur wrap, and an enormous and most becoming black hat, daringly tilted over one eye. Speaking of *La traviata,* we are told that a very great deal of money had been spent on the gown and jewels worn in the third act, and Miss Hempel clasped her hands eagerly, and agreed, "I love the gown. Oh, it is so pretty, and the jewels—it is so easy to be happy and to sing when one can sparkle. I love things that are bright and beautiful."

I don't remember this interview, nor do I remember what I wore that evening, but I do recall the beauty of Rosa Raisa's singing as Santuzza, and the great Tonio that Titta Ruffo created. He had a thrilling voice, cavernous and resounding, and it rang through the auditorium.

The previous Saturday Bonci and I had sung in Des Moines, scoring a great success. I was no longer an undesirable in this city, which had closed its doors to me three years earlier, and I was given an ovation now. "It was an ovation delayed two years by the war, but it demonstrated clearly that Des Moines music lovers were apparently ready to forget the past and appreciate her art," says the review. And in the front row sat the mayor himself!

A Des Moines newspaper had described my new gowns:

> Frieda Hempel, star of *La traviata,* will wear some real Callot gowns, which arrived from Paris a week ago. In the first act, Miss Hempel will wear a gown of blue-green taffeta, with silver lace, and a garland of pink roses. In the rural scene of the second act, she will appear in a white silk mull frock, ruffled and piped with pink satin. A pink sash and a leghorn garden hat complete this delectable costume.
>
> The gown which she will wear in the ballroom scene of the third act is a masterpiece. It is a cloth of gold creation, with a green sheen. Garlands of crimson poppies give an exotic note to this costume. In her hair, tucked close to her neck, she will wear a great green ostrich feather. Each of these gowns is made with hoop skirts, and it is said that Miss Hempel manages these quaint costumes with great dexterity.

Hoop skirts were certainly no novelty to me, and it was true that I was completely at ease with them.

From Sioux City, Iowa, we went to Sioux Falls, South Dakota, and then on to St. Paul, Minnesota. In this city the opera *Rigoletto* was added as a Saturday afternoon matinee, followed in the evening by our *Traviata*. This was the fifteenth season of opera for this city, and the cosmopolitan audience appreciated the quality of singing, according to the St. Paul *Pioneer Press* review: "Attracted by the offering of two extraordinary stars, Frieda Hempel and Alessandro Bonci, opera devotees flocked in numbers that more than balanced the comparatively small attendance at the beginning of the season, and the project once more culminated in success." My association with this organization was now interrupted for several months of concert engagements, and I rejoined for the West Coast tour of March 1921.

The first week of November 1920 took me to Cleveland, Buffalo, Pittsburgh, and Worcester, Massachusetts. For these concerts I shared the program with Mario Laurenti, a gifted baritone.* In Cleveland, however, Mr. Laurenti failed to arrive because he had gone to the wrong city by mistake. He had just arrived from Italy, and apparently he did not know his way around. But Mr. Bos and Mr. Rodeman saved the evening, I offered solos in Laurenti's place, and all went well.

    An engagement with the New York Symphony on 11 and 12 November finally brought me back to New York. As always, this stupendous city throbbed with incessant activity, and the memory of South Dakota fields faded from my mind. These concerts offered an all-Mozart program. I sang "Et Incarnatus est" from the C Minor Mass, and Konstanze's Air from *The Abduction from the Seraglio*. Singing every other day for the past month-and-a-half had limbered up my voice for Mozart, and I see by the reviews that I did well. Mr. Krehbiel wrote in the *New York Tribune* on 12 November 1920:

> Two airs were sung by Miss Hempel, and these, by reason of their exquisite performance, were the delightful features of the afternoon. There could scarcely be too much praise for the manner in which Mme Hempel sang. It was the most astonishing feat of bravura which we have ever heard her perform, and as pure and noble in style as it was brilliant and ravishing in vocal quality. No singer known to us could have rivaled It.

---

*Mario Laurenti (born Luigi Cavadani in Verona in 1890) was studying engineering in Dresden when his voice was discovered. He came to New York in 1914 where he became a member of the Metropolitan Opera Chorus. He was soon given small solo roles and made his official debut as the Innkeeper in *Manon Lescaut* on 6 January 1916 in a cast that included Alda, Caruso, and De Luca. In all he sang seven seasons with the Metropolitan, usually in secondary roles but including the role of Fritz in the U.S. premiere of Korngold's *Die Tote Stadt* (with Maria Jeritza) on 19 November 1921. He died of meningitis in New York in 1922. He recorded extensively for Edison. *Ed.*

Mr. Huneker wrote in the *World*: "Miss Hempel is the most effortless singer before the public today." And Mr. Finck said in the *Evening Post:* "Frieda Hempel, now that Sembrich sings no more, must be looked upon as the best of living Mozart singers."

As usual, my stay in my home city was brief, and on 16 November 1920 I was in Allentown, Pennsylvania. The civic organization responsible for concerts in this little city had secured many great singers over the years. Lillian Nordica, Johanna Gadski, Clara Butt, John McCormack, Louise Homer, Nellie Melba, and David Bispham had all preceded me here. My concert opened this year's series, and despite extremely bad weather the hall was completely filled. I had been engaged for a concert the previous year, but having become ill I had canceled my appearance, and Miss Anna Case had sung in my place. With this concert I compensated for that illness by offering the enthusiastic audience many, many encores. According to the *Allentown Chronicle* my concert was "one of the greatest musical events Allentown ever beheld." The audience was the largest ever assembled. My husband, who came with me, had many friends in this city, and so we were delightfully entertained.

The great success of the Jenny Lind centennial concert in New York, which I had given on 6 October, was fast becoming known. At my Washington, D.C., concert on 19 November, I included some songs from that Jenny Lind program, among these the "Herdsman's Song," which Jenny Lind had made famous. I sang it in Swedish, playing my own accompaniment, and it was an immediate favorite. The "Herdsman's Song" was now included in each of my concerts. The review in the *Washington Herald* attested to my success: "It will be recalled that this famous soprano was chosen to impersonate Jenny Lind at the recent centennial concert in New York City. That this great honor was richly deserved was clearly demonstrated at yesterday's concert. Miss Hempel is a charming and beautiful singer. She has achieved her success without sensational methods." I was honored as well by the presence of Mrs. Wilson, wife of the president.

After a concert in Detroit, Michigan, Mr. Bos, Mr. Rodeman, Rosa, Pitti, and I again headed west, this time to Lincoln, Nebraska; Tulsa, Oklahoma; and Coffeyville, Kansas. In each city we gave a balanced, artistic program, never making any concessions to the possible inexperience of the audience. I still sang my German numbers in English, a procedure which by now seemed almost natural to me. And everywhere I had requests for numbers from the Jenny Lind program, to which I complied. Mr. Rodeman's flute work was excellent, and his obbligatos to my coloratura works were perfect. I was very fortunate indeed to have him with me on these concerts.

On 10 December I appeared in the Liederkranz Hall at 111 East 58th Street in New York City at a benefit for the Women's Clinic of Dresden, Germany. Mr. Bos and Mr. Rodeman assisted me, as usual. This concert resulted in the collection of more than four thousand dollars, for I donated my services and also gave an additional one thousand dollars to the cause. At this time I also announced that the entire proceeds of my coming Carnegie Hall recital would be donated to the relief of undernourished children of Germany.

Boston challenged me again on 12 December. I returned to the German language for my lieder, and I offered this elite audience the finest of selections in my repertory. Wrote the *Boston Globe* critic: "There need be little despair of public taste in America when a singer, who cares—as Miss Hempel obviously does—more about singing the best possible music with all the artistry at her command than about the box-office receipts, can draw an audience which almost filled the hall and insisted on numerous repetitions and extra numbers." And Mr. H. T. Parker says, in his Boston *Evening Transcript* review of 13 December, "Sooner or later the whole town will discover her as one of the signal singers of our time."

Now came two appearances, also in December 1920, with the New York Symphony Orchestra: one in Washington, D.C., and one in Baltimore, Maryland. A review states:

> A combination difficult to surpass—that of the New York Symphony and Frieda Hempel—was listened to with rapt attention by a very large audience. The performance was also noteworthy in that the soloist at a symphony concert was permitted to give an encore. This occurred at the close of Miss Hempel's magnificent rendition of the "Waltz" from the first act of Gounod's opera *Mireille*, when the singer responded with Mozart's "Cradle Song."

We now made what turned out to be a useless trip to Norfolk and Richmond, Virginia, and for a very common reason. The checks bounced! The Southern Musical Bureau, which had handled both concerts, was responsible for my fees, and they paid by check, as was customary. But it was the first time for me that such a check was not valid, and of course the two successful concerts were a thing of the past by the time we discovered this. I don't know what happened afterward, but I suppose the money was finally paid. Some scamp must have run off with the proceeds, leaving it to the management to make good on the loss.

On 5 January 1921 came another of my Carnegie Hall recitals, this time a benefit recital. The hall was completely filled, and my many, many friends and admirers were very cordial to me. Again I earned unstinting praise from the important critics, who increasingly emphasized my perfect vocal art. In the *Times* the next day Richard Aldrich wrote that my recital was "refreshing to lovers of fine singing, and an agreeable reminder that fine singing still exists." He added, "Her voice has rarely sounded more beautiful in its rounded smoothness, its beautiful color, and its equality. Nor has she sung with a more delightful art and perfect command of the higher vocal technique." Of the aria "Non mi dir" from Mozart's *Don Giovanni* he wrote: "Here was the true Mozart style in as near perfection as it is now to be heard; a limpid and translucent delivery of the melody in the most equable tones, in an untroubled legato, in artistic and well-considered phrasing; and, in the last few measures, in finished coloratura." Henry T. Finck commented in the *Evening Post*, "The final group was made up of English, Dutch, French, German and Norwegian folk songs, in the rendering of which Frieda Hempel comes nearer Marcella Sembrich than any other singer of the day."

And in the *Morning Telegraph*:

> Hempel's voice, with its rare quality and coloring, is said to come nearer the mark set by the famous coloraturist of a century ago than any living singer of the day—this is a high compliment, but thoroughly deserved by Miss Hempel, whose attractiveness does not rest entirely with her voice, but in charm of personality as well.

Pitts Sanborn opened his review in the New York *Globe* with the words "Looking positively thin," and I had indeed lost a bit of weight during the summer months in Switzerland. I had spent much time creeping on my hands and knees over the mountain trails, which is the quickest way I know to take off excess weight, and I advise stout women to try it. Of course I had a very good reason for wanting to stay slim. I was a concert artist, and I wanted to look attractive for my public.

After three more concerts in the south, I went to Chicago on 23 January for a few opera rehearsals. I had agreed the previous year to join the company on its 1921 West Coast tour in April. It surprises me now to read in my scrapbooks that in February the story was put out that I had just signed with the Chicago Opera Association on 10 February, replacing Galli-Curci who, the day before, had signed with the Metropolitan Opera Company for the coming season. This is not true. I would not have been willing to "replace" Galli-Curci in Chicago, and I would not have signed a long-term contract with any operatic company, under any circumstances. I wished to concertize primarily.

In February 1921 I gave fourteen concerts, including four performances with the New York Symphony, an appearance with the Harvard Glee Club in Boston, and a joint recital with Alessandro Bonci at the Hippodrome in New York City. The concert in Boston was in a sense a recital, for I did not appear with the Glee Club, but rather I alternated with it. Said the *Boston Post*, "There were several salient features of Miss Hempel's appearance, not excluding that of a quite daring gown with which she graced the occasion. Among contemporary artists she is hardly excelled today as a mistress of song, both as regards finish of vocal mechanism and the sheer beauty of her voice."

H. T. Parker wrote in the Boston *Evening Transcript*:

She is the singer who in these days excels any other of American concert hall or opera house in the richness and luster of a voice now at golden prime; in a skill with ornate and lyric song that she steadily ripens and refines; in the response of vocal intelligence and a just sentiment to the music at hand. It is said that Miss Garden seeks a successor to Mme Galli-Curci for the Chicago Opera. She would not have far to go to find a more excellent singer.

It is because Mr. Parker, Mr. Huneker, Mr. Aldrich, and Mr. Henderson were the peers of music critics in America at this time that I am proud to quote their opinions. In their words the steady maturing of my art is reflected.

The critics also continued to comment on my appearance. About my performance with Walter Damrosch and the New York Symphony in Philadelphia, a critic remarked, "Miss Hempel, radiantly, if rather scantily, attired in a pink costume which set off her still youthful charms to full advantage, sang two arias." I suppose that the Callot gown was unusual, but I don't recall feeling the least bit risqué! All the reviewers mentioned it. One said, "Frieda Hempel was resplendent in an apricot gown that was acutely abbreviated above and below. Her technique was dazzling, but the color of her voice paled beside that memorable apricot gown. She has a delightful personality and she was enthusiastically recalled after both appearances." I read, too, "The quality and flexibility of a beautiful voice were much in evidence." It is important to know that they liked my singing as well as my rainbow gown.

My recital at the Hippodrome with Alessandro Bonci was a great privilege for me. We both appreciated the large audience that turned out despite severe weather. A reviewer called us "both exemplars of the classic art of singing." These Sunday night concerts at the Hippodrome were managed by S. Hurok, today the best-known of concert managers. In New York I sang at Carnegie Hall only once a year, but this offer to appear in concert with an artist of such perfection as Bonci's was not to be turned down. And in a sense it was the knowledge that Mr. Bonci was to be my colleague in *La traviata*, and *Rigoletto* that led me to join the Chicago Opera Association, with a good deal of anticipation, on 19 March following seven more concerts.

During the intervening months following my winter engagement with this company, Mr. Herbert Johnson had resigned as manager, and Mary Garden was now director of the company and one of its members. The artists with whom I associated on this wonderfully successful tour were Bonci, Titta Ruffo, Joseph Schwarz, Edward Johnson, Rosa Raisa, and Mary Garden. Our conductors were Giorgio Polacco, Pietro Cimini, and Alexander Smallens. Polacco was the conductor of my several performances, and of course I had already worked with him at the Metropolitan Opera and thought highly of him.

I was very happy with these friends and with all the other singers who worked with us. We traveled together in two special trains labeled Mary Garden Special instead of the more appropriate name Chicago Opera Special. Many artists in the company complained of this, but it was not of great importance. We never saw Miss Garden in her capacity as a director. She sang in her performances just as we sang in ours.

The tour encompassed seven cities: Cincinnati, Tulsa, Dallas, Houston, Los Angeles, San Francisco, and Denver. Mary Garden appeared in *Carmen, Monna Vanna, Thaïs,* and *Tosca.* Rosa Raisa sang in *Lohengrin, Il trovatore,* and *Otello,* and I appeared in *Traviata, Rigoletto,* and *L'elisir d'amore.* Rosa Raisa was a magnificent Elsa. She often came to me to discuss her portrayal of this role and to analyze fine points of tone coloring. She had a gorgeous voice which she used beautifully. My husband accompanied me on this tour, and although I had little free time, we used it well, visiting friends and sightseeing. We were often able to see a performance of the company, which we enjoyed.

I scored a tremendous personal triumph in every city from Cincinnati and Tulsa to Dallas, Houston, and Los Angeles, earning extraordinary reviews. On 9 April the Los Angeles season closed, and we traveled on to San Francisco. I was delighted to be there again in one of America's most beautiful cities. Situated on a peninsula with the Pacific Ocean on one side and the bay on the other, it commands from its many hilltops a thrilling view of beautiful country for miles around. We all stayed at the Fairmont Hotel, atop Telegraph Hill, and this glorious view greeted us every morning from our hotel windows. Around ten o'clock in the morning the white fog that covered the streets would lift to show us a city already busy at work, sparkling blue waters filled with colorful ships, and beyond all this the outline of the mountains.

Redfern Mason, the fine critic of the *San Francisco Examiner,* wrote:

> It is so much easier to sing Puccini than to sing Verdi, that singers are glad to dodge the exacting strains of *Traviata* on the excuse that the music is old-fashioned. The idiom changes; but wherever music is written from the heart it lives so long as there are people who have the talent to do justice to it. Miss Hempel is one of those people.

And how right he is. This great music lives, and it offers constant challenge. It is not only the music that challenges but also the tradition. As a coloratura soprano I had a great task to perform. My predecessors were the great artists Patti, Melba, Tetrazzini, and Sembrich. In singing their roles I desired to follow in their footsteps.

It is quite simple to sing roles that have never been sung before. One does not have to fear comparisons. To create a new part is not difficult, for the public will accept your portrayal without question if you are an artist. No one can say, "Well, I liked so-and-so better in this part." But how different it is when you appear in a great classic of bel canto singing! Not only is the older music more difficult vocally, but the great high standards have long been set for you, standards of singing, interpretation, and acting.

As Alfred Metzger wrote in the *Pacific Coast Musical Review* of April 1921:

> The sensation-loving people turned out on Tuesday night to hail Mary Garden to the tune of more than 6000 people. But Wednesday night was the real music lovers' and musicians' night. You can well leave it to your genuine music-loving people to select the most efficient and delightful artists as their favorites. There were more curtain calls than on any of the previous nights and even after the performance was at an end, there were more than five calls, a thing that has not been noticed so far this season. . . . Regarding the combination of vocal art and dramatic force, the Violetta of Frieda Hempel is the greatest impersonation of the role we have ever seen, and among the Violettas it has been our pleasure to hear were several of the world's greatest coloratura sopranos.

Ray Brown of the *Chronicle* agreed, "One voice stood out in high relief by virtue of its inherent loveliness and exquisite usage. It was Frieda Hempel's night beyond peradventure."

On 18 and 22 April we presented *Rigoletto* in the Civic Auditorium where all the performances had taken place. Of my singing of "Caro nome," Redfern Mason noted, "She sang it with a brilliance that satisfied even the most exacting lover of coloratura, and at the same time she poured into it a human warmth you would search for in the art of Tetrazzini in vain."

Josef Schwarz, that excellent baritone of Latvian birth who later became one of Germany's finest singers, made his American debut with me in this performance in San Francisco. His portrayal of the hunchback Rigoletto was exceptional—a triumph. He was amazed at his success, and he seemed to feel that he was somehow at fault for detracting from mine. He was very sweet, and it was a great moment for him. Of course I in no way resented his ovation: he deserved it. He was then already engaged to the former Mrs. Sielcken (whose family, the Isenburgs, I had met years before) and some time later they were married.

On 21 April, just before the night of our last appearance in San Francisco, I had great fun singing over a wireless telephone under the auspices of a leading newspaper of the city. All radiophone operators within a radius of 1500 miles were able to hear my voice as I sang "Home, Sweet Home." In these fast-moving days of television it is difficult to recall the time of crystal sets. But it was a great experience for me to realize that people so many miles away were actually hearing me sing, people in Honolulu as well as on the West Coast of America. This was the first of many such broadcasts for me during those early days of radio.

A novel aspect of my last appearance with the Chicago Opera Association, which was *La traviata* in Denver, Colorado, was a long-range combination radio-telephone broadcast. Some five thousand persons, scattered about within a radius of five hundred miles of Denver, lifted their telephone receivers and heard my concert. Other listeners in Wyoming, Utah, New Mexico, Nebraska, and Texas, without telephones, heard my voice by wireless radio if they were fortunate to be near a devotee of the new science.

My voice was transmitted by wireless to the radio stations within this five-hundred-mile limit. At these stations the tones came out of a radio loudspeaker with almost the same effect as if I had been in each receiving room. Here telephone connections were made, and the sound was transmitted to the central telephone station, where it was available to subscribers. This seems primitive today, but believe me, it was exciting then! The realization of what this form of communication meant was thrilling to me. For those listening, it was an actual concert, not a recording. It was something happening as they listened, and they were all moved by the experience. They were everywhere, in the cities, or alone in a mountain camp, or perhaps in a sickbed at a hospital, and I was reaching all of them at once.

The *Denver Post,* which arranged this concert, announced: "It is an event that rich and poor may enjoy, and the *Post* offers it to its big family with the hope that all may be inspired to an appreciation of the greatest that the musical realms have to offer."

Upon my return to New York state, I went directly to Auburn for a concert. At the close of that evening, I was asked if I would sing for the prisoners in Auburn prison, fourteen hundred men in jail for various crimes: murderers, thieves, embezzlers, and arsonists. This idea was not particularly a pleasant one, but because it was for a good cause, I readily agreed.

The next morning I rose early and warmed up my voice as usual. It made no difference to whom I was going to sing—I would still give the very best that was in me to give. I offered the prisoners the same fine music as in Auburn. Warden Jennings, the Auburn manager Mr. James Henessey, Mr. Bos, Mr. Rodeman, and I were driven to the prison and taken into the meeting hall where this noontime concert was to take place.

The "guests" were gathered there, and from behind stage we could hear the talking and the laughing of the men. Then a young man escorted me out upon the platform, where thunderous applause greeted me. This frightened me at first, for I could not help but realize that these men were all criminals and emotionally unstable. Then along each aisle I noticed a guard standing ready, with pistol and stick, and the fear left me as quickly as it had come.

Frieda Hempel on the steps of Auburn Prison, New York, where she sang for fourteen hundred prisoners. Left to right: August Rodeman, flutist; Frieda Hempel, Coenraad V. Bos, pianist; and Warden Jennings. COURTESY METROPOLITAN OPERA ARCHIVES.

I thought to myself, "All right, now. Sing, and see what happens." At the same time I looked at the men. Most of them were bald or clean-shaven, and they were bound together with chains. But each face was different. I fought with the dreadful feelings of condemnation that rose up in me and strove to be all the more charming instead.

I sang Handel, Mendelssohn, Brahms, Schubert, and some lovely waltzes, among them the now-famous "Blue Danube Waltz." The men hung on every tone as complete silence reigned. As I sang the men began to smile, and emotions began to flood the room. I thought to myself, "They cannot be so bad, when one can awaken these emotions in them. And when these emotions are still part of them, then surely they are not completely lost. When good music can move them, then they must be somehow good, themselves."

I learned from the warden that a wonderful system was in use which helped these men to find their self-respect once more. There was an organization of prisoners, with president, vice-president, chairman, and committee members of various rank. The young man who competed for and won the honor of escorting me to the podium was a murderer. But the warden said he was a good man at heart, who had killed once in anger and was then paying for his deed. He would soon be released on parole. These men competed for positions of honor in this prison organization, and their sense of social values was thereby rekindled.

This young man took advantage of the honor accorded him. I promised him that I would help him if I could. He remembered this promise, and one day he appeared at my apartment in New York City and asked to speak with me, saying, "I am from Auburn." After just a moment's hesitation, I went to greet him, and after speaking with him for a few minutes, I realized that he was worthy of help from all of us. I sent him to see my husband in his downtown office, and Will assisted him in finding a good job.

When I had finished my program, the men begged and begged for encores. They cried and laughed as I sang to them, and I did not realize how late it was getting. When we finally left the prison grounds for the station, we realized that we would probably miss the train. But fortunately, after the train had pulled out ahead of our arrival, it was discovered that we were not aboard. The train was stopped, and we were advised at the station to catch up with it by car. Thus I punctuated my memorable visit to Auburn by chasing a train.

I am reminded of another concert. I was singing in a small town, and I learned that a very sick woman wished above all else to hear my voice. I had no time to go to the hospital and see her, so she was brought to the concert hall and placed in the wings. As I entered the stage that night, I greeted her in passing. She was in a hospital bed, placed in the wings just off the stage.

After I had sung my first group, Mr. Bos came on the stage to present his solos. I took this opportunity to speak with the woman. How she clasped my hand in hers! As she spoke I could feel the strength return to her. She said, "I think that no doctor on the face of the earth could have given me this belief that you have given me, this belief that I am going to get well again. Your music has cured me."

I wonder why this great healing strength of music is not used more today, this strength that comes from the flesh-and-blood creation of music by great artists—no radio, no canned music, but living music from those who sing from understanding and who transmit quite unconsciously this healing power to the sick. How much greater this is than vitamins and injections. And no one who is around me remains sick for any length of time. There is a great strength and a great magnetism in music, and in those who live for music.

I prepared to sail for Europe, booking passage with my husband on the *Aquitania* for 24 May 1921. Just before I sailed the writer John Kenneth Gray requested an interview with me. He had seen Sarah Bernhardt, and he had been in San Francisco recently where he had heard me sing *Traviata*. I had been called the "singing Bernhardt" by the critics there, and he wished to write an article on this subject for the *Musical Leader*.

"You did vividly recall the Divine Sarah," he told me, as we began talking. I replied, "Bernhardt is wonderful; please don't misunderstand me. But I don't want to be like her or anybody else. I don't want to inherit anybody's mantle, or wear anybody's halo. I want to be myself." And in his article he says, "No matter how many mantles of other famous folk, seeming a perfect fit, wrap themselves around her; or how many halos of history adjust themselves becomingly over her golden hair, Hempel has a way of tossing them off abruptly and being just herself more completely than anyone I have ever known." He continues:

> Miss Hempel had consented to see me at her apartment the evening before she sailed [with] one condition—that I would not interfere with her work. I did not. No human being could have interfered successfully with that night's activities. The prima donna wrote personal inscriptions and signed her name to dozens of photographs. She made a final inspection of the apartment to see that everything was properly dust-proof and mothproof for the summer, and picked out the music she was to sing abroad.

This was true. I sorted out my Jenny Lind books and letters; and I had spent an hour with my accompanist and my flutist, going over the scores that I would sing in Copenhagen, Vienna, and Budapest. I also picked out the cap which I wanted my husband Will to wear on the boat, answered many goodbye phone calls, received several callers stopping in to say goodbye, and gave my secretary enough instructions to last until November.

All this time my maid Rosa was sorting out and packing my gowns. Mr. Gray was interested in my amazing brocade gown. It was made of six yards of beautiful vari-colored brocade, held together with a few snaps scattered unevenly around the drape. I heard Rosa say to him, "It is easier for Madame to sing a whole concert than to get into this gown!" I laughed because she was not far from right.

On 12 June 1921 I gave my first concert in Copenhagen. I was a little frightened when I arrived there. The Danes had heard so much about my successes in America, and the Europeans were always a little skeptical about people who came from the "Dollarland," the "land of unlimited opportunities." And in this they were not to be blamed. The press-agent system results in such exaggeration. The public is told that you are the most beautiful creature, the greatest singer next to Caruso or Patti, the greatest actress next to Bernhardt, and heaven knows what else. Quite naturally the public takes the attitude, "Well, show me!" For this reason I hated too much heralding.

The ticket sales for my concert had been tremendous, and the demand was so great that I was asked to schedule two additional concerts. The people stood in line for hours to buy up these tickets, too, and for each performance hundreds of people waited outside the packed hall to see me as I left.

The concerts were given in the Tivoli Hall, where a type of arrangement new to me was customary. The symphony orchestra was a permanent feature of this hall, and the audience sat at tables, eating their dinners and drinking. I disliked this atmosphere at first, wondering if the noise of the dishes would disturb me. But when I came out to sing, the hall became silent, and the listeners hung on to every tone. Everything was forgotten but my singing, and the very contrast was exciting and stimulating.

It was a very friendly crowd, and I felt immediately, "Oh, I like to sing for you." It was more like being in my home than at a concert, which is how my audience must feel to me. If I face an audience that is a little reserved, I give them an encore they know and like to loosen them up. I must have them relaxed just the way I am, and then I succeed in making them feel at home. The managers call me a good show woman, but actually I just enjoy my work, and I handle it with real feeling and happiness. I know what my message is, and I give it with all my heart.

These three concerts were so completely booked that Will and I did not have a chance to see much of the city. Even Will had been unable to get a ticket for the first concert, which he considered terrible but I didn't at all! Each concert was a tremendous triumph, and at the last concert I was completely overwhelmed by the tribute paid me. The *Socialdemokraten* critic wrote:

The lights in the concert hall had to be switched out, before the audience would leave the hall. . . . Again she shows that the most difficult part is a trifle for her, and that the tiniest ditty is not too small. . . . She took the audience by assault, nay, by smiles and by her unique, expressive voice. Incessantly tremendous applause was heard, repeatedly she had to appear again, and she did not grow tired of the overwhelming enthusiasm. A full hour she sang to the audience, who did not grow tired either. Cascades of applause streamed up to her, and constantly she returned to acknowledge it, and to sing again. Not until the lights were switched off did the audience awake as from a wonderful dream. And outside the hall an enormous crowd had gathered to catch a glimpse of the artist, and to greet her as she drove away. Her visit to Copenhagen has been an event which will never be forgotten by those of us who had the opportunity to hear her.

Other newspapers sang my praises as well, and so, as it turned out, I should not have feared my debut in Copenhagen. I would have sung there more frequently during the ensuing years if my tight schedule of concerts had permitted me to do so.

I could hardly wait to arrive in Sils-Maria. It was such a tiny village, but every person, every cow, and every goat knew me. All day long I would be outside in the fresh mountain air, far away from the smoke and the drawing rooms full of people. Sometimes I would go out with the townspeople and cut hay, calling out greetings to all the children who waved to us as we passed in our cart. Nobody walked and hiked as much as I did during those wonderful summer months. Alone I would wander through the glorious open country, thinking about nothing, just absorbing the life that streamed forth from sun and air and ground.

Then would come the moment when I became tired of the mountains and the simple life and wanted to see Paris again, buy exquisite gowns, and be once more in the fashionable world. And so off to Paris I was. Will joined me there, and after a shopping spree which included dresses for *Traviata,* which I was to sing in Vienna and Budapest in October, we motored through northern France.

I was not eager to go to Vienna. The Viennese are very chauvinistic, and they had their favorites.* But the concert I gave there for charity was a great success, nevertheless.

Arriving in Budapest, I prepared for the two concerts of 10 and 12 October at the Redoute [Vigadó] and for two performances of *Traviata* on

---

*Referring to Selma Kurz. See reference to performances of 7 October (Vienna) and 10 October (Budapest) 1921 in the Postscript, "An Informal and Selected Chronology." *Ed.*

13 and 16 October. I had given my very first concert in this city years before; now I was warmly remembered by the public and generously praised by the press. In the *Nemzeti Ujság* on 14 October I was called "one of the greatest of living singers." Here the critic also stated: "Her performance was the perfection of vocal art. Her wonderful movements, multifaceted mimic, perfect art of singing, and phenomenally expressive voice were united in such a way that we can find no words to express it. In her, coloratura singing becomes a noble instrument of feeling."

The same high praise was accorded my portrayal of Violetta at the opera house. The performances were completely sold out, and again my husband had to stand until the Regent, Admiral Miklós Horthy, whom he met during an intermission, invited Will to join his party in his box. The prices of tickets had been raised considerably, thus raising great expectations among the public and the press. The *Pesti Hirlap* review, in part: "Since Marcella Sembrich there has not been such an ideal and perfect Violetta Valéry on our stage as that of tonight, in whom the phenomenal coloratura, the intensive magic of the wonderful voice, and the touching dramatic play were united in a wonderful whole. It was an unrivaled, ever memorable performance."

I quote only a small part of each review, but what I have quoted will give you a picture of my great success in Budapest. My husband and I were fêted, and gifts were showered upon me. Instead of floral gifts, however, I received untold numbers of packages of goose livers!

Now, I am certain that these people believed that they were giving me great pleasure, because they knew nothing of my great love for all animals. But these goose livers were each the size of a large lung, and as I knew how such tremendous livers were produced, I shuddered when I saw them. The poor geese were kept in small cages, with food stuffed constantly down their throats, forcing their livers to be overworked and thus grow oversize. What living thing on earth could be forced to overeat without suffering? People who do not love animals and music can never be my friends, for I can never, never warm up to them, and a true animal lover would have reacted just as I did to the gifts of goose livers in Budapest, and he would have been my friend. We left Budapest at the end of October and returned to New York on the SS *Olympic,* where a full year of activity awaited us.

CHAPTER EIGHTEEN

The Jenny Lind Story

O
ne afternoon back in the spring of 1920, I received a telephone call from a Dr. Johannes Hoving, who asked for an
appointment to see me about a concert. I agreed to see him, and we set a
time for the meeting. When he arrived, I found him to be a most handsome
gentleman, with a long white beard that reminded me of the beard of King
Leopold of Belgium. He was charming indeed.

He introduced himself as president of the Swedish Society, an organization representing the Swedish people in America. This group, I learned,
was formulating plans to celebrate the one-hundredth anniversary of the
birth of Jenny Lind. The Centennial Committee, composed of representative men and women of national reputation, wished, among other things, to
erect a statue to Jenny Lind in Sweden. In order to raise the necessary funds
for this project, the members had conceived the idea of presenting a concert.

This concert, however, was to be quite different from the usual concerts. It would be an exact copy of the first concert Jenny Lind gave in New
York in 1850. The singer was to be one who, in voice, appearance, and personality, as well as in the excellence of her art, would most typify the great
Swedish singer.

After having carefully weighed the accomplishments of every famous
soprano in Europe and America, the committee requested Dr. Hoving to
interview me.

"Miss Hempel," he said, "we have considered every soprano before the
public today, and you are our unanimous choice. Would you consider
accepting this offer?"

The first Jenny Lind Centennial Concert, celebrating the one-hundredth anniversary of Jenny Lind's birth, was held on 6 October 1920. Hempel's Callot Soeurs gown was of heavy ivory slipper satin trimmed in lace; the skirt was decorated with morning glories. Hempel was introduced by the actor Tom Weiss who appeared as P. T. Barnum, Lind's famous manager. PHOTO BY UNDERWOOD & UNDERWOOD. COURTESY MICHAEL ASPINALL.

My immediate reply was spontaneous, "Oh, no! I shall be criticized if I presume to impersonate Jenny Lind. When we die, the word goes around, 'How great she was!' People remember our achievements and our art so well when we are dead. Fortunately I am still living, but Jenny Lind is dead and famous. People will compare me unfavorably with her, and they will not understand the spirit in which I would impersonate Jenny, for I would only do so in a spirit of homage."

He was unable to persuade me to change my mind, and so he spent the remaining time of our visit explaining the intentions of the committee regarding the concert, hoping that if I understood more fully, I might agree to appear as Jenny Lind.

I did not become interested in the idea until I began to receive a great deal of literature about Jenny Lind from the committee. Just before I sailed for Switzerland in the summer of 1920, Dr. Hoving called upon me again, pleading once more with me to accept. He promised me that every detail would be taken care of, and that I would have all the help possible in planning and executing the concert. He also promised to inform the press that I had been selected to impersonate Jenny Lind, so that the public would not think I had assumed her mantle myself.

By now I realized that a duplication of Jenny Lind's first concert in America, of 11 September 1850, would be artistically acceptable as well as extremely interesting to the public. And so, much to Dr. Hoving's pleasure, I agreed to sing the concert.

I sailed for Europe, laden with books, pictures, and programs of Jenny. In the mountains of Sils-Maria I studied this material and prepared the music for the program. Before leaving there, I became familiar with all Jenny Lind's mannerisms—her bow, her walk, her gestures, and her posture. Then in Paris I went to Callot Soeurs and ordered an exact duplicate of Jenny Lind's concert gown for the occasion, the details of which I had gleaned from pictures and books. In New York late in September, Dr. Hoving told me about the extensive planning that had already gone into the concert, and together we finished preparations.

Jenny Lind had given her first concert in America in Castle Garden, which later became the Aquarium. This building no longer existed in 1920. It had stood on what came to be known as the Battery. Because the concert could not be given in the original building, it would take place in the foremost concert hall of the city, Carnegie Hall. But it was only in this detail that the evening of 6 October 1920 differed from that of 11 September 1850.

Everything else was to be an exact duplicate, from the program to the costumes. Jenny Lind's original program contained the Scena and Cavatina "Casta Diva" from *Norma* of Bellini; a duet from Rossini which she had sung with Signor Balletti; a trio for two flutes and voice, written expressly for her by Meyerbeer; the "Herdsman's Song," and a "Welcome to America" written for her by her conductor Sir Jules Benedict for the occasion. In addition, there were orchestral selections from Weber and Benedict and a duet for two pianofortes. We copied this program exactly.

I needed an assisting artist to impersonate Signor Balletti, two pianists, and two flutists, in addition to the small orchestra. Even P. T. Barnum himself, the famous manager of Jenny Lind, appeared on the stage that memorable evening, and so we too had our P. T. Barnum.

The committee had arranged everything wonderfully. The firemen, who stood at the head of each aisle, were in costumes of red; the usherettes wore wide crinolines and carried shepherds' crooks. The stage was arranged as it had been arranged in Castle Garden, with a row of little flags of every nation affording colorful decoration. The footlights were candles protected with tin shields. The men in the orchestra were all dressed in the clothes of the period, and my poor Mr. Bos was also costumed! I had a great deal of trouble convincing him and my flutist to dress up.

Both men were perfectly happy in their black suits and white ties, and now all of a sudden a costume! But I told them that if I could dress up, they could, too. After all, it was not just a masquerade—it was a very serious concert. I had a lot of fun making up their faces. I invented a little white lie and told them that one was not allowed to go out on stage in costume without makeup, and they finally fell in with the spirit of the evening and enjoyed themselves thoroughly.

Arthur Middleton* was selected to impersonate Signor Balletti, and two other fine artists appeared as the second flutist and the second pianist. The actor Tom Weiss was chosen to act as P. T. Barnum, and he certainly looked the part. His task was to bring me out on the stage and introduce me to the audience, just as Mr. Barnum had introduced Jenny Lind to her audience.

In the lobbies, young girls in hoop skirts sold programs which were an exact copy of Jenny Lind's programs, and around them stood more firemen with their glistening trumpets, red shirts, and typical fireman hats. Old-time Chickering pianos of the square variety were placed on the stage, one of which bore Jenny Lind's signature.

As I sang, I held in my hand the sheet of music that Jenny Lind habitually held, or rather a copy of the sheet. And when I sang the "Herdsman's Song," better known as the "Echo Song," I copied Jenny Lind by sitting down at the piano, as she did, and playing my own accompaniment. At the

*Arthur Middleton was a well-known concert and oratorio bass-baritone who hailed from Chicago where he received his training. He was at the Metropolitan for three seasons, 1914–17. In two performances with the Chicago Opera he had the dubious distinction of creating Ramatzin in Hadley's ill-fated opera *Azora* (26 December 1917). He recorded extensively for Edison. Middleton died in Chicago 16 February 1929. *Ed.*

end of this song, Jenny Lind had turned away from the piano and then sung several bars with an echo imitation without accompaniment. Returning to the piano, she would strike the last note to show that she was still on pitch. I also did this, and after this song I received a tremendous ovation, for it astonished the audience to hear that I had remained perfectly on pitch. For my last encore I sang "Home, Sweet Home," and indeed I could finish no concert without singing this lovely song. My audience would not let me go until they heard it.

My dress was greatly admired, and Mr. Henderson called me "a vision of loveliness." Callot Soeurs had created a magnificent gown for me, made of heavy ivory slipper satin and trimmed in real Bertha lace. The skirt was decorated with morning glories of all colors, from the lightest blue to the deepest purple velvet, and trimmed with light and dark green taffeta leaves. People had remarked of Jenny Lind that she had no feet, and so of course my dress was very long so that my feet, too, might be covered. I powdered my hair with gold powder after parting it in the middle, for although this style was not very becoming to me, it was the way Jenny wore her hair.

There was great excitement in the audience, and a very elegant group of people faced me as I sang. The house was sold out at the price of ten dollars a ticket and one hundred dollars for a box. When the concert began we received such a tumultuous ovation that the program could not begin for several minutes. And during the intermission, nosegays were thrown upon the stage to me. It was 1850, a wonderfully picturesque and thrilling event for all concerned. As a clipping says:

> Frieda Hempel was so radiantly beautiful that almost every other feature was forgotten, and when she began to sing—she is perhaps the greatest exponent of that sort of singing in the world today—the audience quite rightfully "went wild," even though Hempel, unlike Lind, had not had the great P. T. Barnum to "circus" her but has won her unique position in the musical world by her very great vocal skill.

As we read in the *New York Post:*

> Nothing more lovely could be desired than the picture Mme Hempel presented. Dressed in a beautiful hoop-skirted white satin gown, with her lovely shoulders and neck gleaming above her flowered garlanded corsage, with flowers in her hair, and a most wonderful bodice, she was a dream of beauty. In the aria from "L'Étoile du Nord" nothing was left to be desired in tone or execution. . . .
>
> Then came "Home, Sweet Home," a climax to a great evening of song, and how the pathos of that ballad was brought out! It was sung as it was written and as it should be sung, and the audience hung spellbound upon the wondrous tones of the singer. Never before has the

simple ballad been more gloriously sung. It was a fitting climax to a night of rare music. One can never forget it. It was a night to be cherished forever in the memory.

During the course of the evening a telegram arrived from King Gustav of Sweden, reading, "I send my best wishes for the celebration of the memory of the famous daughter of Sweden, the great singer, and noble personality, Jenny Lind. . . . [signed] Gustav."

This centennial celebration of the birth of Jenny Lind held great interest for New Yorkers, for Jenny Lind had taken the city by storm, and she had not been forgotten. Today P. T. Barnum reminds Americans of the days of the circus. But he was also a genius of a showman who had realized what a sensation Jenny Lind would be in this country. She was then at the height of her powers, and her European fame was enormous, both as an artist and as a woman of great compassion and charity. As Barnum states in his autobiography of 1882, *Struggles and Triumphs; or Forty Years' Recollections*:

> I relied prominently upon Jenny Lind's reputation as a great musical *artiste*, I also took largely into my estimate of her success with all classes of the American public, her character for extraordinary benevolence and generosity. Without this peculiarity in her disposition, I never would have dared to make the engagement which I did, as I felt sure that there were multitudes of individuals in America who would be prompted to attend her concerts by this feeling alone.

"The engagement" was the contract bringing Jenny Lind to America in 1850.

As her steamer, the sidewheeler *Atlantic,* passed Sandy Hook and steamed through the narrows, cannon salutes greeted her, and there was tremendous excitement when her boat landed. Forty thousand people crowded to catch a glimpse of her. Triumphal arches marked her pathway, and crowds surged around her hotel and clamored to see her. Auctions for the sale of tickets attracted thousands of would-be buyers in cities throughout America. And at each concert it was announced that a large portion of the proceeds would be donated to various charities. Extra concerts had to be given to satisfy the throngs, and Jenny Lind herself added more concerts for charity.

Newspaper stories about the centennial celebration made a striking tribute to the memory of Jenny Lind. Every paper printed long, detailed accounts of her original concert and devoted considerable space to the event. The *New York Tribune* printed:

> Life in New York was a one-ring circus in those simple, tuneful days of 1850 when Jenny Lind arrived upon our shores. There was no dispute between the day's headlines; it was an easy task that Barnum faced when

he set out to make a great soprano a national heroine. The hard-put publicity manufacturers of today, competing with one another and with a thousand distractions, can look back with envy to that time when the road to fame was easy—provided only you were entitled to tread it.

Jenny Lind sang only ninety-five of the 150 concerts scheduled for her by Mr. Barnum. While visiting in Boston, she married Otto Goldschmidt and shortly thereafter returned to Europe. After her American tour she never again sang professionally.

My concert had such tremendous publicity and its success was so enormous that I received requests continuously throughout the subsequent season to present the concert in other cities where Jenny Lind had sung and was remembered. And so on 25 November 1921, the first Hempel–Jenny Lind concert outside of New York was given, in Lansing, Michigan.

Of my sixty-nine concerts during the 1921–22 season, we included fifteen Jenny Lind concerts. The pageantry, the color, and the historical interest of these evenings attracted many people who might not ordinarily go to a song recital, and my manager soon realized that even more Jenny Lind concerts could be given during the coming seasons.

In the meantime, I continued to give my regular concert programs. November and December 1921 took me through the Northeast, and at my concert in Chicago on 11 December, I again sang to a packed auditorium. The *Chicago Evening American* critic wrote:

> Before all else, one must say that Miss Hempel's success is always assured before she opens her lips to sing, such is the winning charm of her person and her smile. Then, of course, her voice is Hempel's—fresh, supple, birdlike, unforced, her intonation a veritable pitch-pipe of accuracy, her technic perfection, her concept of the song an enchantment, and her musicianship thorough.

My husband was interviewed in Chicago, and I was amused by his remarks. Although he loved to travel with me when he had time, he admitted to the reporters that it was refreshing to return to New York City and read his own name on his office doors and on his stationery, and to view other unmistakable evidence that indicated his separate identity as William B. Kahn. When asked if I was temperamental, he replied, "How should I know. All women are temperamental with their husbands."

After my Carnegie Hall concert on 27 January 1922, Henry T. Finck wrote in the *New York Evening Post*:

> Wagner has declared that the human voice is more beautiful than any instrumental sound that can be produced. He would have been strongly confirmed in this could he have heard Frieda Hempel sing last night at

Carnegie Hall. What are horns and clarinets, and violins and cellos, alone or in combination, in comparison with such luscious sounds as came from her throat—sounds not only of quality but of golden purity of intonation and phrased with the ripe art of one of the world's foremost concert and opera singers. Couldn't she be persuaded to return to the Metropolitan? To be sure, for a singer of her rank there is more profit in concert work, though it entails more hardship.

My concert work was certainly hard work, but it was a great deal more profitable, as Mr. Finck suggested. My regular concerts brought me fifteen hundred dollars a concert, and the Jenny Lind concerts brought me nightly fees as high as three thousand dollars. For each season I was booked for at least seventy concerts, and so the gross receipts were around $140,000 each year.

And of course nonfinancial considerations kept me on the concert stage rather than on the operatic stage. Above all the concert stage challenged me. The song literature is so rich and varied that it demands the utmost from me. When I sing a song, I must create setting, atmosphere, story, and feeling. I read the title, note the tempo, and already I know much about it. When the first chord is sounded on the piano, I feel the atmosphere, I see the picture, the vision.

In "Wohin" of Schubert, I hear the brook rippling, I see it rushing down the valley, it is all there before me. When I sing "Ihr Bild" of Schubert, I see the blood coming into the face, it appears pink to me, the eyes talk to me in sadness, and I see how they fill themselves with soft tears.

I never think about a song—I feel it too strongly. This is born in a person, and it cannot be learned or studied. One has to have deep feelings to sing these songs, and often I have left the piano because I am moved too deeply, and I start to cry.

As a young girl I studied a song by Schubert, "Die Mutter an der Wiege," but I have never been able to sing it. I have to stop; I cannot finish it. Each time I come to the phrase, "Oh Mutter, lieb Mutter, bleib lange noch hier," it just chokes me. For when I was studying this song in Berlin, my mother was sitting in the next room. When I came to this part she cried, and said, "Oh Friedel, don't sing that song!" I remember this so well. And now that she is gone, it affects me even more. I still hear her voice calling to me.

Other songs I look forward to with great joy, and when my heart is full of happiness, I go to the piano and sing them. Many Schubert songs always exhilarate me. They are so young, so fresh, so warm in their feelings. In "Frühlingsglaube" I just see the birches and the apple blossoms, and I know spring is coming. I see the corn weaving in "Du bist die Ruh." I am painting in my thoughts from the very first sound of the piano.

I have seen singers who gaze around the audience while the accompanist plays the introduction, but I could never do that. The first sound grips me immediately, and until the last note of the piano, I am in my vision. In a song recital one cannot be artificial. The artist must really feel the song deeply in order to transmit this to the audience. She cannot act, she cannot pose, she must be honest and sincere. There are some days when the feeling is stronger, and on those days the concert is more perfect.

I must be absolutely free from the thought of notes or words. It does not matter if I hold a note longer than I should: it must be this way if I feel it this way, provided I stay within the limits of the musical line and the accompaniment. Other times the vision of the song is held by the rhythm, and then I do not make even the slightest change in the notes. "Wohin" of Schubert is held tightly within the steady flow of the brook in the rippling accompaniment.

Often I feel differently from the composer, and I sing a *piano* where I should sing a *forte*. If I feel something very intensely, I think a *piano* tone is more moving than a loud tone. It is so interesting to sing songs. There is so much variety of expression. For my temperament I like the gay songs, the Viennese waltzes and the folk songs. Sad songs appeal to me only when they are not too dramatic.

A real artist must be very sensitive in selecting her songs. They must go with her personality and with the color of her voice. And a woman should not try to sing the songs written for a man, although it has been done. Personally, I could not sing "I am a youth with curly hair." There are not too many songs written for women, for most of the songs are love songs, and so it often depends upon how one interprets the text. To me, "Ihr Bild" could be a portrait of my mother, my sister, or some beloved friend, and not necessarily my sweetheart.

I think that the American folk songs are very beautiful, and in a way classical. The spirituals are also very moving, but I feel that they belong to a colored singer, just as I believe the lieder are for the white singer. This is a matter of taste, and I only express here my personal opinion. Also, I don't like to hear a heavy contralto voice singing "The Trout"; nor would I sing "Der Doppelgänger." The conflict between the voice and the demands of the song is too great.

To make up a program has always been agonizing for me. I change numbers around until the very last minute, thinking again, "Now there must be variety in the keys; I cannot sing three sad songs in succession; if I sing too many lullabies, the audience will go to sleep; I cannot sing constantly in a foreign language, they will be bored—I must please everybody, the connoisseur and the layman." You see it is not so easy to select something that appeals to you. I pick out something that I think will be a big success, and it doesn't take at all; and again something I didn't think so much about will become a great favorite. As Barnum said, "You never know what the public wants."

Concert work is much more rewarding than operatic work, but it is also more demanding. As a concert artist, I stand alone on the stage for an hour-and-a-half or longer. I have absolutely nothing to aid me. I come out, stand in the bow of the piano, and there I am. I must create setting and scenery out of nothing but my inner sense of beauty and my art. I must live the song so fully that my audience sees and feels what I see and feel. My imagination must become its imagination.

I am close to the people who sit before me, and every facial expression, every gesture, and every move that I make is observed. Every flaw in diction and in pronunciation is clearly audible over the sound of the piano. I must be complete master of each language, master of meaning as well as of sound. And every word I sing must be clearly understood by the person sitting in the last row of the hall. I must be understood by everybody present, for everyone must know what I am singing about, in order to share with me the feelings and the mood invoked by the music.

It is very important to have a good accompanist. He does not need to be a great technician, but, more important than that, he must understand me and support my interpretations. Sometimes, when I finish a song, I like to have the accompanist wait just a second before playing the final chord. This little pause sometimes tells volumes. I prefer to sing with the same man at each concert, for often the inspiration of the audience affects my interpretation, and I sing the song differently from the way I might have sung it in rehearsal. I feel human nature in front of me, I look into the eyes of the listeners, we speak to one another, and I am giving them perhaps more inflections and more warmth. All this my accompanist must know and follow.

And so, because of all these considerations, it is always a new challenge to stand before an audience. A second recital is even more difficult. The program must be new, the gown and accessories must be new, and the voice must be better. Any indisposition is noticed at once, and comparisons are made with a standard already set.

W. J. Henderson wrote in the *New York Sun* that newspaper criticism went after debutantes with bouquets, and worked thereby incalculable harm. He went on to say, "Severe criticism is reserved for the great personages of the musical world. When the great do not sustain the level of their greatness, either grief or rage or both spring up in the critical breast."

In opera the problem is quite different. The orchestral overture creates a mood, and when the curtain goes up, the scenery tells the public a great deal about the story. Costumes, partners, and chorus all help the singer. You know that the performance does not depend upon you alone. Acting frees the body and relaxes you. And the acting of your partners stimulates you in turn. If you are not sure of a tone, you can turn your back to the audience, and the orchestra can cover up for you. You are not exposed to delicate and refined art; rather you must sing loudly and brilliantly, for the most part.

Of course, opera also lends itself to a wide range of interpretation. It is annoying to me to see a reviewer criticize Calvé, for instance, and say, "I don't like her. She distorts the written score, and the written score is the criterion." He sees the score, and thinks that every spot of ink must be worshiped. It must be intact. But when you are a human being, you cannot be a metronome. You have a heart, and you sing with a heart. It is your business to transmit feeling, and if you are hampered by rigid, dry rhythm, you cannot do this.

You sometimes stay longer on this note or less long on that note. This gives personal color and individuality of expression. A straight reading of the score is monotonous, and no great conductor or composer will object to personal variation if the singer is motivated by great taste.

Caruso was a warm Italian, with more exuberance than the Irish tenor. Naturally he expressed himself differently from John McCormack, for example. And thank heaven we have this variety. We cannot all paint the same picture. You see a tree in one way; I see it in another. We are both right, yet we see and feel differently.

And in music the score is a structure that is not solid. It is fluid and expressive. I know that both Leo Blech and Richard Strauss were happy to have my suggestions regarding the interpretation of their works. For the written score is not alive—it must be brought to life by artists and given personal coloring.

The spring months of 1922 took me through all of Florida, Havana, the Midwest, and the Northwest, for forty-five concerts. Nine of these were Jenny Lind concerts. And you have no idea how many, many gifts I received from the people who attended these concerts, gifts of Jenny Lind tea kettles, Jenny Lind fans, and handkerchiefs and nosegays. All these treasures had been in the homes of these Jenny Lind admirers, and now they were given to me, along with wonderfully sweet letters of appreciation for my concerts.

At one of these Jenny Lind concerts I ran into a little trouble. Mr. Bos always sat at the piano on a round stool, but in this concert he used a long bench. When the time arrived for me to sing the "Echo Song," which I accompanied myself, Mr. Bos stood up, made a deep bow, took my handkerchief and my little book from me, and left the stage. I then sat down on the piano bench and accompanied myself in the song, as Jenny Lind had done before me. But as I seated myself, the audience began to laugh, and they laughed throughout the entire song, much to my annoyance. I did not know what had happened, nor could I explain to Mr. Bos the reason for all the merriment.

Soon we learned that reason. As I sat down on the piano bench, my wide hoop skirt had sprung up in the air, and the gentlemen in the first rows could see my ankles and way up my stockings. Of course, if I had been properly costumed, with pantaloons like Jenny had worn, it would not have been so embarrassing. I then remembered having tried to make the hoop skirt stay down as I sang, but it wouldn't, and I really did not know that the problem was more serious than that. I did not know that those handsome gentlemen could see so much!

After that, I was very careful as I approached the bench, and I would edge in carefully. Whenever I saw a bench, instead of a stool, I knew I could have a bit of fun with the audience, for they understood why I was being so careful, and they would invariably laugh a little at my slyness, and then we would all be in good humor.

During June 1922 Will and I left for London, where I gave my first concert in the city, at Albert Hall. It had been eight years since I had sung the Queen of the Night under the baton of Thomas Beecham, and it was my first concert appearance in England. The English concert-going public is very discerning, and I was most anxious to count the London concert among my successes.

The magnificent reviews the next day reflected the great approval of the audience, and I was asked to return in October for three more concerts. The critic for the *Daily News* wrote:

> The loveliest music, sung with ideal beauty—the voice, the technic, the understanding beyond any fault-finder's grudge were the reward for going yesterday afternoon to Albert Hall. . . . Her singing of [Schubert's] "Ave Maria," with its depth of feeling, and "The Trout," with its lightness and brilliancy and its subtle touches of humor and pathos, were the highest art.

From the *Pall Mall Gazette* came:

> Frieda Hempel combines a beautiful voice with rare technical skill. The former is of warm coloring, flexible and faultlessly true, and she has made of it an obedient instrument that will perform any task intrusted to it. One group was devoted to the songs of Schubert. The performance was transcendental. Perfect moments followed each other like pearls on a string.

Happy with the success of this concert, my husband and I left London to drive up to Great Malvern, in Gloucestershire. I had studied so much about Jenny Lind and had impersonated her in concert, and naturally I wanted to see where she had lived. Her home was at Wynd Point. We motored through beautiful country until we arrived at this charming, quiet place on the side of a sweeping hill. It was landscaped and decorated with many cut hedges.

The caretaker took us in and showed us the house. I sat down at her piano and let my thoughts wander. I thought of her sitting in that very room, practicing, practicing, and letting her soul talk. I saw her in front of me, in her hoop skirt; I sensed that at any moment she would walk in, and I felt great reverence when I touched that piano. Had she been alive, I would not have touched it.

I suppose this is very old-fashioned, but I am almost afraid to touch things that have belonged to outstanding people. To me not everyone is alike. We must give respect and reverence to those to whom God has given a special gift. He has not given gifts to all of us, He has not made us all alike, He has made the distinctions, and we cannot remove them. We must honor them.

Leaving her lovely home, we went up the hill to her grave and laid a wreath on her tombstone. It was all so simple and so quiet there, and the compassionate, warm heart of Jenny Lind still seemed to beat as I stood before her.

Leaving England then for Switzerland, we boarded the Engadine Express at Paris and sat complacently back in our seats on the train, watching the countryside fly past. Everything was fine. The year had been full and rewarding, the weather was wonderful, and Sils-Maria was a few hours away. Suddenly the train gave a tremendous lurch, and we were thrown from our seats. The cars screeched to a standstill.

For the next half hour I hurried from passenger to passenger, applying bandages, stopping wounds, and helping where I could. My early training at Dr. Schaper's was helpful now. Will and I were not injured at all, but many of the passengers were badly cut. It all seemed to make life more precious than ever, and when we finally boarded another train for Switzerland, we felt as if we had been given a gift of great value.

Summer passed all too quickly, and after my three autumn concerts in London, at Queen's Hall and at Albert Hall, we sailed for America on the SS *Olympic.* I remember this trip because we gave a concert of the three Hs— Hempel, Hofmann, and Huberman—for the Seamen's Fund. Chaliapin also took part in the concert, and we were told that more than three thousand dollars had been collected, representing the largest sum ever realized at a ship's concert.

For this 1922–23 season my manager scheduled me for more than forty Jenny Lind concerts, in addition to my regular concerts, which were now of course somewhat curtailed in number. But before beginning my tour, I sang five concerts with the Boston Symphony Orchestra in Canada and in Boston.

The city of Boston was the home of the finest symphony orchestra in America. The achievements of this organization were indeed equal to those of any European orchestra, and I felt it to be a great honor to sing with these

"Jenny Linds of past and present: Frieda Hempel visits grave of famous song bird. Photo shows the famous living soprano, Frieda Hempel, formerly of the Metropolitan Opera Company, who has made her success through the impersonations of the inspired Jenny Lind on the operatic stage. Laying flowers on the grave of Jenny Lind at Great Malvern, England." Press release dated 27 June 1922. PHOTO BY UNDERWOOD & UNDERWOOD. COURTESY METROPOLITAN OPERA ARCHIVES.

outstanding musicians. For this series of concerts Pierre Monteux was the conductor, and I enjoyed singing Mozart under his masterful baton.

I continued to appear as soloist with the Boston Symphony for many years, singing Mozart, operatic arias, and oratorios. And I remember so well the time I sang with Serge Koussevitzky in *Messiah* with Kathryn Meisle and Charles Hackett. We had a private rehearsal with Koussevitzky, and much to our amazement he confessed that he had never conducted Handel's *Messiah* before. He modestly asked us to help him, especially at those places in the score where we turn from recitative to aria. We did this willingly, and when he faced his orchestra later on, he made no mistakes, and everything went smoothly. I have always found that the greater artists are the more modest artists. No false pride hampers them as they learn.

During the forty-two seasons that the Boston Symphony Orchestra had been playing, it had never appeared outside of New England. This trip to Toronto and Montreal, the first of many, was something of an event for members of the orchestra as it was for me. It was my world fame that I had to live up to in Toronto and in Montreal, for I had never sung in Canada. And indeed the performances were successful. A reviewer compared my scales to "a string of perfectly matched pearls" and called me "the ideal interpreter of Mozart."

Following four Jenny Lind concerts in the northern states, I again sang with the Symphony Orchestra in Boston. And a week later, on 3 December, I returned there to sing my Jenny Lind concert. I was quite anxious about this concert, for the Bostonians were very straight-laced, and I wondered if a concert in costume would appeal to them.

H. T. Parker commented in the *Boston Evening Transcript* that I had given many concerts in his city that were more interesting, but none that was more entertaining. He adds, "The real feast of Sunday was Miss Hempel's singing of pieces that suited her voice and skill and fancy no less than they had Mademoiselle Lind."

By this time I had altered the program a little, adding some Schubert and Schumann, which Jenny Lind had sung in her concerts, and "Ave Maria" as well as several encores, all of which Jenny had sung. I no longer included the duet for piano, nor the duet with baritone. Mr. Bos, Mr. Louis P. Fritze, and I were the only performing artists. We no longer used an orchestra, and no actor appeared as P. T. Barnum. These extra elements were too costly. But the costumes, the large velvet banner saying, "Welcome, Sweet Warbler," the usherettes in costume, the nosegays, and the printed programs in imitation of Jenny Lind's programs were all retained. So Mr. Parker heard his lovely songs and was entertained as well by the "excursion into the past," as he phrased it.

Before going to Boston for this concert, I had given a Carnegie Hall recital with great success. As H. E. Krehbiel wrote, "Everybody present seemed to be having a good time, especially Miss Hempel, who bore out a youthful appearance and animated manner by being in excellent vocal trim." I had so many good friends and admirers in New York City that it was a delight to sing there, and of course I enjoyed myself. "As long as Miss Hempel continues to sing as she sings now, and has sung, the lovers of the fine art of song may be comforted and reflect that the art has not yet entirely disappeared," wrote Richard Aldrich. And W. J. Henderson said, "Miss Hempel's voice was always beautiful, but it was not always as opulent in color or as fully charged with expressive eloquence as now. It is a voice in the splendor of its maturity, backed by a richly endowed musical organization."

If I had read all of these wonderful reviews then, I wonder how they would have affected me. At that time, my mind was constantly on the next concert, and I never stopped to wonder much about what the critics were saying. The day after the Carnegie Hall recital, I was headed for Baltimore, then Brooklyn, then Boston, then to Syracuse. What time had I to think back? Packing, traveling, practicing in the drawing room of the train, sleeping in a different bed each night, resting when I could, seeing reporters, and striving to be even more perfect at each concert—all these were my daily activities. Perhaps, if I had read them, I would not have sung so well, for I would have relaxed a little, I am afraid.

It was midnight when my good Rosa and I returned from Syracuse on 6 December 1922. We were met by my husband at the station. He had a magnificent sense of humor, and he managed to make us laugh and forget the trials of travel and performance. This night he told us in all seriousness that I had been robbed of all my furs and jewels. Tired as I was, I managed to laugh and say, "That would be just all I need. Please, Will, don't joke about something like that!"

But he kept right on, saying that my very expensive chinchilla fur was gone, and all my fur pieces, my beautiful old table silver, all my decorations, and many other things. He did not smile as he told me this, and suddenly I began to sense that he was not joking. He was telling the truth. By the time we arrived home, I was fully aware of the meaning of his words. While he was in his office and I was in Syracuse, somebody had broken in through a bedroom window that looked out over the roof of the next building. Of course the window had been fully protected with strong iron bars, but the thief had somehow managed to pry them off. He must have known just how much time he would have for his job.

My concert gowns were all on the floor; the contents of my bureau and dresser drawers were scattered across the room. It was fortunate for me that most of my jewels were not left in the apartment, for I had had them with me for my concerts. I was not fully insured, and I suffered a great financial loss, but the thing that upset me most was the loss of my wonderful chinchilla coat, which I could never replace.

Some months later the burglar was apprehended. He turned out to be New York's Matinee Burglar, Thomas F. Belford. My home was only one of many he had robbed, and like me, the other victims were also of the theater. This "gentleman," as he chose to call himself, wrote a story for the newspapers, called "Entertaining Confessions of a Matinee Burglar," in which he described his burglaries:

Hempel in fur, probably ermine or mink. PHOTO BY HARLIP. COURTESY METROPOLITAN OPERA ARCHIVES.

In the course of my many entries into the apartments of many of the well-known theatrical people, I came across many things of interest. In the solitary stillness of the actresses' apartments I found that I was sharing the most intimate secrets of many stars which only God, the star, and myself knew. . . .

Of course, to a matinee burglar the time when Miss Hempel was robbed was very unpropitious, since everybody knows that when a lovely lady of the opera travels to sing, she must take most of her jewelry with her, and is likely to put many of her other valuables in a safe until she returns. Therefore, that the Hempel house yielded a $40,000 return, with the mistress out of town, speaks for the solid character of the singer.

At the time of the robbery I felt certain that this had not been an ordinary thief. "There's a woman in this," I told reporters. "No ordinary burglar would confuse my intimate wearing apparel with valuables. The wretch has left me without a stocking, except for the ones I am standing in!"

The year sped to an end, and the spring of 1923 found me as busy as ever. Our Jenny Lind concerts were overwhelmingly successful everywhere. In large cities as well as in small towns, we faced packed auditoriums.

Our advance advertising was unusual. The main department stores in each city where we were to appear devoted a large window to a manikin dressed in a copy of my Jenny Lind dress. In a corner stood a placard saying simply, "Jenny Lind." A week later an announcement of my coming Hempel–Jenny Lind concert would appear in the papers. Before the concert, a group of young girls in the city, daughters of the prominent families, would be selected to act as usherettes, and they, too, would appear in costume. The presence of these society girls, feeling proud and important, would bring the concert closer to the listeners and make them feel more at home and relaxed.

We took our large velvet banner, saying, "Welcome, Sweet Warbler," and hung it above the stage whenever we appeared, and so brought Jenny Lind to life. We always gave free tickets to those persons who had heard Jenny Lind herself, and these wonderful elderly guests were given seats of honor near the stage. I loved to talk with them after the concert and hear them recall their experiences.

At a concert in Kansas City on 23 January 1923, I was given a new name which I loved to use. At a ceremony preceding the concert, I was honored by the Camp Fire Girls, and given an Indian name. This name, Wi-Nish-Ta, meant "To Sing All the Night," and I found it to be quite descriptive. It soon became one of Will's pet names for me, which he loved to use at the end of a long and trying tour. And we did laugh together about its appropriateness.

In April we gave a second New York Jenny Lind concert, this time at the Hippodrome before an audience of five thousand people. I would like to quote just one article, for it skillfully evaluates my Jenny Lind concerts:

> The days of sweet song are past, and when Mme Hempel offers us a Jenny Lind program she offers not half, but twice what Lind had to offer, for she adds to the sweetness and virtuosity of Lind the dramatic force, fervor, passion, the entire modernistic, post-Wagnerian point of view of Hempel.
>
> The Hempel-Lind program is an idealization, a reconstruction. It gives a picture of the past fitted to modern eyes and ears. It is a masterpiece in miniature, and serves a useful purpose.
>
> In her march forward Frieda Hempel still has time to look back to do honor to one who carried the banner of art in olden days.

The city of Springfield, Massachusetts, held very special memories of Jenny Lind, for she had sung there in 1851. Enthusiasm for my Jenny Lind concert was tremendous, and when I arrived in that city on 7 April 1923 for a concert to be given that same evening, I was met by a magnificent coach, drawn by four handsome white horses. This coach had carried Jenny Lind to her rooms in the Warriner's Tavern, and now it had been taken out of the city's museum to bring me to the same hotel. When I arrived at this lovely old building, I appeared on a balcony, standing where Jenny Lind had stood, and received the homage of two hundred school children, all dressed in white, singing "America" in their best school-day voices, just as school children had sung for Jenny, seventy-one years before.

The programs contained an additional page, describing the details of Jenny Lind's visit to Springfield and the festivities connected with it. The concert was, in a sense, a civic celebration, and for the residents who had never heard Jenny herself, it was a gratifying experience, judging from the applause and the excitement. A Springfield reviewer commented:

> There is no other singer who holds the peculiar place that Jenny Lind held in the middle of the 19th century, and as certainly there is no singer of our time who would be preferred to Frieda Hempel for a program in honor of Jenny Lind. The costumes and the stage manners of Frieda Hempel and her associates were perfection itself, and the illusion of an old-time concert was masterfully created.

Mr. Bos wore tan trousers, a brown swallow-tailed coat, and a tan brocaded waistcoat. Mr. Fritze, my flutist, wore grey trousers, a blue coat, and a deep purple brocaded waistcoat. Both wore the high collar and florid tie of the period. They looked wonderful!

I had sung in London in June and again in October of 1922, as I have said, and now I was engaged in 1923 to give two Jenny Lind concerts (the first two of many Jenny Lind concerts I was to sing in England) on 27 May and 21 October 1923. Lionel Powell was my manager in England. He was the famous English impresario who managed Dame Clara Butt, Luisa Tetrazzini, Fritz Kreisler, Jascha Heifetz, and many other great artists. He had come to New York in 1922 and had called to see me at my apartment. He had heard of my great successes, and he wished to engage me for London. But he was a man well-versed in the ways of publicity agents, and he wanted to hear me and judge for himself. Only the greatest of internationally known singers and instrumentalists could fill the Albert Hall, which seats nine thousand people, and for this reason I had to be as good as my reputation.

Of all the things I might have sung for him, he only wanted to hear "The Last Rose of Summer." "If you can sing that to my satisfaction, I shall be seeing you in London," he told me. He knew the voices of Patti and Tetrazzini, and so he was in a very good position to judge. He was also a very fine violinist as well as an excellent manager, and knew much more about concerts than just the box-office reports. He had to engage spectacular artists who filled the halls, but he also appreciated very much the fineness of real art.

I never felt lonely in London. I stayed at the Ritz and was very happy

Madame Frieda Hempel.

	OCT. 192_		NOV. 192_		DEC. 192_
1		1		1	
2		Mon 2	Dundee	2	
3		3		Thur 3	Hanley
Sun 4	Royal Albert Hall	Wed 4	Newcastle-on-Tyne	Fri 4	Oxford
5		Thur 5	Middlesboro'	Sat 5	Alexandra Palace
6		6		Sun 6	
Wed 7	Nottingham	7		Mon 7	
Thur 8	Sheffield	Sun 8	London R.A.H.	Tues 8	
9		9		Wed 9	
Sat 10	Cardiff	10		Thur 10	
11		Wed 11	Bradford	Fri 11	Eastbourne PARIS.
Mon 12	Leicester	Thur 12	Halifax	Sat 12	
13		13		Sun 13	
14		Sat 14	Manchester	Mon 14	
Thur 15	Hull	15		Tues 15	
16		16		Wed 16	
17		17		Thur 17	Northampton
18		18		18	
Mon 19	Bristol	19		19	
Tues 20	Eastbourne	Fri 20	Berlin.	20	
21		Sat 21		21	
Thur 22	Liverpool	Sun 22	leave B.	22	
23		Mon 23	Zurich	23	
Sat 24	Dublin	Tues 24	Birmingham	24	
25		25		25	
Mon 26	Belfast	Thur 26	Cambridge	26	
27		27		27	
28		Sat 28	Manchester	28	
Thur 29	Glasgow	Sun 29	London R.A.H.	29	
30		30		30	
Sat 31	Edinburgh			31	

Handwritten schedule for the Jenny Lind concerts. COURTESY EDDIE RUHL.

during those beautiful spring days. It always struck me as curious that the stage in Albert Hall was so tiny. It was as if I stood on a platform in front of nine thousand people gathered in that huge auditorium. I never forced my voice, in spite of the great depths of the hall: one critic had remarked that the tones of my voice as I sang "Sandmännchen" by Brahms "crept into every corner of the hall like a little mouse."

My first Jenny Lind concert in London was attended by many persons of royalty. Lord Aberdare, Lady Florence Pery, Lady Fairbain, Sir Albert Seymour, Lady Michelham, Lady Southesk, Lady Mary Carnegie, Lord Leigh, and many other personages came to hear me. Nellie Melba was also present, as well as Edward Johnson, later manager of the Metropolitan Opera Company.

Jenny Lind had been England's favorite for more than forty years, and there was much controversy regarding my impersonation of her. The origin of these Hempel-Lind concerts had been explained to the public, but still the London music lovers reserved the right to judge for themselves the fitness of our conception of 1923:

> Only an artist whose position in the song world was assured could have dared what Frieda Hempel did, and did most successfully at the Albert Hall. Anybody less accomplished would have incurred the charge of showmanship; but she, having little to gain and much to lose by adopting such methods, is entitled to be judged solely by the resultant effort, which was not only quite charming, but reconciled us to that part of her program which is perennially a bone of contention with musicians. In no ordinary way do we want to hear Bellini's "Casta Diva," or renew acquaintance with Meyerbeer's "L'Étoile du Nord," but wafted back by ocular illusion to the days when such things were admired, one does—as the contemporaries did—admire them. There is, of course, the reservation that they must be done as well as Frieda Hempel did them. In short, it was delightful.

The critic for the *Daily Express* wrote: "It is not easy to write about a singer who is the best of her kind in the world, so let us say that Frieda Hempel has the most lovely lyrical voice of her day, and leave it at that. Her concert at the Albert Hall was something more than a success—it was a triumph."

Frieda Hempel bobbed her hair in 1924, a daring change. COURTESY METROPOLITAN OPERA ARCHIVES.

CHAPTER NINETEEN

Remembering the Twenties

I was happy to get back to New York with its colorful fall sunsets and its crisp, clear days. I had a full 1923–24 season of Hempel-Lind concerts in front of me as well as orchestral engagements and a few regular concerts. I also made several recordings for the Edison Company. But first I had the fun of seeing and enjoying New York for a while with Will, whom I had missed during the summer months while I was in Europe. We dined out, went to the theater, entertained, and walked in Central Park. Feeding the squirrels in the park has always been among my great joys, and I bought peanuts, raw peanuts of course, for they contain more oil, in fifty-pound sacks. When I was away from New York, Will had to feed the squirrels for me, but while I was at home, I never let a day pass without making certain that the squirrels had their food. And of course, if I went out to feed the squirrels, I had to feed the pigeons as well!

Pitti still traveled with me, and whenever we left from Grand Central Station, we never failed to say hello to Mr. Egan. He was the stationmaster, and he had granted me a very special concession in allowing me to keep Pitti with me in my drawing room. The dog was so tiny that he fitted into what looked like a small jewel case, and I carried him in this case as I boarded the train. Mr. Egan knew about Pitti, but the various conductors-in-charge did not. Therefore, once the train pulled out of Grand Central Station, Pitti had to be on his guard. Whenever somebody knocked at the door, he would dash to his case and scramble inside. Not a sound would be heard from him until whoever had entered my drawing room had left. He was so clever and so cute that we always complimented Pitti when he emerged cautiously from his elegant place of hiding and looked around as if to say, "Well, can I come out now?"

I had always enjoyed going to Chicago, where I had such dear friends in Harold and Robert McCormick. But now I disliked going there, and for good reason. On my last trip to the West, which had taken place in the spring of this year, 1923, I had, of necessity, stopped over a day in Chicago. I arrived there early in the morning and did not leave by train until late that same day. So I decided to take rooms in the Drake Hotel for Rosa and me, for the day.

After having unpacked some of our things, I called the bellboy and asked for some ice water. Pitti, who had traveled in his little jewel case, was now romping around the room, and I forgot to tell him to hide. Of course the bellboy reported this third guest to the management, and immediately I was visited by the manager, who informed me curtly that the dog could not stay with me.

I was terribly tired, and I did not want to move to another hotel. And after all, Pitti only weighed five pounds. He could not do much damage to the furniture, and he was a gentleman in his ways. Couldn't we please stay? I would pay for any damage. No, it was impossible; I would have to move. I offered to send Pitti to Rosa, whose room was of course much less elegant, but that would not do, either. Well, I simply refused to move, and I asked the "gentleman" to leave.

A detective was put in front of my door, and my telephone was cut off. I was furious, and I stormed out of the hotel to find a phone, so that I could call Harold McCormick and get some help. He was enraged when he heard how this hotel manager had treated me. He sent a car immediately and had my things transferred to the Congress Hotel. Here I was warmly greeted by the manager, who was only too happy to have me as his guest. A beautiful floral arrangement was sent up to my room, and I was treated with the utmost courtesy. Pitti was made most welcome, and we were very comfortable there.

I was still crying bitterly when Harold met me at the Congress Hotel, and he insisted on taking me to see *Tea for Two* in order to cheer me up a little. It was not long before we were laughing together, and all was forgotten for the time being.

But ever since then, the Drake Hotel has symbolized something inhuman and unfeeling. I never recommended the Drake Hotel to my friends after that experience. How inhuman people can be! After all, a well-trained pet animal is as worthy of respect as any human. In Germany, animals are even allowed in the dining rooms. Any civilized person knows how to watch his dog, and I find some people, with their uncouth manners, far more objectionable than any dog. I cannot forgive injustice to animals. When I next came to Chicago in December of 1923, it was the Congress Hotel that had my patronage.

For my Chicago concert on 5 December I planned an aria that Mr. Henderson had praised in New York the week before. Regarding a cadenza that I sang in Meyerbeer's "Shadow Song," Mr. Henderson had written in the *Sun*: "The soprano delivered a chromatic scale, twice ascending and descending the octave in one breath, with flawless accuracy and smoothness and with irresistible elan. It was a burst of old-fashioned florid song such as one very rarely hears in these days. And the artist sang the entire number brilliantly." Galli-Curci, whose concert was scheduled for 9 December, also included this aria on her program, and so of course there was much interest in my singing of it: "When the singer gave the 'Shadow Song' from *Dinorah*, she made her hearers fairly gasp by a cadenza which no one seemed to remember and which took the chromatic scale twice up and down in one breath. It was sung flawlessly and with a flexibility as rare as it is beautiful." Edward Moore wrote in the *Tribune*:

To the world at large she classifies as a coloratura, but this is only a part of the truth. For, while she sings both high and low with all the sky-rocketing fireballs of coloratura display, she does other things with the same degree of ability. One will seldom hear much better Mozart singing than Miss Hempel accomplished with the aria "Deh vieni, non tardar." It was restrained but supple, vital without the aid of any interpolated high notes, in good taste and good tone.

My one deviation from the classical concert platform occurred in Detroit on 13 December 1923. Following an appearance with the Detroit Symphony Orchestra, I stepped upon the theatrical stage to join, for a brief time, the Ziegfield Follies. The Detroit Athletic Club had scheduled a benefit performance of the "Follies of 1923" for their Christmas Fund, and I had been asked to appear. I accepted. When I announced that I had joined the company and was going to sing, all the male members of the company insisted on escorting me to the footlights. I sang "Way Down Upon the Swanee River," "Carry Me Back to Old Virginny," and "Dixie." As Charles Pike Sawyer put it in the *New York Post*, "Her singing of 'Dixie' finished them, on stage and off. Nobody wanted anything more but Hempel, but, you see, she had given her three numbers, called for in two-a-day contracts, and the show had to go on."

Spring of 1924 was memorable in one way. It had become quite impossible for me to keep my hair in condition, as I was giving as many as twelve Jenny Lind concerts in one month. The constant application of gold powder to the hair above my forehead, and the continuous grooming of my long hair in a way different from that to which it was accustomed, had made it unruly and bothersome. So one day, in Nashville, Tennessee, of all places, I just walked into a beauty parlor and said, "I want my hair bobbed!"

In no time at all the long silky tresses were snipped off, and my hair fell loosely around my neck in soft waves. I did not tell Will of my plans, and his anger at seeing me shorn of my beautiful hair was quite frightening. It took a good deal of courage to bob one's hair in those days, and few men approved of the new style, but Will soon became reconciled to what was after all an accomplished fact, not to be remedied for some time. At the same time, I purchased a sort of toupee which fitted across the front of my head, on the top of my own hair. It enabled me to look like Jenny Lind for an evening, without upsetting my own hairdo, and it made everything so much simpler. There was much comment in the press about my daring new haircut, and I suppose many angry husbands blamed me for the bobbing of their wives' hair. I only hope that the women enjoyed the new style as much as I did.

My first visit to Palm Beach, Florida, in 1924 was delightful. This beautiful place seemed like paradise. The waving palms, the warm, calm ocean with its stretch of dazzling white beach, the magnificent mansions, the Everglades Club, and Bradleys Gambling Casino were all part of an atmosphere I had never before known. One could sense that people had come here to rest and to play. It was so easygoing, and there was no sense of pressure. First there would be morning bathing in the ocean, then luncheon on a veranda, followed by an afternoon rest, and then cocktails and a dinner party, perhaps at the Everglades Club.

At that time, this club was very exclusive and elegant. Every guest had to be personally invited by some member. A well-known orchestra would play for dancing in the open, and outstanding artists would entertain during the floor show. There were wonderful lighting effects, which reminded me of the famous Château de Paris in Paris. And at the tables sat persons of fame or fortune, beautiful women and elegant gentlemen.

I met Mrs. Ed Hutton at this time. She was one of America's richest women as well as one of the most beautiful, and later married Ambassador Davies. She invited me quite often to visit her handsome estate near Palm Beach. And on several occasions Beniamino Gigli and I spent happy evenings there, for I went to Palm Beach for a few weeks each year following this first enchanting visit.

Mrs. Davies was famous for her magnificent costume balls. Everyone came in costume, and of course I appeared as Jenny Lind. Hundreds of guests were present, and I always enjoyed myself thoroughly. I had little time during tours to just let go and have fun, and so when I came to Palm Beach, usually in February, I participated in these social events with great verve and pleasure.

Mr. Stotesbury's birthday was always celebrated at this time of year, and I sang "Happy Birthday" to him. He was a prominent Philadelphia banker and an active participant in the Palm Beach social affairs at that time. I met other socially prominent persons as well: the Walter Chryslers; Mr. Willys, the automobile manufacturer; Jules Bache, the banker; Mrs. Hay-

warth, the beautiful blonde wife of Colonel Haywarth; Mr. and Mrs. Atwater Kent; and others.

At Bradleys I had the most fun, and I was often reminded of those days
in Ostende, where I had first ventured to gamble at the tables. Walter
Chrysler, a most charming man, generous and kind, loved to supply me
with chips, and whenever he noticed that my supply was running low,
because of an unlucky streak, he rushed to my side and gave me a new stack
of chips. It was so gallant of him that I did not spoil his pleasure by refusing.
In fact, it was much more fun this way, and to win was all the more exciting.
Emil Winters, or perhaps Frank Storres, or Arthur Hopkins would be at a
table with me, and we all found it amusing to win or lose.

I was frequently with the Walter Chryslers, and, curiously enough, years
later I met the daughter of the locomotive manufacturer Mr. McNaughton.
Laura McNaughton and I have since become close friends, and she told me
that her father had employed Walter Chrysler as a brakeman, and that he
had worked for the railroad before going into the automobile business.

During the short weeks spent in Palm Beach each year, I received many
social invitations, and it was my pleasure to return these invitations whenever I was in New York at the same time these friends were. I recall one evening when I entertained Mr. Chrysler as well as Otto H. Kahn, Harold
McCormick, Mrs. Parish, and Mrs. Ann Austin, the wife of Dr. Austin of
Greenwich. She was a beautiful, intelligent woman, and we became close
friends. She opened up her heart to me, and spoke with me of her great un-
happiness. I was sad when I learned of her tragic death in an automobile
accident. Her daughter, Mrs. Luce, later Ambassador to Italy, had at that
time just begun to write, and I often saw her working, surrounded with
manuscript pages. How proud Mrs. Austin would have been if she had been
able to share her daughter's great success. Palm Beach is no longer what it
was, and I have not been there for many years, but I remember it fondly.

On 1 June 1924, we all sailed for Europe, to be gone this time for seven
months. The apartment was mothproofed and all the furniture covered,
with windows sealed against dust and rain. The packing for this trip was
more difficult than usual: winter clothes had to be taken along as well as
several Jenny Lind dresses, for I was to tour England in the fall with my
Hempel-Lind concerts.

We spent the summer in Sils-Maria, as always. This summer, however,
my father came to visit with us. I did not want to take the time to go to Berlin to see him, and I knew that he would enjoy a trip to the mountains. He
was wonderful company, and he walked with us often on our jaunts through
the valleys.

On one of these lovely walks I met Mr. Stokowski and his wife, Olga
Samaroff. He had a bundle of edelweiss in his hands, and he gave me these

flowers. This was quite a present, when you realize how hard they are to find. They grow high in the mountains, and it is always dangerous to climb to pick them from their hiding places. They are beautiful, delicate little flowers, and I still have them pressed between the leaves of a book.

Early in July, Pitti fell ill. I was heartbroken, and I sat with him day and night, trying to nurse him back to health. But it was to no avail. His strength gradually failed, and he died early one morning. I buried him in a little grave, high up in the mountains, weeping bitter tears for the loss of this wonderful, faithful, innocent companion of many, many years.

Lionel Powell heard of the death of my beloved dog, and one day he appeared in St. Moritz, bringing with him an adorable little Pomeranian, weighing about five pounds at the most. She had a beautiful blond coat, and she was so petite and alert that I accepted her gratefully. Mr. Powell evidently knew how much I loved my four-footed friends, and he did not want to let me suffer too much. He was a wonderfully understanding person.

Early in October I left for Paris, from where I would fly to Hull, England, for my first concert on the twenty-third of the month. While in Paris, I learned of a strict quarantine of dogs in England because of an outbreak of rabies. I was in no mood to be parted from my little Betsy, and so I evolved a plan to get her into England with me. First of all, I searched the city for a lynx coat to match the color of Betsy's fur. When I carried her under this coat, in my arms, she would not be spotted so easily if she peeked out at the wrong time. Secondly, I had Betsy sedated so that she would sleep. I had heard that Sarah Bernhardt had always done this with her dogs so that she could carry them under her coat without detection. Sweet soul, she, too, knew how difficult it was to part from such friends.

As we finally boarded the plane, Betsy snuggled under my coat and fell fast asleep. To my relief no one saw her, but shortly before landing, we suddenly hit an air pocket. The plane took a sickening dip, and Betsy woke up and began to whimper. She poked her head out from under my coat and begged for help. I was quite airsick myself, but the stewardess came to our rescue. She must have loved dogs also, for she did not betray our secret.

When we landed, I tucked Betsy under my coat again and rushed for the gate where Mr. Powell awaited us. He drew the attention of the gatekeeper by firing questions at him, and the poor man had no time to notice the bundle under my coat. Our ruse succeeded, and Betsy, who certainly had no rabies, traveled on with us.

CHAPTER TWENTY

Great Britain

*T*he *1924 tour,* beginning in Hull and ending at Eastbourne on 16 December, encompassed thirty concerts. I was one of several artists touring the country that season under the auspices of the International Celebrity Series managed by Mr. Powell and his associate, Mr. Holt. Among the other artists appearing were Dame Clara Butt, Fritz Kreisler, Wilhelm Backhaus, and Amelita Galli-Curci. Galli-Curci preceded me by one week in most of the cities, and the others followed throughout the season.

We traveled by train, but because I was so accustomed to the long, tiring train trips in America, these short jaunts from city to city were almost enjoyable.

I was quite surprised to discover how old-fashioned the hotels were, but I did not mind. On the contrary, I liked the quaintness, and it was fun to stay in a room like my grandfather might have had. When I entered a hotel, the chambermaid would follow me to my room, place the luggage there, and then say to me, "Oh, Madame, I would advise that you wait downstairs for half an hour. I have to make a fire, and I don't think you would enjoy the smoke from the fireplace." Sometimes, when we arrived late at night, it was not comfortable to sit up and wait, but the smoke from the fires burned my throat and choked me, and I could not afford to irritate my voice.

I don't think Empress Josephine could have made more commotion with her scented baths at Versailles than I did with my requests for a hot bath after an evening concert. Hot water had to be carried up to my rooms in pails, and with typical English apology, my bath would be prepared. And this was so unlike life in America that it had a certain charm and color.

Mr. Bos frequently registered for me at these hotels, and sometimes he would write the date of my birth as 1821, which was of course the date of Jenny Lind's birth. That would make me 103 years old, yet nobody ever commented on my youthful appearance. But we had fun with this little joke anyway, and Mr. Bos enjoyed his humor.

I must say that I preferred to sing in England in the spring. The winter fogs were so thick in London that often, when I was riding with Mr. Powell in his car, the driver would have to get out and walk in front of us so that we could follow behind safely, Mr. Powell taking the wheel. It looked as though the world were tumbling down when, at noontime, big bonfires were lit in the middle of the streets, casting a weird glow on the dark, heavy fog. It was so theatrical and so mysterious that I enjoyed it at first, but I preferred the renowned English springtime.

The cold of winter also gave me some concern. One very cold night when deep snow was on the ground, I gave a concert at Alexandria Palace in London. This auditorium is as large as Madison Square Garden in New York City, and it was unheated! I faced the audience with bare shoulders and evening gown, and I steamed like an engine every time I opened my mouth. To avoid pneumonia I finally had to put on my fur coat, and I finished the concert all bundled up. The audience shivered and so did I, but we stuck it out together to the last moment. They all came to hear me, and they all stayed. Afterward, I went back to the Hotel Ritz and had a good champagne dinner, thus avoiding any illness.

In general, the concert halls in England are wonderful to sing in. They are of normal size, and they have excellent acoustics. In particular, I liked the halls in Liverpool, Manchester, and Birmingham, where I felt so close to my audiences. They stimulated me in a very special way with their warmth and their enthusiasm. The musical audience in England is like no other audience in the world. Once it has taken you to its heart, it never forgets you. It is wonderfully loyal. I loved to sing in England.

As I said, train travel was quite comfortable there. The compartments were cozy, and our little group, consisting of my husband, my secretary Miss Lois Willoughby, my maid Rosa, and me, was well taken care of. Also traveling with us were of course Mr. Bos and my Australian flutist John Amadio, the greatest of flute virtuosos.

Mr. Amadio entered into the spirit of the concerts willingly, and if Mr. Fritze's costume had fitted him, he would have worn it with pride, I am certain. But he was much taller than Mr. Fritze. As it was, he looked very handsome in his black swallowtail, high collar, and lace tie. He carried three flutes with him—one of gold, one of silver, and one of wood—which he played interchangeably, much to the delight of the audience. He was a great showman, and both he and Mr. Bos played solos at each concert, allowing me time to rest a little. I was very fortunate to have two such excellent musicians with me on this tour.

Amadio was amused at our reactions to English food, for of course he was quite satisfied with it. But I confess that I was not, and out of desperation, I ate practically nothing. Cheddar cheese! I cannot stand the sight of it any more. Mutton, cabbage, and cheddar cheese were the constant bill of fare on the trains, and this food was much too heavy and dreary for me.

Most of my appearances with Mr. Amadio and Mr. Bos were as Jenny Lind. I had originally intended to sing only a few Jenny Lind concerts in England and to give a much greater number of straight Hempel concerts. But the demand for the Jenny Lind concerts was so great that Mr. Powell booked us for these in all the major cities.

There had been some difficulty with the daughter of Jenny Lind, who had publicly protested this use of her mother's name.* I thought this rather foolish, for I was bringing the name of Jenny Lind back into notice in the most artistic way, and she had every reason to be grateful. This protest kindled a heated controversy in the press, and many important newspapers defended us in our endeavor to recapture for the English audiences the spirit of the days of the great favorite. Others objected to what they called "showmanship," but the public decided in our favor, and the halls were filled to capacity in each city.

Our program for these Jenny Lind concerts differed somewhat from the original program that we had followed in Carnegie Hall. The "Dedication to America," the flute duet, the piano duet, the orchestra, and the impersonation of P. T. Barnum were omitted. We now presented favorite songs and encores of Jenny Lind.

The program included the aria from *The Marriage of Figaro* of Mozart, Handel's "Oh, Had I Jubal's Lyre," the "Shadow Song" from *Dinorah* of Meyerbeer, "Ave Maria" and "Die Forelle" of Schubert, sung in German, "Der Nussbaum" of Schumann, sung in English, "The Last Rose of Summer," and the "Herdsman's Song." Sometimes I sang the beautiful Vesper Hymn. For encores, I sang popular songs such as "Dixie," "Way Down Upon the Swanee River," Taubert's "Bird Song," and other Lind favorites. I confess that "The Blue Danube Waltz" was so frequently requested that I sang it, even though Jenny had never sung it. I always closed with "Home, Sweet Home."

We opened our tour in Hull with tremendous success, and we knew, from that time on, that the objections of a few persons had not in any way

---

*In 1926 Jenny M. C. (Mrs. Raymond) Maude, O.B.E., published a biography of her mother (*The Life of Jenny Lind*) in which there is no mention of Frieda Hempel. *Ed.*

dissuaded people from attending my concerts. "The visit of Miss Hempel caused something of a sensation," wrote the critic in Hull, and this phrase was echoed in newspapers wherever I appeared. In Liverpool, a critic commented: "One felt that this was a genuine act of homage from one artist to another. This new Jenny Lind has a voice of exquisite purity. If Jenny Lind was a better artist—if she had a finer vocal instrument than Miss Hempel—then she must have been a heaven-sent singer."

On 26 October I gave my own recital, appearing as Frieda Hempel at Albert Hall in London. Such was the enthusiasm in the crowded auditorium that I had to sing two encores after every song on the program, and the encores at the close of the program seemed endless to me. I could not give them enough. The *Times* critic wrote:

> Miss Hempel showed us at once, in "Oh, Had I Jubal's Lyre," how lovely coloratura singing can be. Her voice is extraordinarily flexible and true, while its quality is warm and capable of great variety of color. She has the power of making the finest pianissimo clearly audible throughout the hall, and perhaps her most wonderful achievement was her singing of Brahms's "Sandmännchen," an exquisite miniature that reduced the vast auditorium to an intimate drawing room.

I treasure my many notices from Ernest Newman, that gifted music critic of London. He was a great musician, and his writings reflected grand judgment and knowledge. He was quick to praise my singing of German lieder, noting the finest details of phrasing and coloring and commenting on them in a masterful way. His reviews in the *Times* were definitive.

The *Evening Standard* reviewer declared, "Mme Frieda Hempel is a great—a very great—singer," and the *London Telegraph* printed, "All this was as near perfection of vocalization, of beauty of tone, of phrasing as is humanly possible. It was, in a word, a crowded hour of glorious life that Mme Hempel gave us yesterday, and such hours are all too rare."

I always had great success with my lieder in London. One must not make the mistake of considering the English unmusical. In no other country are German composers so deeply appreciated and honored. And in London, when I sang these songs of Schubert, Schumann, and Brahms, the people seemed to hang on my lips and absorb every tone. They were warm, almost Latin, in their expression of appreciation. A review in the London *Referee* of 9 November 1924 describes this English awareness of tonal quality:

> The three most important elements of attraction are beauty of tone, ease of delivery, and the conveyance of the spirit of the song interpreted. In no country is the quality of musical tone more keenly expected than in England. It is the first element to excite attention in an English audience. In Italy, it is power that tells; in France, the dramatic timbre; in

Germany, heaviness. Ease of delivery means a perfected technique, and the expression of the spiritual part of the song is the result of clear thinking. The enthusiasm created by the singing of Mme Frieda Hempel should impress young singers with these facts.

Betsy, who traveled with us, was the one privileged "person" who remained in my dressing room during a concert. After the concert, when excited friends and admirers flocked to greet me, she would retreat into her jewel case and watch us from the safety of that sanctuary. She would not come out at all, unless Will came into the room, and then she would rush to greet him and to be taken up in his arms. There she would let herself be admired and petted by the guests, paying no attention to the fact that it was I who had given the concert. At her first concert in London, Betsy made many friends, and by the end of the season, after I had sung seven London concerts, she was among the most famous dogs in the city. She was present during all my interviews with the press, and she was such a delightful little bit of a thing that she captured the hearts of all.

Following my second London appearance at Queen's Hall, on 2 November, I sang in Birmingham. Here again, the Jenny Lind concert was received with great interest:

> Miss Hempel attracted a large audience, easily succeeding in putting them in a state of rapture, which, let us hasten to explain, was a quite legitimate success earned by the extraordinary beauty of voice, skillfully managed, and certainly one of the most seductive of the half-century to date. As an artist, she is excellent in the Jenny Lind pieces, and one wonders if Jenny could possibly have been any better.

Belfast and Dublin were next. Unfortunately, I had so little time in Ireland, only three days, that I could not capture any impressions of the country or of its people. My Jenny Lind concerts were much discussed before my arrival and interest was high. The audiences were very animated in these two cities, and certainly any opponents to the Jenny Lind idea were made aware of the success it enjoyed. "No more attractive concert has been given in Belfast for a long time," commented one critic. Another wrote, "Her art does not thrill, perhaps, at once—it is too exquisite for that—but it is an art which does not pall. In this it is like the art of Mozart, and what can one say more?"

In Dublin, a critic said, "Hempel's singing is characterised by sweetness and purity rather than by dramatic intensity and force. Her voice is musical throughout, and does not depend upon the penetrating brilliance of a few high notes. Her effects of climax are not those of violent fortes but of the most thrilling pianissimos."

On 12 November we gave a Jenny Lind Tea Party in London for thirty guests, all of whom had heard Jenny Lind sing. One woman of eighty-five had heard Jenny when she was a young girl of fifteen, and she told us all about her experience. Several others had been pupils of Jenny. I cannot remember all that was said, but I have a film of the party,* and it is wonderful fun to see myself in what is, sadly enough, the garb of thirty years ago. It is so true that a woman's hat dates her. If I had not worn the hat in the latest style of the day, a cloche, the film would not betray its vintage. The elderly guests, who also appear in this film, are so sweet and so excited as they bustle about, talking to one another. The film had no soundtrack, and so what was said is lost, but the happy spirit of the occasion is certainly caught on the faces of those who were perhaps enjoying their first visit to London.

My concert in Manchester evoked a magnificent review in the *Manchester Evening News*: "Birds have no publicity agents. The poets who sing their praises do so out of fullness of heart, and pure joy at their exquisite music. It is in the same spirit that men and women speak, write, and dream of Frieda Hempel. Their praise may seem immoderate and extravagant before one has heard her. After hearing her one feels they can never have said quite enough."

Another concert at Albert Hall, on 16 December, was different in form from most of my concerts. I presented the first half in my own name, and I was gowned in a modern pink and gold satin creation of Parisian lines. For the second half, I wore the Jenny Lind dress and sang her songs. The audience seemed to enjoy the contrast, and many persons had been turned away from the doors, unable to get tickets. Of course, there was some criticism in the press from those who felt that I had so much to offer as Frieda Hempel that I should no longer limit myself to the repertory of Jenny Lind, even for half a concert. But I satisfied them by returning for three extra concerts at Albert Hall, all straight recitals. After one of these recitals, someone wrote an article commenting upon my back!

> Quite the most interesting news is the back-talk about Hempel. Hempel has the most perfect back imaginable, and the Parisian designers have built her new gowns around it—so to speak—without obstructing the view. Miss Hempel has a delicate way of insinuating, "Excuse my back," when she turns around—but apologies are out of order. It is nice to be face to face with great musicians when they sing, but I will never grudge the stage audience Hempel encores when I am in the stalls.

---

*This film, which runs five minutes, thirty-four seconds, was produced by Gaumont Graphic, UK. Although the film itself is undated, Hempel can be seen autographing records with the date 1924. The final screen says, "With Hempel as his star, Barnum could have conquered more than one world." *Ed.*

On 25 November Mr. Lionel Powell and his associate Mr. Harold Holt gave a dinner for artists of the Celebrity Series at the Royal Automobile Club in London. A photograph, appearing in the newspapers, shows Galli-Curci, Dame Clara Butt, and me seated together. And it was at this dinner that Amelita Galli-Curci and I met for the first time during this season of concerts. A journalist subsequently commented:

> With the meeting of Frieda Hempel and Galli-Curci at dinner the other evening, a situation of some humor has come to an end. Although for weeks past the two prima donnas have occupied rooms in the same London hotel, neither has dared to speak to the other. When they passed in the hotel corridors or in the lounge, or rubbed sables in the lift, they had not dared to speak for the simple human reason that each has been waiting for the other to say the first word. Now the spell is broken at last, and—well, there are some wonderful soprano duets.

We were both aware of the critics' frequent attempts to compare us, but I don't think it mattered to either of us what conclusions were drawn. As one writer put it in the *Literary Digest*, "It seemed no more solvable than to decide which was better, a peach or a pear." I don't recall meeting Galli-Curci in the hotel lobby, but I am certain that we would have spoken, had we met. The rivalry that existed in the minds of so many other persons did not exist in our minds, and certainly we knew that there was room for both of us.

In December I went to Scotland for concerts in Edinburgh and Dundee. "Not for a number of years has so completely satisfying a vocal concert been given in Edinburgh," said one critic. Our success in Dundee was just as complete. Commenting on my singing of "Home, Sweet Home," the Dundee critic wrote, "Other great singers have sung the melody in Dundee, but Miss Hempel eclipsed them all."

Here in Scotland I felt it necessary to make a public statement concerning certain remarks made by members of Jenny Lind's family. I had inquired as to whether anybody knew of any "lost" songs of Jenny Lind, and the daughter of Jenny had replied, curtly, in a news article, that there were no "lost" songs, that she had Jenny Lind's complete repertory in her own library. Now I wanted to make it clear that by "lost" songs, I meant songs that her hearers remembered having heard her sing. No one had access to this library; certainly I did not. But perhaps certain songs which I did not know about remained in the memory of persons, and I wished to learn of them.

Also, the daughter stated that Jenny never wore a crinoline. Perhaps she didn't, but the centennial gown I was asked to copy in Paris, from a picture sent me, certainly looks like a crinoline, and neither Callot nor I could tell the difference. In any event, it was not the dress that mattered, nor the songs. I had been able to stir into life long-smoldering memories. That was my privilege and my only consolation for submerging my own personality.

CHAPTER TWENTY-ONE

Washington, D.C.

After my concert in Eastbourne, which closed this tour, we went to Sils-Maria again, this time for winter sports. We spent almost a month at Sils-Maria and St. Moritz, and returned to New York just in time for me to prepare for a concert in Plainfield, New Jersey, on 19 January 1925. It was about this time that my husband and I decided to separate. My constant traveling and continued absences from home had not made things easy, and differences arose between us more and more frequently.* So we finally decided to live apart, and we separated on the most friendly terms. I stayed in my home on Central Park West, which I had established before my marriage, and Will moved into a hotel. We had been close friends for some years before our marriage, and we are still the best of friends as I write these words today.

My managerial organization, to which Will had given much of his time and effort, was dissolved, and I engaged George Engles as my manager. Mr. Engles was currently handling Elena Gerhardt, Ignacy Jan Paderewski, Emilio de Gogorza, and other noted artists. I was fully booked for the year, and my career continued to occupy my time completely.

A second tour of England was scheduled for the fall, and now the spring months were crowded with concerts throughout the East and on the West Coast. Mr. Bos and Mr. Fritze traveled with me as usual for the Jenny Lind concerts. I sang only a small number of straight recitals because the public demand for the Jenny Lind concert was overwhelming.

---

*Here our author exercises her autobiographical prerogative and is far less than candid with her readers. See Postscript, "Hempel and the Lawyers." *Ed.*

And as had been the case each year, I sang this spring again in Washington, D.C. Indeed, Washington had become almost my second home, thanks to my friend of many years Nana Wilcox. Nana and her husband Walter had a beautiful mansion, with a room ready for me whenever I came to Washington, and so each year I spent pleasant days there. She entertained lavishly for me and often had more than one hundred guests at her parties. Through her I met many interesting, cosmopolitan people and made many friends. The Wilcox mansion is now a club for diplomats, for neither Nana nor her husband is still living.

During my very first visit with Nana in Washington I met her sister, Mrs. Gist Blair. Mr. and Mrs. Blair owned the lovely mansion that has since become famous as the Blair House, where former president Harry Truman lived while the White House was being remodeled. Mrs. Blair also entertained a great deal, and at her parties I met many diplomats from foreign countries. As I chatted with them, I was reminded of those days in Schwerin and in Berlin when I attended court functions and when colorful uniforms and stunning evening gowns caught the eye.

Mr. Blair had a collection of glassware of great value, and he loved to show me his newest acquisitions whenever I came to Washington. Mrs. Blair had furnished their home exquisitely, with elegant furniture and beautiful oriental rugs. But she seemed to prize her French chef above all her possessions. He was famous in Washington for his magnificent dinners, and she was very proud of him.

I had other friends in Washington as well. Early in 1918, Will had introduced me to the Wilbur Carrs. Mr. Carr served with the State Department under ten presidents, from Harrison to Roosevelt, and he had been instrumental in helping Will to have my papers cleared in Germany in 1916, as I mentioned before. The Carrs invited us to their home and subsequently to many gatherings of diplomatic circles.

I was only too happy to repay the kindness of the Carrs by singing occasionally for their guests, as I had done at the Wilcoxes and the Blairs. Once while singing in the Carrs' home, I met Chief Justice Charles Evans Hughes. He became a great admirer of my voice and my art, and I was asked to sing for the State Department Club at the Wardman Park Hotel. I gladly did so and was honored to have the chief justice himself introduce me to the audience.

The Carrs were very kind to me, and Mr. Carr gave me many letters of introduction to American diplomats serving in Europe so that I might more quickly solve any problems that arose in traveling. Ambassadors Steinhard in Sweden; Tony Drexel Biddle in Denmark; and Ruth Bryan Owen in Norway were all helpful and entertained me during my visits to those countries.

For many years the firm of Steinway and Sons arranged concerts in the White House. This custom is no longer observed, but it would be wonderful if it could be revived. Washington is one of the world's important meeting places, and regular concerts at the White House by the great artists of the day would surely enhance the dignity of the office of the president.

My first appearance at a White House concert was during the administration of Herbert Hoover. The concert took place in the Music Room, which accommodated from two to three hundred guests. The long French windows were draped with heavy damask curtains, and at the front of the room was a little podium for the artists, encircled with potted palms. To the side was a golden grand piano. And of course we had a lovely dressing room at our disposal. These intimate concerts were presented following some social function or dinner given in the White House, and the guests were therefore important dignitaries, many of whom I had the pleasure of meeting after the concerts.

Mr. and Mrs. Hoover were extremely gracious to me that evening, and they both presented me with personally inscribed photographs which I have kept on my lovely marble-top table here in my home.

A few years later I had another enjoyable evening at the White House. Josef Hofmann and I were invited to be the performing artists at a concert given by the Franklin Delano Roosevelts. A dinner for members of the Supreme Court preceded the concert, and we were invited to attend. I was interested in meeting all these wise judges, and so I accepted, even though I could not eat so close to the time of a concert.

I sat at the dinner table, and each time the waiter came to serve me, I would say, "No, thank you." It amused him, and he would smile and shake his head. Another person had observed that I was not eating, and after the dinner ended and the president had left the room, she came over and asked with some concern why I had not eaten. She was Mrs. Roosevelt, and I thought it very sweet of her to inquire about this. I assured her that she need not worry, and explained to her that I never ate before singing. She then suggested that I should go up to her room, and that she would send up a cup of coffee. I appreciated this thoughtfulness. She had such a warm, compelling voice that she put me immediately at my ease. She looked lovely that evening in her attractive blue gown, and her forceful personality filled the room as she talked with her guests and with me.

After a little rest in Mrs. Roosevelt's room, I joined Mr. Hofmann in the artists' room just off the Music Room, and the concert began after President and Mrs. Roosevelt and their guests had assembled. At the end of the concert, as an encore, I sang "The Blue Danube Waltz," and as I sang it, I noticed that Chief Justice Charles Hughes kept nodding his head vigorously in time with the waltz rhythm. After accepting the warm applause from the audience, I returned to the artists' room, only to be met by Mrs. Roosevelt who was somewhat out of breath. Chief Justice Hughes, she explained, loved "The Blue Danube Waltz" so much that he had asked her if she might persuade me to repeat it. She had then left the Music Room and rushed around to ask me. But I felt that it was too long for an encore, and perhaps I should not delay Josef Hofmann any longer, for he still had a group of numbers to perform. I suggested that she ask the chief justice if he would as soon hear "Home, Sweet Home." So she rushed around to speak with him again and then returned to tell me that "Home, Sweet Home" would be fine as a substitute. And so I sang this song for Chief Justice Hughes. I have always remembered Mrs. Roosevelt's busy share in this incident, and how very thoughtful it was of her to be certain that every wish of her guests was fulfilled.

For my part, I sent Chief Justice Hughes a record of "The Blue Danube Waltz" for Christmas, telling him that now he could hear me singing this song as often as he wished. I received a charming letter of thanks from him, written 21 December 1933 on the stationery of the Supreme Court of the United States, assuring me that he would do just that. But he added, "You must not ask which song I like the best for I love them all."

From Mr. and Mrs. Roosevelt I received personally autographed photographs, framed in wood from the old roof of the White House. At the time of repairing the White House, all the old wood from the parts that were torn down was kept and distributed as gifts. This wood was rosewood, I believe, and it made handsome frames for these photographs which now hang on the wall of my salon.

After many of the guests had left following the concert, we artists gathered with Mrs. Roosevelt and her daughter, Mrs. Dahl. The president had thanked us and had left the room. Then we chatted freely about music and replied to Mrs. Roosevelt's questions about our profession. I was again made aware of her thoughtfulness when supper was served to me. She had felt that I must be hungry by now, and had consequently made these arrangements. The other artists, Mr. Bos and Mr. Hofmann, were served refreshments, and we had a cozy evening. As always, Mr. Bos entertained us with wonderful jokes and stories, and it was late when we left the White House that evening.

Turning back to the spring of 1925, I returned from Washington to give a Carnegie Hall concert on 25 March. For this concert, I planned to sing the aria from *The Daughter of the Regiment,* which I had sung for many years. But this music from the opera which had caused me so much grief in my homeland was bad luck for me, I guess. That afternoon, before the concert that was to take place in the evening, I took a walk in Central Park as usual. But this time I slipped and fell, turning my ankle as I did so. I managed to get back to the apartment, and Rosa put hot compresses on the injured ankle. I was able to give my concert that evening, although I was still somewhat shaken, and I had trouble with my breath. The next day I discovered that two ribs were broken! I was taped up, and soon all was well, but I avoided the *Daughter of the Regiment* for some time after that.

It was difficult having to make decisions alone now. My husband and I had been married for seven years, and naturally I missed his love and care and his watchful eye. I had an almost childlike trust in people, and I completely lacked the ability to judge them. I had never had any reason to mistrust anyone, and those whom I met seemed honest and kind to me. But now I began to realize how much I had been protected from those situations that were unpleasant and from those persons who were dishonest. Now I had to do everything alone and make important decisions by myself. It was very difficult.

But for the present, things went smoothly. Rosa and I went to Switzerland for the summer, as usual, and then I returned to England for my second International Celebrity tour, this time appearing as myself, not as Jenny Lind.

Hempel, holding a Pomeranian, poses with Leo Slezak (left) and Walter Slezak (right) in Tegernsee, Germany, 1927. COURTESY METROPOLITAN OPERA ARCHIVES.

Hempel with Rosa Seidl in the Swiss Alps. COURTESY METROPOLITAN OPERA ARCHIVES.

In the country house of Lionel Powell, Hempel's manager in England. PHOTO BY
UNDERWOOD & UNDERWOOD. COURTESY METROPOLITAN OPERA ARCHIVES.

CHAPTER TWENTY-TWO

Luisa Tetrazzini

This 1925 English tour also included some thirty concerts and followed the same itinerary as that of the previous year. Lionel Powell and I had become good friends, and this season he drove me through the renowned English countryside to many of the cities where I appeared. He had a big Daimler limousine, and travel in this manner was much superior to train travel. We ate in delightful restaurants and drove through beautiful country, much of which I had never seen, enjoying ourselves thoroughly.

Mr. Powell was a true English gentleman, elegant and cultured. I once spent several weeks at his ancient country house. This building had stood since the thirteenth century, and although sections of it had been rebuilt, it still retained its imposing outline. His wife and daughter were charming to me and made my stay very pleasant. His beautiful mother was a true patrician, and it seemed so right that such a noble person should live in such a noble building. I also fell in love with the many handsome dogs that belonged to the family and to Mr. Powell personally. Everything about this ancient English manor, its inhabitants, and its grounds, was storybook-perfect, and England was somehow personified there.

My first concert was in London at Albert Hall on 4 October. Upon arriving in the city just prior to that day, I decided that this season I would take an apartment, where I would be free to practice whenever I was in London. I was alone, for Rosa had stayed in Paris and had then gone to Berlin to stay with her son. She had taken Betsy with her, because without Rosa I could not properly watch Betsy. The apartment I found was small, but it was pleasantly furnished and it exactly fitted my needs.

Knowing the temperament of the London musical audience, I pro-
grammed several German lieder for this first concert, and I was richly rewarded with prolonged applause after each song. As Leigh Henry wrote the
next day:

> Personally, I am always happy when Hempel sings the adorable Schu-
> bert; here is precisely the lyric grace which her voice shows best in. She
> certainly has one of the purest vocal lines I know. . . . In Schubert's
> "Nacht und Träume" one got the real Hempel in her rare office of spir-
> itual interpretation, singing not only intrinsically beautifully, but also
> illuminated by those more distinctive things of the mind and spirit which
> go to making the greatest interpretative as well as the greatest creative art.

Among the wonderful reviews came this tribute: "Madame Hempel has
a gloriously beautiful voice and a tone far purer than that of her rivals in
vocal fireworks—Tetrazzini and Galli-Curci—and she can sing (which they
cannot) lieder perfectly." Galli-Curci had sung the previous season in London, and Luisa Tetrazzini was touring the country this season. I hoped very
much to meet her, because I admired her art greatly, and I asked Mr. Powell to arrange this.

I am ever so grateful to him, for Luisa and I subsequently became very
close friends. Whenever she had a concert that season and I could possibly
attend it, I did. She, in turn, came to hear me, and I would see her, sitting
down there in the front row, smiling up at me and nodding her head. I was
very proud of her interest in me and in my singing, and I must have fairly
burst with pride to know that she had come to hear me.

I considered her way of singing magnificent, and I admired her art above
that of Sembrich and Melba. Next to Patti, whose voice I had heard only on
records but which I could judge very well, Tetrazzini was my ideal. Her elegance in singing, her dashing way of composing new cadenzas on the spur
of the moment on the concert stage, her absolutely perfect breath control,
her brilliant coloratura fireworks, and her magnificent high tones were all
part of her consummate artistry.

I had been told that in facing Tetrazzini, I would have to face a great
competitor. This had been said to me years before, but it was not true. We
admired each other, for I knew what she had and she knew what I had. She
showed me her wonderful control of breathing and her exercises, and I in
return sang songs for her. Being an Italian, she had concentrated on the
development of her high tones, for brilliant high tones had the greatest effect
upon the audiences. But in later years, when she wished to express her deeper
feelings, there was not enough voice, not enough body of voice to sing songs
in the middle range. This was her greatest sorrow, and how often, in later
years, she said to me, "Fridolina, if I could sing songs as you sing them, I
would never touch coloratura again!"

Hempel with
Luisa Tetrazzini.
LONDON NEWS
AGENCY PHOTOS.
COURTESY S. HENIG,
HISTORIC SINGERS
TRUST.

Her great ideal had been Adelina Patti, whom she admired not for her high tones nor for her technique but for her great art, her phrasing, coloring, and taste in singing. She told me that one evening, after a concert of Patti's, she had gone backstage and kissed the hands of that great artist, who had just sung "Pur dicesti, o bocca, bocca bella," performing a remarkable trill in the middle register and imbuing that delicate song with magic.

The art of singing, as Patti knew it and as Tetrazzini knew it, is all but gone today. It is an art which knows no age in the voice, and which can never die in a singer. It is an art based on the true vitality of perfectly trained muscles schooled to perform. The desire to practice every day, to keep up your chest, to exercise your breathing muscles, and to maintain your technique will preserve your voice for you.

I often hear singers say, "No, I had to give it up. I do not have the strength anymore." This lack of "strength" is age in the voice. But underneath the "strength" to sing lies the strength of the deep-breathing muscles. Deep breathing not only supports the trained voice, but supplies the body with life-giving, clean oxygen and keeps it healthy.

If we had to pay for fresh air, we would appreciate it more and pay greater attention to its value. Students in school should be taught to breathe correctly, and exercises should be carried on throughout the school hours. Often, however, when a teacher says to a child, "Breathe deeply," the child raises his or her shoulders and collarbone and develops very shallow high breathing instead. Nothing could be worse for the body. I showed my breathing exercises to a friend, and he introduced them to soldiers and finally became an instructor in the army. He had great success with these exercises there.

My advice to young singers is: never slouch, keep your shoulders back, and take your breath slowly and deeply—then half the battle is won. I would give this same advice to people who have sleepless nights and to those who suffer from asthma or tuberculosis. A straight spine and lungs filled with air are keys to health as well as to a beautiful voice.

But let me return to my beloved Tetrazzini. Years passed and we met again in New York. She had come to America to give farewell concerts—in former years, the great singers gave many "farewell" concerts. Luisa had rooms in the Ritz Towers, and I visited her often. She was giving "personal appearances" in the movie houses, and following an appearance in Boston, she was engaged to appear at the Paramount in New York City in March 1932. She decided to buy a new dress for the occasion, and together we selected a lovely yellow lace dress made by Madame Nicoll. I presented her with a huge yellow feather fan. She looked very attractive in spite of her heavy figure.

Her engagement at the Paramount was very successful. She gave several shows a day, singing "Caro nome" and other arias to what must have been an unusual audience for her. But the work was tiring, and she became ill with the grippe and had to end her contract.

I went to see her at the Ritz Towers and offered her the hospitality of my home while she was recovering from this severe illness. She accepted, much to my delight, and she stayed with me for more than six months. She was a very jolly, happy soul, always laughing and gay. She sang all day in my home, and no matter what she was doing, there was always this gentle singing, very sweet and lovely.

We had marvelous times together. She talked to me about her career and about all the great singers she had known. She told me of her very unfortunate marriage to a young man who eventually made off with all her money. She was often depressed, for she did not get the engagements she had expected, and she was quite poor.

One day she said to me, "Fridolina, whenever I pack my trunk, I get engagements." Probably that had happened in former days. Perhaps whenever she was ready to leave a town, they begged her to stay and give another concert. Underneath my door I could see the light burning in her room late at night. Then I would hear her moving about. She would pack her trunk and then shove it with her big stomach into the closet, hoping that the next day an engagement would come. But it did not come, and so she would take that big trunk out of the closet and unpack it again so that she could repack it the next night.

She had great faith in the power of unseen forces, and she believed strongly in spiritualism. I have a dear friend, Madame Sophie Tavarozzi, who is a well-known clairvoyant and who possesses many degrees in theosophy. She and Luisa became friends, and she was the medium through whom Luisa spoke with her ideal, Patti.

I later learned that Luisa would get up in the middle of the night, leave my apartment, and go to the home of Sophie to speak with Patti. At two in the morning she would ring Sophie's doorbell, as Sophie related to me later, and Luisa would say, "Forgive me, Sophie dear, but I must speak with Patti. May I come in?" And the two of them would sit at a table to contact the spirit of Adelina Patti. At other times she spoke with Enrico Caruso and Francesco Tamagno, the great Italian tenor with whom she had sung in her youth. Communicating with the spirits of these artists seemed to give her courage to face the uncertainties of this life. At one time, during a séance, Caruso spoke of a rose he had given Luisa, and she remembered that he had given her a rose in 1906 in San Francisco. Tamagno also recalled events to her mind. This may sound fantastic to those of us who have not experienced such séances, but Luisa was not to be shaken from her belief that she had spoken with and received help and encouragement from these spirits.

I shall never forget the wonderful evenings when we would chat together until midnight or so, playing her records, my records, and the records of Patti, Caruso, and others, and talking about them. To illustrate some point, Luisa would often burst into song.

One evening Luisa, Edward Lankow,* the Metropolitan Opera basso, and I were sitting in the kitchen. Lankow was a friend of mine, a "basso profundo" as Luisa had nicknamed him, and I think that she liked him very much. He was tall and handsome, and he had a great jovial sense of humor. They were helping me to dispose of old clippings and papers that had cluttered up my trunks. Luisa would open the clippings, remove the clips from

---

*Edward Lankow was born Edward Rosenberg in Tarrytown, New York, in 1883. His teacher and foster mother was Anna Lankow, whose name he took when he made his concert debut in 1904. He was a member of the Dresden Royal Opera from 1906 to 1908, then joined the Frankfurt Opera where he remained until 1910 before a season with the Vienna Imperial Opera. He was with Henry Russell's Boston Opera for the 1911–13 seasons, followed by five performances as Sarastro in the Metropolitan's new production of *Zauberflöte* (with Emmy Destinn and Leo Slezak) in 1912–13. He made four recordings in Berlin in 1908 and two in Paris in 1926. *Ed.*

With Hempel and Will Kahn are (left) Sophie Tavarozzi, Hempel's close friend, a fortune teller and psychic who helped Tetrazzini; and (right) Laura McNaughton, a friend in New York. COURTESY METROPOLITAN OPERA ARCHIVES.

those papers I wished to throw away, and give them to me to tear up. It was Lankow's job to first lift them out of the trunk and sort them. We all had quite a task, and when we finished we were tired. Luisa suggested that we make some coffee, and just as we finished with the coffee and sandwiches, she surprised us by saying, "Now I am going to sing!"

And so at two o'clock in the morning, she stood up and sang the difficult aria "Ah, non credea mirarti," from *La Sonnambula*. She took a high C *pianissimo*, swelled it like a fireball, and then diminished it to whisper. It was like nothing I had ever heard. Then she sang another aria, and trilled on a high D in a way that was incredible. Her voice had no tremolo, no quiver—it was as steady as a violin, never breathless, and always on pitch. Any person in the next room would have judged this singer to be twenty-five years of age, and Luisa was then well past sixty. But she practiced every day, for she needed to sing as much as she needed to breathe. And she sang until the last moment of her life, I am certain.

I am reminded of the many long walks in Central Park with Luisa and Lankow. One Sunday I suggested that they stay home because Luisa was tired, and that I go for a walk alone. "When I return, we can all go to a movie," I told them. But when I returned I brought company with me. I had found a stray dog in the park, a Great Dane, and I could not bear to see him wandering around lost. I had two dogs of my own, and so I could not keep him. So I suggested that we take him down to the Speyer Hospital for Animals.

Off we went. Luisa weighed about two hundred pounds, Lankow weighed more than that, I wasn't the slimmest thing, and the Great Dane was as big as any dog I have ever seen. What a load for the poor taxi! We just barely squeezed in, but the poor dog didn't know what to do with his legs. He was good about it, though, and we finally arrived at the hospital, where I am certain he was well cared for, and the next day he was given to a new master.

When Luisa had become ill, a well-known doctor treated her. Thinking her to be rich, he had sent her an outrageous bill of $850 for treatment. Of course she did not want to pay this bill, and we agreed with her that she had been overcharged. The doctor sent bill after bill, and finally, learning that she was leaving for Italy by boat, he threatened her with a summons. But we were ready for him. The boat was to sail at midnight, and the man with the summons arrived that afternoon at my front door. In the meantime we had whisked Tetrazzini away by the back elevator! As we rode down that service elevator, she said, "Look at poor Tetrazzini. She is leaving America, and down the back elevator she has to go!" But we reminded her of the reason, saying, "Never mind, darling. You have saved $850!"

We spirited her away to the boat and cautioned her, "Now, don't open your cabin door to anyone, until after the boat has sailed. No matter who knocks on your door, no matter what they do, don't answer. Just stay locked in your cabin, and everything will be fine." From her voyage to Italy, she wrote to me that she had taken our advice. Her letter is dated 26 May 1932:

> I do not know how I can begin to thank you for all your kindness to me and perhaps also for accepting the way I may have disturbed your routine. I hope I may be able to thank you in kind by helping you to perfect your lovely voice, and if you come to Italy, I hope to offer you the hospitality of my home in such a way as will be worthy of you. After you left last night someone knocked four times on my cabin door, but I did not answer and went straight to bed. . . . Lots of kisses and good wishes to you, dear Frieda: a little kiss to Sophie—many thanks to Rosa and hearty greetings to the Basso Alto profondissimo. Remember, my dear, to cover your high notes as much as you can and make them round.

My memory of Luisa in Italy remains vivid, but it pertains to a much earlier visit my husband and I made to Lugano long before I ever met her. Will and I were in St. Moritz for the summer, and we decided to drive down to Lugano where she lived at the time and call upon the great soprano. We just dropped in, you might say, and unfortunately, we did not find her at home. But certainly the spirit of that warm, lovable person permeated the little house and garden on the lake. And in every corner of the rooms, shown to us by her maid, we found signs of that love. For there stood the stuffed bodies of all the dogs she had ever had! She had never been able to part with her beloved pets, and in this manner she kept them always with her.

Luisa was a very great person, and her death in Milan in April of 1940 saddened me, as it saddened everyone who loved her and admired her supreme art.

CHAPTER TWENTY-THREE

Jekyll and Hyde

*R*eturning to our British tour of 1925, I might ask for whom we should sing our concerts. In Sheffield a critic wrote, "Much of Frieda Hempel's success in the concert world is due to the bestowal of her rare gifts of phrasing and interpretation upon the rendering of songs and ballads known and beloved by the people as a whole." My encores usually included just such favorites as "My Old Kentucky Home," "Dixie," "The Cuckoo Clock," and "The Spinning Song," an old German song. And every one of my concerts ended with "Home, Sweet Home." These wonderfully simple, sweet songs were a joy to sing, and I never tired of them.

In Dublin, where we appeared on 24 October, a critic wrote: "The audience indeed enjoyed every moment of 'Roulade' and 'Bravura' singing, but I found her rendering of Brahms's 'Sandmännchen' so right, and so restful, that I must hope my discovery of the real artistic self of Madame Hempel in mere lyrical simplicity is right. That, and a silver voice. What more should one expect?"

I must confess that all the critics in those days scolded me for singing coloratura. As Arnold Gyde wrote:

Now comes the fly in the ointment—the air of amazing intricacy, replete with trills and thrills, now up the whole register, now down, round the corner and up again, all of it most meaningless, if it were not for the happy temperament of Hempel catching the right spirit. But why this lovely singer should bother her head about such pieces one cannot imagine.

But after all, in giving a concert, don't we artists have to cater to everyone who buys a ticket? Should I only concern myself with the reactions of the severest music critic? I could arouse the layman to wild applause with these acrobatics and these exciting high trills; the long scales and the high notes thrilled him. But he could not understand the subtlety of my German lieder. These were for the real music lovers who understood the human expressions embodied in these songs and lived them with me. I sang these songs with all the deep, genuine feeling required, and apparently I made the music lovers jealous of the time spent on "meaningless" music.

To impart these same human feelings to untutored listeners, I sang the lovely folk songs, and I will hazard the guess that the professionally trained listeners also enjoyed them, although some stalwart critics flayed me unmercifully for singing "Dixie." In Bradford we read, "The somewhat startling, if not humiliating, incident of a prima donna wasting time on 'Dixie' was witnessed last night." Quite naturally one finds in his review these words, "The great feature was the singing of Schubert, Brahms and Wolf. The Brahms lullaby was perhaps the finest song of the evening." When he writes, "This is one of the condescensions of the age, when artists with great reputation manage sometimes to forget their artistic sensibilities in order to give the public what they think it wants," he is wrong. In the perfect singing of folk songs, artistic sensibility cannot be forgotten. Concealing art and technique within the framework of a simple song, so that the folk song itself becomes a work of art, is challenge enough for even the greatest of artists.

I must say, in addition, that unfortunate as it may seem, the box office is important, and even today a long trill on a high note will "get" the audience more than "Immer leiser wird mein Schlummer" of Brahms. The obvious is more easily understood than the subtle, and if the obvious is expertly presented, as well as the subtle, both can have value, and the purse is not empty.

I strove to do all things well. The critic for the *Birmingham Post* wrote during this tour:

> A singer who can give us Wolf so finely, and in the same programme win us with a "Mad Song" of Bellini is a vocalist beyond ordinary. Not often do we get the "Jekyll" of "Lied" and the "Hyde" of the "Coloratura" embodied in a single personality. It was no mere triumph of voice which won us, though her soprano tones are exquisitely pure, and have fullness and power at command when needed. Rather was it her musicianship which held us captive—the feeling for line and rhythm. One rarely hears the rhythmic cast of a song made to yield so much as in Madame Hempel's singing. It was good also to find her able to cater for every taste without descending to the banalities some celebrities indulge in.

In Belfast I opened the Celebrity Series for Mr. Powell on 26 October:

> If the other concerts of this series come up to expectations so fully as did last night's, Belfast concert-goers can wish for nothing better. A great number of singers have come to Belfast, and although many of them have charmed, and a few have left a more abiding impression upon us, yet, on the whole, it has been the instrumentalists rather than the vocalists who have given us the most memorable things. One of the few exceptions to this rule is Frieda Hempel. She gave us one of the most perfect examples of bel canto that the writer has heard. There are few singers whose vocal quality is so ravishing in its beauty or whose production is so delightfully easy and effortless. So easy and effortless is it, indeed, as to appear almost artless, which is to pay her the highest compliment that one can accord to any true artists.

That is a review of which I am very proud.

I was somewhat worried at this point. I was scheduled to sing a Jenny Lind concert in Edinburgh on the thirty-first of October, and unexpectedly the port authorities, controlling the shipments to England from Paris, had decided to refuse acceptance of my brand new Jenny Lind costume, just in from Callot Soeurs. And why? Because the slippers were made of silk! My London agent, in response to my frantic appeal, motored to Croydon, where the costume was being held, and finally succeeded in getting a release. I suppose he vouched for the good health of the silkworms. Anyway, my costume arrived in time for the concert, and that worry was over.

I had become fond of appearing before English audiences in my beautiful modern gowns, and although I enjoyed singing the Jenny Lind concert in Edinburgh, I was happy to appear in Dundee on 2 November in modern dress. "Frocks!" I said, when interviewed on the subject in Dundee, "There is not much to talk about now. They are getting shorter and shorter!" I was certainly not one of those who criticized the modern style. I thought the clinging lines were much more womanly than the straight gowns, and I loved the short skirts. .

And here I would like to quote Arnold Gyde again. In a review of my London concert he said:

> To state that she had a perfect method is but to repeat what every critic says every time she sings. No, the supremacy of Hempel lies in things that are deeper, and at the same time, more natural than that.
>
> To begin with, the sight of her is cheering. In theory a woman's perfect figure should not sway one's opinion of her voice. But in fact it does, and when the perfect figure is dressed—no longer in the long train and stupid great hat which once reigned on the concert stage—but in a simple frock of apple-green, whose sole and entirely permissible extrava-

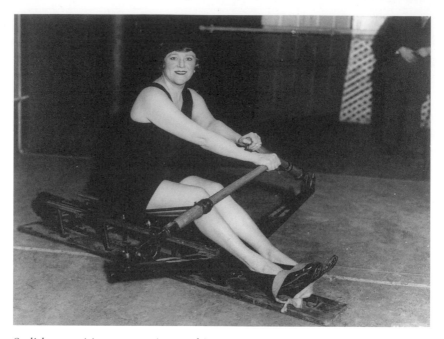

Stylish excercising on a rowing machine. PHOTO BY UNDERWOOD & UNDERWOOD. COURTESY METROPOLITAN OPERA ARCHIVES.

gance is a slit in the slender skirt, allowing a perfect cascade of chiffon and flowers to burst from it, surely seven thousand Londoners may be excused for being disposed towards enthusiasm!

Then there is the Hempel smile as she prepares to sing—a smile which is a real smile and no grimace, even to the people crowded near the Steinway Grand, and which can register its presence at the back of the furthest loggia. It is as if she says, "I am happy. I have been happy all my life, and shall be happy until I die. Song is like life; there is every-thing in it—moonshine, sunshine, darkness, blaze. And whatever hap-pens I am happy in it all, because it *is* life. And now ..." And so she begins to sing.

He was right. I had smiled and won friends with my smile and with my warmth even as a child in Leipzig. I have always been essentially happy, and this innocent happiness remains mine today. Singers must be happy, for singing is a joy and a blessing.

November found me in England again, singing in ten cities. And after giving three more recitals in London itself, I closed my tour with an appear-ance in Eastbourne on 11 December.

CHAPTER TWENTY-FOUR

Then and Now: Reflections on the Golden Age

"*M iss Hempel stands midway* between two ages of singers. The one she cannot ignore, the other she would not ignore." Thus H. T. Parker opened his *Evening Transcript* review of my Boston concert of 22 January 1926, shortly after my return with Rosa from Europe. It is a review that most ably describes my position in the concert world during the later years of my career. Mr. Parker continued:

> the dignitaries, the mannerisms, the poise, the whole atmosphere of the Sembrichs, the Tetrazzinis she desires not to lose; while the directness, the "chic" qualities of many of the latest ones, she also wishes for her own. The stage appeared clothed with the pathway of white so indispensable a decade ago. . . . Miss Hempel upon the stage was graciousness, in a modern version, personified. . . . Miss Hempel's voice is an instrument that produces a tonal marvel of beauty. Its flexibility is unlimited. Such tone it clothes with color superb, lustrous.

Judging from the opinions expressed by critics of my many concerts these last several decades, I have been successful in maintaining this stance midway between the two ages. I have clung dearly to my hard-won vocal technique, and I have brought it with me into this modern world.

In November of 1926, the *Boston Herald* critic wrote that my voice was "amazingly beautiful, at its best," and he said, "Her technique, on the whole, stands superior to that of almost any singer of today. Her musicianship is second to none. And her vitality, and her keen insight into the meaning of a song, these qualities are beyond compare."

There were many wonderful reviews through the years.* My 1935 Queen's Hall concert in London magically transported the *Manchester Guardian* critic back to the Golden Age of Song, or so he said, and after I sang in Amsterdam in October of 1938, Leo Riemens of the *Het Nationale Dagblad* wrote:

> The season gave us back one of the greatest personalities, Frieda Hempel. The admiration of a full house quickly passed into enthusiasm, and reached a pinnacle higher than any that we recall at any vocal recital of the last few years.
>
> Hempel's voice was so youthful and fresh, her personality so vital—and always the boundless ability, the masterful interpretation. She is better than ever before, and as an interpreter of the "Lied," her position is unique. The audience soon learned how much more personal and alive this art of the "Lied" is than the inadequate interpretation by tiresome contemporaries of ours—for in this long and variegated program, there was never a dull moment.
>
> A comparison with most other singers who have appeared here shows definitely how far this artist surpasses all her colleagues.

Theo van der Bijl, writing in *De Tyd,* said of that concert:

> Last night there stood in the Concertgebouw an artist of true greatness, real and true greatness. There is only one description for her singing—masterful. The singer is not only a vocalist but also what so many are not—a thorough musician. She is incomparably precise and possesses complete technique and musical virtuosity. And how completely such a great singer masters her language! The night was a blessing because

---

*Singers and athletes have much in common: the activities of both are invariably subject to the passage of time. Some profess that peak performance can only be maintained through the passage of the years by constant and diligent pursuit of active careers. Intelligent artists, like Frieda Hempel, learn to compensate for the inevitable decline in physical prowess by a constant adjustment of repertory to emphasize artistic presentation and to match remaining vocal abilities. Most critics attempt to be lenient in reporting on late-in-life performances by our waning stars and will stress the positive elements which can be found in a recital. Those who feel they must also be honest will search for kindly or merciful ways to point out that time has taken some toll. An editor only can be in complete sympathy with the perfectly natural desire of an author to be quite selective in the choice of reviews (or portions of reviews) which leave a favorable impression; thus the material chosen by Mme Hempel has been left as she wished it. From the standpoint of history, however, in order not to leave the impression that we are dealing with a superwoman who had found the fountain of youth, additional (likewise selected) reviews and excerpts are to be found in the Chronology appended within this volume. For example, see the (complete) review of the Town Hall recital of 6 October 1939. *Ed.*

something great happened . . . because we were face to face with a personality of the first rank . . . a rare combination of craftsmanship in the highest sense of honestly inspired musicianship.

Following the recital in New York on 7 January 1939, the critic for the *New York Times* wrote:

As strikingly handsome and attractive as ever, the soprano, who graced the Metropolitan stage so unforgettably in the heyday of her splendid career, quickly proved to a large and ardently responsive audience that she still remained an outstanding exponent of her art.

An inborn talent as interpreter was made manifest in everything Miss Hempel essayed. Few singers are left today with her rich imagination, unerring sense of style and ability to bring home to an audience the particular mood and meaning of a song. Her diction, phrasing and intonation were above cavil, and in all respects her singing was that of a vocalist in complete command of the technique of her metier. One would search long among singers of the day for more perfect legato or finer breath control.

The concert in Town Hall on 3 October 1948 was described in the *New York Post:*

Frieda Hempel returned to Town Hall yesterday and showed once again her extraordinary qualities as a personality and artist. Renowned as one of the world's great singers, Miss Hempel still manifests a compelling artistry and an electric projection of personality. She creates a remarkable illusion of youth, and is the essence of charm and grace. She has mastered the art of "Lieder" singing, and in my experience this is a unique feat. Dressed in a pink satin gown which should make her a contestant for the best-dressed-woman list, Miss Hempel received an ovation when she entered the hall.

A *Musical America* review of my Town Hall concert on 4 December 1949 reads, "There are few singers of this generation who can equal, let alone surpass, the supremely right and beautiful placement of her voice, the completeness of her vocalism, or the magnificently vital and flexible rhythmic sense that is hers."

Alfred Frankenstein, reviewing another concert of that year in San Francisco, said, "Miss Hempel's style of singing remains as vivid, fresh and appealing as ever, and her artistry in creating and projecting a phrase remains as masterful as ever. The mood and character of each song was profoundly understood and profoundly shared."

I gave my last concert in November of 1951 in New York. And of this concert the *New York Times* critic wrote, "She has charm and joyousness

Hempel singing for convalescing soldiers at Walter Reed Hospital, Washington, D.C., 2 July 1944. COURTESY METROPOLITAN OPERA ARCHIVES.

and interpretative skill that few young singers can match. As a musician, too, she showed command of the melodic line such as one seldom hears nowadays."

My art has stayed young with me, and the most precious hour of the day is that hour devoted to my voice. The songs that I sing remain forever fresh, and each time I sing them, I find new meaning and new sources of beauty. And so, if the thrilling ring of youth is gone from my voice, perhaps a richer essence has remained.

I am reminded that I am one among very few singers living today whose career was at its height during the early years of this century. It is very difficult for me to realize this fact. Time has passed so quickly, and life has always been a very present thing to me, something without past and without future, something so immediate that all yesterday is one. Only yesterday I was singing with Caruso, with Amato, and with Emmy Destinn. Was it really so long ago?

And yet, if I consider the well-known expression, "the Golden Age," it does seem as though a hundred years have passed. So few singers of today have thoroughly trained their voices, and so few conductors demand performances of high caliber. The art of bel canto singing, as we knew it, has all but disappeared.

I received a letter recently from a person unknown to me. He writes: "After having become acquainted with your singing on records, and with the voices of your contemporaries, I can hardly believe that there was a time not long ago when such voices were actually heard by the public. And until I heard these records myself, I knew nothing about 'The Golden Age of Singing.' If the younger singers would but pay more attention to these records!"

One must not blame the younger singers for a situation in which they are caught up. Acceleration in the tempo of living and very complex problems of survival have so altered our lives that we can no longer devote the proper time to a cultivation of the subtle arts.

Before the First World War, during the last years of the past century, and during the early years of this century, when my colleagues and I were young, distance still had meaning, monarchies dictated the mode and manners of life, and the craftsman in the village was contented and proud of his achievement. It was a time of economic simplicity, political clarity, and social stability. It was the Golden Age of Singing. My appearances in Europe and at the Metropolitan place me among the last group of artists to be included in this term, for after the First World War great changes were manifested in every phase of living, and the art of bel canto singing declined.

In my day the jet plane could not whisk a young singer across the waters and carry her rapidly to and from cities on a strenuous tour for which she was not ready. The advertising wizards did not exist who today would build a reputation for this singer out of words. Radio and television were unknown, those two modern means of communication which skyrocket a public favorite to fame in twenty-four hours. And the enormous, fast-moving, highly publicized managerial chains had not yet been organized which could tempt a singer with promises.

A young singer in former days knew that her success and fame would rest solely upon the solidity of her technique and upon the thoroughness of her training. She knew that for many years she would sing in small, obscure opera houses, and that only when she had gained complete mastery of her art could she expect to sing in the major opera houses of her country. For her, the Metropolitan was the highest achievement of all, because here the greatest artists of each country performed magnificently.

If she were a German citizen, she would strive to earn the title of court singer, for this would be a measure of her artistry. All artists and all craftsmen strove to be honored by the king or emperor, for such an honor singled them out as being the best in their chosen profession. And this is what each person strove to be.

In this manner, extremely high standards of performance and of workmanship were maintained. And the singer engaged by a court theater, performing for the king or for a grand duke or a prince, living in the atmosphere of nobility and gracious manners, became a finer person herself. She strove constantly to please the court with the excellence of her art and her deportment and so became an artist of repute in her country and perhaps eventually in the world.

Such slow, sure growth had its reward in that excellence of singing now characterized as Golden Age singing. The coming together of many great voices at the Metropolitan was the culmination. Each great artist inspired the other, and the resultant performances were of a perfection never again to be obtained. Having been on that stage at that time myself, having been electrified by the genius of Caruso, of Toscanini, and of Amato as I sang with them, and remembering how earnestly we all worked for the highest perfection in performance, I feel certain that there was a Golden Age of Singing, for I lived it.

Today, singers are expendable. A fresh young voice is destroyed in a few years because not enough time is taken to develop a secure technique. The great mobility of voice, the perfect control of breathing muscles, and the ability to color and blend tones are acquired only after several years of cautious, quiet work. A beautiful instrument cannot be exploited; on the contrary, it must be protected and made secure. But today the managers, knowing the commercial value of a beautiful voice, exploit it immediately. The singer must face important audiences before she has had her period of apprenticeship, and this is impossible. I could not have succeeded in this manner.

I sang before a most important audience, the audience of the Royal Opera House of Berlin, but my debut was followed by three years of apprenticeship in Schwerin. I was not engaged immediately by the Royal Opera House. I was given time to learn how to handle my voice; I gained experience in coloratura roles, in lyric roles, and in dramatic roles. I sang the Queen of the Night, and I sang Elsa. In this capacity to manage my instrument I was not unique. Tetrazzini, Lilli Lehmann, Emmy Destinn, Caruso, all the great singers of my time sang roles in each category. Caruso was often described as having two completely different voices.

We all were blessed with the opportunity to study correctly and to acquire skill slowly and quietly. We learned to treat the voice according to what was demanded of it in a role. Great technical knowledge enabled us to make this constant adjustment. Emmy Destinn sang *Aida* one day and then *Faust, The Flying Dutchman,* and *Mignon,* all to perfection. I sang *Traviata* one day and *Der Rosenkavalier* the next, Fiordiligi in *Così fan tutte* and then *Lohengrin.* This ability was not unusual—it was expected of us, and we were given ample opportunity to develop it.

The present division of voices into precise and limited categories is quite naturally disturbing to me. I very much dislike a tiny coloratura voice, a voice without depth and body, a voice, to my mind, only partially trained. But I cannot rightly blame the singer, for I know that she has been engaged to sing only the coloratura roles. In addition, I know that she has no exemplars before her of great bel canto style, other than records; she cannot hear the coloratura of a Lilli Lehmann in her prime, nor a Tetrazzini, a coloratura of thrilling dramatic, emotional import. She has neither the idol to emulate, nor the opportunity.

A dramatic voice of great power and no virtuosity is equally distasteful to me; but here, again, the same reasoning can explain the problem. Lack of time for study, lack of standards to be maintained, and lack of interest in the reestablishment of standards result in a complete lack of artistry as was known in the Golden Age.

The ability of the average listener to recognize exceptional singing should inspire young singers to seek some way of overcoming their handicaps. There has never been a Wagnerian singer like Kirsten Flagstad, and the public knows this. But Flagstad learned all her roles in little Norway, and her mother told me that she and Kirsten worked together three hours every day, for three years, on the score of *Isolde,* perfecting the placement of every vowel, and carefully molding the vocal line. And before that study began, Flagstad had sung for many years without notice, quietly perfecting her art.

But there will be few singers indeed who will have the economic means to afford such training. Few will hazard the long road to artistic achievement of this caliber. Today the problems are almost unsurmountable, and even the shorter road to fame is a difficult one. Musical education is so expensive in

America that it is impossible for a poor girl to study with any hope of success. The positions are few, and the experience needed to acquire those positions is difficult to obtain. Managerial fees are high, and salaries are low.

Fortunately, the great desire to sing is born in some of us, and we shall sing. If there are obstacles in our path, we shall overcome them, if we can. We shall always sing, and there are those of you who shall always listen. It is perhaps enough, in this day, that there is singing. For singing heals the spirit and lightens the heart. Great music, beautifully sung, bears a message from heaven.

CHAPTER TWENTY-FIVE

On Mozart and Coloratura Singing

inging Mozart is a delight of which I shall never tire. To me, Mozart is always fresh, always new, young, and sparkling. His expressions are so perfect. He seems to know everything and feel everything just as it should be known and felt. Friendship, love, anger, sadness: all are expressed to perfection in his music. How young he was when he wrote his great music, and how young he is with us today. I know of no other composer who lifts me in spirit as he does. It is like drinking champagne.

Mozart was my first love, his music the first real music I ever studied, and I feel that I understand him ever so well. He is so pure, so clean, so elegant in his musical line, that everything has to be sung beautifully, with beautiful sounds, first of all, and with matchless legato. There must be no tremolo, no chopping off of phrases and no bombast. Mozart must always be dignified, and never so dramatic that the beautiful legato line is lost.

I think that Mozart should only be sung in small houses, as we had in Germany. The Residenz (Cuvilliés) Theater in Munich was ideal for his music, and he, himself, conducted his operas there. Only in such small, intimate theaters can one recognize the divine genius of this man, and it shines forth in his music.

And what command of the voice his music demands! For the role of Queen of the Night in *The Magic Flute,* for example, he writes a dramatic recitative, followed by a spinning lyric legato in the andante, and then a brilliant allegro with coloratura figures and the highest notes. And within this tremendous gamut of expression, everything must be kept delicate, refined, and bathed in beauty. Luxurious scenery and overacting cannot camouflage an inadequate performance of Mozart. His particular style has to be respected and perfectly performed vocally and histrionically.

If I want to be happy, I sing Mozart. I take out any of his scores from my library and place it in front of me on the piano. As I turn the pages, singing one phrase and then another, I forget the problems that beset me, and my happiness returns. There is an indescribable quality, a vitality in Mozart's music, which renders it eternally young. It is intoxicating and exciting. When I sing Mozart I feel like a young girl going to her first dance, and the exhilaration permeates every tone. There is great alertness inside of me, a de-lightful tension.

In *The Marriage of Figaro,* as I start the recitative "Giunse alfin il mo-mento," I am immediately in the spirit of fooling Figaro, who is listening to me. The musical line, the phrasing, and the words offer me a consummately natural expression of the dramatic situation. The exaggerated dignity of my masquerade is marvelously reflected in this music. In the following "Deh, vieni, non tardar," the delicate legato line is so animated that I do not under-stand how some singers can make a sobbing, dramatic aria out of it. I am try-ing to make Figaro as jealous as possible, and naturally I put longing into it, but underneath there is a delicate humor that I must not lose.

Everything must be as clear-cut and crisp as possible. The youth, the sparkle, the freshness, the silver, the champagne must be present in every note. There must be very little portamento, and the *messa di voce* must be skillfully employed. The tones must be spun out from *piano* to *forte* and back again to *piano* with a sureness indicative of the highest technical virtu-osity. The coloratura passages demand an accuracy of technique that can only be mastered after long and arduous study, and the lyric lines in their purity and simplicity, betray the technically imperfect tone immediately. Mozart reveals the great singer, and exposes the lesser singer.

Each coloratura role is unique. Just singing scales and staccatos for the sake of technical display is meaningless. The passages must be imbued with appropriate feeling and expression. Coloratura must be used to portray joy, the hate, the anger, the happiness—whatever mood or quality the composer had in mind when writing the role. Rosina, in *The Barber of Seville,* is not a dull person who can vocalize swiftly and expertly. Rosina is a graceful, witty young woman with a good deal of feeling. The first part of her aria "Una voce poco fa" should be sung with great warmth and feeling, while the sec-ond part should reveal a person who is mischievous, gay, and happy. The coloratura of the Queen of the Night in *The Magic Flute* is, on the contrary, angry and brilliant. In *Traviata,* the aria of Violetta, "Sempre libera," must suggest abandon, an "I-don't-care" feeling.

The performance of coloratura arias demands great artistry and taste. A well-known singer destroyed this artistry when she tacked on a "Lucia" cadenza to the end of the "Blue Danube Waltz." I wasn't quite sure what I had come to hear. I immediately thought of a Viennese skirt and a Scotch blouse, and I was shocked to realize that such a misconception of the art of coloratura could be fostered by the public.

A tiny, inexpressive coloratura voice may be artistically vapid, but a large, pushed dramatic voice is perhaps an even greater betrayer of vocal art. Screaming and yelling are not singing, even though the audience may react with excitement, just as it does to pyrotechnics. One of the greatest evils of singing, and the surest way to destroy the fine balance of an acquired technique, is the forcing of a voice beyond its natural limits. And, paradoxically, the safest way to obtain volume is to perfect the coloratura flexibility so that the volume may grow naturally.

Lilli Lehmann sang the coloratura aria from Mozart's *The Abduction from the Seraglio* and Wagner's "Liebestod," both on the same evening in concert. Schumann-Heink sang in *Lucrezia Borgia, Parsifal, The Flying Dutchman, The Magic Flute, Martha, Rheingold,* and *Walküre* on successive nights. I sang a Queen of the Night one evening and the Marschallin the next evening. This adaptability was expected of us, as I have mentioned before. We were not accomplished singers if we failed in this.

In our ears, constantly, was the sound of beautifully placed tones which implied such adaptability. We heard no tiny, bodyless coloratura, no forced bigness, and in this we were fortunate. Our model was the perfectly placed tone, beautiful in sound, and capable of expression, flexible, and rich in modulations of shading.

In my mailbox nearly every day are letters from youngsters who have never heard my colleagues, nor me, in person. Yet they feel impelled to write me and tell me of the great joy and inspiration they derive from the sound of our voices on records. They hear the beautiful sounds, they sense the desire that was in each of us to produce perfection, to create beauty, and to inspire. They seem to have an instinctive appreciation for the haunting, moving quality of voice that is associated with the singers of the Golden Age.

Many of these young people who write to me and many of you who read this book aspire to become great singers, and before I close this book, which has become dear to me, I want to talk to you, a little, about singing.

CHAPTER TWENTY-SIX

To the Young Singer

ach of you dreams of being a future Patti, a future Caruso. Your friends tell you that you have a beautiful voice, and I am certain that you have a lovely quality and easy high tones. But do not listen to your friends when they tell you that you sing better than so-and-so at the Metropolitan. Close your ears to such statements, for they are usually made by persons who have no knowledge of our profession.

Your beautiful natural voice is only a fourth wheel on the wagon. So much, much more is needed. Many of you will begin your studies, and before long you will find the work too difficult, the demands upon you too great. You will turn to different professions.

Others of you will persevere in your desire, and you will succeed. But you must discipline yourself. You must be determined to practice faithfully at least an hour a day. You must be as faithful to this hour as you are faithful to your hours of eating. Never skip a day and say, "I'm tired. I'll practice longer tomorrow." No matter how talented you are, you must work at your vocal technique.

Your mind and body must be kept alert, for it is that alertness which we need in singing—not relaxation, not tension, but this alertness, this alert feeling in every fiber of the body. You must live for your voice, and your voice requires a healthy body.

Be gracious and smiling. Carry yourself erect and hold your chest up in its natural position. Never slouch, even though all your friends may slouch. As a singer you cannot indulge in this lazy habit so prevalent today. It will hinder your career.

Go to as many vocal concerts as you can. Train your ear to recognize the good and the bad in production. Watch the singer carefully, and when you return home, write down your observations. Notice the singer's breathing, mouth positions, and manners. Try to imitate those things that you believe are good.

If you think that you are not beautiful, do not let yourself be disturbed by this realization. Your personality is more important than your physical beauty, and if you radiate from within, you will be beautiful. Take lessons from a dancer to limber up your body and impart grace to your movements. Listen to great actors, and study their dramatic expression. Imitate them, if you cannot afford to take lessons. Observe their breathing technique, and their faultless pronunciation.

Be fanatically precise about your diction in singing. This precision will solidify your tone placement and bring about great freedom in your tone production.

Study languages so that you may use them with understanding. It is not necessary to speak them fluently, but you must know what you are singing about, not just through your knowledge of the translations but because you understand the foreign words themselves. Then sing from your heart, and the singing will be a great joy, and it will be correct.

A perfectly placed tone cannot be described in words. It must be heard, and then imitated. Therefore, never study with a teacher who has never sung. You cannot learn a language from a teacher who cannot speak it. You must hear the sound of the word you wish to use. Likewise, you must hear the sound of the perfectly placed tone you wish to imitate.

There is not an Italian method as distinguished from a German method of singing. There is only "the free tone." The Italians have the advantage of a naturally placed tone, because the Italian language is spoken where the perfect tone is sung. The Germans, on the other hand, have advanced beyond the Italians in the science of tone production, in my belief. They have methodically analyzed the problems of tone placement, and they are able to create word pictures that aid the pupil in her efforts to imitate the perfect sound.

When you have found the teacher with whom you are satisfied, your voice will grow, you will sing well, and you will be happy. But there will always be disappointing days when your voice will not respond as you wish it to. Do not be influenced by this setback. Do not give up.

Those of you who keep trying in spite of all difficulties will succeed. Be steadfast with yourself, and most honest. Dream, live, and pray only for your voice and for its perfection. Smile, smile, and surely you will win your heart's desire. "Kein Meister fällt vom Himmel." Practice makes perfect.

CHAPTER TWENTY-SEVEN

Other Years, Other Endeavors

Certainly my life has been eagerly dedicated to my art. And I am grateful beyond measure for what I have received in return. My tools—the healthy body, the vital spirit, and disciplined living, tools which serve my voice—have served me as well. My life has been singularly free from illness, and severe trials and heartaches which have heavily burdened me have not broken me in spirit, nor in health.

In 1929, as a result of the stock-market crash, a young business venture of mine, a cosmetic firm, failed, and I suffered severe financial losses. Then, in the early thirties, I had to face several legal proceedings. All were decided in my favor, but this personal victory was small compensation for the toll exacted from me physically and mentally.*

For years I could not find the peace of mind needed to pursue my art extensively. I devoted most of my time to teaching the essentials of my vocal art to young students, and to animal welfare work. I would have also enjoyed reestablishing my cosmetic business, but I was financially unable to do so by then.

I have always had great interest in medicine and in the care of the body. In fact, my initial venture into the cosmetic business came about because of this interest. During my many years in the theater and on the concert stage I was obliged to take exceptional care of my complexion. The continuous application of stage makeup might well have been injurious to my face if I

---

*See Postscript, "Hempel and the Lawyers." *Ed.*

had not taken great care of my skin. Fortunately, I found some scientific preparations in Paris which excelled anything I had ever used, although they were virtually unknown on the cosmetic market.

These creams interested me very much, and after some difficulty I succeeded in locating the manufacturer. I could not find his products easily, and I wished to purchase a large supply for myself so that I would not find myself without them when I returned to America. Soon my friends noticed the wonderful condition of my skin and begged me for some of my facial creams. Before I knew it, I was besieged with requests from other women who had heard about them, and I realized that they could be successfully marketed in America.

A promoter took charge of the financing and the business arrangements, I gave permission for the use of my name, and in 1927 the firm of Frieda Hempel, Inc., was established, with offices at 225 West 57th Street in New York City.

I invested a great deal of money in this firm and worked personally with the chemists in the preparation of the products, after having spent several months in France with the parent firm learning the manufacturing processes. My early training in the offices of my brother-in-law, Dr. Schaper, himself a famous skin specialist, now stood me in good stead, and I was able to handle the formulas with success.

In a short time we achieved national distribution, and the company stock was selling well. I had great hopes for the future growth of the firm, but I had not counted on the stock-market crash of 1929. We did not have enough capital to weather the depression, and although I tried desperately to help by investing more money, my help was not enough and the firm failed. My losses were well over fifty thousand dollars, and, in addition, many other stocks became worthless at the same time. Thus much of the money I had earned with my voice was gone.

Several years later I began making some new products for my personal use, and again my friends begged me to put them on the market. And so, in 1947, I started my own company, under the name of Delfrie, Inc. I kept it quite small and personal, and it was very successful. Our pharmaceutical items were developed by famous chemists, and these dermatological preparations helped countless persons afflicted with skin troubles. I worked occasionally with the chemists in our laboratory and made certain that only the finest ingredients were used. I loved the entire change from music to business, and I found it very stimulating. Many of my colleagues also engaged in enterprises outside of their special field, and so of course I was no exception to the rule. We all found such contrast challenging and interesting.

Thinking again of those very difficult years in the 1930s, I must stress the great comfort and solace one gains from participation in the activities of animal welfare organizations. There is always work to be done, and in help-ing one finds a tranquility of spirit. My own home was dedicated to ani-mals, and a sparrow fallen from its nest, a baby squirrel too young to be left alone in the park, or a pigeon with a broken wing would find itself resting in a basket in the sun, somewhere in one of my rooms. Stray dogs from the park would command my complete attention, until I had found a good home for them, and animal lovers in the city knew that they could count on my help to find homes for stray dogs they had found.

Thus in 1937 I began the story of Brownie.

CHAPTER TWENTY-EIGHT

My Date with Brownie

*C*entral Park covers an area of more than 820 acres in the center of New York City, a section about fifty blocks long and over five blocks wide. From my apartment at 87th and Central Park West, I can see the whole park as it extends north to 110th Street, and south to 59th Street, and beyond it the Empire State Building, Rockefeller Center, the United Nations Building over on the East River, and the skyline of New York City for miles to the north. As I look to the east I see the handsome apartment houses along Fifth Avenue, which borders on this beautiful park.

Across from me, toward the eastern side of the park, is the city reservoir, around which runs a bridle path. The south-bound thoroughfare for automobiles, cutting through the western side of the park, flanks the bridle path at this point. And between this road and the western edge of the park are beautiful lawns and a great variety of trees and foliage.

Each day I watch the city folk walking along the numerous footpaths, the cars driving through, and the seagulls settling on the water. From my windows high up on the eighth floor, the panorama is beautiful, and I gaze many times a day upon it. I describe this view and this park so that you will understand me as I tell this story.

It was a Monday morning in 1937. I had promised to attend a Bagby Musical Morning at the Waldorf Astoria at eleven o'clock, and after the concert I was expected to stay for lunch as the guest of Mr. Bagby. These concerts had continued throughout the years, and they were still a part of the musical life of the city. I looked forward to the occasion, for I was always interested in the artists, and I enjoyed meeting my friends at the luncheon.

Naturally, I dressed in my newest clothes, and when I was ready to leave, I glanced out of my bedroom window to make certain that it was not going to rain. But as I looked down upon the park, I noticed a lost dog limping along the bridle path.

There wasn't a moment of hesitation on my part. I knew what I had to do. Off came my stylish clothes. Hastily I put on a street dress, grabbed my walking shoes and a coat, rushed to the kitchen to get some roast beef, and flew to the elevator. I rang the bell furiously, and when the elevator man arrived, I told him to hurry. "But Madame Hempel," he objected, "I cannot change the speed of the elevator!"

Once in the street, I ran two blocks to the 90th Street park entrance and raced across the lawn to the bridle path. I could still see the dog some distance ahead of me, limping along painfully. I hurried after him, calling and throwing him food. He was forced to move slowly because of his sore foot, but still I could not catch up with him because the faster I moved, the faster he ran. So I stopped chasing him and turned back. At that point a mounted officer, Mr. George Fullner, came riding along the bridle path, and I told him about the dog.

"Oh, yes!" he said, "We all know about him. He has been wandering in this park for over a year now."

"But where does he get his food? Where does he sleep? Does he belong to anybody?" I asked. The answer to my questions was a shrug of the shoulders: "Nobody knows." I felt frightfully sorry for the poor animal, and I returned home dejected. The next morning, as I stood looking out of my window thinking about the dog, I saw him again, a little distance up on the bridle path. I knew better than to go after him, but I began to wonder if there were some way to help him.

For the next few days I watched for him, and I discovered that he passed by each morning around eleven o'clock. With my opera glasses I would see him appear from the southern end of the reservoir, cross the thoroughfare, come down on the lawn, stop at a certain tree, cross back up over the road into the bridle path, and finally disappear at the northern bend of the reservoir. He had his own plan worked out, and it seemed amazing to me. He reminded me of a watchman who makes his rounds and punches a certain clock at eleven each morning. I remarked to a friend, "He must have a wristwatch. He is so punctual!"

One morning I decided to go out at ten-thirty and be there to meet him around eleven. I sat on a bench near his favorite tree and pretended not to notice him. But he saw me from a distance, and he detoured around me. Obviously he mistrusted people and avoided them. He was a large dog and seemed to be a cross between a chow and a collie. He was not starving, for his body was strong, and he moved swiftly in spite of the injury to his foot. He had a coat of beautiful auburn fur, and so I decided to name him Brownie.

His months of wandering about alone had made him very resourceful and cunning. I admired him for his independence and his courage, and I wanted him for a friend. How had he managed to keep well during the winter months, when heavy snows covered the ground and rains drenched the paths and roads? Where had he found food and water? This wild dog commanded all my respect, and I wanted to help him.

At this time I was not touring the country with concert engagements, and I had a good deal of time to myself. So I started to look for Brownie's hiding place. I had decided to feed him, but this open part of the park was too populated, and he wouldn't have eaten here. I had to find out where he rested and slept.

I wandered all over the park, looking in bushes, under bridges, and along the pathways. I had no clue as to where his hiding place might be, but I knew that when I found it, I could leave good meat for him with the certainty that he would get it. In the meantime I carried dog biscuits with me, and I left them at different spots along that part of his trail that I already knew, hoping that he would find some of them. Then I continued beyond where I had seen him disappear from sight, looking for signs of his hiding place.

I went out daily in all kinds of weather, paying no heed to such foolhardiness, thinking only of that dog. I set up my own trail with those crackers I left for Brownie. Terrible winds and rains did not keep me at home, because I knew that more than ever on those days Brownie would have to rely on me. Nobody else was in the park, and there were no crumbs around. I even left him meat on these days and prayed that he would find it.

Months went by without success, and then one day Mr. Fullner, seeing my desperate efforts, said to me, "I want you to meet another officer who knows all about the dog. He might be able to help you find his hiding place." And so Mr. Jim Flanagan was introduced to me. He was a mounted policeman, extremely handsome, very polite, kind, and honest. He told me that formerly Brownie had slept down in the bushes opposite the American Museum of Natural History at 81st and Central Park West. Now he had moved uptown. I must confess that I could not cover the whole park by myself, and I begged Mr. Flanagan to watch out for Brownie during his tours of inspection and to let me know if he found out anything.

A few weeks later he called me late one night. "Miss Hempel," he said, "I think I know where Brownie's new hiding place is. Meet me tomorrow at twelve-thirty on the bridle path, and I will show you."

This was wonderful news! I could hardly wait for morning to come, and around noon I met Mr. Flanagan. I walked beside him as he rode his horse along the bridle path, and when we got to the spot where the path turns southward on the eastern side of the park, he said to me, "Now look down there in the bushes but don't say a word!" I looked through the high wire fence that borders the bridle path, and down below me, across from 104th Street, I saw Brownie sleeping in the bushes. Even though it was winter and the leaves were gone, the matted branches still covered and protected him.

We walked on, so as not to disturb him, and left some food where we knew he would pass when he awoke and started wandering again. Now I was happy for I knew where I could leave a good meal for him. Soon, I thought, I will be able to pet him, tell him that he is a good dog, and bring him home with me. I thanked Mr. Flanagan and returned home with my mind at rest for the first time in months.

Now I began to feed him properly. Every day I brought a pound-and-a-half of boiled beef with fresh vegetables, and sometimes I added a little cod-liver oil. I was careful to give him only the best food so that he would gain strength. But my hopes of making a friend out of him right away were soon dashed. I could not come close to him even here. If I approached his hiding place while he was there, he would move out slowly, look around, and then run away. So I had to put the food down and then go some distance away and wait to see if he returned. When he wasn't there, I followed the same procedure.

I fed him every day for two years on this spot. I sat on a bench up on a footpath, and when he appeared I would sit motionless, so as not to frighten him. He must have come to recognize me, for he often saw me sitting there, with my five-pound Pomeranian, Hansi, by my side. I always had a leash with me, because each day I hoped to bring him home. But he never came near, and he never let me approach him.

When a dog becomes wild, he is very difficult to catch. One must have great patience to match his patience. Only when he is exhausted or starved will he beg for help. And Brownie would never starve, even without my food. I think that he was a "one-man" dog. He seemed to be waiting for his master, but, alas, his master never came.

Sometimes I would not see him for a while, and I would worry. Then Mr. Flanagan, who had become my good friend, would look for him. And there were other people who rode regularly in the park, and they gave me information about Brownie.

The multimillionaire Fred Pearson rode his four horses around the reservoir every day, and Mrs. Judy Meehan, the beautiful wife of Mounted Police Inspector Meehan, and one of the finest of horsewomen, practically spent her days in the park. I would question Mr. Pearson and he would tell me, "Oh yes. I saw Brownie down by the playground this morning. He is fine." Or Judy would say, "Don't worry, Frieda. I saw him this morning." Jim would report that Brownie was around, and so it would turn out that I had missed him for some reason; perhaps he had come earlier in the day for a change, or perhaps later.

I still looked for him along the trails of the park, because he sometimes rested in other places, but he always saw to it that he had exits on all four sides, so that he could not be cornered. If I saw him before he saw me, I would just watch him for a while, thinking that perhaps today he would let me come close to him. But as soon as he noticed me, he would get up and in a flash would completely disappear from sight.

My daily trip to Brownie might be pleasant or it might be an ordeal: I had to be prepared for sudden changes of temperature and perhaps rain or snow, even when the day seemed normal. When it was really too severe in the morning, I would walk over to Jim's post and beg him to ride up to 104th Street and put Brownie's dinner down for him. But for no other reason would I miss seeing Brownie.

I planned my day so that I might go to him. I dressed plainly and left all my jewelry at home. It wasn't too safe for me to walk around the park alone in those out-of-the-way places, and the officers, who were all my friends by now, warned me to be careful. They advised me never to stay too late. But I don't think that I realized what dreadful things might have happened to me. I was just hoping to see Brownie.

From the very first time I laid eyes on him, I had admired him. I admired his intelligent planning, his sense of awareness, his cleverness, and his quietness. I knew that he had a strong, fine character, and later on I found out that his good qualities exceeded all my hopes. In the boiling heat of summer he would find his way to the lakes where he could cool off his hot body. He drank water from the overflowing drinking fountains, for the reservoir was fenced in, and he kept away from the open, sun-drenched fields.

During the winters he was less able to protect himself. Judy would tell me, "Oh Frieda! I saw heavy icicles on Brownie's fur today. He looked frozen to death!" He would often be soaked to the bone, and his body looked black with the rain. All year long he fought off the sticks and stones of the young boys and fled from those who chased him. Poor Brownie, he could never sleep with his two eyes closed. He had to be on the alert night and day. But he never bit anybody, and he never barked.

The ASPCA received many calls about him from people who, not knowing that he was being fed, worried about him and wanted him to have a home. I believe that they made several attempts to catch him, but it was impossible. No one could catch a wild dog as clever as Brownie in so large an area. I never betrayed his hiding place, and neither did Jim, because we knew that if anybody tried to catch him there, he would never return and our search for his hiding place would begin all over again.

One day I saw Brownie being chased around the bridle path by a police car. The poor animal was so frightened that he just kept running straight ahead along the bridle path, instead of turning off into the bushes where the car could not follow him. He must have been exhausted by the time he finally evaded his pursuers, but he got away. I was furious over this cruel procedure, and I wrote a strong letter to the police. I begged them not to hunt Brownie in this manner but to let me catch him with kindness, and they left him alone.

A short time later I discovered that Brownie had not taken his food one day. He did not pass by my windows the next day, and I became worried. I called the ASPCA, and they assured me that they had not caught Brownie. I asked Mr. Pearson and Judy if they had seen him, but they had not. Jim looked for him further down the park without success. I was terribly afraid that something had happened to him, that he was lying somewhere, injured or sick.

I was therefore overjoyed when Jim called one evening. "I have found Brownie," he said, excitedly, "He must have been sick this past week, because he seems a little weak, but don't worry. He will soon be fine. Meet me this evening around six-thirty at the water station, and I will show you his new hiding place." Whether Brownie had suffered with a sickness or an injury I don't know, but nothing could break the spirit of that remarkable, wonderful dog. He had simply rested somewhere until he felt well again, and now he was up and about.

His new hiding place was in the bushes near 87th Street and Fifth Avenue. This spot was directly across from the mansion of Mr. Jimmy Speyer, that wonderful man who created the famous Speyer Hospital for Animals, a hospital where stray dogs were cared for. How ironic, I thought, for Brownie to choose this spot!

Jim had seen him resting here about seven o'clock in the evening, and so we knew that we could put his dinner down a little before that time. Close by the deep bushes where he hid was a large tree, on the edge of the bridle path. And at the foot of this tree I began to leave his meal of freshly cooked beef and vegetables. Then I would cross the northbound auto thoroughfare that skirts the eastern side of the park and sit down on a bench along the footpath to wait for him.

I could see him coming from a distance, usually down from his old hiding place at 104th. He would stop, look around to make certain nobody was waiting for him, go to the tree and pick up the familiar brown paper bag containing his dinner and carry it between his teeth to an open spot about a hundred feet away and eat his meal.

It was so cute to see him walking with the paper bag in his mouth just like a trained dog. But he was smarter than a trained dog, for he figured out everything by himself. He was smart enough to know that he should be very careful when on the auto thoroughfares, and so his trail was counterclockwise to the traffic. He knew that when he was on the bridle path he might be chased, and so he dug several holes under the high wire fence. When his pursuers got too close, he just ducked out under the fence and slipped away.

There was something about Brownie that made all of us who knew him think that he was more than just a dog. He did everything so correctly and so intelligently. Many times he was in danger, but he always saved himself. Some unknown power seemed to arrange everything for Brownie and protect him. Not only did he have my food, but now he had a large black cat to protect that food from the rats! I saw her several times, lying there beside Brownie's food. She never touched the meat herself, she just guarded it, and when Brownie came she would leave. Her very presence would frighten the rats away, and for days they would disappear from the spot. I was very happy to have her as an ally.

Brownie didn't always eat his food on the cleared spot. Sometimes he took it farther away. An officer told me one day, "Miss Frieda, I saw Brownie way over here on the west side. And he must have been shopping, because he had a brown bag in his mouth!" This remark brought a big smile to my face, for I could just see Brownie trotting along for blocks, with that precious parcel between his teeth.

This paper bag gave me some difficulty at first. At 104th Street I never saw him pick up the bag and leave his hiding place. Now he always walked away with it, and one evening he taught me a good lesson. I saw him spill the contents of my bag on the auto thoroughfare. The food was lost, and Brownie missed his dinner. Of course, I thought, he doesn't know which end is the top. So the next day I put brown glue paper all around the bag. I sealed it tightly, and left just enough of the bag exposed for him to chew open a hole and get his food.

There were times, of course, when I didn't see Brownie pick up his food. Whenever I went to a cocktail party in the afternoon I would take my brown bag with me, and a little after six I would try to make my excuses, so that I could get to the park and leave the food before Brownie arrived. But I was sometimes late, and then I would miss him. Or I might have an evening engagement and not be able to wait for him, if he happened to be late.

Jim was a great help to me now. Whenever he had late duty, which kept him in the park until midnight, he would drive home by way of the Eastside thoroughfare, past Brownie's spot. If I had asked him to check, he would then call me on the phone and give me the good news that the food was gone and that in all probability Brownie had been fed.

I also thought up another way to check on Brownie when I missed him. I began to put dates on all the bags. If then I found a discarded bag of a certain date, with a large hole in it, Brownie had found it. If the bag had several small holes in it, the rats had beaten him to it, and he had been cheated out of his dinner.

In the years just preceding my first visits to Brownie, I had been through the most trying experience of my life;* I cannot talk about it, but I don't know what I would have done if Brownie had not been sent to me. I had no interest in social activities, and I had very little desire to sing. There were moments when even the thought of singing brought tears to my eyes and a constriction to my throat. My belief in humans had been sorely tried, and I clung more than ever to the animal world and to those creatures who had given me so much. They have in excess those qualities of loyalty, trustworthiness, devotion, love, companionship, and gratefulness which are so difficult to find in human beings.

I felt that in helping Brownie I would find an answer; I wanted to repay his kind for all the love and devotion I had known. I wanted to show Brownie loyalty, devotion, and trust so that he would come back to a human being, and I wanted to be that person.

One rainy night I put his dinner down for him about six-thirty and left for an appointment. I returned at eight-thirty, and since his bag was not yet gone, I decided to wait a while for him.

I was walking up and down the footpath, my music bag under my arm and an umbrella over my head when a car suddenly stopped beside me. A heavy-set man, over six feet tall and dressed in a dark suit and overcoat, climbed out of the car and came over to me.

"What are you doing here?" he asked me.

"I am just taking a walk."

"Yes," he said, "And how often do you do that?"

"Well," I said, "I don't know. Why do you ask me?"

"What is your name?" he then asked me, and I began to get a little angry.

"Now, why should I give you my name. Who are you?"

He grabbed my bag from under my arm, and I quickly said, "You can't take that. It is my property."

"Oh yes?" he answered, and then he showed me some kind of a badge.

"That means nothing to me. Anybody can have something like that."

At that point I noticed a second man getting out of the parked car. He was also tall and strong, and I began to fear for my safety. As he spoke to his partner, saying, "Did you get anything?" I began screaming for help.

A doorman in a building on Fifth Avenue heard me and came running across the street. He climbed quickly up a six-foot wall that encloses the park and ran over to us. But the two men, now standing one on either side of me like two giants, assured him that they were detectives and that they were taking me to the police station.

---

*Perhaps the Heckscher Affair? See "The Heckscher Affair" in the Postscript, "Hempel and the Lawyers." *Ed.*

"Haven't you been putting a mysterious package down over there every night for the past three weeks?" they asked me.

"No," I said, "I have been putting a package down over there every night for the past three years, and there is one there right now. You can go and look at it, if you wish!" Now I knew what they were about, and I was angry.

"Will you get the package, lady?" one of them said.

"Oh no! You're going to get it, and then we shall see what is in it. And if a park-police car comes by, in the meantime, you might ask them about all of this. They know me well."

Finally one of them crossed over the road, climbed up through the bushes, and picked up the brown bag. Then he brought it back to the bench and showed it to his partner. They turned to question me again, but I said sharply, "I will not talk to you. We will go to the police station, as you suggested, and you will soon be sorry for what you have done. Please be careful with that bag and do not open it here."

"Who the hell do you think you are?" one of them said.

"I am not much of anybody, but you are less than I am," I answered, and then stepped into their car.

"Why don't you go back to the country you came from?" the other man sneered.

"And why don't you both do just that!" I spit back, because I knew that they were Irish by their accents.

Then I stopped talking, because I could not compete with their rudeness. I was boiling inside. All this, I thought, for five years of kindness! We arrived at the police station in the center of the park, and I was taken into the building and ordered to stand before the desk sergeant. The sealed brown bag was placed on the desk before him.

"What is the charge against her?" the desk sergeant asked.

"Well," replied one of the detectives, "We got a telephone call informing us that this woman puts a mysterious package down every evening in a certain spot of the park, and in the morning it is gone. It must contain either stolen goods or sabotage material, and someone picks it up during the night." The desk sergeant looked at me for a moment and then picked up the bag. He studied it carefully and then tore it open. "It looks like pretty good beef to me," he commented.

"And mighty good beef it is," I said, and I picked up a piece and ate it. "Let me call up officer Jim Flanagan," I said to the desk sergeant. "He can explain everything to these two detectives." But he did not answer. I spoke to him again, and still I got no answer. Then one of the policemen standing around told me to go ahead and use the phone.

I reached Jim and told him what had happened. As he lived in Mount Vernon, some distance out of New York City, he could not come to the station, but he asked to speak to one of the policemen. I don't know what was said, but the two detectives disappeared in a hurry after that! Perhaps they learned that I was a good friend of Mayor La Guardia.

It was still pouring outside, and I naturally expected to be driven home. But nobody said anything to me. Finally I spoke up and said, "I'm going back to feed my dog." Picking up the bag at the desk, I turned to go. Still no one offered to accompany me. How rude, I thought to myself as I left the building and headed into the rain. I walked back through the park to Brownie's spot, put the bag down, and then hurried over to Fifth Avenue to hail a taxi, all the while holding my umbrella tightly against the wind and rain.

It was close to ten o'clock when I arrived home. Naturally I was very excited and angry by now, and I called a close friend and told her what had happened to me. The next thing I knew, a reporter from the *Times* was at my front door. I did not hesitate to tell him my experience and how I had been treated. "Well," he said, after he had heard me, "That's some story! I'm going over to see the desk sergeant now to check on the details, and I'll call you from there."

The phone rang in a little while, and the reporter was on the line: "Everything you told me was correct, Miss Hempel. And, by the way, you wanted to know why the sergeant didn't answer you when asked to use the phone. Well, I'll tell you. He is almost stone-deaf! I had a hard time with him myself."

The next morning these headlines appeared in the *Times*, dated 7 February 1942: "Singer and Police in Row over Dog. Frieda Hempel Seized in Park as She Leaves Meat for a Mongrel She Fed 5 Years. Eats It to Prove Story." The story was copied by all the afternoon and evening papers. "Frieda Hempel in Jail" and "Frieda Hempel Arrested" were alarming captions, even though the articles clarified their meaning. I opened the *New York World-Telegram* to see my picture on the front page, just under the war headline "Pacific Situation Is Critical." This story started off, "Central Park's animal kingdom today was as it has been. The crazy duck still went screaming around the duck pond, the squirrels still were sponging for food, and Brownie was still being fed by Frieda Hempel, the singer. Only thing was, Miss Hempel was sore at the cops."

I had no intention of pressing charges against the two detectives who had arrested me, but nevertheless Police Commissioner Valentine ordered an investigation. And so a few days later I reenacted the events for his officials who came to my home, and then assured them that all I wanted from the detectives was an apology. I had been pestered by lawyers who offered to handle what they termed an airtight case against the city, but I refused even to listen to them. On the following Sunday the two detectives came to my home to call. They presented me with enormous bouquets of roses, and I in turn gave them each a good highball. We all shook hands, and soon the unpleasantness was forgotten.

Now that I had had time to think things over, I was really angry with the person who had called the detectives in the first place. The police would not tell me who the man was, but eventually I found out. He should have had the decency to come away from his window on Fifth Avenue and cross the street to find out for himself what was in the packages instead of causing so much trouble for so many of us.

The *New Yorker* of 25 April 1942 had a long story about Brownie in their "Talk of the Town." It stated, "An opera star eating cold raw meat in a police station, under the stern eye of Authority, seems to personify love of animals better than almost anything else." After describing my daily habit of feeding Brownie, they wrote, "The rats, so abundant in Central Park, might be a hazard to this system of feeding except that, by good luck, a wild cat lives near Brownie's hiding place, and the cat scares the rats away. Thus have Miss Hempel, Brownie, and the cat established their own peculiar balance of nature."

The war had started, and because I had been born in Germany I found myself in a difficult situation as a result of all this publicity. Some people still might think that the mysterious packages left in the park each night contained more than just meat for a stray dog. If they came snooping around looking for signs of sabotage, they might frighten Brownie away or perhaps even harm him.

And there were other problems now. Blackouts occurred rather frequently, and at these times the park would be pitch-black unless the moon was out. The soldiers, guarding the reservoir against possible poisoning of the water, might shoot Brownie if he came too close. Jim told me that one soldier even reported seeing a fox in the bushes, but of course the fox was Brownie! Meat-rationing had also started, and I was going to have to give Brownie something other than boiled beef. He was bound to be suspicious of anything strange and different, and I just couldn't say to him, "Now, Brownie, you're going to have to eat something different. I can't give you any more beef."

We didn't want to lose Brownie for any of these various reasons, and so Jim and I decided that it was time to try and catch him. We drove down to the offices of the ASPCA and spoke to the director, Mr. Coleman. At first he was doubtful that he could help us, noting, "You know that we have tried many times to catch this dog. He is just too smart." I agreed and then said, "But I have been feeding him for so long that he trusts my food, and perhaps if you come and see him when he picks up his dinner, you may find a way." He agreed to send up Mr. William Ryan and a helper, and we thanked him.

The next day toward early evening, Jim and I met with the two gentlemen at the benches opposite Brownie's spot. I put the food down, and then Jim drove along near Brownie's trail, calling out, "Come here, Brownie. Come here, Brownie." And just as though we had rehearsed it all with him,

Brownie soon appeared, picked up his food, and walked on. We were lucky that day, and we didn't have to wait at all.

Mr. Ryan was quite surprised at this appearance of Brownie, and he said, "You are right. We can catch him now. We will bring a trap here tomorrow morning, and meet you both again tomorrow afternoon." I was unhappy that to catch Brownie we had to trick him, because we were going to trap him by using the food he had come to trust. But I felt that somehow he would soon understand.

When Jim and I arrived the next afternoon, the men had leveled the ground near the tree and placed a big wire trap there which they had camouflaged with leaves and branches. Jim put the bag of food inside the trap, and then we sat down to wait while Jim drove around again, looking for Brownie with his "love call." After some time Brownie appeared.

He sniffed around the trap several times, became suspicious, and walked away. Then he changed his mind and returned, noticed my bag inside, and very carefully stretched his paw inside and scooped out the bag. He picked it up between his teeth and ran away. "Isn't he smart!" I cried, "Nobody can catch him." I was so overjoyed that Jim said, "Friedel, you're not making sense. I thought you wanted to catch Brownie!" But I was glad Brownie had tricked us, too. It served us right.

We tried again the next day, and this time Jim suggested that the food be tied to the back of the trap. Brownie would have to go all the way in to get his food, and then the door would spring shut. This was done, and when Brownie came for his food, he did not hesitate as he had the day before, but crawled right in. Down came the door, and Brownie was trapped. I rushed over and looked closely at him for the first time in five years. His eyes were clear, his fur was thick and beautiful, and he had a clean appearance about him. I heard him bark for the first time, and it was a wonderful sound to my ears. Proudly he sat there, protesting loudly against such a mean trick, and he was right.

I was glad that my wonderful friend, Mr. Ryan, who understood animals so well and knew how to calm them in their fright, was handling all the details. He supervised the loading of the trap into the wagon and rode with Brownie to the ASPCA while Jim and I followed in Jim's car. There Brownie was unloaded like a trapped lion and put into a cage by himself. I had to wait until the next morning to see him again.

My night was sleepless, and morning never seemed to come. Then Jim called for me, and we drove to the ASPCA. Under my arm was the familiar brown package. Mr. Ryan met us and took us to Brownie's room, where Jim put the food down. Brownie didn't even look at it. I said, "Come here, Brownie," and although he recognized my voice, he just whined, as if to say, "What are you going to do with me now?"

Several reporters and photographers arrived to cover the story, for evidently the society had notified the papers of Brownie's capture, and that was news. After five years as a stray in the park, Brownie was bound to be a little unpredictable, and nobody expected him to act like a lap dog. And although I am not afraid of any animal and they usually take very quickly to me, I must confess that I was a little doubtful as to just how Brownie would act. But I wanted to try and give him a dog biscuit, and so I asked Mr. Ryan to let him out of his cage. Brownie stepped out and looked around, and then sat down on the floor in the center of the room. He would not take my biscuit, but he let me pet him gently, and it was a wonderful moment for me. I knew then that he would come home with me.

The bulbs began to flash right and left. The photographers took Brownie's picture from all sides, and Brownie was photographed just like a movie star. It was all new and strange and baffling to him, and after a while he started to whine. I knew that he had had enough, and I asked Mr. Ryan to put him back in his cage so that he could rest. His picture appeared in all the papers the next day. We laughed at one of the captions, "Frieda Hempel Traps Pet Dog. Dog Previously Trapped Miss Hempel."

The next day Jim and I took him out for a walk, and thank heavens we had the foresight to put three collars on him, a choker, a neck collar, and a harness, because as we walked along the street a man came along with a large Doberman, and Brownie jumped like a horse. If we hadn't had a tight hold on him, we would have lost him. We let him run loose in the big open pen of the ASPCA, we took him up and down the elevators, and we walked him among the other dogs until he became acclimated. In the meantime we had him thoroughly checked physically. He weighed more than thirty-five pounds, and the doctors found him to be in magnificent condition. One doctor commented that his five-year diet of beef and vegetables had been a diet not many house pets enjoyed, let alone a stray dog!

Now he was ready to be brought home, and so one morning I took a taxi to the ASPCA and informed Mr. Ryan that I had come to fetch Brownie. He was happy to hear this, and he immediately made all the necessary arrangements. Then he brought Brownie out to me on a double leash, called a cab, and put us in safely. I thanked him again for his kindness. I was very grateful to him for his willingness to help, and I shall always remember his many kindnesses in later years when I have asked him to help me with sick and lost animals that have come my way.

Brownie jumped up on the seat beside me as we drove off. He looked at me out of the corner of his eye, and I looked at him out of the corner of my eye, but neither of us spoke. We drove home in perfect silence. Arriving at my apartment building, I climbed out of the cab and motioned to Brownie to follow. As though he had understood and wanted to please me, he climbed down from the seat and stood on the curb beside me as I paid the driver. His leashes were on, but I didn't need them, for he followed me

closely into the foyer of my building and entered the elevator with me. I
rang my doorbell, and Rosa opened the door.

She stood back a little for she had fed this dog on many a sweltering
summer day, hoping, for my sake, that he would one day stand on this very
carpet where he now stood. Then she bent over him and said, "Welcome to
our home, Brownie." We took him into a big room with French windows
overlooking his park, and let him jump up on the velvet-covered couch.
And there he was, as much at home as if he had been born in that very room.

I brought him his food and water and took care of him. After a few days
indoors, his protective layer of excess hair just naturally fell off to the floor
in handfuls. He didn't bark, and he had beautiful manners. And how he
loved that couch! He never wanted to leave it. He was spotlessly clean, and
I always knew when he wanted to go down to the street. I didn't have to
teach him anything. We asked him to roll over, and he did so. We asked him
for his paw, and he gave it to us. Who had taught him all of this, or did he
just understand everything that was said to him? What an extraordinary animal! A few days after he came home with me, I took him down to my photographers, and we had some excellent pictures taken. It was no problem at
all. He was gentle, obedient, and kind.

My Pomeranian, Hansi, was frightfully jealous of this new guest, and he
had big ideas. He wanted to kill Brownie whenever he saw him, and so I
could not let the two of them alone together. I didn't want to keep either of
them behind locked doors, nor did I want trouble, so I had two large
wooden gates made for the doors of Brownie's room. One day I would put
Brownie in there and give Hansi the run of the house, and the next day they
would exchange places. They could see each other through the slats in the
gates, but they could not disturb each other.

The newspapers, which had carried the story of Brownie's capture on 2
December 1942 now followed them up with clever descriptions of
Brownie's new life. Under the headline "Brownie in Hempel Guest Room,"
I read:

> Brownie, the Central Park stray that Frieda Hempel fed daily for five
> years, is home at last. He is a chow-collie of uniformly molasses color,
> described by Miss Hempel as "brown like the leaves."
>
> Today his kennel is the green and gold guest room in Miss Hem-
> pel's elegant apartment, where the dog looks down on miles of grass
> where many a time he ran for his life, eluding policemen and SPCA
> catchers.
>
> When Miss Hempel brought him home, he was allowed to nose
> around all over the nine-room apartment. He sniffed at the grand piano
> beside the great window where many a day Miss Hempel had one eye on
> the music and the other on the park. He rested his chin on a needlepoint

With Brownie in the Adirondacks, 1943. COURTESY METROPOLITAN OPERA ARCHIVES.

chair, strolled over to a satin brocade sofa, then, with a question in his soft brown eyes, looked up as if wondering what to do next.

The article continues in this vein. Another one is entitled, "Frieda Hempel's Dog, in Luxury, Looks Wistfully at Central Park." It begins:

> Brownie has a room to himself, the former guest room of the apartment. Its furnishings include high shelves of books, English prints in gold frames, and pink and green furniture.
>
> There are servants on call, a fine quilt and green scarf to chew on, and the heat in the apartment is turned off at nine each night, so that Brownie will not be distressed by too much warmth.

The rags-to-riches aspect of Brownie's story seemed to interest everybody, and the papers made the most of it. I received hundreds of letters from people whose warm words of thanks touched me deeply. I had not realized that so many New Yorkers knew Brownie. So many wrote to tell me that they had seen Brownie in the park and expressed their gratitude to me for the love and care I had given to him:

> I was so pleased to know that you are the Lady who has fed Brownie every day for five years. It is so sweet, and wonderful to be born kind to animals. You had my blessing every day, for I have seen Brownie a few times, and so have my friends. Please, Madame, accept my deepest wishes of blessing, and the best to Brownie, my pal, too.

Yes, Brownie had been watched over by many friends. Another letter reads:

> I recall with great pleasure our meetings several times, several months ago, when you were on your daily visits to the park, on your missions of mercy. And how strange that I did not recognize you! For I have heard you sing many times in opera and concert, and have been one of your warm admirers. But you were so modest and reserved as to your identity that I never tried to penetrate it. However, I have thought of you often, and it is wonderful now to know that you have brought Brownie home with you.

I cannot begin to quote the many lovely things that were written, but I treasured every single letter.

In 1943 I took a house for the summer high up in the Adirondack Mountains, and of course Brownie and Hansi went with me. I thought that I would give Brownie a treat and let him run loose in the woods, but he never left my side and was only too glad to return to the house. I returned each summer for many years, and never once did Brownie romp alone through the woods. It was "Home, Sweet Home" for him now.

Shortly after Brownie had arrived in my home, I had an experience that had its humorous aspects. One day I returned from a shopping trip to find a police car in front of my building. In the doorway a policeman stood talking to a little dark-haired woman.

"Madame Hempel, we have been waiting for you. This woman claims that you are holding her dog."

"Well," I said, "if I have her dog, of course she can have him." To myself I thought, how strange it was that after five years she should suddenly remember her dog.

"What did you call your dog?" I asked politely.

"Whitey!"

"That's surely a strange name for a brown dog," I remarked.

"Was your dog male or female, lady?" asked the policeman.

"Well," she said, as she hesitated a moment, "I don't really know."

"What's the matter, lady? Don't you know who gets the pup?" said the policeman, and we both laughed.

Anyway, I decided to go up and fetch Brownie, and let him have a look at her. I brought him down and put him up on the seat in the foyer. She walked over to him, and cooingly she said, "Whitey, Whitey." Brownie knew what to do. He very severely gave her some rough "woof-woofs," and that was that.

I thought that of course the matter had been settled right then and there, but a few months later the doorbell rang. There stood the same woman, this time with another policeman and a warrant for me to appear in court the following morning at nine o'clock! The charge was stolen property. Jim offered to go up with me, and he suggested that we take Mr. Ryan along also. The three of us arrived at the courthouse and waited for my case to be called.

Then this woman produced a tiny, tiny sweater, the kind a lap dog wears, and insisted that it had belonged to her Whitey, who was now my Brownie. The judge had read all about Brownie in the papers and of course he knew that a thirty-five-pound dog would never have been able to wear that silly sweater. The woman kept on talking and talking, until finally the judge interrupted her.

"Didn't you testify falsely, about six weeks ago, that a man had raped you? Now, if you don't stop all this nonsense I shall see that you are sent to Bellevue Hospital for observation." Of course she lost her case. Perhaps she had figured that if she could have proven her claim, then I would have paid her any amount to keep Brownie. But that sweater and that name made us think that in all probability she was actually just a little crazy and that the judge was right.

Brownie showed his gratefulness to me in many ways. He wasn't slushy in his affection but, quite the contrary, very subtle. When he licked my hands, which wasn't too often, I knew that what he wanted to express came from the bottom of his heart. Whenever I left the house he would lie down near the front door and not move until I returned. Then he would carry on like a puppy, barking, jumping all over me, and giving me much more than a royal welcome. Of course he had to take turns with Hansi.

Jim and I had become good friends, and I often invited him to my house. Brownie was extremely fond of Jim, and he must have remembered his voice from the park, for he went wild with joy whenever Jim arrived. Without Jim's help I never would have gotten Brownie, and it was good to see that Brownie was grateful to Jim as well as to me.

In 1945, three years after Brownie was caught, the King Features Syndicate ran an article in the *Saturday Home Magazine* by Mel Heimer, entitled "Frieda and the Wild Dog." "I decided to see how the years had treated Brownie," he starts out,

> So I went up to see Miss Hempel, and after a lot of small talk, I asked to see the sturdy beast. I expected to see him charging out, flashing-eyed, and fang-bared.
>
> He came trotting out into the sitting room. No flashing eyes. No fangs. While I waited for a display of the old outdoor spirit, he climbed wearily up on a settee, patted it down in bored fashion and dropped off to sleep. Miss Hempel burst into laughter.
>
> "He's a complete cake-eater now," she said, still laughing, "and I mean that literally. His favorite food is cake, and it has to be sweet cake at that. All he does is eat and sleep."

The article closes: "'Don't you miss the park, old boy?' I asked Brownie, as I took my leave. Maybe it was just my day for hearing things—but I thought I distinctly heard someone say, 'Don't be a sap, sap!'" Along with this article is a large cartoon by Ralph Stein, showing Brownie lying on his back, lounging on an elegant settee, while a pretty maid in uniform serves him with a large piece of frosted layer cake. It is very well done, and I have to smile whenever I think of it.

Poor Hansi died in 1947 at the age of twelve years. Brownie was then over fourteen years old, for, according to the doctors at the ASPCA, he was over nine years of age in 1942. He had the whole apartment to himself after Hansi's death, and he often sat near me in the music room as I taught my students. Sometimes I heard him sigh deeply, and then I knew that he didn't approve of the sounds he was hearing. Hansi had loved songs, but he couldn't stand to hear scales, and he would leave the room until my students had finished with their technique. Brownie was content to listen to everything, sighing just now and then.

As the years went by, he lost most of his sight and his hearing. He lived on my bed then, for he knew that place and felt safe there. One evening he suffered one hemorrhage after another, and I knew that I was losing him. I took him to the Speyer Hospital for Animals, and there he fell asleep on the twenty-first of June 1952. He was over nineteen years old when he died, and I had had his love for ten long years. He is buried next to Hansi in the beautiful Hartedale Animal Cemetery, high up on the green hills.

I have never had a friend and a companion as true as Brownie. He is still deep in my heart, and I shall never forget him. He gave me so much devotion, so much love, so much of everything when I needed it most, and few human beings can equal him in character. I believe that the Lord has selected those whom he wishes to take care of the poor, and those whom he wishes to take care of the sick. And I am ever so grateful that he has selected me to take care of animals.

A portrait from the 1950s by Bruno of Hollywood, inscribed to Elizabeth Johnston "mitt all good wishes." COURTESY ELIZABETH JOHNSTON.

CHAPTER TWENTY-NINE

Singing Is My Life

Every artist retires eventually. Every singer bids adieu to the opera stage and the concert platform. The usual comment from the public is that she or he has aged a great deal and that the voice is gone. I think that most people misunderstand this situation. Gigli gave his last concert, he "retired," and yet those knowledgeable people who heard him realized that his voice was as beautiful as ever, and that he certainly had not grown old.

The end of an artistic career and the number of calendar years completed have little in common. We artists often retire when people in other professions feel that they are in the prime of life. Furthermore, our voices are still in very good condition, certainly better than is assumed. It may naturally occur that a singer has aged early in life and that the voice is tired and broken. But this is the exception rather than the rule.

We admittedly become tired of being confronted from day to day with those many challenges that belong to a singer's career. For twenty, thirty, or forty years one has "worked," spending most of the time in train compartments, hotel rooms, or airplanes. Tired or not, we must rehearse with the accompanist at the appointed time in the morning of the performance, and even though we may have a headache, a fever, or a sore throat, we must appear on the stage in the evening and sing.

Perhaps I should have written more about these things: How strenuous it is, and how uncomfortable, to have to dress and redress five or six times a day, to have my hair done five or six times during the day by the opera hairdresser and while she is busy with my hair to think of my next entrance.

When the evening performance is over and the applause has been gratefully acknowledged, my thoughts turn to my next deadline, a song recital initiating a new concert tour. Did Rosa get the suitcases properly packed with the right dresses and costumes? Must I remind Mr. Bos of the piano music? Ah, I must remember to call my New York apartment later on for surely important mail will have come which must be answered immediately, and so on.

Singing is wonderful—to be a singer is not so wonderful. It is very tiring, and the greater the reputation, the harder it is. We all feel this, so one fine day we say enough of this strain and tension, and we retire. But does this imply that singing no longer concerns us? Certainly not. We will continue to sing for our friends and ourselves.

I have given up a great deal for the joy of mastering the great art of singing. I was often very, very lonesome, but I never felt that I was alone. I had singing, which filled my heart and consoled me, and I always had true friends as well as my beloved animals. Many important things had to recede into the background because singing dominated my life. I have always been essentially happy, and this innocent happiness has never left me. I said before that singing heals the spirit and lightens the heart. Great music beautifully sung becomes a message from heaven. In my heart I still belong to song, and indeed singing is my life.

The Final Years

by Elizabeth Johnston

Among the admirers at Frieda Hempel's final recital in Town Hall in November of 1951 was a young soprano, composer, and musicologist from San Francisco, Elizabeth Johnston. Johnston had trained in Germany and Italy and had earned a Master's degree at U.C. Berkeley, subsequently serving as lecturer in music. Also a professional singer, she had moved to New York hoping to find a voice teacher who could help her repair vocal cords damaged by overwork. Frieda Hempel became her teacher, and Ms. Johnston soon devoted all her time and efforts to the needs of the older singer. Here Elizabeth Johnston tells the story of Frieda Hempel's final years.

It was my good fortune to be in New York City in the fall of 1951 and to attend Frieda Hempel's final Town Hall recital. There I was able to experience and judge appreciatively her technical mastery and the wonder of her voice and personality. I phoned her the following morning and requested an audition. She agreed to see me and subsequently accepted me as a pupil.

In 1951 I began working with Frieda once a week on voice technique. After a while she invited me to move in with her as her secretary in exchange for room, board, and lessons. This was the beginning of a friendship and companionship that were to absorb all my time and effort and end only after Frieda's death in 1955.

I moved up from Bleeker Street in the Village to Central Park West and was given a nice room and bath overlooking the park with its brilliant morning and evening skies, as I had known them from the hills of Berkeley.

Rosa and I soon became good friends. She accepted me gladly as she knew that Frieda liked me and needed my help. Rosa was a cheerful, good-hearted German woman, simple and modest, still living just for Frieda and dedicated to making her home life comfortable. She served us wonderful dinners every evening in the beautiful dining room, where occasionally Sophie Tavarozzi and Laura McNaughton, Frieda's dear friends, came to join us.

The lessons gradually stopped, since we both realized that the results did not warrant the effort. I began working on her accounts and her correspondence, and soon felt quite at home. Frieda was still a beautiful woman—she had the wonderful carriage of a singer and walked with a delightful lilt. Her voice was clear and bell-like, and above all her laughter was infectious and sparkling. She was a joy to be around, always cheerful and good natured, although somewhat reticent and with a certain pride in her bearing which forbade familiarity.

Frieda had long been interested in Christian Science, and her faith continued to guide her. As she wrote from the vantage point of her later years, "I am grateful for the shedding of great fears and the ability to accept disappointment which this way of thinking has prompted in me." We both strove to be good Christian Scientists (I had been raised in Christian Science), and perhaps for this reason also we understood each other so well.

Brownie was still around. He was a big dog, blind and crippled but still eating well and enjoying the good care of Frieda and Rosa. He never left the apartment and he smelled, as old dogs will, but this bothered neither Frieda nor Rosa, and I was seldom around him.

It wasn't just Brownie in the apartment at that time. Frieda had brought home a stray female cat from the park just before I arrived, and she already had the run of all the couches, chairs, and drapes. We decided to call her Phtha, since she looked very Egyptian. She was a pure white cat of long Siamese build with typical black face markings. She had evidently been a family pet, for she had been spayed and was immaculately clean. Frieda had already taught her to retrieve a rubber sink stopper which she would repeatedly throw down the long hallway. Phtha, of her own accord, would bring the stopper every morning to Frieda's bedroom and drop it on Frieda's chest. Frieda would have to repeatedly toss it across the bedroom for Phtha to retrieve. We both had much fun with Phtha, since I, too, was a cat lover.

One special guest was a squirrel with an injured hind leg. I did not meet him but Rosa told me about him. He finally healed enough to hobble around, and soon took to climbing up Frieda's satin bedroom drapes. They became tattered and Rosa was angry with Frieda, she told me, and so Frieda obediently took him back to the park where he could climb trees.

I saw the proof of Frieda's genuine love for all animals not only in the bedroom's tattered drapes but also in the frazzled chair covers, scratched furniture legs, and torn couch coverings, the furniture still being the French period pieces chosen by Elsie de Wolfe in 1917. This damage was not immediately noticeable to the unschooled eye, and so Frieda did not bother to get anything repaired. She loved animals too much and knew that more damage would follow when the next sick animal needed a home. She and I would feed the squirrels and birds and pigeons every day in the park, except in bad weather.

Frieda no longer saw any of her former colleagues in New York when I knew her, and never had any social engagements. She never listened to music during the day and seldom went to the piano to play for herself. She seemed far away from music.

During my years at 271 Central Park West, I was dismayed to learn that the Metropolitan Opera Company paid no attention to the fact that Frieda was living in New York, but apparently she did not care. She had no visitors other than her close friends Sophie and Laura, and her former husband, Will Kahn, still very handsome and full of good humor. I do recall that Jussi Björling once called on Frieda and spent the afternoon "talking voice techniques" with her, as she told me.

I gradually got her accounts in order, except for the confused tax records. Here nothing could be done, so Frieda told me to continue to ignore the problem as she had for years. Later, when I wrote to Mr. Keating in 1955 about the pending Internal Revenue Service auction of Frieda's estate, he replied, "I am amazed that she owes that much in back taxes. On two separate occasions I gave Frieda some money to apply against her tax debt to the Government. I had hoped that it was used for this purpose."

He had warned Frieda several times of the possibility of losing all her estate to the Internal Revenue Service for back taxes, but apparently Frieda did not grasp the seriousness of the situation. So at the time I just followed her advice. I knew nothing of Mr. Keating's generosity to Frieda, and his checks to her were never entered in the account books. Her private income came from the monthly checks from the settlement from the Heckscher legal proceeding.

Mr. Jim Flanagan, the handsome, tall policeman who had helped Frieda to catch Brownie and bring him to the apartment in 1942, had spent many evenings with Frieda and Brownie in the apartment. He became ill with liver cancer in 1944, and Frieda was desolate. She and Brownie were then alone for the next eight years. When Brownie died on 21 June 1952, Frieda was completely alone, for I was visiting relatives in Florida.

In July after Brownie's death, Frieda flew to Europe, with Mr. Keating paying all the expenses. When she returned in the fall of 1952, she had decided to reactivate her cosmetic business with my help. We were to manufacture and sell her famous cream. She had previously placed her equipment in storage, and now she had it moved to a large workroom across the park.

She was very secretive about her formula. I recall her standing in one

Frieda Hempel and Elizabeth Johnston in Central Park feeding the birds and squirrels, 1952. COURTESY ELIZABETH JOHNSTON.

corner of the room and calling out to me in the opposite corner what to pour into the mixing vat from the containers of ingredients: so much lanolin, so much pure oil, so much perfume, and so on. We spent many an hour waiting for the mixture to finally acquire the proper consistency, doing other jobs in the meantime such as getting the cream jars clean and shiny, pasting on the labels, filling the various containers with ingredients, and tidying up the room. Frieda enjoyed the work, just as she had in her youth.

The cream was exceptional; to sell it, Frieda had only to notify an established clientele from former years. Most of them were wealthy women living on Manhattan's Upper East Side. My task was to deliver the cream person-

Hempel and Elizabeth Johnston making facial cream, 1952. COURTESY ELIZABETH JOHNSTON.

ally. Business thrived, but we kept it small because all Frieda wanted was to be kept busy. She asked far too little for her cream, considering the quality of the ingredients. I recall that a director of a famous cosmetics firm came to the apartment and wanted to buy her formula and sell the cream under her name, offering to cover eighty percent of advertising costs and twenty percent of the costs of ingredients and manufacturing. Frieda refused, of course. Unfortunately the formula book was never found.

We continued to manufacture the cream until Frieda left for Europe in the summer of 1953, again as Mr. Keating's guest. While in Berlin, she signed a contract with Argon Verlag for the publication of her autobiography. When she returned she closed down the cosmetic business, since now we had to get the English text ready for Argon's translator, Mr. Fritz Engert. This work was completed in late 1954.

We were often quite tired in the evenings and would just watch television with Rosa. Frieda would sometimes send me by taxi to a specialty shop on the East Side, open evenings, to purchase a pound of chocolate creams and chews. She loved these candies, and so did Rosa and I.

One evening in December of 1954 Rosa was serving our meal, and just as she was asking if fish would be all right for dinner the next evening, she toppled over. Frieda rushed to her and tried to comfort her, for she was fully conscious. She could not move her limbs. I immediately called the family doctor, who came right over. Rosa had had a severe stroke, so we carried her with all our combined strength to her bed. She was soon taken to a hospital where she lay motionless for two weeks, with no sign of recovery. She decided that she wanted to return to Germany, where she had a nephew living in Münster. Frieda contacted him, and in Regensburg he located an excellent home for the disabled elderly. Frieda arranged for transportation and of course accompanied Rosa on this sad, final journey. Ironically, Frieda had to be transported in the same manner to Germany a year later. The two good souls never saw each other again.

When Frieda returned home from Regensburg she began to cook for us. I remember above all her roast chicken, which we had frequently. However, we soon found a housekeeper and cook, and things gradually returned to normal. Early in May 1955, sadly, Frieda discovered that she had cancer. She thought at first that the bleeding had come from a special diet she was following to lose weight, but she was mistaken—it was indeed cancer. She seemed to have expected this problem, for she had lost her mother, her father, her sister Helene, and her brother Emil to this disease.

She bravely went to Memorial Hospital, and I remained in the apartment to put away personal things and prepare the apartment for rent. I then placed an announcement in the papers stating that Frieda Hempel's apartment was for rent, fully furnished, for one year. A younger man from the entertainment world came highly recommended and seemed the ideal client.

I had him visit Frieda in the hospital, and she gave him the apartment for one year.

I moved into a furnished room near the hospital so that I could see Frieda every day. She underwent two operations, and after being fitted with the necessary catheters and bags, she was finally told that she could go home. Her first wish and indeed her need was to go to her hairdresser at the beauty shop just off Fifth Avenue and 57th. The physician advised against this, but we went anyway and I had no difficulty tending to her medical problems in the shop. She did look lovely as we drove to the furnished apartment on Central Park West just south of 271 which I was able to rent for July and August. I had called Will Kahn, and he was there to greet us.

All the nurses whom I engaged came only once, saying that the work was too unpleasant, so I had to become a trained nurse twenty-four hours a day. I found a woman to keep house and cook for us. Will Kahn visited us often and brought much cheer and good humor into Frieda's new life. It was very hot in July, almost 96°F day and night, and so Sophie and Laura came only once, much to their shame, I felt. Mr. Keating had had a heart attack and unfortunately could not come to New York. He told Frieda that he had to go to Mexico on urgent business but would try and come as soon as he got back. He never came, and so I never had the pleasure of meeting him even though he covered all of Frieda's and my travel and living expenses.

Frieda felt that she had to make the trip to Berlin, and I knew that she needed to experience the joy of seeing her autobiography published, so I agreed to take her despite the family doctor's disapproval. He finally advised that she should remain lying down in a special separate compartment behind the pilot's cabin, so that I could adjust her catheters and change her bags without bothering the other passengers on the plane. We decided to do this, and I made the necessary arrangements.

Although Will Kahn, Sophie Tavarozzi, and Laura McNaughton had come to the apartment on the sweltering day of departure in August of 1955, none of them would accompany Frieda and me to the airport. They simply waved goodbye from the curb of Central Park West. I could not understand this, as I thought they were true friends. Were they all afraid of an airport adieu? Perhaps.

At the airport I could not leave Frieda standing alone while I hurried about to take care of all the formalities, so I arranged a wheelchair for her. I shall never forget her bewildered looks; I am certain that she was wondering why Will, Sophie, and Laura were not there with her, and I could not explain—there was no acceptable explanation. Was the weather too hot for such effort?

In any event the Red Cross personnel with whom I had spoken helped us to the plane and got Frieda settled. She was a "real trooper," as Mr. Keating said. He later wrote to me, "You have been with a very great soul." How true this was! Frieda was patience itself during the entire trip to Berlin. The lovely stewardess was very efficient and helpful, and so we had no real trouble. Red Cross personnel met us in Frankfurt and had a wheelchair ready for Frieda's transfer to the Berlin plane.

In Berlin where it was also sweltering hot we were met at the airport and taken in an ambulance to Franziskus-Krankenhaus in the center of West Berlin, just a block from the zoo. Since war damage had leveled the streets, we could hear the calls of the animals throughout the day, much to Frieda's delight. Professor Hüdepohl told Frieda that he could not share her hope of recovery, since no further operation was possible. Frieda took this news quietly, and bravely settled down to life in the hospital.

I was given a hospital room next to Frieda's. I was not even aware at first that the nurses were taking my blood pressure and my pulse every day and trying to find out why I was there. I eventually began to notice what was going on and complained to the head nurse. The matter was promptly settled, much to the amusement of all. Frieda was comfortable and well taken care of in this Catholic hospital. Her medication soon made her mind confused in the evenings, and her large, sunny room seemed to remind her of earlier times in her Central Park apartment. She would tell me every now and then to invite so-and-so to her party and make certain that the food was right. Or she would have me go and see who was at the door. Clearheaded during the day, she would work with Mr. Engert, or talk with her brother Walter, who lived in Berlin and whom she had not seen for many years. Some days she would chat with Michael Bohnen (1887–1965), once a renowned bass-baritone but now spindle-thin, starving we thought. Frieda helped him out financially and talked with him about the great days of the Met, where he had also sung (from 1923 to 1932).

In the early evening hours she would often sing folk songs to herself in a quiet, soft voice. I was greatly moved, and the attending doctor suggested that we place a microphone under her bed and catch these songs for posterity. I refused to allow this, feeling that it would be a violation of Frieda's privacy. Perhaps I was wrong?

Mr. Keating was very caring and sent me frequent letters. "You are a brave, fine friend," he wrote. "I am so glad that Frieda has you rather than just relatives who have not been with her enough these past few years to be of the necessary comfort. I enclose a draft for flowers several times a week, so that she can look on beauty." In another letter he said, "I know what you must be going through each day, and God be with you and give you strength. I am happy that Frieda has you, now that Rosa cannot help, you who can give her that spiritual lift she so much needs, she who gave so many people happiness during her lifetime."

After learning from me that Frieda was dying, Mr. Keating wrote:

You know, you and your dear patient are in our prayers. . . . I can think
of no other help for you, so devoted to her and with her in these last trying hours. You will never forget this experience for the rest of your life.
I enclose a further check. I want the nicest flowers for her, something
special. For a great diva, for my Brünnhilde. God be with you, young
lady, and keep your head up very high. She would have wanted you to.
"The play must go on," she would have said. What a grand trooper, the
old Golden Age kind! You were her very best friend, a friend when one
really and truly needs one. You have been with a great artist and a very
great soul.

He also wrote, "I am glad that she has come 'home' where her great heart
is; Germany is in her blood, nothing could change that very natural feeling
for her homeland, her birthplace, and the scenes of her early struggles and
triumphs."

Death came quietly to Frieda on the morning of 7 October 1955. With
me in a circle around her bed were the Catholic sisters of the hospital in
their white habits, with the splendor of Mr. Keating's fragrant, beautiful
flowers blessing the room. This very peaceful scene remains in my memory
as a wonderful Italian oil painting of perfect harmony, illuminated by the
morning rays of sunshine flooding in from the window and outlining
Frieda's soft smile.

A great number of Berliners attended Frieda's funeral service. Her
brother Walter with his wife and his two nieces sat in the family pew, and
afterward we were together in Walter's home in Lichtenrade, a suburb of
Berlin. Frieda did not live to see the publication of her autobiography, but
she did hold in her hands the red book cover with its photo of her as Verdi's
Gilda, which she had selected for this purpose. This had given her great joy.
Her ashes were laid to rest in her home soil, at Heerstrasse Cemetery in Berlin, the city where her career had started fifty years earlier and where her star
had risen suddenly and brilliantly in the heaven of great song.

Upon learning that Frieda Hempel had died, the Internal Revenue Service scheduled an auction of her estate in New York on 23 March 1956, in
order to collect the thousands of dollars she owed in back taxes, just as Mr.
Keating had predicted. I was not in New York at the time and do not know
who got what. Nor was Mr. Keating able to be there. He had commissioned
Will Kahn to bid for certain items. I do hope that Frieda's favorite belongings found loving and respectful buyers.

One of her last wishes soon touched my life in a way she could not have
foreseen. She had realized that Michael Bohnen and his wife were penniless
and had sensed that he would not willingly accept cash from her. But she
thought that if I would take voice lessons from him, the lesson money would

Notice of auction of Frieda Hempel's estate at 271 Central Park West, New York, 23 March 1956. COURTESY ELIZABETH JOHNSTON.

enable them to eat. After Frieda's death I was thus obliged to study with Michael Bohnen.

Michael was a fascinating man with wonderful tales to tell about his life as an actor and singer, but he was a brutal teacher. Although he wrote that I had one of the most beautiful contralto voices he had ever heard, under his insensitive treatment I soon became dreadfully hoarse. At least he began to gain weight and feel better, now that his wife was cooking lunch regularly for all three of us. He was also a psychic and lived by the predictions of the cards he read.

In February after Frieda's death I had flown to New York and had to fly to California immediately, for my mother had taken seriously ill. Michael had read the cards for me just before I stopped singing and left for New York, and had told me that a close woman friend, probably a family member, would die shortly. How right he was. He had seen my mother's death in the cards. She died before I arrived in Berkeley, just as Michael Bohnen had prophesied.

Frieda's life was one of great highs and tragic lows. Her last years were empty of any real happiness and public recognition. Indeed, her life was like that of all naive artists. Just as Tetrazzini was robbed of nearly all her life earnings by her handsome young male companion and Bohnen lost his life's earnings through careless investments, so Frieda lost her wealth through tragic circumstances. But I never heard a bitter word from her. She knew how to accept whatever came her way and remained, as she writes, an "essentially happy person." She lives on in her wonderful records as the great lyric soprano and impeccable musician that she was. We are all grateful to her for having given us such beauty.

Postscript

by
William R. Moran

An Informal and Selected Chronology:
Frieda Hempel's Career as Reported in the Press

Hempel and the Lawyers:
The Heckscher Affair and the IRS

George T. Keating, Friend and Benefactor

An Informal and Selected Chronology: Frieda Hempel's Career as Reported in the Press

Frieda Hempel was born on 26 June 1885 in Leipzig, where she began her musical studies with piano lessons at the conservatory. Later, when her family moved to Berlin, she enrolled at the Stern Conservatory, working for three years under the tutelage of her only voice teacher, Selma Nicklass-Kempner. We find first mention of her in a July 1905 review of a Stern student recital at the Berlin Beethovensaal: "The greatest individual success won by any singer was that attained by Fräulein Frieda Hempel of Leipzig. . . . This young lady has all that is necessary to the making of a truly great artist."[1] Her operatic debut as Frau Fluth (Otto Nicolai's *Die lustigen Weiber von Windsor*) at the Berlin Royal Opera in September 1905 was so successful that she was promised a permanent engagement at Berlin's Royal Opera as soon as she had acquired the routine experience to be gained only at a smaller theater. There followed two years at Schwerin, after which she returned to Berlin and the Royal Opera where she signed an exclusive five-year contract, taking the place of Geraldine Farrar (as Gilda).

In Berlin she had great success especially in coloratura and lyric roles. Her Berlin contract prevented her from accepting offers from the Metropolitan in 1906[2] and again in 1910[3] but allowed her to make many guest appearances throughout Europe, in Munich, Vienna, Brussels, Paris, Monte Carlo, and other major cities. In June 1907 she was heralded for her debut as Eva (*Meistersinger*) at Covent Garden.[4] In October of the same year, she sang Gilda (*Rigoletto*) and Lucia in Berlin with Caruso, singing in Italian while he was on the stage, otherwise in German.[5] She was in great demand for coloratura roles, especially as Königin der Nacht (*Zauberflöte*) at various

Mozart festivals, where she was "quite at home in that difficult role, and not content with the three high Fs which the composer had already demanded, put in an extra one."[6] Hempel's reviews were not all entirely favorable. Berlin critics found that her Marguerite de Valois in the revival of *Les Huguenots* at the Court Opera "lacked the necessary power and coloratura accuracy,"[7] and a *Musical America* correspondent wrote, "Frieda Hempel is developing well as a coloratura soprano; unfortunately she has neither soul nor personality."[8] Later the same season, in a review of *Rigoletto* at Théâtre de la Monnaie in Brussels (with Anselmi and Sammarco), *Musical America* remarked, "As for Fräulein Hempel, her popularity grows a pace. One of the few German singers who have any conception of the art of singing, she has steadily grown artistically at a rate that augurs well for the future stretching out before her. At present, Selma Kurz is the only coloratura soprano on the German or Austrian stage who overshadows her."[9]

Hempel herself had probably begun to realize that her fabulous coloratura technique was not sufficient foundation for an entire career. Richard Strauss had Hempel in mind from his initial concept of the role of Zerbinetta (*Ariadne auf Naxos*) and still hoped he could persuade her to create the part just a few months before its premiere in October 1912.[10] Instead the role was created by Margarethe Siems in a new version with somewhat simplified coloratura. Hempel was anxious to become involved in the first production of *Der Rosenkavalier,* which was scheduled for Dresden (26 January 1911) with roles assigned to established Dresden artists, but second in importance was the Berlin premiere which took place 4 April. Hempel tells us that Strauss asked her to prepare the roles of Octavian, Sophie, and then the Marschallin; she chose the latter rather than the more obvious Sophie, no doubt to make a public statement and wisely establish her capabilities in roles more serious than those usually available to so-called "empty-headed coloratura canaries." She had already sung Eva (at Covent Garden in 1907) and was to add Elsa and other lyric parts in the near future.

In March 1910 she sang the role of Berta in a revival of *Der Prophet.*[11] In April, headlines proclaimed her "conquest of Paris" as Gilda and the Queen (*Les Huguenots*).[12] Charles Henry Meltzer of the *New York Times* reported from Brussels, "The sensation of the hour here were the appearances of the great Russian basso, Chaliapin, and of Frieda Hempel, the famous coloratura soprano with M. Smirnoff, the wonderful Russian tenor, in *La traviata*."[13] In July and August, Hempel was found at the Mozart Festival in Salzburg organized by Lilli Lehmann. "In *The Magic Flute . . .* honors were pretty evenly divided among Hempel as the Queen of the Night with the formidable colorature flights, Johanna Gadski as Pamina and Frau Lilli herself as the First Lady."[14] The press carried little news about Frieda Hempel in concert; one exception was a review of a recital in Vienna on 6 December 1910 in which she sang several arias with orchestra and songs with piano. "In the arias she gave fresh proof that she shares with Hermine Bosetti of Munich the honor of being the best coloratura singer in German. The songs, while charming, were less effective. One felt that she belonged on the stage."[15] According to a letter and notes dated 1911 in the Gramophone Company files, a publicity film of Hempel in the recording studio and enjoying her records in a drawing room was shown in Berlin movie theaters at the time.

In May of 1911 Hempel took part in an opera season in her native city, where she was acclaimed for her *Traviata* and Marie (*Die Regiments-tochter*);[16] the year 1912 was to see the end of Hempel's restrictive contract with the Royal Opera of Berlin. The international press had been reporting for some time negotiations which would allow her to appear with both the Metropolitan and the Royal Opera,[17] and plans were announced for her to open the Metropolitan season of 1912–13 with a revival of *Zauberflöte* to be sung in Italian, conducted by Toscanini, with Gadski, Berger, and Amato.[18] However, it was announced on 13 October that Hempel "has been taken suddenly ill in Buda Pesth [Budapest] where she is playing a two-weeks engagement . . . the date for her Metropolitan debut may have to be postponed."[19] The long-anticipated debut finally took place on 27 December with Hempel singing the Queen in a new production of *Les Huguenots* (with Caruso, Destinn, Scotti, Rothier, and Didur). In the 1912–13 Metropolitan season, she repeated this role four times. Her second role at the Met was Rosina (*Barbiere di Siviglia*), which she sang three times, then Olympia in *Les Contes d'Hoffmann* in the first production in the house on 11 January, which she repeated six more times. Next was the long-promised revival of *Zauberflöte*, which was heard four times with Hempel's spectacular Queen of the Night.[20] In addition this first season Hempel was heard as Gilda once, Violetta five times, and Lucia once. In her first Met season, she was also heard in two galas and two performances of Beethoven's Ninth Symphony conducted by Toscanini. Boston heard her Violetta in a special non-Metropolitan production 28 February. Hempel was back in Berlin for a special production of *Rosenkavalier* conducted by the composer on 26 May, which elicited rave reviews.[21]

Hempel began her operatic activities for the 1913–14 season at the Royal Opera "as the feted darling of the Berlin public,"[22] with her first *Bohème* on 19 September; her first American concert of the season was in Hartford on 3 November followed by a recital with orchestra in Boston on the ninth.[23] November 19 saw her return to the Metropolitan in *Zauberflöte*, followed on the twenty-second by the long-anticipated new production of *Un ballo in maschera* under Toscanini. Hempel "sang with brilliant effect as a charming and seductive Oscar,"[24] with fellow cast members Caruso, Destinn, Matzenauer, and Amato. W. J. Henderson wrote: "It would be more than unkind to make detailed comment on the singing of yesterday's cast.

Mr. Caruso alone stood forth as the artist commanding the respect of the connoisseur. Even his delivery of the music of Riccardo was by no means impeccable, but at its best moments it was admirable." (Hempel received no mention.)[25] Four days later came a revival of *Lucia* before a "not very large nor enthusiastic house . . . Mme Hempel was a very pleasing Bride of Lammermoor, though she effaced no hallowed memories,"[26] while 9 December saw the first American performance of *Rosenkavalier.*

All the New York critics had much to say in detailed evaluation and appraisal of the new opera; few had more than a brief line or two about the singers. Herbert F. Peyser wrote, "Mme Hempel made of the Princess an attractive and genuinely poetic figure and proved that she is even more satisfying in pure cantabile than in colorature."[27] Richard Aldrich (in the *New York Times*) had most praise for the Octavian of the evening, Margarete Ober, and concluded, "Also, wholly admirable is Frieda Hempel's impersonation of the Princess; an impersonation fully denoting all the nuances of the character as the poet has shown it, and expressing them with passion that yields to gentle melancholy most befittingly; and her bearing has then great repose and dignity. There is abundant opportunity for the pure brilliancy of Miss Hempel's voice to count for much."[28]

In January 1914 Hempel managed to find time between her Metropolitan performances for her debut in Chicago 5 January in *Traviata,* with Giorgini and Polese, followed by a *Lucia* on 7 January with Giorgini[29] and her first Eva (*Meistersinger*) in the United States, in Boston 29 January. Olin Downes wrote, "Mme Hempel's Eva was by some warmly praised. We found it a rather characterless impersonation, in spite of Mme Hempel's undoubted skill and musicianship."[30] However, in an unsigned article that looked back over the year we also read: "Her Eva came as another happy surprise, for in addition to her thrillingly beautiful delivery of the music, she presented a portrayal that realized in every detail of winsomeness, ingenuous charm and simple coquetry Wagner's conception of the Nuremberg goldsmith's daughter. That this soprano had not been earlier exploited in this part amazed all lovers of Wagner."[31] More performances of *Rosenkavalier, Traviata, Ballo in maschera,* and *Zauberflöte* followed before the Metropolitan season ended. Richmond, Virginia, was the setting for a festival on 11 and 12 May, which saw Hempel in the company of Amato, Braslau, Althouse, Gluck, Kline, and Homer "for the finest brilliant concert . . . not even excepting Tetrazzini has any artist sung *Ah fors'è lui* here as Frieda Hempel sang it, for in spite of Tetrazzini's top notes she has bad spots in her voice and Miss Hempel has none. In runs, trills and cadenzas it ripples and flows without a quiver; in sustained passages it veritably sings itself, so pure and smooth and perfect is its legato."[32] By 26 May Hempel was back in Berlin for a *Bohème* at the Royal Opera "for a welcoming ovation and storms of applause"[33] followed by a *Rosenkavalier* on 14 June. Next came a concert at Queen's Hall London with orchestra directed by Percy Pitt.[34] While Hempel was in London there were performances under Beecham at Drury Lane (the Marschallin on 4 June and the Queen of the Night on 6 June)[35] before her return to Frankfurt for *Fledermaus* and two performances of *Barbiere* on 10 and 13 June. In both she sang her role in Italian and German, depending on the nationalities of her fellow artists on the stage at any given time,[36] then returned to close the festival at the Berlin Royal Opera with *Rosenkavalier*, conducted by the composer, on 14 June.[37] During July, Hempel joined Amato, Campagnola, Chenal, American soprano May Peterson, and many others at the summer festival at Ostende which came to an abrupt close because of the German invasion of Belgium.[38] An English concert tour beginning at Manchester on 10 October had been planned before the singer's return to New York, but this had to be canceled.

Hempel opened the Metropolitan season for 1914–15 in *Un ballo in maschera* (with Destinn, Matzenauer, Caruso, and Amato, conducted by Toscanini); the opera was repeated once. She was also heard in *Rosenkavalier* (with Elisabeth Schumann as Sophie) (five performances), *Zauberflöte* (nine), and *Traviata* (six). Excitement for the season was provided on 19 December by a new production of the seldom-heard Weber opera *Euryanthe*, conducted by Toscanini with Hempel in the title role. Herbert F. Peyser reported: "As a very virtuous but very stupid Euryanthe, Mme Hempel won a fresh triumph. The greatest singer in the world would be hard taxed to make the character convincing, but the noted soprano gave a tender, winsome and sympathetic portrayal at all events, and most important in this case, sang the lovely music that has fallen to her share with ravishing purity and loveliness of tone and true capacity for emotional expressiveness."[39] It was performed six times. *Les Huguenots* was given an "Italian Revival" on 30 December, with Hempel, Destinn, Garrison, Caruso, Scotti, and Rothier. *Musical America* reported "Mme Hempel was the Queen. She sang the empty, florid passages of the part in which she made her American debut brilliantly enough. But happily one does not now readily associate the great artist who has given us the matchless Marschallin, Euryanthe and Eva with this silly role."[40] It was given four performances. Hempel sang Eva in *Meistersinger* on 12 March, repeated twice. She sang one Gilda and took part in one gala (Act 1 of *Traviata*) and five concerts. In addition to her work at the Metropolitan, Hempel was heard (with Amato and Rudolph Ganz) at the Biltmore Morning Musicals and as soloist at the Ann Arbor Festival.[41]

The *New York Sun* for 14 July 1915 reported:

There is strong feeling among subscribers against the performance of German operas at the Metropolitan Opera House next season. The writer does not believe that the departure for Germany of Frieda Hempel means that she thought there would be little opportunity here in German opera next season. It is explained that although by her agreement with Mr. Gatti-Casazza Mme Hempel had no right to leave the United States this summer, she was obliged to go home by the grave illness of her father and will return as soon as his condition is improved. Thus her departure had nothing to do with any movement to eliminate German opera from the Metropolitan repertoire.[42]

Her safe arrival on 15 July in Copenhagen was duly noted. There was a concert for wounded German soldiers in the auditorium of the Royal Surgical Society in Berlin on 15 September,[43] three days before her departure for New York.

Musical America commented:

> Once more it has been demonstrated that a German singer, no matter how pronounced a favorite with the home public, automatically forfeits a large measure of hard-won popularity by heeding a call from Dollarland, or more elaborately, Dollarika as German writers have dubbed this country. This time Frieda Hempel is the victim of this unfortunate prejudice, though in her case the resentment over her defection from the Berlin Royal Opera has found expression not so much in any changed attitude of the Berlin public toward her as in the tone of the reviewer's comments. When, a few weeks ago, this popular Metropolitan soprano gave a concert in Berlin in aid of the soldiers, she announced that the special purpose to which the funds would be devoted would be to augment the available financial resources for a home she proposes to establish for German soldiers physically wrecked by the war. Ungracious, to say the least, is the reception this announcement has met with at the hands of the *Allgemeine Musik-Zeitung*, which in zealously espousing the cause of the overlooked but none the less needy and deserving members of the musical profession does not hesitate to attribute egotistic motives to Miss Hempel's efforts. This is the comment made: "To be charitable is certainly an admirable trait, but leaving out of consideration the fact that this act of charity ostensibly planned for effect smacks somewhat emphatically of personal acclaim, Miss Hempel should have directed her sense of generosity primarily toward her German colleagues who are in downright want. For our heroic soldiers an endless amount is being done both by the State and by countless private societies and individuals, but for the non-combatant victims of this world war, the innocent servants of Art who have been plunged into bitter need, practically nothing has been done. Who, then, should have an eye and a heart for these suffering ones if it is not their few fortunate colleagues? But of course, singing in aid of needy artists does not achieve the same showy publicity effect."[44]

A lengthy fall tour began 15 October in Lynchburg, Virginia, and included concerts in Minneapolis, Kansas City, Chicago, and Pittsburgh. Samuel Chotzinoff was her accompanist, and for some concerts she was joined by baritone Pasquale Amato.

Hempel began her Metropolitan 1915–16 season with *Rosenkavalier* on 20 November and repeated the role of the Marschallin four times, but she shared it with Melanie Kurt after the latter's arrival. She was given Rosina (*Barber*) in the first two performances of the season but was replaced first by Alice Nielsen and later by newly arrived Maria Barrientos, who was also to take over the roles of Gilda (in a new production of *Rigoletto*) and Lucia. Eva in *Meistersinger* Hempel shared with Johanna Gadski, while Oscar in *Un ballo in maschera* went this season first to Edith Mason and later to Mabel Garrison. *Traviata* was only given twice this season, both times with Hempel, but she retained her exclusive right to the Queen of the Night in *Zauberflöte*. Hempel was given the lead in the revival of Flotow's *Martha* on 11 December (with Ober, Caruso, and De Luca): "Frieda Hempel's Lady Harriet may not rank with her Euryanthe, her Eva, or her Marschallin, but that is only because the part itself is infinitely less significant. Yet in charm, in effervescence and delicate gaiety her portrayal stands beside some of the finest Marthas heard here. Vocally, her work was brilliant, both in the numbers spiced with *fioriture* and in passages of smooth *legato*. The *Last Rose of Summer* took the audience by storm, and with good reason. She was obliged to repeat it *da capo* and on the second hearing gave it in flawless English, which pleased the hearers better than the Italian version."[45] Hempel sang the role four times; Barrientos twice. Hempel proved herself to be a trooper of the old school on 15 February 1916 when she sang a lengthy concert of opera and lieder at Carnegie Hall and then rushed to Brooklyn to substitute for an ailing Gadski in a Metropolitan production of *Meistersinger*. Both performances drew extravagant praise from critics.[46]

Richard Aldrich wrote:

Miss Frieda Hempel, who is now and has been for several years the chief reliance of the Metropolitan Opera House in coloratura singing, gave a song recital in Carnegie Hall yesterday afternoon. There was a large audience present, and Miss Hempel gave a delightful exhibition of an art that she has unquestionably made finer and more finished since she first came to this country. Miss Hempel is one who takes thought about her art, and has raised herself to a higher artistic stature thereby. Her program yesterday was made up almost wholly of music particularly well adapted to her voice and style, and there was much artistic enjoyment to be derived from the way in which she presented it. She began with the air that ought to be *Divinités du Styx*, from Gluck's *Alceste*—an air that has been introduced into *Orfeo* in the New York performances of recent years. It was not *Divinités du Styx* because she sang it in German, a transformation not altogether to its advantage. There were breadth and passion in her delivery of it; but this air, alone of all her music, needed more weight and power of voice, more dramatic vehemence than belong to the singer. Handel's *O had I Jubal's Lyre* in English which followed, she took at a rapid pace, and sang the "divisions" with great brilliancy, flexibility and precision. Miss Hempel is thoroughly at home in German Lieder within a certain range of expression. There were warmth and sincerity in her singing of Schumann's *Widmung*; there was a greater charm of tenderness and grace in his *Nussbaum*, of arch and mischievous humor in Schubert's *Forelle* and Brahms's *Vergebliches Ständchen*; for these it would not be too much to say that she struck quite the right note of expression and found an infinity of exquisite detail; and likewise for Mozart's *Warnung*. Nor could there be wished a greater perfection of diction than she showed in these German songs—a diction whose finish is allied with the beauty and freedom of her production of tone. To this group she added Mozart's *Das Veilchen* in a manner worthy of the rest. She sang another operatic air, *Ernani involami* from Verdi's *Ernani*, with much of the large and expansive style of the finish and freedom of phrase that belongs to it, and then added *The Last Rose of Summer* in English as she does it in *Martha*. More English songs followed. A beautiful and characteristic *Song of the Nile* by Courtland Palmer, in which Oriental color is used with skill in avoiding excess; *Phyllis has Such Charming Graces*, *The Lass with the Delicate Air*, and two vivacious German songs, Wolf's *Elfenlied*, which she had to repeat, and Pfitzner's *Gretel*. Miss Hempel's English pronunciation was very good, indeed; scarcely more than a few of the vowel sounds betray the foreign accent. At the end she sang the brilliant arrangement for soprano solo of Strauss's *Blue Danube* waltz, with Italian words and some additional vocal ornamentation in which she has already been heard this season. Coenraad V. Bos played her accompaniments with the hand of a master.[47]

Reviews of Melanie Kurt's Marschallin (9 March) were polite but left little doubt who owned the role in New York: "[Kurt] sang the music well . . . but one missed the variety of delivery, the beautifully chiseled enunciation, the subtle appreciation of the import of every phrase to which operagoers have been accustomed in the past. And the characterization as a whole lacked the repose and grace as well as the delicately wrought psychological delineation which made Miss Hempel's embodiment a veritable masterpiece of character drawing."[48]

The Central New York Music Festival opened its sixteenth season on 12 May 1916, with Stokowski, the Philadelphia Orchestra, and soloist Frieda

Hempel,[49] who ended her spring concert tour in Boston 28 May.[50] On 4 June she took part in an open-air performance of Mendelssohn's *Elijah* in Boston, with Schumann-Heink, Elvira Leveroni, Marie Sundelius, Johannes Sembach, and Clarence Whitehill, directed by Walter Damrosch conducting an orchestra of 165. Hempel was selected for special praise by Olin Downes.[51] The press was kept busy during the late spring and early summer announcing Hempel's summer plans and their many alterations. First she would spend the summer giving concerts in Germany to raise money for war refugees and resting in Switzerland. Then she would remain in the United States for the summer, taking a house in the Adirondacks. Next it was Europe again, because the managers of our most exclusive resort hotels had refused to welcome Miss Hempel's dog, Pitti, as a fellow guest: "In Europe there are so many attractive little places where I can rest and Pitti will be happy and well cared for. In Europe the little dogs are welcomed and you know my little Pitti. She never barks or makes any trouble, so I must sail and get some rest for us both."[52] So Pitti and Frieda sailed for Bergen 15 July. On her return, her Norwegian-American liner was stopped and searched by the British. "Miss Hempel spoke of the shortage of food in Germany which resulted in making the German woman more thin and elegant. . . . If only I could get a personal audience with President Wilson I would tell him that now is the most acceptable time for him to offer to mediate the differences between the warring nations."[53]

The 1916–17 Metropolitan season opened 13 November with a new production of Bizet's *Les Pêcheurs de perles* with Hempel, Caruso, De Luca, and Rothier. Peyser reported that "Frieda Hempel has done few things better than the forsworn vestal virgin Leila. She was in delightful shape, and the music of the role is congenial to her. Of her one occasion for florid display in the first act, she availed herself handsomely, but she won her hearers no less by the smooth and lovely treatment of sustained legato phrases and pure cantabile."[54] The opera was only repeated twice. Eva was given twice to Gadski and twice to Hempel, "perhaps the loveliest Eva in the experience of New York operagoers . . . the role might have been created to fit her personality and voice."[55] *Rosenkavalier* received only three performances, all with Hempel. Adina in *Elisir d'amore* became a new role for Hempel at the Met on 30 December (with Caruso, Scotti, and Didur). She was given three performances, and Barrientos, who also shared *Martha*, the same number. Excitement for the season was provided by a revival of *Le nozze di Figaro* with Hempel as Susanna, Farrar as Cherubino, and Matzenauer as the Countess, with De Luca as Figaro and Didur as the Count. H. E. Krehbiel said: "All that can be called a survival of the Mozart style was summed up in the performance of Frieda Hempel. She alone knew equally well how to act her part, sing her airs and speak her recitatives. [She] was in many respects the most satisfying member of the cast. She seems naturally fitted for humorous parts and, as in *Martha*, she acquitted herself charmingly."[56] Peyser (?) in *Musical America*, wrote: "Mme Hempel's mercurial nature and silvery voice fit her admirably to the needs of Susanna. Her singing was tasteful and exquisite. The *Deh vieni non tardar* provided the supreme vocal joy of the evening."[57] The soprano's busy day of 12 February was reported in detail: in the morning she spent "considerable time" with conductor Richard Hageman of the Metropolitan going over some songs, in the afternoon there was a concert at Carnegie Hall "before a crowded house," and in the evening it was her final appearance in opera this season in *Le nozze di Figaro*, after which she took a late train for Ohio to open her concert tour.[58]

Upon the declaration of war with Germany (6 April 1917), Frieda Hempel along with thousands of other German citizens in the United States became legally "enemy aliens." Individual artists reacted differently: some scampered for home; others sought a safe neutral haven. Still others decided that the United States was a pretty good place to be and adopted individual methods of contending with the problems which arose. In June it was reported that "Miss Hempel has taken a long lease of a beautiful apartment overlooking Central Park and has been giving much attention during spare moments of the past season to the furnishing and decoration of this home."[59]

During an interview at the time of a joint concert in Detroit with Giuseppe de Luca (30 October), the soprano announced that she would be making her debut in motion pictures in California during the following summer. On 3 November at a concert in Providence, Rhode Island, "excitement ran high against artists of German origin, and a concert of Mme Hempel was held up by local authorities until it was arranged that she should sing *The Star Spangled Banner*." Her champion on this occasion was Mr. William B. Kahn, an American and head of the W. B. Kahn Silk Company of 95 Madison Avenue, New York. A week later Mr. Kahn went to Youngstown, Ohio, where a women's club threatened to cancel a concert "until persuaded that Mme Hempel intended to become an American. Mme Hempel has made no secret of her matrimonial plans since then, but it was said that should she marry before the end of the war she would forfeit considerable property in Berlin, the earnings of her operatic career before she came to the Metropolitan."[60]

The 1917–18 Metropolitan Opera season began for Hempel with *L'elisir d'amore* on 15 November, with Caruso and Scotti. It was repeated three times with Hempel, but in the performance of 19 April, Barrientos took over the role of Adina. Hempel was given all four of the season's Violettas, all six Maries (*Fille du régiment*), all three Suzannas, and three of the five Lady Harriets (*Martha*) but only one of the season's seven Gildas. Rossini's Rosina became the exclusive property of Barrientos, as did all performances of the revival of *I puritani*. The revival of *La Fille du régiment* was exclusively for Hempel (11 December 1917). Herbert F. Peyser wrote, "The *Rat-a-Plan* number passed off so infectiously that Mr. Papi had to bow to the will for an encore. No doubt Miss Hempel's drumming, which was of virtuoso quality, had more or less to do with this. . . . Her Marie is vivacious, volatile, loveable. She conquered her audience completely as she waved the large tricolor in the last act, making this episode the climax of the whole evening."[61] A friend said to Oscar Thompson, "Well, that settles Hempel. She can never go back to Germany, that's certain." When asked to explain himself, the friend noted "Because in the opera she has just fallen down before the French Flag and kissed it. . . . When they hear that she has kissed the French Flag instead of resigning her position [rather] than do it, they will never accept her again." The comment was of course made in jest, but it unfortunately proved prophetic, as the German press later made much of this bit of stage business in New York.[62]

The 4 May 1918 issue of *Musical America* reported:

Eighteen members of the Metropolitan Opera Company chorus were dropped last week. It is reported that a searching investigation is being conducted and that every person in the artistic corps, chorus and orchestra suspected of enemy alien affiliation will be immediately dismissed. Not even first papers of naturalization will avail, it is stated. No contracts will be renewed with any person of German sympathy. It is understood that Frieda Hempel, coloratura soprano, Margaret Matzenauer, contralto, and Artur Bodanzky, conductor, are among those who have been dropped. Miss Hempel's forthcoming marriage to an American, W. B. Kahn, will make her automatically an American Citizen; Mme Matzenauer's divorce from her Italian husband has not been recognized by the Italian government, and in consequence her status is that of an Italian Citizen, and Mr. Bodanzky had taken out his papers as an American Citizen.[63]

The same issue of *Musical America* carried a note: "The eloquence of Percy Hemus, who spoke for the Liberty Loan [war bond drive] at the Eltinge Theater . . . resulted in Frieda Hempel adding $3000 to her already sizable subscription to the Loan. This subscription was made in $1000 lots. . . . Miss Hempel has subscribed liberally to the third Loan as well as to the two previous issues."

William Armstrong tells us that with Will Kahn it had been "love at first sight,"[64] which had been the moment Mme Hempel walked on the Metropolitan stage in her debut in 1912. Kahn appears to have been a constant suitor since then—at least he spent a lot of time making himself useful to the singer. For example, his name appears as witness on a contract Hempel signed to make recordings with Edison 30 November 1917; Edison was apparently perfectly willing to accept Kahn's legal authority when some alterations to the original contract were made by letter signed by Kahn on 20 February 1918.[65] The formal engagement announcement came on 7 March in Los Angeles, during a concert tour, and drew attention to the fact that Mme Hempel would become an American citizen upon her marriage.[66] The couple obtained their marriage license on 4 May—the story in the *New York Times* stated that Mme Hempel was an "enemy alien" but that her marriage would make her a citizen. The article further states that neither had been married before and that Kahn was thirty-five.[67] (Hempel was about to turn thirty-three.) She had a concert in Macon, Georgia, on 8 May[68] and was in the Edison studios 28 and 31 May and 3 and 5 June.[69]

The much-anticipated marriage took place in New York on 8 June 1918 at St. James Lutheran Church. The *New York Times* headline reads, "Frieda Hempel Wed; is American Citizen,"[70] and the "American Citizen" part was stressed in publicity releases for some time. On 10, 11, and 15 June Hempel was recording in Edison's New York studios; on 18 June the couple left on their honeymoon trip to Watkins Glen, Lake Placid, New York.[71]

Hempel's newly acquired American citizenship was not an end to all hostility. The Edison files contain correspondence from irate customers: in a letter dated 3 July 1918 a Nebraska customer asks, "Are there no American singers with sweet voices whom you can feature? This German Hempel who has given us insult upon insult. . . . Be an American Concern. Feature American singers. We've had enough of the Hun for all time. This page ad. of yours is an insult to all good Americans." On 18 September 1918 the general supervisor of the Edison plant wrote a vice president of a Des Moines company (a record dealership?) noting:

> Your section of the Middle West appears to be laboring under a misapprehension regarding Miss Hempel's status and character. So far as I can learn Miss Hempel has never been identified with the German clique at the Metropolitan. She has definitely thrown her lot with America by marrying an American who has been prominently active in cutting off necessary supplies to Germany shipped through neutral countries. For several years *In the Daughter of the Regiment* [sic] she has kissed the French flag on the stage of the Metropolitan Opera House. I doubt if any German who expected to return to Germany or who cared for German favor would do that. It would be astonishing to read the newspaper article which you sent me and which assumed of course that Miss Hempel's loyalty is in doubt if I were not familiar with the conditions which have brought about so much criticism of Miss Hempel in your locality. . . . I think that the Des Moines newspaper might better be engaged in encouraging the populace to conserve sugar or some other commodity or to buy War Stamps or subscribe to the next Liberty Loan than in devoting really valuable space to the perpetuation of a feud

which bears the earmarks of personal vindictiveness and malice. It seems to me they are grinding somebody's axe with no possible benefit to themselves or the community at large.

> Yours for the 4th Liberty Loan.
>
> Thomas A. Edison, Incorporated.

In our so-called more enlightened age, it is sometimes difficult to believe the extent to which anti-German feeling was whipped up in the United States during World War I. The trade publication *The Talking Machine Journal* printed a story entitled "Collecting German Records in Cleveland" in September 1918 (p. 34):

> The Northern Ohio Talking Machine Dealers' Association have put the ban on talking machine records in German, or of German origin, and are carrying the idea even further than internment. Pittsburgh has interned these records for the time of the war. The Cleveland dealers decided to handle the matter with even a firmer hand. Consequently, A. L. Maresh, treasurer of the Association, and C. K. Bennett, president, have been constituted as a committee, and are calling upon dealers to gather in these records. It has not been decided what will be done with the records after they have been collected, but opposition to this move is being mollified by a statement that the Department of Justice has requested that steps be taken to prevent the distribution of talking machine records in German on the grounds that it keeps alive the spirit of Germanism in American communities.

The 19 October 1918 issue of *Musical America* carried a photo titled "Frieda Hempel Singing on the Steps of the Sub-Treasury in Wall Street in Aid of the Liberty Loan" before an audience that packed every inch of space for more than a city block. She sang "The Long Long Trail" and "Dixie" and promised an encore ("Annie Laurie") for an additional $1000 subscription, which was immediately forthcoming. "On Saturday evening Miss Hempel sang at another Liberty Loan rally at which Colonel Roosevelt was present, at the Academy of Music, Brooklyn."[72] In a reference to the Metropolitan performance of *Daughter of the Regiment* on 14 November 1918, Grenville Vernon of the *Tribune* was somewhat severe, even while noting that Mme Hempel had recently become an American citizen: "Miss Hempel had better be told at once that the introduction of such phrases as 'Gee Whiz, what are you fellers doin here,' and such songs as 'Keep the Home Fires Burning' into a Donizetti opera will not endear her to her adopted countrymen. The bestowal of American citizenship ought to be thought an honor and not a patent to vulgarity." The audience, three days following the armistice, felt differently and demanded an encore![73] Robin Legge in the London *Daily Telegraph* picked up the story and suggested substituting "Tipperary" for the Soldier's Chorus in *Faust* and that Caruso should use "Over There" in the scene of Radames' triumphal return in *Aida*.[74]

On 18 January 1919 the first (of only four) Metropolitan performances of the Ricci brothers' *Crispino e la comare* took place, conducted by Gennaro Papi. It was to be Hempel's last new role at the Metropolitan. Herbert F. Peyser wrote:

> Saturday's representation sped on its way under an implosion of comic exuberance and animal spirits that lifted it to a level of diversion never attained by the Hammerstein productions. It moved with all the progress of finely co-ordinated ensemble. But the efforts of Frieda Hempel, Sophie Braslau and Mr. Scotti ranked preëminent. Annetta allows the apt and pretty comic propensities of Mme Hempel such play as they have in *L'elisir* and *The Barber*. Her humor, arch and exhilarating, never fails the touch of delicate distinction. Some altitudinous tones may have grieved her admirers last week. But apart from these paltry blemishes her song was minted silver. She followed the Patti-Tetrazzini precedent with the diabolical *Carnival of Venice*. If anything on earth could justify the procedure, her singing of these damnable variations did.[75]

On 6 February Hempel announced that she would no longer be under the management of Winton & Livingston. She had established a new organization called Frieda Hempel, Incorporated, with her husband as president and principal stockholder. "A force of four people will devote itself exclusively to the direction of Miss Hempel's various interests, concerning which many interesting rumors are circulating. All concert dates will be booked from that office."[76] On 15 February a private showing of a new life-sized Hempel portrait by the Hungarian artist Louis Mark was held at the artist's studio. Enrico Caruso was among the guests.[77] In its issue of 27 March 1919, the *Musical Courier* "learns on good authority that Frieda Hempel has declined an offer from Giulio Gatti-Casazza for a renewal of her contract on the terms upon which she has been appearing at the Metropolitan Opera House for the last five seasons."[78]

April 1919 saw Hempel on an extended concert tour of the southern states. "She has advised all the local, Victory Loan committees that she will be glad to subscribe through them for the amount of the bonds equal to the gross receipts of her concerts in their cities. . . . Miss Hempel will buy bonds in sixteen cities."[79] The bitterness of the recent war lived on:

> There has been a beautiful row in the Oratorio Society of which the distinguished industrial leader Charles M. Schwab is the president. . . . The row is said to have been precipitated by a discussion as to whether the Society should engage for its soloists singers of pronounced German sentiments or sympathies. The storm center was Frieda Hempel.

Rudolf Bing and Anna Case with portrait of Hempel. PHOTO BY LOUIS MÉLANÇON. COURTESY METROPOLITAN OPERA ARCHIVES.

> . . . A resolution was finally put through to the effect that the Society would bar those singers who have been outspoken in their sympathy with the Teuton nations. The decision seems . . . eminently just. In the first place, there are too many American singers of standing and reputation who need all the engagements they can get. Then too, there are foreigners here, Germans among them, who have been either discrete in their attitude or have become thoroughly Americanized. Indeed many of them have become citizens. With regard to Frieda Hempel, it is but just to that lady to state she is today an American Citizen by right of her marriage to an American businessman. In the next place, we believe that Mme Hempel has conducted herself with scrupulous consideration for our feelings all during the war period. An effort was made . . . at one time to decry her but it had no basis in anything the lady had said or done.[80]

A story datelined Paris, 16 August 1919, stated: "I was somewhat astonished to hear frequent remarks about Frieda Hempel from a number of Berliners and I gathered that her conduct during the war had not altogether found favor among her compatriots in Germany. She was accused of having deserted Germany in its hour of peril and further of not having shown herself sufficiently anti-allied or, if you like, rabidly pro-German,"[81] while in September we read: "It would appear as if a concentrated effort was being made to discredit Mme Hempel as being so distinctly pro-German that she should not be accepted by American audiences, even now that the war is over."[82]

In the fall, winter, and spring of 1919–20, Hempel continued with a busy concert and oratorio schedule, reported in detail by the press. Much was made of her use of an airplane to fly from Fort Worth to Austin to keep a concert date.[83] She and Will Kahn sailed for Europe on 10 June to spend the summer in England, France, and Switzerland.[84] The press continued to keep track of her activities, even noting that perhaps the reason she did not give a concert in Berlin was the way "a part of the press attacked her" over the old charge of kissing the French flag.[85] We learn in September that the singer was bringing back with her from Paris a "Jenny Lind gown, an exact copy of the one in which New York music lovers first saw the Swedish Nightingale."[86] This was the first the public had heard of Hempel and the Jenny Lind concerts, but it was far from the last. Herbert F. Peyser reported his reaction:

> The Centennial of Jenny Lind's birth was commemorated in Carnegie Hall October 6, 1920, with Frieda Hempel as Jenny Lind, Thomas A. Wise impersonating P. T. Barnum; Arthur Middleton as Signor Belletti; Coenraad V. Bos and Daniel Wolf, pianists; and an orchestra

under Ole Windingstad. Hempel sang "Casta Diva," a trio for two flutes and voice from Meyerbeer's *The Camp in Silesia*, "The Herdsman's Song" and "Greeting to America" by Sir Jules Benedict. She gave "Home Sweet Home" as an encore. Middleton sang several Rossini arias, including a duet "Per piacer alla Signora" from *Il Turco in Italia* with Hempel. Frieda Hempel, in billowing white satin, looked sufficiently like available pictures of Jenny Lind to convey the desired illusion and her manner was charm and graciousness itself as she came into view on the arm of Signor Belletti-Middleton. The soprano enjoyed hearty applause throughout the evening and did her best work in the Meyerbeer trio and in the echoing "Herdsman's Song" in which last she accompanied herself on a kind of spinet, the veritable one used by Jenny Lind and lent for the occasion by Mrs. John W. Tobin of 490 Riverside Drive. This she had to repeat. Strict honesty of record requires the admission that she has sung much better as Frieda Hempel than as Jenny Lind.[87]

Hempel must have felt she had a real winner as she continued to give Jenny Lind concerts (minus most of the trappings) in the United States and England as late as 1931, although in the later years these were "by request."

Later in October 1920 Hempel made a first appearance with the Chicago Opera Association in a pre-season *Traviata* in Milwaukee (with Bonci and Rimini under Alexander Smallens). She was not listed as a regular member of the company which had both Galli-Curci and Garden in performances at its home base.

On 20 December Hempel took part in a performance of *Messiah* at Carnegie Hall with the New York Oratorio Society under Damrosch.[88] She was soloist with the Harvard Glee Club on 17 February; the reviewer called attention to the number of songs in German which were included.[89] On the twenty-sixth, Hempel appeared in a joint recital with Alessandro Bonci at the New York Hippodrome "in a program of songs and operatic airs delivered in a manner to satisfy the many admirers of these two exponents of bel canto."[90] Hempel (and Forest Lamont) gave a much-heralded radio concert from San Francisco on 21 April by DeForest Radiophone which was unusual for the fact that "every radio station within a radius of 1500 miles had been formally notified" to pick up and rebroadcast the program, so that it was "heard from Alaska to Mexico and as far west as Hawaii and 1500 miles to the east."[91]

On 24 May 1921 Hempel and Will Kahn sailed from New York to spend the summer in Europe. Plans were announced for opera and concert programs in Spain, Denmark, and Italy, including a Toscanini invitation to sing at La Scala,[92] but like many such press-released plans, the La Scala visit did not take place. The tour extended to Vienna, where Hempel sang a children's benefit concert and a *Traviata* (under Weingartner, 7 October), and to Liverpool.[93] On 10 October reports from Budapest read, "All appearances sold out. . . . Thousands turned away. People offering ten times box office price for *Traviata* tonight."[94] On 6 September 1921 the *New York Times* reprinted a story (datelined Berlin the previous day) under the headline, "Flurry Over Hempel's Return to Berlin: Nationalist Newspaper Attacks Singer for Wartime Pro-French Demonstration in New York." The story repeats the business about the flag-kissing and says, "It is well that she transfer her field of activity elsewhere . . . as conditions today make it appear imperative to us that no new occasion be given for awakening passionate excitement. . . . Mme Hempel should not dare attempt to sing in Germany. . . . Apparently the Nationalists and reactionaries are determined to break up any concert Mme Hempel may give in Berlin."[95]

On 13 January 1922 Hempel was enthusiastically welcomed back to Carnegie Hall.[96] She made her debut in Havana at the Capitol Theater 5 February, followed by a second recital three days later. "The large crowd which attended was enthusiastic and the concert proved an unusual success."[97] On 19 February Hempel gave a joint recital with Titta Ruffo at New York's Hippodrome. Bos accompanied Hempel and Charles Gilbert Spross accompanied Ruffo, who was reported to be suffering from bronchitis.[98]

Richard Aldrich had a rare opportunity in his review of the activities at Carnegie Hall which took place the afternoon and evening of 21 March. First he commented on what became an "informal" concert by Emma Calvé, who "sang what she wanted to sing at the moment" without regard to the limitations of the printed program. "Of course, the voice of a singer approaching 60 years is not that of a singer of 27 [and] though the voice does show signs of what the years do to voices, there was much beauty in it, and there was much that was fine, noble, searching, charming in her singing. And it was quite appreciated by her listeners." When Frieda Hempel presented her fourth song recital in the evening, she "appeared to be in the best of voice, and her best of voice is very good indeed—surpassed indeed by very few now before the public. She seems at the height of her powers. The voice has not often sounded more beautiful, more vibrantly rich and penetrating than it did last evening—a true sfogato quality."[99]

Hempel (and Will Kahn) left for Europe on 23 May 1922. They celebrated their fourth wedding anniversary with a dinner at the Ritz in London, followed by a concert at Albert Hall, London, 11 June. The next day she went to Malvern to visit the grave of Jenny Lind. During May and June *Musical America* and *Musical Courier* announced plans for Copenhagen and a *Rosenkavalier* in Budapest, and a royal concert to celebrate Jenny Lind's birthday in Stockholm. In August *Musical America* reported, "The music critics for the leading London papers seem to have fallen in love with Frieda Hempel . . . who was welcomed back with enthusiasm when she sang a number of concerts at Albert Hall and elsewhere. They think she is now singing better than she did when she visited the English metropolis before." And she "had the unique experience of having to sing the same song [Farley's *The Night Wind*] four times before the audience would permit her to proceed with the program."[100]

Hempel returned to the United States on 1 November and began a tour with the Boston Symphony Orchestra, conducted by Pierre Monteux, in Toronto on 6 November, followed by a concert in Providence and two (24 and 25 November) in Boston. It was reported that she was scheduled for "over ninety appearances in practically every part of the United States" and that some fifty of her concerts would be Jenny Lind events.[101] Both Hempel and Coenraad Bos received extravagant praise following a 28 November Carnegie Hall recital.[102] Much coverage was given to a break-in of the Hempel apartment with a loss of some $30,000 in jewels, furs, and personal trophies which were listed in detail by Will Kahn.[103]

A brief article appeared in the press in early January 1923, to be noted in view of events which took place two years later:

> To judge by Mme Hempel's vivacity and all-pervading happiness, she has evidently solved the matrimonial problem which has been the cause of trouble to so many beautiful and talented prima donnas from time immemorial, and no wonder. Right at her side stood her tall handsome husband, Mr. Kahn, who is not only a man of charming manner but a good businessman who looks after his wife's interests with scrupulous care as well as consummate ability. If some of the other prima donnas who are now engaging the press because of trouble with their husbands would have exercised the same discrimination that Frieda did, instead of being in the law courts most of the time, they would be pursuing successful careers and increasing their bank accounts beyond the dream of avarice.[104]

The article is signed "Mephisto," who was, at least in 1934, Oscar Thompson.

On 9 January 1923 Hempel again appeared in a revival of her now-famous Jenny Lind program, this time before an audience of five thousand at the Hippodrome. The review mentioned her singing "Home Sweet Home" and noted that the song would have its one-hundredth anniversary on 8 May, which anniversary she celebrated by broadcasting the song from the Westinghouse radio station WJZ in the Waldorf Astoria.[105] The singer and her husband sailed for Europe 12 May. In a report from London dated 27 May, Lionel Powell reported: "Frieda Hempel's 'Jenny Lind' concert at Albert Hall today was the sensation of the London season. More than 7000 persons were in the audience. All royal boxes were occupied until the last encore."[106]

By July a vacation seemed to be in order:

Cable dispatches from Europe, published in various New York papers on 17 July, stated that Frieda Hempel . . . had been warned by a faction of monarchists that on account of "unfaithfulness to Germany" during the recent war, she would not be permitted to sing in Germany. The accounts further stated that Miss Hempel was notified that if she attempted to appear, she would be "howled down." W. B. Kahn, husband of Miss Hempel, when spoken to concerning the statement, said: "Miss Hempel was asked by leading impresarios to sing in Germany last year and again this year, so I do not understand the story. When I left her in Paris two weeks ago, she had refused many offers from various opera houses in Europe, as she wishes to have the entire summer for her vacation. She does not intend to sing anywhere in Europe except the return 'Jenny Lind' engagement in London [21 October] just before she sails for home."[107]

Hempel (and Bos) returned to New York 2 November and began her season with a Jenny Lind concert in Lynn, Massachusetts, noting that "80 concerts will keep her busy until May when she returns to Europe in time for engagements in London."[108] On 27 November Hempel gave her annual Carnegie Hall recital with Bos but without the Lind trappings.[109]

Carnegie Hall was again busy on 12 February 1924, with a Reinald Werrenrath concert in the afternoon and another Jenny Lind–Hempel affair in the evening, reported as "sold out."[110]

Hempel sailed for Europe on 7 June, and Will Kahn followed on 5 July on a business trip to the continent, after which he was to join his wife in Switzerland.[111] An announcement from Berlin dated 2 September stated, "Frieda Hempel will return to Berlin for the first time since the war this season to give recitals,"[112] but there is no later mention of Berlin this season, so plans appear to have changed. The first recital of the season at Albert Hall took place on 26 October. "She was in marvelous voice and was greeted with tremendous enthusiasm by a capacity audience. . . . At the close of the program she was recalled seventeen times."[113] She returned on 17 November, and an extra concert (her sixth London concert this season) had to be scheduled for 7 December, followed by a tour of thirty concerts in the British Isles.[114] Meanwhile *Musical America* carried a two-page spread that reproduced reviews of her London, Liverpool, and Birmingham concerts, several of them containing derogatory remarks about Galli-Curci, whose name had been excised.[115]

Back in the United States, Hempel opened her 1925 season on 19 January with a concert in Plainfield, New Jersey, a benefit for the Greater Goucher College Fund. On 10 February it was Carnegie Hall in a concert given as a benefit for the New York Women's League for Animals. She first

appeared as herself, then as Jenny Lind.[116] There was a Massey Hall,
Toronto, recital of 16 February and on 25 March a "Last Concert of Season," a request program at Carnegie Hall.[117] The singer was "preparing to
start for a two-month's tour of the Pacific Coast" on 6 April. Her "last
appearance of the season" was on 14 June in Providence, when she sang at
the Rose Festival "at the first anniversary of the Benedict Monument to
Music" (a benefit?). On 17 June she had her one recording session (for Edison in New York), and on 20 June she sailed for Europe for a six-month stay.
The press announced, "Before returning to America during Christmas week,
she will make another tour of the British Isles giving thirty concerts. A recital
in Albert Hall, the first of four to be given there, will open the tour in October (1925)."[118]

 "Like a voice of Spring [Hempel] returned from a recent Florida tour for
her first recital of the season in New York," reported the *New York Times*.[119]
A new journal, *Singing*, in its second issue for February 1926, reports on a
Hempel concert with the New York Symphony but does not give the date.
In the same issue W. J. Henderson, under the banner "What I Think of
Living Singers, II," remarks: "Frieda Hempel, who occupies much of her
valuable time in impersonating Jenny Lind, was one of the best singers that
ever trod the Metropolitan boards; but her voice has taken on a slight acid-
ity and her singing betrays a descent in artistic idealism. In her opera days she
was a lyric soprano of the first rank, and no lover of fine interpretation will
forget her Princess in *Rosenkavalier*."[120] In April came an announcement
that "Frieda Hempel will be under the management of Baldini & Engel-
hardt for the season 1926–27. Miss Hempel recently returned from a tour
which covered territory from New York and Florida to Denver where she
sang to nearly 14,000 people. On this tour G. A. Baldini acted as her personal representative. Miss Hempel will sail for Europe on April 30."[121]

 A "Special to the *New York Times*," datelined Chicago, 13 May, advises
readers: "ADMITS MME IS SEEKING DIVORCE. Suit Brought in Paris, Says
W. B. Kahn, Husband—Plan to Wed Heckscher Denied." The story read:

> Reports of marital discord between Frieda Hempel, famous prima
> donna, and her husband, William B. Kahn, . . . were confirmed today
> when Mr. Kahn made a statement admitting impending divorce, and in
> which he said: "I deeply regret to say that it is true that my wife, Mme
> Frieda Hempel, has gone to Paris and has there instituted an action to
> divorce me. It is merely a question of incompatibility; no other man or
> woman has ever come between us. We therefore retain for each other
> mutual respect and esteem. I do not know anything about a contem-
> plated marriage between Mme Hempel and August Heckscher, 78-year
> old New York millionaire. Whether Mme Hempel marries again or
> remains single, however, I shall always keep her in my memory as a

Hempel appeared in the *New York Times*, 2 June 1924, in a campaign by the Women's League for Animals to raise funds for watering places for horses in Central Park. PHOTO BY UNDERWOOD & UNDERWOOD. COURTESY METROPOLITAN OPERA ARCHIVES.

woman of beauty, charm and grace, of beautiful voice and magnificent art. Evidently I failed to make her happy. This I sincerely regret, as no woman who has brought so much happiness to millions throughout the world should herself be unhappy." It was said last night at the home of August Heckscher, 277 Park Avenue, that there was no truth in the report that Mr. Heckscher planned to marry Mme Hempel as soon as she could obtain a Paris divorce from her husband.[122]

This article appears to be the first time the name of August Heckscher was associated with that of Frieda Hempel in the press, but stories about what came to be known as the Heckscher Affair would continue to appear even after Heckscher's death in 1941. (See "Hempel and the Lawyers," below.)

An Associated Press report datelined Paris, 25 June, states:

Frieda Hempel . . . within thirty days will receive a decree of divorce. . . . Mme Hempel and Mr. Kahn were summoned by the judge two days ago for the usual effort to effect a reconciliation. . . . She presented herself in court, but Mr. Kahn failed to appear. Although it is understood he is in Paris, he has taken no part in any of the proceedings. Mme Hempel charges her husband with abandonment and refusal to support her. The singer has a permanent residence in Paris and will remain here or in some French resort during the summer, or until the beginning of the opera season.[123]

A further story dated 17 July reported that the final decree of divorce had been granted 15 July. The story goes on to tell that the singer's engagement to Kahn had been made early in the spring of 1918 "when feeling ran high against artists of German Origin." It then relates how Kahn and his mother had journeyed to Providence and later to Youngstown, Ohio, where a women's club threatened to cancel a contract until persuaded that Mme Hempel intended to become an American.[124]

Hempel returned to the United States 5 October 1926 and announced the opening of her current concert tour at Ann Arbor on 18 October and Carnegie Hall 5 November, with Richard Hageman as her accompanist.[125] An unidentified clipping states that Mme Hempel will be heard on 14 November on the Atwater Kent Radio Hour. The next news of the singer's professional activities is found in April 1927 in which great plans for Europe are announced—concerts and opera in Paris ("early in June"). "*Rosenkavalier, Manon, La bohème,* and *Traviata* are the operas she is scheduled to sing. After several months in Switzerland, Mme Hempel will fulfill engagements in the opera houses of Berlin, Munich and Budapest. . . . The Christmas holidays will bring the singer to the United States. For her American concert tour she is planning a novel program as unique in character as her Jenny Lind recital programs."[126] Yet when she left for Europe 11 June, she stated,

"I may sing during the summer in Europe, but not professionally."[127] During the summer, American readers were treated to a veritable barrage of newspaper articles with claims and counter claims from both sides of the Atlantic with respect to the Heckscher affair, with occasional references to concerts (not opera) in St. Moritz, Berlin, Munich, Hamburg, Bonn, Budapest, and London (22 October). These articles seldom contain dates, but just plans, and there is little evidence for just which engagements were fulfilled.[128] The singer returned to the United States on 22 November.

She said she had sung concerts in London, Hamburg, Berlin, and Budapest. "My audience in Berlin loved me and they received me most kindly."[129] An article reviewing "New Productions in Germany" had this comment:

> Frieda Hempel came back to Berlin in recital last month for the first time since the war. There were some cheers from the audience for one who had been an opera idol throughout Germany, but there were hisses from those who remembered her conduct toward Germany during the war, when she kissed the French tricolor before an American audience. The critics seemed willing to forgive her trespasses if only she had not sung. As for her performance: We are poorer by one more artistic illusion. We have to go even further and say that Frieda Hempel is "done" as they say across the ocean. The clarity and brilliance of her voice are gone; her forte is shrill and disagreeable to hear; her coloratura, upon which she depended so much, has lost its mobility and refinement. She still can sing charmingly in the more subdued passages, but that will not make up an entire program. The chief complaint against her was that she made inordinate use of pantomime in her songs—which the one reviewer describes as "Wild West" antics, and which he says would not have been tolerated in Boston or New York.[130]

On 18 December 1927 Hempel opened a tour with the Boston Symphony Orchestra, under Koussevitzky, with a performance of *Messiah* with Kathryn Meisle, Charles Hackett, Fraser Gange, and the chorus of the Handel & Haydn Society.[131] It was noted that she "will sing in Detroit, Chicago, and other midwestern cities. An extensive tour of the South and festival appearances will occupy her time until the middle of May (1928)."[132]

On 29 April 1928 Hempel gave a recital at the Studebaker Theater in Chicago. Albert Goldberg noted: "Her taste in songs and her understanding of them are still exceptional but in excursions into the coloratura realm, such as "Qui la voce" from *I puritani*, the tone tended to become thin and labored, and there were deviations from pitch."[133] In August we hear that "Frieda Hempel has been in Paris for some little time, not giving concerts, but buying clothes. . . . Mme Hempel announces that she was a candidate to sing at the Paris Opera—Gilda or Violetta maybe, but the invitation hasn't as yet been issued. She plans on staying abroad until late in September or October, part of the time in Switzerland. No, she is not going to Germany."[134] On 30 September she is reported to have given a concert at Albert Hall (with thirteen encores). On 8 October it was a concert at Queens Hall, London, and on the following day, a concert at the Paris Opera the night before her departure for the United States.[135]

After two years' absence, Hempel returned to Carnegie Hall on 21 October 1928, with two groups of lieder, "Come per me serena" from *Sonnambula* and a group in English. "The present singer is not, unfortunately for us, the Hempel of our fond memories, but still she is Hempel, which means that no one can fill her place. Her charm and artistry are undimmed, but the voice is clearly on the decline. Those electrifying top notes are so far gone that not even the Hempel skill can conceal their loss. But the middle and lower registers retain more of the old warmth and sweetness than most other singers can dare to hope for. As was to be suspected, there were superb interpretative insight and style, felicitous phrasing and clean vocalization, especially in the descending scales and in stacatti, when they did not lie too high."[136]

Some news of interest (about which we hear no more) appears in a note signed by Hollister Nobel of *Musical America*: "At [the Metropolitan Opera premiere of Strauss's *Die Aegyptische Helena*, 6 November 1928] was Frieda Hempel with fiancé Jack Taylor of Florida, chatting with her late [that is, former] husband Kahn and Elsie Ferguson."[137] There was a recital in Massey Hall, Toronto, on 26 November, and a guest appearance with the San Francisco Symphony on 18 December, where Hempel sang "Ernani involami" ("which was a gem") and an aria from *The Marriage of Figaro*.[138] Back in New York, the soprano was heard as guest soloist on the General Motors Hour on WEAF, conducted by Papi. To celebrate Thomas A. Edison's birthday on 11 February, Hempel took part in a broadcast of "The Edison Hour" on WJZ, portions of which were recorded. Another of those press stories which told of great plans ahead, often never fulfilled, read, "Following an appearance in Atlantic City on 8 June [1929, with Albert Spalding, and which was broadcast] Mme Hempel sailed for Europe where major appearances include engagements in London and Paris. Upon her return to this country in the Fall, she will actively take up her work in concert, radio broadcasting, and sound pictures, also her Jenny Lind concerts and solo appearances with major orchestras. She will seek the earliest opportunity to fulfill engagements in Australia and the Orient. Mme Hempel is maintaining her own Management Bureau."[139]

Musical news about Frieda Hempel was scarce in the press of the 1930s, although her name is frequently found in the papers with respect to other matters (see "Hempel and the Lawyers," below). "Frieda Hempel, following a retirement from the musical field of about two years, made her re-entry at

Carnegie Hall on Friday evening (14 February 1930) before a large and representative audience. The renowned coloratura presented an attractive appearance and was given an enthusiastic reception. The impression gained by this writer was that the singer was in excellent vocal form, her voice being notable for its freshness, and her admired facility being as remarkable as ever. In a word, the Hempel art is still great and afforded her listeners an evening of distinct artistic pleasure." (Frank Bibb was at the piano.)[140]

On 15 March we are informed that Hempel "plans to continue next season with Jenny Lind concerts of which she has given seven hundred. She also has active plans in progress for sound picture arrangements,"[141] while in July we learn that "Frieda Hempel sailed recently . . . for Europe where she will sing in Paris, Ostende, and Vienna. Upon her return in the Fall she will make an extensive concert tour in addition to radio, picture work and stage appearances, under the exclusive management of William Morris."[142] A brief note advises us that "Frieda Hempel sang her first Town Hall recital 19 Oct. 1930 to a capacity audience. Frank Bibb was her accompanist,"[143] but no reviews can be found in the New York papers. Aside from a mention that she sang at a White House dinner given 18 December by President and Mrs. Hoover,[144] her musical activities seem to be ignored.

Things appeared to be looking up in 1931. The 31 January issue of the *Musical Courier* reported, accompanied by a photo, "Frieda Hempel . . . will be under the management of the Betty Tillotson Concert Direction for the coming year. Miss Hempel will be heard frequently from now on, both in concert and on the radio. She sang on the Maxwell House Coffee Hour January 27."[145] A few days after the announcement that Betty Tillotson was to take over the management, a *Musical Courier* representative visited the office.

> As you know, Miss Hempel has not sung extensively throughout the country for several years, but next season she will go to the Pacific Coast. In fact, she will tour all over the country; also go into Canada to Vancouver and Calgary. She is the luckiest person. . . . Miss Hempel plays golf and well enough to enter the amateur championships. Besides she's a good swimmer and is a daily attendant at the pool. She also skates and rides horseback. . . . As far as looks are concerned, she is always exquisitely groomed. . . . We plan to have her give a Carnegie Hall recital early in November [1931]. This summer she will go to Europe to fulfill some engagements, making several appearances in London. . . . Although Miss Hempel will present her Jenny Lind programs it will be done on request. She will sing more straight recitals.[146]

In April we read:

> Frieda Hempel, who will sing from coast to coast during the season 1931 and 1932, will be one of the first artists to appear at the new

With this photo came the announcement, "Frieda Hempel, world famed opera singer, will give a New York concert at Carnegie Hall on Friday evening February 14th. Recital Management Arthur Judson." COURTESY METROPOLITAN OPERA ARCHIVES.

Waldorf Astoria in the grand ballroom. The New York Diet Kitchen announces they have engaged Miss Hempel for their annual morning concert which is to be given at eleven o'clock on December 12, 1931. It is announced by Betty Tillotson, Miss Hempel's manager, that she will open the season in New York, after which she will immediately go to the Middle West starting her tour at Ripon, Wisconsin. She will sing in the principal cities of the United States, and many of the leading cities of Canada. Miss Hempel will fulfill social engagements this Spring, and will spend part of the summer in Europe.[147]

We find no mention in the press of the fulfilment of the plans announced in April unless this note in December may refer to the "social engagements": "Frieda Hempel's Sunday afternoon teas attract many fashionable and artistic personages."[148] The singer reported to tax authorities that her gross receipts from her "professional activities" (i.e., singing) in 1931 were $2063.10, while her "professional" expenditures in order to earn this income were $15,664.52, for a net loss in her professional activities of $13,901.42.[149]

Hempel opened her 1932 season with a recital in New York's Town Hall on 17 January before a large and enthusiastic audience. The concert opened with "Dich, teure Halle" from *Tannhäuser*, as Howard Taubman wrote, "on the whole, not a felicitous choice. For, while Miss Hempel revealed immediately that she still knows how to phrase and sing with feeling, the quality of her voice has not retained its beauty intact; there was some hardness in the upper tones in the Wagner aria, and some insecurity of pitch. In the next group, however, Miss Hempel dissolved any doubts that might have arisen concerning her mastery of German Lieder. It is still there. . . . Frank Bibb provided admirable piano accompaniments."[150] From the *Musical Courier* we learn that "Frieda Hempel gave a large tea party at her home . . . after her Town Hall recital last Sunday. Frieda's concert gown was a dream . . . and maintained her position as one of the smartest dressed women in the metropolis." The same publication noted in February that Mme Hempel was a soloist with the National Symphony Orchestra and went on to list all the dinners and social events the singer attended while in Washington.[151]

On 13 May 1932 Hempel wrote a note to Gatti-Casazza at the Metropolitan Opera:

Dear Commandatore [sic]: This letter is to let you know how sorry I am not to be with you at the Metropolitan. It is not my fault, nor is it yours, having always given me proof of so much kindness and genuine friendship; rather it is due to a third person: my husband. This is why we cannot give recitals of *Rosenkavalier* or other things. If you wish I could give you a private audition to prove to you how good my voice is. Dear sir, have no concerns about my cachet—we will come to terms. You have known me for many years, and you know that I have always been good, kind and a lady. I know that you are leaving soon, but I beg you to read this before you depart and to give me a long-cherished hope. . . . You know my repertoire, Elsa, Elisabeth, Daughter of the Regiment, Traviata, etc.

Gatti's reply was dated 16 May, and read in part as follows: "My Dear Mme Frieda, As you will have seen from the newspapers the next season of the Metropolitan will be much shorter than the previous one. This fact compels me to leave out of the company several artists who have appeared with us in these last seasons. And the same fact prevents me from using your valuable services. I always remember you with sympathy and sincere admiration but it is now a material impossibility which even the best sentiments and the best disposition cannot eliminate."[152]

The singer reported on her 1932 federal tax return that she had no income but expenses of $9801.28, and she deducted a net loss of that amount.[153]

For the year 1933, we have a report that Hempel impersonated Jenny Lind at a "Save the Metropolitan" ball on 28 April, and that she and Frank Bibb, along with Josef Hofmann, were on the program for a state dinner at the White House 14 December. Once again, the singer reported no gross receipts and expenses of $11,703.80 on her tax return.[154]

A first recital for the year 1934 took place in Town Hall on 4 February, and was reported as well attended; Frank Bibb was her accompanist. "Her songs, with a few exceptions, were chosen with shrewd wisdom, for her vocal abilities and limitations. Her gifts as a stylist projected them with unerring taste. The result was a recital that, for sheer artistry, has had few if any equals this season. . . . One was struck again and again by the singer's mastery of style. . . . [There were only certain songs] which require a dramatic, rich vocal timbre and a tender warmth of tone which the singer could not supply. . . . Her voice is too limited in volume [so that she] could make them mere simulations of what they should be."[155] A second recital at Town Hall took place on 27 March with Árpád Sándor at the piano.

A *New York Times* story on 3 June 1934 details a legal row with the singer's sister, Mrs. Helene Schaper, who we learn for the first time is a resident of New York. (See "Hempel and the Lawyers," below.)

Because the "present tendency on radio was to neglect the works of the great composers," the singer offered to sing for the radio audience over WNYC, the municipal broadcasting station. "She proffered her musical services in appreciation of the happiness she has found in this city. . . . Mayor La Guardia . . . said he could not find words to thank Mme Hempel."[156]

When it was announced late in 1934 that the Metropolitan was planning a new production of *Rosenkavalier*, Hempel wrote Gatti-Casazza on 18 December 1934:

Having had a very friendly relationship with you for many years, I believe it is not impertinence on my part if I allow myself to write this letter. I note that you are about to produce *Rosenkavalier*, could you not let me sing a single performance of this opera? I believe that there are many friends and critics who would gladly see me once more in this role, and I for my part would make my best effort to sing as I have always sung to make you satisfied and proud for having given me this opportunity. I would thus realize the dream of my life. I have suffered so much disillusionment, so much injustice, and so much humiliation, that by you acceding to my request I would have a new lease on life, or at least I would be heartened to continue living. . . . I have lost a lot of money, and it is a hard struggle to go on, so this opportunity would be an enormous help to me. Because I don't have my own manager nor anyone else to assist me, I am writing this most confidentially. . . . If you could spare a few minutes for me, I would ask you, if possible, to see me for these few minutes if you can.[157]

Gatti's answer has not survived, but the new production of *Rosenkavalier* took place on 4 January 1935 with Lotte Lehmann singing her first Marschallin at the Metropolitan.

Hempel received a letter dated 31 December 1934, from her attorneys, warning her that Heckscher was in great financial distress and that the security for future payments from this source was in considerable question (see "Hempel and the Lawyers," below). She consulted with Will Kahn and her former secretary, Lois Willoughby, and decided it was necessary to make a European tour to raise money. For 1934, Hempel claimed a gross income of $750.25 and expenses of $12,130.39 for a net loss of $11,380.14.[158]

News of Frieda Hempel in the local press virtually disappeared for most of 1935. We know she had a recording session in Berlin during the summer, although nothing from it was commercially published. In November, notes appeared in *Musical America* ("Frieda Hempel, returning to give a recital at Queen's Hall on October 29, was welcomed back to the concert platform with an enthusiastic response from audience and press that shows her place in the affection of music lovers is unsurped. Singing with great brilliance, charm and artistic verity, the soprano was at her best in a 'prima donna' program of arias, songs and Lieder. . . . Gerald Moore accompanied. . . . Mme Hempel is singing several additional recitals in England, Holland and Sweden, and will go to America at the end of December")[159] and *Musical Courier,* which added that she would have an extensive schedule of radio broadcasts when she returned.[160] Cesar Saerchinger reported surprise at the remarkable preservation of her voice. "She was at her best in the lighter, lilting Schubert songs, but never less than good." For 1935 her tax returns showed zero income against an expense of $7,121.87.[161]

Frieda Hempel did not return to the United States in 1935 nor in 1936, but remained in Europe. This time she was not forgotten by the American press: unfortunately the publicity, which sometimes ran to several articles a month, was mostly concerned with her legal battles which went on unabated. Now and then a musical reference appears: a 20 January concert in London had to be canceled because of illness; she sang three times for the BBC; a note on a Stockholm concert (undated) merely mentioned "Frieda Hempel's vocal artistry was admired in an evening of Lieder."[162] A review of a later concert in Copenhagen noted: "The last time this reviewer heard her previously—that was years ago in London—her tone quality and interpretations were exquisite, but he has to confess that the years have somewhat told on her once lovely voice. Formerly she was a coloratura, now she is more of a Lieder singer. Mme Hempel opened with Handel and Mozart arias, which proved to be somewhat of a mistake. Some of the high notes have lost their brilliancy, but one could still admire her art in forming a song, and her musical sensibility."[163] There were other concerts in London, but they are merely mentioned without comment. For 1936 Hempel's tax returns gave gross income as $1165.21 against expenses of $10,641.17.[164]

Hempel returned to New York on 17 February 1937, "from a month's vacation abroad that started two years ago."[165] "After a short stay in New York, Miss Hempel is going to California for concerts. It is said that while there, she is to discuss an offer she has had to appear in a movie version of _Der Rosenkavalier_."[166] On 29 July she sang Viennese songs with orchestra over the NBC Red Network.[167] "During 1937 she sang several concerts for charity and for Pan American Company for which she received no pay." Reported to IRS: gross receipts $99.00; expenses $9592.42.[168]

Hempel left for Paris 22 April 1938 and returned to New York 25 October. There were vague plans for concerts in Holland, Paris, Hungary, Germany, and Romania before her return to the United States, but as so often with announced plans, one can find few actual dates. Tax returns show no income. Concerts in The Hague (3 October) and Amsterdam (8 October) were on a percentage basis but were not successful. In an interview she speaks of her recital at Town Hall on 6 January, and then mainly of plans for the new year. "Next Spring I must return to Europe for engagements in Rumania and Bulgaria and France. I am to sing _Rosenkavalier_ again in Paris." The story continues, "She insists that she never retired—that court-aired and much publicized agreement which kept her from singing in public for so long to the contrary."[169] Tax returns for the year 1938 show gross receipts of $16.20 against expenses of $12,001.98 for a loss of $11,985.75.[170]

The Town Hall recital scheduled for 6 January 1939 did come off. "Her recital proved that her art remains elevated even though the voice now has some limitations. However, they seemed as nothing for Hempel knows how to select a program in accord with her present tonal equipment, and for the rest she pleases continuously through her sincerity, charm and brightness of delivery. . . . Celius Dougherty's pianistic partnership was altogether understanding and delightful."[171] Noel Straus wrote in the *Times*: "Miss Hempel had devised a program of German Lieder astutely chosen, in character and range to meet the present limitations of her voice. . . . One would search long among singers of the day for a more perfect legato or finer breath control. Miss Hempel never ventured more than a tone or two above the staff, and for the most part her voice was hard and white in its upper reaches except in mezza voce work. But the rest of her tones were not only pure and sweet but capable of unusual expressiveness and charm."[172] A flyer, which reproduces excerpts from eight reviews of this concert, announces a coast-to-coast tour for 1939–40, with a return to Town Hall in October 1939. It proclaims the management of Annie Friedberg of New York. Again there were changes in plans: a European tour mentioned for the summer did not take place, but we do find Hempel on a radio broadcast of recordings with host Stephen Fassett on 30 March, and in a performance at Robin Hood Dell on 11 July.[173] On 6 October came a recital at New York's Town Hall. "Despite passages and whole songs that did not measure high on a critical yardstick, she proved herself indisputably an artist worthy of her own reputation. Viewed in sum, Miss Hempel's art asks no charity. For the sake of the record those details are an uncertain pitch, an occasional pallor on quietly sustained tones, tightness and unsteady control in the upper register. . . . In one or two songs, Miss Hempel offered interpretations that belied musical meaning, as when she imposed a blatant whinny on Schubert's delicate *Die Forelle* . . . there were many compensations even in these weaker items of the program, just as, in her best efforts, Miss Hempel was not flawless. . . . Here and in other songs Miss Hempel was the artist of clear, firm conceptions, authoritatively conveyed with mature control. She was ably accompanied by Celius Dougherty."[174] On 30 November Stephen Fassett gave a program on WQXR with Hempel commenting on her own Mozart recordings. Tax returns for 1939 show gross receipts of $981.95 and expenses of $14,922.03.[175]

For the year 1940 the press appears to be silent on Hempel's musical activities. One undated notice from the New York *Mirror* stated that she was active in the Wendell Willkie presidential campaign. She must have taken part in some recitals and possibly radio broadcasts, as her 1940 tax return shows gross receipts of $1350.00 and expenses of $11,624.60.[176]

On 30 March 1941:

> Frieda Hempel, who was last heard here two seasons ago, gave a recital in Town Hall. The eminent soprano, for many years one of the leading exponents of the art of song in its loftiest estate, was still able to evoke an enthusiastic response from her audience at this latest appearance by the musicianship and intelligence of her work. When last listened to in

the same auditorium, Miss Hempel's voice still retained enough of the qualities of its glorious prime to make it possible for her to deal triumphantly with a program carefully restricted to selections well suited to a voice no longer what it had been. Yesterday the artist was less discreet in the choice of material presented. Beethoven's *Neue Liebe* and other offerings on the list proved to be too high in their tessitura, and it would have been far better had no attempt been made to enter the colorature field with the *Zeffirretti* aria from Mozart's *Idomeneo* or to venture songs like Schubert's *Die junge Nonne* or that composer's *Ungeduld,* making such exacting demands. For the voice at this recital proved to have lost its rich texture to such a degree that it was nearly always edgy and metallic, even in the lower half of the scale . . . Paul Ulanowsky provided impeccable accompaniments.[177]

The death of August Heckscher at the age of ninety-two in Florida on 26 April 1941 again opened the floodgates in the press, which took delight in reviewing past court battles and reporting new legal moves by Hempel against his estate. For the year she reported gross receipts of $627.50 and expenses of $10,692.01.[178]

For 1942 no reviews of Hempel recitals could be found, but the New York press delighted in the epic of Frieda Hempel and her dog, Brownie.[179] Tax returns for 1942, the last available, show gross receipts of $350.00 and expenses of $14,133.38.[180]

The Hempel press was again busy with Brownie and the Heckscher estate during 1943.[181] From 7 March through 30 May, the soprano hosted a series of fifteen-minute (later extended to one-half hour) Sunday evening radio programs broadcast from WNYC. The selections were listed in the radio pages of the *New York Times,* which did not always note the accompanist. (Celius Dougherty opened the series, sometimes replaced by Herman Neuman and Paul Meyer). Some of these broadcasts have been preserved on recordings (see Discography). August 30: "Frieda Hempel, who is nothing if not versatile, is to appear in the new Ed Wynn Vaudeville show, 'Big Time' . . . opening in Boston."[182]

On 11 October it was again Town Hall time: Noel Straus reported that a recital on that date was greatly to her credit.

The eminent soprano's youthful appearance and the excellence of her singing were alike remarkable for an artist who has been before the public for nearly four decades. Still more remarkable was the fact that instead of showing any deterioration since her last recital here two years ago, her work on this latest occasion was the finest heard from her in many a year. Discounting Wolf's *Verborgenheit,* that composer's *Er ist's* and Strauss' *Nichts* which were not well chosen, every one of the fifteen selections presented proved masterly both as regards to vocalism and interpretation. . . . A few slips from pitch occurred on the upper tones, which showed the ravages of time, but otherwise the intonation was secure and the scale notably even, the voice being used with a ductility, expressiveness and interpretive subtlety that lent real distinction. . . . Paul Meyer was the efficient accompanist.[183]

Jerome Bohm wrote:

> In far better vocal form than she was heard here last two seasons ago, Miss Hempel, although no longer able to cope with such altitudinous affairs as the music of Mozart's *The Queen of the Night* with which she won fame here three decades ago, is still an artist to be seriously reckoned with. Her program, more wisely chosen to meet her present needs than the one presented previously, contained many songs which were delivered in a manner which brought pleasure to the most fastidious ears. There were, to be sure, in the course of the afternoon occasional tones in the upper register which left something to be desired in quality. . . . Everything Miss Hempel undertook bore the earmarks of stylistic perfection. Every nuance, every turn was flawlessly delivered. Even the gestures with which she sought to enhance her interpretations and which are nowadays thought to be out of place on the concert platform by many, were made with such good taste and appositeness, that it was difficult to find them objectionable.[184]

A notice of a Town Hall recital on 26 March 1944 mentions that this is Hempel's second recital of the season. The first must have been that of 10 October 1943. The notice remarks that the program was varied, the audience large, many encores were demanded, and Árpád Sándor "provided support at the piano."[185] A clipping from the *Times-Picayune* of 16 April 1944 advises that Frieda Hempel will be at the Municipal Auditorium in New Orleans 25 April.

"Miss Hempel Gets Ovation" reads the headline for 26 March 1945, in reference to her concert at Town Hall the previous afternoon.

> The passing years have robbed her of none of her youthful enthusiasm, which combined with her magnetism and charm, lent an allure to her work that the large audience found irresistible, an audience containing many singers of note. There was an unusually long ovation for the artist when she came on stage, looking remarkably young and handsome. And after each of the offerings the demonstrations of approval were so marked that four of the songs bore repetition and many encores were demanded. . . . The delivery of these varied items could be commended for steadiness of tone, accuracy of pitch, carefulness of phrasing and excellence of diction. In fact, from the technical standpoint, Miss Hempel's singing was on its accustomed high plane. But the voice was not in

the condition that made it possible for the singer to do herself justice at her two recitals here last season. Yesterday the lower half of the compass was mellow, but the rest of the range proved pushed and extremely edgy, while there was a constant resorting to fussy gesturing quite out of place on the recital platform. . . . Occasionally there were beautifully sung phrases in the Lieder and folksongs, but on the whole neither her vocalism nor her interpretations matched those at her previous recent appearances in the same hall. Árpád Sándor furnished discreet and sympathetic accompaniments.[186]

During 1946 Hempel gave two recitals, both in Town Hall. The first was on 19 January: "Miss Hempel's voice is no longer in its prime, and the singer appeared at times to have difficulties in vocal production. But of artistry there was no lack, and the concert as a whole was an engrossing display of outstanding musicianship. . . . Despite vocal problems, Miss Hempel's voice is still an agile and pliable instrument. . . . It was only in such songs as Brahms' *Botschaft* where the vocal demands are heavy—both in volume and range—that Miss Hempel did not seem quite equal to the task."[187] The second 1946 recital took place on the first of December

before an enthusiastic audience. . . . Comely and gracious, as always, Miss Hempel was a treat to the eye, and her work could be commended for its impeccable phrasing, highly perfected legato and clean-cut diction. But the voice, though still voluminous, steady and true to pitch, rarely escaped edginess in the upper half of the scale, and except in a few offerings, had little variety of color. Of the superb tones and magnificent vocalism of old there was no hint in the first half of the program, nor were the interpretations during that part of the recital communicative or convincing, despite the attempt to add vividness to them by means of gestures and facial expression. But in the later half of the schedule . . . a turn for the better occurred. . . . That the voice broke on the final tone of Wolf's *Er ist's* was purely accidental, as Miss Hempel proved by repeating the song, but the sum total of her singing was disappointing. . . . Paul Meyer was the able accompanist.[188]

Reviews for Hempel's Town Hall recitals of 1948 and 1949 testify to her spirit and loyal following. "Frieda Hempel can still pack them into Town Hall," wrote C. H. in the *New York Times* on 4 October 1948:

And the noted soprano, young looking in a sumptuous pink creation, gave the audience what it wanted yesterday afternoon in a program of love, spring and folk songs, sung with stage manners to match. The listeners reciprocated with warm and prolonged applause.

Traces of the great voice remain, and the musicality, the knowing phrasing, the clear diction and, to a lesser extent, the sense of pitch were all in evidence. But the tone was edgy throughout its register, although an occasional pure note came through, and except for the lightest of folk-songs which concluded the program, there was little difference in color or dynamics between one piece and another.

The singer achieved a rather gay impulse in Schubert's "Das Lied im Gruenen," but made perhaps more of his "Fruehlingstraum" and Beethoven's "Ich liebe dich," among the Lieder, by way of [more] dramatic inflections and free tempo changes than the songs demanded. She pleased listeners into laughter with "Lolly du dum day" and Brahms' "Och Moder ich will en Ding han," and sang many encores.

On 5 December 1949 R. P. wrote in the *Times*:

Perhaps of all human gifts, imagination, charm and sympathy are the ones most impervious to time. And because Frieda Hempel has them in such abundance her recital yesterday afternoon at Town Hall was a singularly touching experience, even though old-time admirers had to admit her voice was not at the best.

A few complained that she took some liberties with the music. Others felt that she gestured too much. But for one listener neither seemed to matter. She gave a recital that few young singers could match, for all their fine voices, musical rectitude and unbending deportment. . . .

There was an audience of more than 1,000 persons, and the soprano was greeted with prolonged applause on her first appearance. The enthusiasm continued all afternoon so that she was obliged to sing four encores during the course of the program and four at the end. . . .

It should be noted how much spirit the singer had. And though her selections had moments of sadness—about the passing of time, especially—most of her program reflected her own joy of living.

The final encore was a surprise for it was one of her few selections in English, "Home, Sweet Home." And it was a measure of her artistry, her sincerity and her depth of sentiment that she was able to hold the audience with that old song as if it were being heard for the first time.

In her memoirs she says that her final Town Hall recital, 7 November 1951, was her last concert.

Frieda Hempel missed giving a recital last season, but she was back at Town Hall last night and her admirers turned out in force to greet her with an ovation, to applaud her continually, to load her piano with flowers and to hold her singing until after she had extended her program with five encores.

The truth should be faced that very little of the soprano's singing was actually beautiful in sound. But she still has so much charm and innate joyousness and such interpretative skill that she can give a recital few young singers can match. . . .

As a musician, too, she showed a command of the melodic line such as one seldom hears nowadays, so that each of her lieder were genuine songs as well as miniature dramas.[189]

A lengthy article on 8 October 1955 reported Hempel's death in Berlin the previous day and reviewed her career in considerable detail.[190]

An advertisement headed "Public Administrator's Sale" announced that an auction sale of the "Estate of Frieda Hempel, Decd., Famous Opera Star," would be held at 10:30 A.M. at 271 Central Park West (eighth floor) Friday, 23 March 1956. "Nine room apartment, period and antique furnishings, rare and important paintings by old masters, clocks, art objects, grand piano, Tiffany sterling silver platters, trays, tea sets, original records by famous opera stars Gluck, Caruso, Tetrazzini etc., music, books on music, collectors items, autographed photos and mementos of famous people, large quantity of theatrical costumes, and many other items too numerous to mention."

Will Kahn attended the auction. Her old friend George Keating, to whom she had dedicated the German edition of her memoirs, was ill in California and could not attend.

How fortunate that Frieda Hempel did not have to suffer this final indignity.

Hempel and the Lawyers:
The Heckscher Affair and the IRS

If there is such a thing as a litigious gene, then Frieda Hempel was bountifully supplied. In the old newspaper files the number of stories about litigation in which Hempel was involved is a source of constant wonderment. Since most are long-forgotten disputes, a sampling is more than enough to paint the picture.

Budapest, 10 May 1910. F. H. has been fined 1000 Kronen by the Budapest District Court for breaking her contract with a local concert agency.[1]

Berlin, February 1912. F. H. sued a Berlin newspaper recently for questioning her right to the Leopold Medal, the order of the late King of the Belgians. She won her case.[2]

Berlin, 13 December 1912. "Before sailing for New York tomorrow [Hempel] made a deposition in a libel suit begun as a result of insinuations in a local newspaper [*Klein's Journal*] to the effect that she was a participant in an orgy at the villa of Baroness Vaughan, morganatic wife of King Leopold of Belgium."[3]

Berlin, 15 November 1913. F. H. won her criminal libel suit against the editor of *Klein's Journal*. The editor was sentenced to a month's imprisonment.[4]

New York, 26 June 1919. "F. H. received service on her birthday . . . of a summons and complaint in an action begun in the Supreme Court by Winton & Livingston, Inc., concert managers, to recover $8400 for the alleged violation of an oral agreement made between the singer and them . . . six concerts had already been booked and she then refused to have anything more to do with the plaintiffs." (Hempel had opened her own booking office 6 February.)

Paris, beginning 30 April 1926. Filed for divorce from W. B. Kahn on arrival in Paris. Divorce announced 14 May; rumored plans to marry August Heckscher as soon as her Paris divorce was in hand were denied;[5] Kahn fails to appear at divorce hearings;[6] divorce granted.[7]

New York, beginning May 1926. "Mystery has surrounded the Hempel-Heckscher suit since it became known last May that Miss Hempel had brought an action in the Supreme Court to compel the 78-year-old widower to pay her nearly $1,000,000 based on an alleged contract. . . . Previous to the filing of the suit there had been persistent rumors that the singer would marry Mr. Heckscher following her divorce in Paris last year from W. B. Kahn."[8] (See "The Heckscher Affair," below.)

New York, 10 June 1928. Printer wins suit against F. H. for nonpayment of 1924 bill for printing 10,000 window cards "before her announcement that she had retired from the stage because of the agreement with August Heckscher."[9]

New York, 5 February 1929. "Voice teacher sues Hempel for $50,000. Berlin Professor says singer broke agreement to supply him with pupils here. Alleges he saved [her] voice. Defendant denies compact. Denies she needed treatment and plans counter suit because he said so."[10]

New York, 8 February 1929. "Hempel loses two Pleas. Singer fails in move for New Complaint in Professor's suit."[11]

New York, 17 April 1930. "Frieda Hempel, Inc. Sued; Promoter asks $2,958 for services to concern endorsed by singer. An attachment against the property of Frieda Hempel, Inc. of 225 West Fifty-seventh Street, a cosmetic concern in which Frieda Hempel, concert singer, is a director, was levied yesterday by Sheriff Bernstein in a suit by Thomas La Prelle to recover $2,958. The plaintiff asserts he was hired as sales director and was to get $10,000 the first year and $12,000 the second year. . . . Attached to the papers was a prospectus of the Hempel Underwriting Corporation, fiscal agent for Frieda Hempel, Inc. saying that 325,000 shares of no par value common stock had been issued out of a total authorized issue of 1,000,000 shares, and a letter from Miss Hempel endorsing the concern."[12]

New York, 6 January 1931. "Hempel Concern Enjoined by Court: State Charges Opera Singer's Name was used to Obtain $150,000 in Stock Sales. Her loss put at $10,000. . . . The name of Frieda Hempel, opera singer, was used to obtain more than $150,000 from German and Austrian servants, waiters and other small wage earners through the fraudulent sale of stock. [A court order was obtained] enjoining Frieda Hempel Inc. . . . from further dealings in securities. . . . More than 300,000 shares were issued to Frieda

Hempel for a number of formulae for beautifying preparations and for the use of her name."[13]

New York, 6 June 1931. "Frieda Hempel won a dismissal of the suit filed against her by Johannes Alder-Selva." (See 5 February 1929, above).[14]

New York, 3 June 1934. "Mme Hempel Wins Suit Against Sister; Obtains Court Ruling for Sale of Jewelry pledged for $3,550 Loan. Justice Albert Conway, in the Supreme Court in Brooklyn, yesterday signed an order directing Mrs. Helene Schaper to turn over to her sister, Mme Frieda Hempel . . . a diamond crown and platinum chain valued at $10,000, in order that the jewelry may be put up at public sale. Three years ago, Mrs. Schaper brought suit against Mme Hempel for the jewelry or its equivalent in money. Mrs. Schaper said at that time she gave the jewelry to her sister for safe keeping. Mme Hempel replied her sister owed her $3,550 and had given her the ornaments as collateral for the loan. She said she was willing to surrender the gems if the loan were paid. The case was tried before Supreme Court Justice John S. Johnston but was dismissed when an agreement was entered into whereby the jewelry was given in escrow to Mrs. Schaper, her attorney, and a representative of Mme Hempel for two years. Under the agreement which expired last November Mrs. Schaper was to try to sell the jewelry and if she was unsuccessful it was to be turned over to Mme Hempel at thirty days' notice. Mrs. Schaper was unable to sell it. In her application for the order from Justice Conway Mme Hempel said she demanded the jewels from her sister but the latter took the position that the arrangement between them provided for continued joint control. In his decision, Justice Conway said that Mme Hempel clearly received the right to sell the jewelry after a period of two years and the right to sell indicated the right of possession in order to offer it for sale. If the jewelry brings more than $3,500, the balance is to paid to Mrs. Schaper."[15]

The Heckscher Affair

The name of August Heckscher is not widely remembered today, nor is he often mentioned in popular accounts of social and business affairs in the financial centers of the United States during the first half of the twentieth century. Yet his death at the age of ninety-two on 26 April 1941 was front-page news in New York, throughout the United States, and in Europe. That he was a bit of a mysterious figure during his lifetime generated a good many pages of newsprint at his death: it is from these obituaries that the following facts have been gathered.

"A common impression, intensified by frequent publication, is that August Heckscher came to this country a friendless immigrant boy of 19 with little education and less money. Almost the reverse is true. His father was a statesman and diplomat in Germany, and the son came here under the protection of a wealthy branch of his family, members of which owned about 20,000 acres of anthracite coal land in Schuylkill County, Pa." begins his obituary on page one of the *New York Times* on 27 April 1941. August was born in Hamburg, 27 August 1848, when his father was, according to the obituary, Minister of Justice there for Archduke John of Austria. He was first sent to school in Switzerland, then apprenticed for three years to an exporting house in Hamburg. He took passage for New York in 1867 with $500 in gold. His first business was to teach himself English, which he accomplished in three months by spending twelve to fifteen hours a day reading English books. He then joined a cousin in the management of a coal mine in Pennsylvania; after two weeks the cousin became ill and August took over. Fifteen years later, he sold the mine to a railroad and invested in the zinc business, merging with New Jersey Zinc in 1897 and managing the company until 1905, when he "retired" by investing in mid-Manhattan real estate. He reportedly sold one property for $3,000,000 more than he had paid for it after holding it six years. He became interested in the Society for the Prevention of Cruelty to Children, eventually founding the Heckscher Foundation for Children, to which he gave valuable land on which he erected a major building.

Heckscher's first wife died in 1924. He apparently met Frieda Hempel sometime in 1925, and in April 1926 she entered into an agreement with him which provided that she would not accept any professional engagements which would require an absence of more than two days at a time from the City of New York during the rest of her life and would sing exclusively for charitable organizations whenever he requested her to do so. Heckscher agreed to pay Hempel $48,000 annually beginning with quarterly payments on 1 July 1926. After the first payment by Heckscher, payments ceased, and in 1927 Hempel commenced an action in the New York Supreme Court for breach of contract. Before the case came up for trial, it was settled out of court. This settlement provided for Heckscher to set up a trust fund (in May 1928) under which Hempel was to receive $15,000 annually during "the remainder of her natural life." The trust instrument provided that if the net income of the trust was not sufficient to pay $15,000 per annum, Heckscher during his life and his legal representatives after his death would make up the difference. Part of this agreement agreed to hold Heckscher harmless for any "action by William B. Kahn on account of or because of or by reason of and relation of Heckscher to Frieda Hempel." A second instrument provided:

after reciting the consideration, the parties, Heckscher and Hempel, agreed to surrender and to deliver to each other, all writings, communications, letters, telegrams, cablegrams and radiograms from each to the other. They further agreed that they would neither publish nor suffer to be published any of the contents of the writing or communications, nor any facts nor statements of or concerning any business, financial or personal relationship or transaction between them, and that neither would publish or cause or suffer to be published any statement with respect to or concerning any financial or other adjustment made or promised to be made, and that neither would leave or preserve any such writing concerning the matters for publication at any time, either before or after the death of either. Further, neither would at any time, communicate with or molest or otherwise interfere with the peace and happiness of the other, or permit or suffer the same to be done with her or his knowledge or consent. They also agreed to cremate the above mentioned writings upon delivery and receipt of them, and to execute and deliver a joint certificate or letter of cremation in such form as their respective counsel might approve.[16]

The agreement continued in a like vein, seeming to suggest a paranoiac obsession on the part of Mr. Heckscher, no doubt instilled by the actions of Mme Hempel or her attorneys in letting slip to the press from time to time quotations from materials allegedly written by Mr. Heckscher. Some of these were a bit poetic in nature and had no doubt become an embarrassment to the financier (or his second wife whom he married in July 1930) when they were woven into tabloid accounts.[17] As late as 1943, when the whole story was again told, we find: "Recalling their exciting romance, still as fresh to him as newly minted money, August averred 'it was like champagne with not one bubble left out; followed also' he agreed in a somewhat disenchanted manner, 'by the inevitable headache.'"[18]

The payments provided by the trust agreement were made until the latter part of 1934 when Heckscher alleged that Hempel had violated the agreements, and she was informed that the payments would be discontinued and the trust terminated. Hempel brought suit against Heckscher and three trustees; she was declared the winner and received payment for the judgment, less attorneys' fees, in January 1937. Hempel reported receipt of $13,500 for 1937 and $15,000 for 1938 as income from the Heckscher Trust.[19]

The Heckscher affair was again headlines in 1943: "Frieda Hempel Gets Heckscher Estate Annuity: Executors Reveal $15,000 Payments Made During Life Are Being Kept Up."[20] From the fact that she appeared to be abiding by the restrictions and terms of the Heckscher agreement when she wrote her autobiography, and from the apparent absence of references in the daily or legal press to further actions between the Heckscher estate and

Hempel, we assume that Hempel continued to receive the annual Heckscher estate payments until her death.

In the end, Frieda Hempel's romantic attempt (if indeed that is what it was) to turn back the clock and establish in twentieth-century New York the life of an eighteenth-century "courtesan" must be deemed a failure.[21]

The Internal Revenue Service

Frieda Hempel died more than forty years ago, her tax problems with the Internal Revenue Service unresolved after years of struggle involving experts on both sides. To attempt to sort out her complicated financial affairs from this distance is of course a useless exercise. Anyone interested in details may wish to consult some ten pages of fine print in the *Tax Court Memorandum Decisions* published in 1947.[22] Briefly, Hempel's problems appear to have arisen because her income tax reports from 1931 to 1942 showed gross professional receipts generated by her singing to be some $10,216 against claimed expenses connected with these activities of some $140,416. While the tax authorities found that she "was attemptiing to make profits, and was not merely spending money in a social way or as mere living expense," some of her claimed expenses, such as those for the support of a niece living in Germany and other charges which were not properly substantiated, were disallowed. Also at question was whether various payments in connection with the Heckscher Affair were taxable. Again, the 1947 tax publication proves to be of considerable value in clarifying that perplexing matter.

George Keating, who was privately assisting Hempel in financial matters at the time, had an accountant and lawyer from his New York firm try to help Hempel straighten out her tax problems with the IRS. They must have agreed on a compromise figure, for he wrote me that twice he had sent Frieda checks with which to settle the IRS accounts. She may have used these funds for other purposes, for Keating expressed surprise, at the time of her death, that the accounts had never been closed.[23]

The funds received from the auction of Hempel's personal effects held at her New York apartment 23 March 1956 were applied to the IRS claims.

George T. Keating,
Friend and Benefactor

Webster tells us that something inscrutable is "incapable of being searched into and understood; incomprehensible; an enigma: something which hides its meaning under obscure or ambiguous allusions. A riddle . . . a conundrum." I knew George Keating (1892–1976) for the last twenty-five years of his life, and all the above apply. He seems to have been inscrutable to all who knew him, and most especially to the members of his family. It was as though he had a compartmentalized life, so that few could know the details from more than one compartment. I used to think of him as a vast jigsaw puzzle: one had to watch for missing bits and pieces in personal discussions with him and in his many letters. I most certainly never had access to many of the pieces, and many who did have refused to help fill the gaps. Thus I can only summarize what I know about him, fully realizing that the mosaic is far from complete.

George Thomas Keating was born in Brooklyn, New York, 17 July 1892. His father, also named George, an alcoholic, was killed in a bar fight around 1904. His was a "picture which was turned against the wall," as the old song says. He was not to be discussed, nor his name ever mentioned. Son George became the head of the family at the age of about twelve; he had to drop out of school and look for a job as he was the sole support of his mother, Louise Gentil, and one sister. The job he found was as office boy at the firm of Moore & Munger, 33 Rector Street, New York, dealers in clay, ceramics, and paper products and owners of clay mines in Georgia. The firm was privately owned, so that records of corporate history were not public documents. George advanced to a job of traveling salesman for the firm. He married Harriet G. Martin about 1912. Aside from this, the record is a complete blank until approximately 1922, at which time George had become an owner and general manager of the firm and a very wealthy man.

He could afford to engage in such sophisticated pursuits as collecting original manuscripts along with first and autographed editions of Joseph Conrad's works, which he purchased from the finest (and most expensive) London and New York antiquarian book specialists. We have no details to help us understand the metamorphosis from a traveling salesman for a paper products supplier without even so much as a high school education to a thirty-year-old tycoon intent on making a play in the ranks of the intelligentsia at the Yale University Library. Where did the emphasis and drive come from, and who were the mentors (there must have been more than one) who planted the seeds and nurtured and guided the plant? George would never discuss the subject with me, and members of his family claimed to be as ignorant as I was.

George was engaged in correspondence with Joseph Conrad in 1922. A letter from Conrad dated 18 October reads in part: "Here are two pamphlets for your Conrad Collection, by which I feel most honored." Again, 28 January 1924: "Your project of a marvelously illustrated catalog is almost too much for my modesty"; and on 29 May of the same year: "I venture to add to it four pages of another preface. . . . I hope you will put those very scratchy pages away with your other MSS. as a memento of our friendship and the affectionate esteem in which I hold you."[1] Keating's purchases of Conrad manuscripts, letters, first editions, and other memorabilia from Conrad and, after his death, from his widow, must have formed a substantial portion of the Conrad family income for some years. Keating probably contributed financially to the expenses of Mr. and Mrs. Conrad's only visit to America in 1924.

The year 1929 saw the publication of the massive *A Conrad Memorial Library: The Collection of George T. Keating*, an elegant volume of artistic design, printed on special paper, and limited to an edition of 501 copies.[2] Keating appears as its sole author, but the work obviously was put together by bibliographic experts who had knowledge and skills far beyond those possessed by George himself. In addition to noting each of the many items "personally dedicated to Mr. George T. Keating" by authors and others, the work describes in meticulous detail the individual items in the collection, the whole

made resplendently uniform in appearance by their enclosure in blue solander cases and bindings of full levant morocco. . . . [The collection's] scrupulous completeness is altogether remarkable. In it has been assembled—for the first and, without any question whatsoever, the last time—every known issue of the first English and American editions of Conrad's works . . . the first issue of *The Inheritors* of which but four copies were printed . . . two of the seven copies of the first edition of *The Nigger of the Narcissus* only three of which were not sent to the British copyright libraries . . . the sole copies definitely known to exist of the first issues of *Nostromo*.[3]

William McFee in his remarks at the opening of the exhibition said:

> It is customary among tough-minded "practical" citizens to deride and deplore the time and money wasted (as they call it) by the collectors of manuscripts and first editions. This attitude is also to be found among those authors whose manuscripts and first editions are never, for some reason, collected by anyone except the garbage man. But it is perfectly obvious that all the great libraries of the world were built up from what were originally collected items. It is equally obvious that if such things were not collected and cared for by individuals with the enthusiasm and the money for the task, they would be lost to us forever. So I have always maintained, although destitute myself of the collector's passion, that such men and women should be cherished by all authors and honored by all institutions of learning.[4]

With the required deep pockets, obvious personal dedication, and encouragement and help from similarly dedicated experts, George Keating had accomplished a truly remarkable feat in assembling this collection honoring a great author. When he presented the collection to Yale, he too was indeed honored for this job of assembly and thanked for the gift. Yet during the years I knew George Keating, I tried many times to engage him in discussions about the content and literary significance of the works of Joseph Conrad, but I always drew a blank. I always came away with the feeling that he had passed the place in his life in which Joseph Conrad was important: he had collected every scrap by and about the man, had had it all bound in expensive morocco leather, and had given it all to a great university. Conrad became a thing of the past. I am not sure just how much of the truth really sank in that all these years of dedication and all the wealth expended had made him a great Conrad *collector*, but by no means a Conrad *scholar*. Many times I was struck by the impression that George Keating had read little of the mass of material he had collected and that he had little idea of its significance. I believe that this truth eventually dawned on him, in a sense as a rejection by academia, which soured his relationship with Yale and had a good deal to do with his "escape" to the West Coast when he retired from business.

During his Conrad Collection period, George Keating established his family, consisting of his wife Harriet, a son, and a daughter, first at Douglaston, Long Island, and later at a seventy-eight-acre estate called High Oaks near Watchung, a few miles from Plainfield, New Jersey. About 1929 a new member was added to the family in the person of a four-year-old boy. It was generally understood that he was "adopted." In later years he told of an unhappy childhood and said that he always felt like a "fifth wheel" in family undertakings and that his stepmother always seemed to resent his presence. He saw George and Harriet for the last time in 1960 when he tried to discuss his parentage and was told it was none of his business. In George Keating's will, dated 26 February 1970, he acknowledges this "adopted" son as his own and states that he "intentionally and not as a result of any accident . . . omit[s] in this Will to provide for [this son and for] the issue of said [son] whether natural or adopted." No clue is offered as to this son's mother, an unsolved mystery to this day.

In 1985 this younger son of George Keating contacted the writer, requesting a meeting for the purpose of discussing Frieda Hempel. This was arranged, and we spent a long evening in discussion. There seemed to be as many questions about his father, George, as about Frieda Hempel, and when I noted my patchwork view of his father's past, I suggested and he agreed to sit down and put some memories and impressions on paper for me. This he did, and with the help of a word processor, produced two essays: one called "George" runs to sixteen pages; the other, titled "Frieda," some thirteen pages. Each fills, in a fuzzy sort of manner, a good many missing holes in the Keating jigsaw puzzle. This is not the place or time to publish them because they contain many unverified statements and impressions involving people who are still alive. They will be preserved should they be of value to future researchers. The son's lengthy research suggests and does not eliminate the possibility that Frieda Hempel was his mother.

We have no information on how and exactly when George and Frieda first met. George was apparently on good terms with Will Kahn, and George frequently tried to assist Frieda in business matters. We have Keating's statement that he supplied the funds for Frieda's last several trips to Europe, and he seems to have been involved in the decision that she return to Europe in 1935. He was well aware of her financial difficulties and apparently supplied needed funds on many occasions through the years. In a letter to me, dated 1 February 1955, Keating wrote: "Miss Hempel has been a close friend . . . for many years. She brought over a little German baby some years ago who is now legally adopted by our daughter." George had accompanied Hempel to Germany around 1946 for this purpose; he paid all expenses and engineered the legal adoption by his daughter. I have been told that the girl was raised by Keating and his wife as well as by his daughter, that she was neither loved nor wanted by either and had a tragic and unhappy upbringing.

George Keating disposed of his New Jersey estate by presenting the property to the Salvation Army in 1941[4] and moved to California. He first settled in the rather exclusive community of Rancho Santa Fe, where he was a neighbor of Amelita Galli-Curci and her husband, Homer Samuels, with whom he made friends. Fortunately he was also introduced to Stanley L. Sharp of Palo Alto, who was on the staff of Stanford University.

George craved praise and recognition. The Conrad experience had

In 1955 George Keating wrote, "She brought over a little German baby some years ago who is now legally adopted by our daughter." COURTESY KENNETH LANE.

introduced him to the collection mania which gave him a previously unrecognized passion in life. He learned that his wealth could open doors for him in a world where he never dreamed doors could be opened and in effect buy him position and a place that he felt had been denied him by his lack of formal education. His Conrad efforts had allowed him to make personal contacts within academia which he never would have made otherwise, creating a lifestyle that satiated a long-suppressed need to be considered an important person. He loved the opportunity to mix with and be on a first name basis with the famous. The connection with a major university was stimulating and satisfied his needs. After his move to California, George sought a new outlet for his talents. Where could he now turn to build an important and unique collection of *something* which could carry his name and which could hold an honored and permanent place in an institution of higher learning? Stan Sharp was seeking funds with which to establish a suitable memorial to those Stanford students who had lost their lives in the recently ended war. Sharp, together with J. E. Wallace Sterling, Stanford's president and former head of the Huntington Library in Pasadena, and Nathan van Patten, recently retired as Stanford's head librarian, developed the idea for a Memorial Library of Music, which became a part of Stanford's War Memorial.

Nathan van Patten was a delightful gentleman who carried the title of Professor of Bibliography. He and George hit it off from the first. With hindsight we can suggest that the resulting collection might have been far more focused if a trained musicologist had served on the selection team, as in the end the collection turned out to be a rather mixed bag, though certainly one that includes a wealth of remarkable material. It contains original manuscripts, first editions, and unique items representing major and minor composers, the great majority inscribed by their authors. It is quite an experience to view in one collection autograph manuscripts by Bach, Beethoven, Bellini, Berlioz, Bizet, Brahms, Cherubini, Chopin, Cimarosa, Debussy, Donizetti, and so on, through Richard Strauss, Stravinsky, Verdi, and Wagner. Letters and signed photographs and other memorabilia abound. Keating had an eye for "association" items (for example, books autographed by the author to someone named therein), and wherever possible, materials are inscribed for the collection. A "first catalog" of 310 pages with 1226 entries was prepared by van Patten and printed at Keating's expense by The Ward Ritchie Press in 1950. In what was becoming a Keating trademark, the entire collection was bound in handcrafted cardinal levant and matching slip cases, at immense expense.

Keating was displeased when the university could not find funds to take care of the catalog printing and when his suggestions for use of university funds to continue adding to the collection were not immediately adopted. Private universities do not have unlimited funds with which to carry on the entrepreneurial collecting habits of all its donors, and once again, George had pushed his luck too far: he began to believe that he was an expert, which he was not. Nor was he able to spread a thick enough coat of polish to cover revealing blemishes, which further caused some to question his expertise. He purchased first editions and manuscript scores but could pronounce neither titles nor roles, nor the composers' and artists' names. Yet he would never know he was out of step. As far as he was concerned, he never was: it was the other fellow. Thus began yet another adventure in disenchantment with academia in general, which unfortunately carried over to George Keating's next inevitable collecting binge.

This was to be the putting together of a library of super-rare phonograph recordings by famous artists. He began this enterprise with characteristic zeal: dealers in the United States, Europe, and South America were alerted to the fact that a wealthy collector was now in the market, and they would be advised to give him priority and apprise him of all rare material which came their way. If George Keating wanted something, never mind the price: there would be no haggling. Send together with bill. Of course this worked. Keating had first choice of important material which disappeared from the market until he had had first refusal, and dealers' prices skyrocketed to the detriment of all except the dealers. George's interest in the musical content of recordings of classical music was typically only skin-deep, but the physical record had to be a first pressing (a first edition) and preferably rare. About the same time, George had also become interested in a Civil War general named George Thomas, largely because he shared two-thirds of his name. Our George was trying to get the general installed in the Civil War Hall of Fame, and had dealers hunting for manuscripts and letters which might accomplish this event. (I never tried to follow this one.)

George began a correspondence with me in the early 1950s from what was then his home in Los Altos, California, near Stanford University. I knew of his involvement with the Stanford Memorial Library of Music, and of his global search for rare recordings. I first met him in person when I accepted his kind invitation to dinner at his home, having anticipated an enjoyable evening engaged in an interesting discussion about Joseph Conrad and his work, as well as an exciting time listening to some of the world's rarest recordings. My first shock was Harriet, Mrs. George. Try as I would, I could not find a single subject for conversation in which she had the remotest interest. George was no help and only came to life after Harriet had excused herself and departed to be seen no more. But he could not be led into a discussion related to his Conrad collecting days and adventures. He did not want to talk about the music library, except to complain that Stanford didn't appreciate it. He did warm up on the subject of records, and we were soon involved in examining his choice rarities which he seemed proud to own; he delighted in telling me what he had paid for them, sometimes numbers so astronomical they made my head spin. He seemed a bit hesitant when I asked to hear some of them, and for good reason. His only phonograph equipment was a cheap tabletop turntable equipped with a turn-over cartridge which could be made to play the old 78s and the then-new LPs. It played through an inexpensive radio. There was no way to adjust the speed, so necessary in reproducing the old 78s. Nor could the size of the sapphire stylus be adjusted to the wide variance in groove size of the old recordings. The result was that none of the old recordings could be played at proper pitch, and the rattling stylus created such a roar of background noise that one could hardly identify the music, much less get any feel for the character of the voice. George seemed unaware of any problems and accepted the racket as perfectly normal and proper. To be fair, some time later, after he had visited my home and had a demonstration of the quality of sound which could be produced from old recordings, he made an effort to improve his play-back equipment, but he never understood the importance of playing his recordings at proper pitch. It did not seem to bother him if a bass sounded like a tenor or a contralto like a soprano.

In 1960, because of a combination of health and family problems, George rather suddenly decided to move back to Southern California. He had had enough of phonograph records, didn't want to move them, and offered his collection for immediate sale. Considering the rarities involved and what Keating had paid for the collection, the price was reasonable, set on condition that the collection would end up in an archival institution such as a university. I received his letter about this in Alice Springs in the middle of Australia. By the time I could reply, the collection had been sold to a New Haven book dealer who sold part of it and eventually deposited some of the rarer items at Yale in a collection bearing his own name, but without giving any credit to Keating.

I have said that there was much about George Keating I did not know and much that I did know I never really understood. I was certainly given the impression that he seemed dictatorial and difficult to his children and his family relationships were generally not happy ones. On the other hand, he seemed to flourish away from his family. He was kindly and generous in the extreme and was looked upon as a paragon of virtue by those who benefited from his largess. He certainly acted as a guardian angel to Frieda Hempel, providing her with substantial financial assistance for many years, which the two of them apparently had agreed would remain a private matter between them. We have no way of knowing how many others his generosity privately benefited: I suspect perhaps there were many. He left substantial physical legacies to both Stanford and Yale. These no doubt could have been of much greater importance had the donor's egocentricity been removed, but one does not look a gift horse in the mouth. Considering his background and education, George Thomas Keating went far and did many good things. He died in Pomona, California, 23 April 1976.

Frieda Hempel's Operatic Repertoire

Adam	*Le Postillon de Longjumeau*	Madame de Latour (Madeleine)
Auber	*La Muette de Portici* (Masaniello)	Elvira
	Le Domino noir (The Black Domino)	Angela
Bizet	*Les Pêcheurs de perles* (The Pearl Fishers)	Leila
	Carmen	Micaëla, Frasquita
Blech	*Versiegelt* (Sealed)	Gertrude
Boieldieu	*Jean de Paris*	Princess from Navarra
Cornelius	*Der Barbier von Bagdad* (The Barber of Baghdad)	Margiana
Donizetti	*L'elisir d'amore* (The Elixir of Love)	Adina
	Lucia di Lammermoor	Lucia
	La Fille du régiment (Daughter of the Regiment)	Marie
Flotow	*Alessandro Stradella*	Leonora
	Martha	Lady Harriet
Frederick II, King of Prussia	*Der grosse König* (The Great King) singspiel after the king's melodies	Barbarina
Gluck	*Orfeo ed Euridice*	Euridice
	Iphigénie en Aulide	Iphigenia
	Armide	Armide
Goldmark	*Ein Wintermärchen* (A Winter's Tale)	Perdita
Gounod	*Faust*	Marguerite
	Roméo et Juliette	Juliette

Halévy	*La Juive* (The Jewess)	Princess Eudora
Humperdinck	*Hänsel und Gretel*	Gretel
	Die Königskinder (The Royal Children)	The Goose Girl
Leoncavallo	*Pagliacci*	Nedda
Lortzing	*Der Wildschütz* (The Poacher)	Baroness Freimann
Mascagni	*Cavalleria rusticana*	Lola
Méhul	*Joseph*	Benjamin
Meyerbeer	*Les Huguenots*	Marguerite de Valois
	Le Prophète	Bertha
Mozart	*Bastien und Bastienne*	Bastienne
	Die Entführung aus dem Serail (The Abduction from the Seraglio)	Constanze
	Le nozze di Figaro (The Marriage of Figaro)	Susanna
	Così fan tutte	Fiordiligi
	Die Zauberflöte (The Magic Flute)	Queen of the Night
Nicolai	*Die lustigen Weiber von Windsor* (The Merry Wives of Windsor)	Mistress Ford
Offenbach	*Les Contes d'Hoffmann* (The Tales of Hoffmann)	Olympia, Giulietta,
Antonia		
Puccini	*La bohème*	Mimì
Ricci	*Crispino e la comare*	Annetta
Rossini	*Il barbiere di Siviglia* (The Barber of Seville)	Rosina
Smetana	*Dalibor*	Jutta
Strauss, Johann	*Die Fledermaus*	Rosalinda
Strauss, Richard	*Der Rosenkavalier*	The Marschallin, Princess von Werdenberg
Suppé	*Die schöne Galatea* (The Beautiful Galatea)	Galatea
Thomas	*Mignon*	Philine
Verdi	*Rigoletto*	Gilda
	Il trovatore	Leonora
	La traviata	Violetta
	Un ballo in maschera	Oscar

Wagner	*Rienzi*	Messenger of Peace
	Lohengrin	Elsa of Brabant
	Die Meistersinger von Nürnberg	Eva
	Das Rheingold	Woglinde
	Die Walküre (The Valkyrie)	Helmwige
	Siegfried	Waldvogel (Forest Bird)
	Götterdämmerung	Woglinde
	Parsifal	Flower Maiden
Weber	*Euryanthe*	Euryanthe

The Recorded Legacy of Frieda Hempel

by William R. Moran

Recording session for Odeon with Frieda Hempel singing, Eduard Künneke directing, 1908. COURTESY ROBERT TUGGLE.

I. Odeon Records, Berlin, 1906–1913

(xB = 27 cm; xxB = 30 cm)

Discog. No.	Matrix No. -Take	Date	S/f Cat. Nos.	D/f Cat. Nos.	Speed	Re-issues
1.	Il Bacio (Gottardo Aldighieri; Luigi Arditi) (I) (pf. Robert Erben)					
	xB 1503-1	Aug. 1905	50131	RO200	73.47?	
2.	s'Lerchle (Wilhelm Taubert) (G) (pf. Erben)					
	xB 1504-1	Aug. 1905	50126	—	73.47?	
3.	Wiegenlied (Schlafe, mein Prinzchen) (Friedrich Wilhelm Gotter; Bernhard Flies attrib. Mozart) (G) (pf. Erben)					
	xB 1505-1	Aug. 1906	99998	—	73.47	
	-2	Aug. 1906	50127	—	73.47?	
4.	MARTHA: Letzte Rose (The Last Rose of Summer) (Old Irish air intro. in Flotow opera) (G) (pf. Erben)					
	xB 1506-1	Aug. 1906	50134	RO200	73.47	
5.*	TRAVIATA: "Arie der Violetta" (Possibly Er ist es) (Ah! fors' è lui) (Verdi) (G) (pf. Erben)					
	xB 1507-1	Aug. 1906	50133	—	73.47?	
6.*	TRAVIATA: S'ist seltsam . . . Er ist es, dessen wonnig Bild (E Strano! . . . Ah! fors' è lui) (Verdi) (G) (pf. Erben)					
	xB 1508-1, -2	Aug. 1906	50247	—	73.00	
7.	TRAVIATA: O Torheit! . . . Von der Freude Blumenkränzen (Follie! follie! . . . Sempre liberal) (Verdi) (G) (pf. Erben)					
	xB 1509-1	Aug. 1906	50132	—	74.00	
8.	ENTFÜHRUNG AUS DEM SERAIL: Ach, ich liebte, war so glücklich (Mozart) (G) (pf. Erben)					
	xB 1510-1	Aug. 1906	50135	—	74.00	

9. MARTHA: Letzte Rose (The Last Rose of Summer) (Old Irish air intro. in Flotow opera) (G) (Or. Friedrich Kark)
xB 2270-1   1 Oct. 1907   50254   ——   72.00

10. TRAVIATA: Er ist es 'Ah! fors' è lui) (Verdi) (G) (Or. Kark)
xB 2271-1   1 Oct. 1907   50248 99993 118531   0-5529 R0296   72.00

11. TRAVIATA: Von der Freude Blumenkränzen (Sempre liberal) (Verdi) (G) (Or. Kark)
xB 2272-1,-2   1 Oct. 1907   50313 99994 118532   0-5529 R0296   72.00   Okeh 70101

12. Il Bacio (Aldighieri; Arditi) (I) (Or. Kark)
xB 2273-1   1 Oct. 1907   50249 99995 98109   0-5511   72.00   Lp

13. FIGAROS HOCHZEIT: O säume länger nicht (Deh vieni, non tardar) (Mozart) (G) (Or. Eduard Künneke)
xB 2644-1   2 Oct. 1907   50335   ——   72.00?

14. BOHEME: O du süssestes Mädchen (O soave fanciulla) (Puccini) (G) (w. Hermann Jadlowker) (Or. Kark)
xB 3376-1   3 Oct. 1907   99887   ——   72.00?

15. LUCIE VON LAMMERMOOR: Nach trüben Tagen (Ardon gl'incensi) (Mad Sc., Pt. 2) (Donizetti) (G) (flute: Emil Prill; Or. Kark)
xxB 3634-1,-2,-3,-4   Oct. 1907   76033   0-8189 RX22   73.4   Lp

16. LUCIE VON LAMMERMOOR: Welch' holder Ton (Il dolce suono) (Mad Sc., Pt. 1) (Donizetti) (G) (flute: Prill; Or. Kark)
xxB 3635-1,-2,-3,-4   Oct. 1907   76032   0-8189 RX22   73.4   Lp

17. LUCIE VON LAMMERMOOR: Wenn er entzückt im Auge mild (Regnava nel silenzio, Pt. 2) (Quando rapito) (Donizetti) (G) (Or Kark)
xB 3643-1   Oct. 1907   64861   0-5524 R0563   ——   Lp

18. LUCIE VON LAMMERMOOR: In tiefem Schweigen lag die Nacht (Regnava nel silenzio, Pt. 1) (Donizetti) (G) (Or. Kark)
xB 3644-1   Oct. 1907   64852   0-5524 R0563   ——   Lp

Discog. No.	Matrix No. -Take	Date	S/f Cat. Nos.	D/f Cat. Nos.	Speed	Re-issues
19.	Wiegenlied (Schlafe, mein Prinzchen) (Gotter; Flies attrib. Mozart) (G) (Or. Kark)					
	xB 3645-1	Oct. 1907	64835 118533	0-5531 R0521	74.00	Lp
20.	Villanelle (Eva dell'Acqua) (F) (Or. Kark)					
	xB 3649-1	Oct. 1907	64853 118534	0-5531 R0521	75.00	Lp
21.	HUGENOTTEN: O glücklich' Land (Huguenots: O beau pays de la Touraine) (Queen's air, Pt. 1) (Meyerbeer) (G) (Or. Kark)					
	xB 3827-1	1908	64968	0-5522 R0524	73.4	IRCC 3006(rr); Lp
22.	HUGENOTTEN: Dies einz'ge Wortchen Liebe (Huguenots: A ce mot seul) (Queen's air, Pt. 2) (Meyerbeer) (G) (Or. Kark)					
	xB 3828-1	1908	64969	0-5522 R0524	73.4	IRCC 3006(rr); Lp
23.	TRAVIATA: So hold, so reizend (Un di felice) (Verdi) (G) (w. Franz Naval) (Orchestra)					
	xB 3829-1	1908	53252 80032	0-6423	——	Lp
24.	TRAVIATA: O lass' uns fliehen (Parigi, o cara) (Verdi) (G) (w. Naval) (Orchestra)					
	xB 3830-1	1908	53253 80033	0-6423	——	Lp
25.	CARMEN: Ich sprach, dass ich furchtlos (Je dis que rien) (Micaëla's air) (Bizet) (G) (Orchestra)					
	xB 4250-1	1908	99172		——	
26.	Variationen (Heinrich Proch, Op. 164) (Proch's air and variations) (Pt. 1) (G) (Or. Kark)					
	xB 4330-1	1908	99217 99996	0-5532	73.4	
27.	Variationen (Proch, Op. 164) (Proch's air and variations) (Pt. 2) (G) (Or. Kark)					
	xB 4331-1	1908	99218 99997	0-5532	73.4	

No.	Title	Matrix	Year				Lp
28.	RIGOLETTO: Teurer Name, dessen Klang (Caro nome) (Verdi) (G) (Orchestra)	xB 4332-1	1908	99219	R-0726	72.00	
29.*	CAVALLERIA RUSTICANA: (a) Szene zwischen Lola und Turiddu (Comare Lola . . . Vado a casa) (Mascagni) (w. Franz Naval); (b) Trinklied (Brindisi) (G) (Franz Naval and Chorus) (Or. Kark)	xB 4357-1	1908	50605	——		Lp
30.*	CAVALLERIA RUSTICANA: O süsse Lilie (Lola's ditty: Fior di giaggiolo) (Mascagni) (G) (w. Frances Rose and Naval) (Or. Kark)	xB 4360-1	1908	50608 52562	0-5066		Lp
31.	PERLE DU BRESIL: Charmant oiseau (Couplets du Mysoli) (Pt. 2) (David) (F) (Or. Künneke)	xxB 4809-1	1909	75056	RX-72		Lp
32.	PERLE DU BRESIL: Charmant oiseau (Air du Mysoli) (Pt. 1) (David) (F) (Or. Künneke)	xxB 4810-1	1909	76057	RX-72		——
33.	ERNANI: Sorta è la notte . . . Ernani involami (Verdi) (I) (Or. Künneke)	xxB 4811-2,-3	1909	76058 81057	0-8180		Lp
34.	REGIMENTSTOCHTER: Weiss nicht die Welt (Fille du Régiment: Chacun le sait) (Donizetti) (G) (Or. Pilz)	xB 4862-1	1910	99517 52926	0-5091	79.00	Lp
35.	REGIMENTSTOCHTER: Heil dir, mein Vaterland (Fille du Régiment: Salut à la France) (Donizetti) (G) (Or. Pilz)	xB 4863-1	1910	99518 52927	0-5091	79.00	Lp
36.*	ZAUBERFLÖTE: Zum Leiden bin ich auserkoren (Mozart) (G) (Or. Künneke)	xxB 4895	1910	76069 80310	0-8195	79.00?	
37.	ZAUBERFLÖTE: Der Hölle Rache (Mozart) (G) (Or. Künneke)	xB 4896	1910	99541 50335	0-5521	79.00	

Discog. No.	Matrix No. -Take	Date	S/f Cat. Nos.	D/f Cat. Nos.	Speed	Re-issues
38.	BARBIER VON SEVILLA: Frag' ich mein beklommnes Herz (Barbiere di Siviglia: Una voce poco fa) (Pt. 1) (Rossini) (G) (Or. Künneke)					
	xxB 5058-1,-2,-3,-4	1910	76901 80328	0-8023 RX-501	77.00	
39.	BARBIER VON SEVILLA: Sanft bin ich, treu und gut (Barbiere di Siviglia: Io son docile) (Pt. 2) (Donizetti) (G) (Or. Künneke)					
	xxB 5059-1,-2,-3	1910	76900 80329	0-8023	78.00 (tk. 3)	
40.	PERLE VON BRASILIEN: Arie der Mysoli (Charmant oiseau) (David) (G) (Orchestra)					
	xxB 5099-1	1910	76906 53244 81051 80163	0-6406	——	
41.	CARMEN: José! Micaëla! (Me voici) (Bizet) (G) (w. Jadlowker) (Orchestra)					
	xB 5178-1	1910	52896 98069 99900	0-5064 RO-2001	78.00	Okeh 35003; Lp
42.	CARMEN: Einen Kuss meiner Mutter (Un baiser) (Bizet) (G) (w. Jadlowker) (Orchestra)					
	xB 5179-1	1910	52897 98070 99901	0-5064 RO-2001	78.00	Lp
43.	TRAVIATA: O lass' uns fliehen (Parigi, o cara) (Pt. 1) (Verdi) (G) (w. Jadlowker) (Orchestra)					
	xB 5180-1	1910	52940 98071 99902	0-5102	78.00	Lp
44.	TRAVIATA: Jetzt, mein Alfred, gehen wir (Ah, non più . . . Ah! gran Dio!) (Pt. 2) (Verdi) (G) (w. Jadlowker) (Orchestra)					
	xB 5181-1	1910	52941 98072 99903	0-5102	78.00	Lp
45.	TRAVIATA: So hold, so reizend (Un di felice) (Verdi) (G) (w. Jadlowker) (Orchestra)					
	xB 5182-1,-2	1910	98108 99904	0-5511	78.00	Lp
46.	HUGENOTTEN: Ach, wär ich wie and're Frauen (Huguenots: Ah! Si j'étais coquette) (Pt. 2) (Meyerbeer) (G) (w. Jadlowker) (Orchestra)					
	xxB 5184-1	1910	76903 80159	0-8186	78.00	Okeh 45012; Lp

47. HUGENOTTEN: Wer uns Vertrauer gab (Huguenots: Pareille loyauté vaut son prix) (Pt. 1) (Meyerbeer) (G) (w. Jadlowker) (Orchestra)
xxB 5185-1,-2   1910   76902 81058   0-8186   78.00   Okeh 45004; Lp

48. REGIMENTSTOCHTER: Wie, du liebst mich? . . . Nicht zweifeln darf ich länger (Fille du Régiment: Quoi! vous m'aimez? . . . Depuis l'instant où dans mes bras) (Donizetti) (G) (w. Jadlowker) (Orchestra)
xxB 5187-1   1910   76906 76460 76996 80361   0-8095   78.00   Lp

49.* LUCIE VON LAMMERMOOR: An des Tods heil'ger Stätte (Sulla tomba) (Donizetti) (G) (w. Jadlowker) (Orchestra)
xxB 5188-1   1910   98081 99905   0-5525   78.00 (See note)   Lp

50. RIGOLETTO: Teurer Name, dessen Klang (Caro nome) (Verdi) (G) (Orchestra)
xxB 5195-1   1910   76907 81052 80309   0-8195   80.00   Okeh 44005

51.* STUMME VON PORTICI: Den Geliebten vermählt; O Tag voll heller Wonne (Muette de Portici: Plaisir du rang suprème) (Pt. 1) (Auber) (G) (Orchestra)
xxB 5196-1   1910   76904 81049 80305   0-8196   78.00 (See note)   Lp

52.* STUMME VON PORTICI: O Tag voll süsser Lust (Muette de Portici: O moment enchanteur) (Pt. 2) (Auber) (G) (Orchestra)
xxB 5197-1   1910   76905 81050 80308   0-8196   80.00 (See note)   Lp

53.* LOTTERIELOS: Nein ich singe nicht, mein Herr (Le billet de loterie: Non, je ne veux pas chanter) (Pt. 1) (Isouard) (G) (Orchestra)
xB 5198-1   1910   98065 99908   0-5523   78.00   Lp (x2)

54.* LOTTERIELOS: Einst klagte man in süssen Romanzen (Le billet de loterie) (Pt. 2) (Isouard) (G) (Orchestra)
xB 5199-1   1910   98066 99909   0-5523   78.00 (See note)   Lp (x2)

55. BAJAZZO: Vogellied der Nedda: Ach, die lustigen Vögelein (Pagliacci: Qual fiamma) (Leoncavallo) (G) (Orchestra)
xB 5201-1   1910   99888   ————————

Discog. No.	Matrix No. -Take	Date	S/f Cat. Nos.	D/f Cat. Nos.	Speed	Re-issues
56.	ROMEO UND JULIA: O Nacht! du machest mich erbeben (Romeo et Juliette: O nuit divine) (Pt. 1) (Gounod) (G) (w. Jadlowker) (Orchestra)					
	xB 5371-1	1911	98069 99885 52930	0-5095	75.00	
57.	ROMEO UND JULIA: Nein, nein, du sollst nicht gegen (Romeo et Juliette: Ah! ne fuis pas encore!) (Pt. 2) (Gounod) (G) (w. Jadlowker) (Orchestra)					
	xB 5372-1	1911	98070 99886 52931	0-5095	75.00	Lp
58.	ROMEO UND JULIA: Ja, ich habe verziehen (Romeo et Juliette: Va! je t'ai pardonné) (Pt. 1) (Gounod) (G) (w. Jadlowker) (Orchestra)					
	xxB 5373-1	1911	76290	——	75.00	Lp
59.	ROMEO UND JULIA: Ach, du sprachst wahr (Romeo et Juliette: Ah! tu dis vrais) (Pt. 2) (Gounod) (G) (w. Jadlowker) (Orchestra)					
	xxB 5374-1	1911	76291	——	75.00	Lp
60.	BOHEME: O du süssestes Mädchen (O soave fanciulla) (Puccini) (G) (w. Jadlowker) (Orchestra)					
	xB 5375-1	1911	99887 99941 52538	0-5061	75.00	Lp
60.^*	MARTHA: Letzte Rose (The Last Rose of Summer) (Old Irish air intro. in Flotow opera) (G) (Orchestra)					
	xxB 5567-1	1912?	76920	——	77.00	
61.*	TRAVIATA: O lass' uns fliehen (Parigi, o cara) (Pt. 1) (Verdi) (G) (w. Jadlowker) (Or. Künneke)					
	xB 5780-1	1912	99902	——		——
62.	TRAVIATA: Jetzt, mein Alfred (Ah, non più . . . Ah! gran Dio!) (Pt. 2) (Verdi) (G) (w. Jadlowker) (Or. Künneke)					
	xB 5781-1	1912	99903	——		——

63. TOREADOR: Ah! vous dirai-je, maman (Based on Mozart's Variations for pf. K. 265) (Pt. 1) (F) (Adolphe Adam) (Or. Künneke)
xxB 5793-1   1912   76909   —

64. TOREADOR: Ah! vous dirai-je, maman (Based on Mozart's Variations for pf. K. 265) (Pt. 2) (F) (Adam) (Or. Künneke)
xxB 5794-1   1912   Unpublished

65. Parla! (Walz) (Arditi) (I) (Orchestra)
xxB 5913-1   1913   76948 80316   0-8177   75.00   Okeh 44005; 50102

66. MARTHA: Letzte Rose (The Last Rose of Summer) (Old Irish air intro. in Flotow opera) (G) (Orchestra)
xxB 5914-1   1913   76947 80359   0-8089   78.00   Lp

67. ENTFÜHRUNG AUS DEM SERAIL: Martern aller Arten (Mozart) (G) (Orchestra)
xxB 5915-1   1913   76949 80304 81054   0-8180   75.00   Lp

68. FIGAROS HOCHZEIT: O säume länger nicht (Deh vieni, non tardar) (Mozart) (G) (Orchestra)
xxB 5916-1   1913   76950 80358   0-8089   75.00   Okeh 50101; 45004

69. BOHEME: Man nennt mich Mimi (Sì, mi chiamano Mimi) (Puccini) (G) (Orchestra)
xB 5918-1   1913   76951 80500   0-8177   75.00

70. ROMEO UND JULIA: Walzer (Roméo et Juliette: Je veux vivre dans ce rêve) (Gounod) (G) (Orchestra)
xxB 5920-1   1913   76952 53245 80164 81053   0-6406   74.00

71. Wiegenlied (Ebeling; Humperdinck) (G) (Orchestra)
xxB 5921-1   1913   76946 80317   —   74.00   Lp

II. The Gramophone Co. Ltd., Berlin, 1910–1915

(all 30 cm)

Discog. No.	Matrix No.	HMV/Opera Disc	Date	S/f Cat. Nos.	D/f Cat. Nos.	Speed	Re-issues
72.*	507s	BARBIER VON SEVILLA: Arie der Rosine (Barbiere di Siviglia: Una voce) (Pt. 1) (Rossini) (G) (Or. probably all Bruno Seidler-Winkler)	21 Sep. 1910	Unpublished			
73.	508s	BARBIER VON SEVILLA: Arie der Rosine (Barbiere di Siviglia: Io son docile) (Pt. 2) (Rossini) (G) (Orchestra)	21 Sep. 1910	Unpublished			
74.	509s	RIGOLETTO: Teurer Name (Caro nome) (Verdi) (G) (Orchestra)	21 Sep. 1910	043153 76035	DB 272 85286	75.00	
75.	516s	BARBIER VON SEVILLA: Frag' ich mein beklommnes Herz (Barbiere di Siviglia; Una voce poco fa) (Pt. 1) (Rossini) (G) (Orchestra)	6 Oct. 1910	043151 76033	DB 455 85285	78.00	
76.	517s	BARBIER VON SEVILLA: Sanft bin ich, treu und gut: Arie der Rosine (Barbiere di Siviglia: Io son docile) (Pt. 2) (Rossini) (G) (Orchestra)	6 Oct. 1910	043152 76034	DB 455 85285	78.00	
77.	530s	LUCIE VON LAMMERMOOR: Schon glimmt der Weihrausch (Wahnsinnsarie) (Lucia: Ardon gl'incensi) (Mad Sc., Pt. 1) (Donizetti) (G) (flute: Prill; Orchestra)	13 Oct. 1910	043159 76036	DB 365 85287	78.00	
78.	531s	LUCIE VON LAMMERMOOR: Wahnsinnsarie (Lucia: Mad Sc., Pt. 2) (Donizetti) (G) (flute: Prill; Orchestra)	13 Oct. 1910	Unpublished			

79. FLAUTO MAGICO: Infelice, sconsolata (Zauberflöte: Zum Leiden bin ich auserkoren) (Mozart) (I) (Orchestra)
529m   4 Feb. 1911   Unpublished

80.* TOREADOR: Ah! vous dirai-je Maman (Based on Mozart's variations for pf. K. 265) (Adam) (F) (flute: Hendrick DeVries; Orchestra)
530m   4 Feb. 1911   DB 352   85281   75.00   Victor: (76017); 88404; 6364; Lp

81. TRAVIATA: Follie! follie! . . . Sempre libera! (Verdi) (I) (Orchestra)
542m   13 Apr. 1911   053262   76127   DB 272   85292   78.00

82.* Il Bacio (Aldighieri; Arditi) (I) (Orchestra)
543m   13 Apr. 1911   053261   76126   DB 298   85295   78.00

83. NOZZE DI FIGARO: Deh vieni, non tardar (Mozart) (I) (Orchestra)
544m   13 Apr. 1911   053263   76128   DB 353   85293   78.00

84. FLAUTO MAGICO: Infelice, sconsolata (Zauberflöte: Zum Leiden bin ich auserkoren) (Mozart) (I) (Orchestra)
545m   13 Apr. 1911   053260   76125   DB 331   85288   78.00   HMV VB 21

85. PERLE DU BRESIL: Charmant oiseau (David) (F) (Orchestra)
2221c   9 Jun. 1911   Unpublished

86. HUGUENOTS: O beau pays de la Touraine (Meyerbeer) (F) (Orchestra)
2222c   9 Jun. 1911   033125   76021   DB 276   85282   80.00   Victor: 88382; AGSB 59; Lp

87. MIGNON: Titania ist herabgestiegen (Polonaise) (Je suis Titania) (Thomas) (G) (Orchestra)
2223c   9 Jun. 1911   043174   76038   DB 366   85286   80.00

88. PERLE DU BRESIL: Charmant oiseau (David) (F) (flute: DeVries; Orchestra)
2227c   10 Jun. 1911   033126   76022   DB 295   85283   80.00   (Victor 88435); Lp

Discog. No.	Matrix No.	HMV/Opera Disc					
		Date	S/f Cat. Nos.	D/f Cat. Nos.	Speed	Re-issues	
89.	2228c	ERNANI: Sorta e la notte . . . Ernani, involami (Verdi) (I) (Orchestra) 10 Jun. 1911	Unpublished				
90.*	2229c	ERNANI: Sorta e la notte . . . Ernani, involami (Verdi) (I) (Orchestra) 10 Jun. 1911	053265 76129	DB 296 85294	80.00	Victor 88383	
91.	2230c	Variationen (Proch, Op. 164) (G) (Orchestra) 10 Jun. 1911	Unpublished				
92.	2246c	Villanelle (F. vander Elst; Dell 'Acqua) (F) (Orchestra) 23 Jun. 1911	033127 76023	DB 297 85283	80.00	Victor 88410; Lp	
93.	2247c	ZAUBERFLÖTE: Der Hölle Rache (Mozart) (G) (Orchestra) 23 Jun. 1911	Unpublished				
94.	2248c	MUETTE DE PORTICI: O moment enchanteur (Auber) (F) (Orchestra) 24 Jun. 1911	Unpublished				
95.	2249c	MUETTE DE PORTICI: O moment enchanteur (Auber) (F) (Orchestra) 24 Jun. 1911	033128 76240	DB 276 85281	80.00	HMV VB 22; Lp	
96.	2250c	LAKME: Où va la jeune Hindoue? (Air des clochettes) (Delibes) (F) (Orchestra) 24 Jun. 1911	Unpublished				
97.	2386c	ZAUBERFLÖTE: Der Hölle Rache (Mozart) (G) (Orchestra) 12 Sep. 1911	043185 76039	DB 365 85288	75.00	HMV VB 21; Lp	

98. ROMEO UND JULIA: Ich will in dem Traume (Walzer) (Romeo et Juliette: Je veux vivre dans ce rêve) (Gounod) (G) (Orchestra)
2387c   12 Sep. 1911   043186 76040   DB 774 85287   75.00

99. LAKME: Où va la jeune Hindoue? (Air des clochettes) (Delibes) (F) (Orchestra)
2411c   15 Sep. 1911   033144 76024   DB 295 85284   75.00   IRCC 161; Lp

100. Variationen (Proch, Op. 164) (G) (Orchestra)
2412c   15 Sep. 1911   Unpublished

101. MARGARETHE: Ach, welch ein Glück (Juwelen-Arie) (Faust: Air des bijoux) (Gounod) (G) (Orchestra)
2413c   15 Sep. 1911   043192 76041   DB 360 85289   75.00

102.* Wiegenlied (Schlafe, mein Prinzchen) (Gotter; Flies attrib. Mozart) (G) (Orchestra)
608m   9 Apr. 1912   043193 76042   DB 774 85132   76.00   (Victor 88446)

103. MIRELLA: O d'amor messagera (Mireille: O légère hirondelle) (Gounod) (I) (Orchestra)
609m   9 Apr. 1912   053290 76242   DB 373 85292   76.00   AGSB 29

104. PURITANI: Vien diletto (Bellini) (I) (Orchestra)
610m   9 Apr. 1912   Unpublished

105. PURITANI: Vien diletto (Bellini) (I) (Orchestra)
610 1/2 m   9 Apr. 1912   053289 76241   DB 296 85291   76.00   Lp

106. WILDSCHÜTZ: Auf des Lebens raschen Wogen (Lortzing) (G) (Orchestra)
716m   28 May 1913   Unpublished

107. Parla! (Arditi) (I) (Orchestra)
717m   28 May 1913   Unpublished

Discog. No.	Matrix No.	HMV/Opera Disc		D/f Cat. Nos.	Speed	Re-issues
		S/f Cat. Nos.	Date			
108.*	CONTES D'HOFFMANN: Les oiseaux dans la charmille (Offenbach) (F) (Orchestra)					
	718m	033164 76025	28 May 1913	DB 352 85282	78.00	Lp
109.	RATTO DAL SERAGLIO: Che pur aspro al cuore (Entführung aus dem Serail: Martern aller Arten) (Mozart) (I) (Orchestra)					
	719m	053326 76332	30 May 1913	DB 331 85293	78.00	Lp
110.	ROBERT LE DIABLE: Robert, toi que j'aime (Meyerbeer) (F) (Orchestra)					
	720m	033165 76026	30 May 1913	DB 297 85284	78.00	AGSB 29; Lp
111.*	GLI UGONOTTI: Salute, o cavalieri (Huguenots: Une dame noble et sage) (Meyerbeer) (I) (Orchestra)					
	721m	Unpublished (except for dubbing of a test pressing. See note)	30 May 1913			
112.	Parla! (Arditi) (I) (Orchestra)					
	1089s	Unpublished	10 Jun. 1913			
113.	Parla! (Arditi) (I) (Orchestra)					
	1089 1/2 s	Unpublished	10 Jun. 1913			
114.	WILDSCHÜTZ: Auf des Lebens raschen Wogen (Lortzing) (G) (Orchestra)					
	1090s	Unpublished	10 Jun. 1913			
115.	ROBERT LE DIABLE: Robert, toi que j'aime (Meyerbeer) (F) (Orchestra)					
	1091s	Unpublished	10 Jun. 1913			
116.	BOHEME: Si, mi chiamano Mimi (Puccini) (I) (Orchestra)					
	1173s	053327 76130	18 Sep. 1913	DB 353 85294	78.00	

117. WILDSCHÜTZ: Auf des Lebens raschen Wogen (Lortzing) (G) (Orchestra)
1174s   18 Sep. 1913   043247 76047   ——— 85291   78.00   IRCC 161; AGSB 59; Lp

118. Parla! (Arditi) (I) (Orchestra)
1175s   18 Sep. 1913   053329 76131   ——— 85295   78.00

119.* ROSENKAVALIER: Kann mich auch an ein Mädel erinnern (Monolog der Marschallin) (Richard Strauss) (G) (Orchestra)
1176s   18 Sep. 1913   043248 76048   DB 373 85289   78.00   Lp

120.* TROUBADOR: Es glänzte schon das Sternenheer (Trovatore: Tacea la notte) (Verdi) (G) (Orchestra)
892m   1915   043276 76049   ——— 85290   78.00   Lp

121.* TROUBADOR: Ein unnennbares Sehren (Trovatore: Di tale amor) (Verdi) (G) (Orchestra)
893m   1915   043277 76050   ——— 85290   78.00   Lp

III. The Victor Talking Machine Co., Camden, New Jersey, and New York, 1914–1917

(B = 10"; C = 12")

Discog. No.	Matrix No. -Take	Date	Victor/HMV S/f Cat. Nos.	Victor/HMV D/f Cat. Nos.	Speed	Re-issues
122.*	Il Bacio (Aldighieri; Arditi) (I) (Or. Rogers)					
	C-14362-1	22 Jan. 1914	88476	053261	DB 298	76.00
123.	NOZZE DI FIGARO: Deh vieni, non tardar (Mozart) (I) (Or. Rogers)					
	C-14363-1	22 Jan. 1914	88450	—	—	76.00
124.	TRAVIATA: Ah! fors' è lui . . . Sempre libera! (Verdi) (I) (Or. Rogers)					
	C-14364-1	22 Jan. 1914	88471	2-053100	6163	
	-2	5 Mar. 1914			DB 294	76.00
125.*	Parla! (Arditi) (I) (Or. Rogers)					
	C-14365-1	22 Jan. 1914	—	—	—	
	-2	5 Mar. 1914	88463	—	—	
	-3	5 Mar. 1914	88463	2-053098	6364	DB 298	76.00
126.	PURITANI: Qui la voce (Bellini) (I) (Or. Rogers)					
	B-14539-1,-2	5 Mar. 1914	87179	7-53012	DA 248	76.00
127.	PURITANI: Vien, diletto (Bellini) (I) (Or. Rogers)					
	C-14540-1	5 Mar. 1914	88470	2-053099	—	76.00	Lp
128.	BALLO IN MASCHERA: Amici miei, soldati . . . La rivedrà nell'estasi (Verdi) (I) (w. Caruso, DeSegurola, Rothier, Met. Opera Chorus/Giulio Setti) (Or. Scognamiglio)					
	C-14659-1,-2	3 Apr. 1914	89077	2-054052	10005	DM 103	76.00	Lp; CD

129. BALLO IN MASCHERA: Così scritto è lassù . . . È scherzo od e follia (Verdi) (I) (w. Caruso, Duchêne, DeSegurola, Rothier, Met. Opera Chorus/Setti) (Or. Scognamiglio)

C-14560-1,-2 3 Apr. 1914	89076	2-054050	10005	DM 103	76.00	16-5000; Lp; CD

130. TRAVIATA: Dite alla giovine (Verdi) (I) (w. Pasquale Amato) (Or. Setti)

C-14716-1,-2 16 Apr. 1914	89079	2-054054	—	DB 135	76.60	15-1020

131. TRAVIATA: Imponete! (Verdi) (I) (w. Amato) (Or. Setti)

C-14717-1,-2 16 Apr. 1914	89081	2-054058	—	DB 135	76.60	15-1020

132. RIGOLETTO: Figlia! Mio padre! . . . Ah! Deh non parlare al misero (Verdi) (I) (w. Amato) (Or. Setti)

C-14718-1,-2 16 Apr. 1914	89082	2-054060	—	—	76.60

133. Wiegenlied (Schlafe, mein Prinzchen) (Gotter; Flies attrib. Mozart) (Or. Rogers) [12" recordings (E), 10" (G)]

C-16027-1,-2 17 May 1915	Unpublished			
B-16027-1 8 Jun. 1915	87234	—	—	74.23

134. Sulle onde del Danubio (An der schönen blauen Donau) (Blue Danube Waltz) (Johann Strauss, Op. 314) (I) (Or. Rogers)

C-16028-1,-2 17 May 1915					
-3,-4 8 Jun. 1915	—	—	—		74.23
-5 9 Jun. 1915	83540; 88664	2-053184	6162	DB 293	74.23

135. Ben Bolt (Thomas Dunn English; Nelson Kneass) (E) (Or. Rogers)

C-16029-1 17 May 1915	—	—	—	74.23
-2,-3 8 Jun. 1915	88451	—	—	74.23

136.* ERNANI: Sorta è la notte . . . Ernani, involami . . . Tutto sprezzo che d'Ernani (Verdi) (I) (Or. Rogers)

C-16041-1 24 May 1915 (no recit.)	—	—	—		74.23
-2,-3 9 Jun. 1915	88383	2-053051	6163	DB 296	74.23

137. Ma Curly-Headed Babby (words and music: George H. Clutsam) (E) (Or. Rogers)

C-16042-1,-2 24 May 1915	88543	—	78.26

Discog. No.	Matrix No.	-Take	Date	Victor/HMV — S/f Cat. Nos.	D/f Cat. Nos.	Speed	Re-issues
138.	**BALLO IN MASCHERA: Volta la terrea (Verdi) (I) (Or. Rogers)**						
	B-16086	-1,-2	9 Jun. 1915	7-53026 87235	—	74.23	DA 138
139.	**Just You (Harry T. Burleigh) (E) (Or. Bourdon)**						
	B-17782	-1,-2	2 Jun. 1916	87261	—	76.00	—
140.	**"Go to Sleep, my Dusky Baby" (Based on Dvořák's "Humoresque") (Frank Rix) (E) (Or. Bourdon)**						
	B-17783	-1,-2	2 Jun. 1916	Unpublished			
		-3,-4	27 Jun. 1916	Unpublished			
141.	**"Voices of the Woods" (a k a "Welcome, Sweet Springtime") (Based on Rubinstein's Melody in F) (Michael Watson) (E) (cello: Bourdon; harp; Str. Qt.)**						
	B-17784	-1,-2	2 Jun. 1916	87250 2-3402	—	76.00	DA 250
142.	**MARTHA: The Last Rose of Summer (Old Irish air intro. in Flotow opera) (Thomas Moore) (E) (Or. Bourdon)**						
	C-17785	-1,-2	2 Jun. 1916	88567 03684	—	76.00	—
143.	**The Bird's Song (Fågelns visa) (Z. Topelius; W. Th. Söderberg) (E) (Or. Pasternack)**						
	B-18914	-1	20 Dec. 1916	87268 2-3400	—	76.00	DA 250
144.	**When I was Seventeen (Swedish folk tune) (När jag blef sjuton år) (Henry J. G. Chapman; H. Lilljebjörn, 1797–1875) (E) (Or. Pasternack)**						
	B-18915	-1,-2	20 Dec. 1916	87270	—	76.00	—
145.	**Vino, donne e canto (Wine, Women and Song) (J. Strauss, Op. 333) (I) (Or. Pasternack)**						
	C-19858	-1,-2	16 May 1917	88588 2-053152	6162	76.00	DB 293
146.*	**Elfenlied (Eduard Mörike; Hugo Wolf) (G) (cello: Bourdon; Or. Pasternack)**						
	B-19859	-1,-2	16 May 1917	(87279)	Unpublished		

IV. Thomas A. Edison, Inc., West Orange, New Jersey

Vertical cut, acoustical 1917–1925; Electrical 1928–1929
(All discs 10″, 80.00 rpm, in English unless otherwise noted)

Discog. No.	Matrix No. Takes	Date	Disc. Cat. No.	Cyl. Matrix No.	Cyl. Cat. No.	Re-issues
147.	Air and variations (Proch, Op. 164) (I) (Orchestra)					
	5937 A-B-C	9 Dec. 1917				
	F-G-H	14 Jan. 1918	82134			
	J-K-L	5 Jun. 1918	82134	14170-3	29013	Lp
148.*	Lullaby (words and music: Joseph Kline Emmet) (w. Criterion Qt.) (Orchestra)					
	5942 A-B-C	21 Dec. 1917	82550			
	F-G-H	31 May 1918	82550	14380-1	29030	
	J-K-L	26 Sep. 1919	82550			
149.	Long, Long Ago (words and music: Thomas Haynes Bayly) (Orchestra)					
	5948 A-B-C	31 Dec. 1917	82550			
	F-G-H	28 May 1918	82550	14206-2	29069	
150.*	My Old Kentucky Home (Foster) (w. Criterion Qt.) (Orchestra)					
	5966 A-B-C	11 Jan. 1918	82551			
	F-G-H	31 May 1918	82551	14369-2	29008	
151.	"Ave Maria" (music based on *Cavalleria rusticana* Intermezzo) (Mascagni) (I) (vln. Marie Zentay) (Orchestra)					
	5972 A-B-C	11 Jan. 1918				
	F-G	7 Feb. 1918	82549			
	J-K-L	28 May 1918	82549	14326-1	29027	

Discog. No.	Matrix No. Takes	Date	Disc. Cat. No.	Cyl. Matrix No.	Cyl. Cat. No.	Re-issues
152.*	Aloha Oe (Liliuokalani) (w. Criterion Qt.) (Orchestra)					
	5992 A-B-**C**	31 Jan. 1918	82551	14201-3	29007	
	F-**G**-H	3 Jun. 1918	82551			
153.	DINORAH: Ombra leggiera (Pardon de Ploërmel: Ombre légère) (Shadow song) (Meyerbeer) (I) (Orchestra)					
	6214 A-**B**-C	10 Jun. 1918	—	—		
	F-G	13 Feb. 1919	—	—		
	J-K-**L**	18 May 1921	82251	—		Lp
154.*	There's a Long, Long Trail (Stoddard King; Zo Elliott) (w. Criterion Qt.) (Orchestra)					
	6217 A-**B-C**	11 Jun. 1918	82145	—		
155.*	Little Alabama Coon (words and music: Hattie Starr) (w. Chorus) (Orchestra)					
	6223 A-**B**-C	15 Jun. 1918	82562	14130-4	29023	
	F-G-**H**	26 Sep. 1919	82562	—		
156.	RIGOLETTO: Caro nome (Verdi) (I) (Orchestra)					
	6508 A-B	16 Dec. 1918	—	—		
	F-G-H	2 Apr. 1919	—	—		
	J-K	28 May 1919	82568	—		
157.*	ERMINIE: Lullaby (Dear Mother, in Dreams I See Her) (Harry Paulton, Claxson Bellamy; Edward Jacobowski) (w. Chorus) (Orchestra)					
	6585 A-**B-C**	24 Jan. 1919	82174	—		
158.	CRISPINO E LA COMARE: Io non sono più (Ricci) (I) (Orchestra)					
	6628 A-**B**	19 Feb. 1919	82563	—		

159. FIGLIA DEL REGGIMENTO; Evviva la Francia (Fille du Régiment; Salut à la France) (Donizetti) (I) (Orchestra)
6695 A-B-C   18 Mar. 1919   82568   14461-2   29034

160. (a) From the Land of the Sky-Blue Water (Nelle Eberhart; Charles Wakefield Cadman, Op. 45 No. 1); (b) Dixie (words and music: Daniel Decatur Emmett) (Orchestra)
6709 A-B-C   7 Apr. 1919   82174   ———   Lp

161.* Silent Night (Stille Nacht) (Joseph Mohr; Franz Gruber) (Orchestra)
6714 A-B-C   9 Apr. 1919   82171   ———
F-G   5 May 1921   82171   ———
J-K-L   4 Jun. 1924   82171   ———

162. Onde del Danubio (Waves of the Danube) (Ivanovici) (I) (Orchestra)
6807 A-B-C   26 May 1919   82198
F-G   14 Jan. 1920   82198

163.* O Holy Night (John Sullivan Dwight; Adam) (Orchestra)
6817 A-B-C   4 Jun. 1919   82171   14481-1   29040
F-G-H   6 May 1921   82171   ———

164.* Kentucky Babe (Richard Buck; Adam Geibel) (w. Lyric Male Qt.) (Orchestra)
7092 A-B-C   7 Jan. 1920   82189   (C)14653-2   29053

165. (a) By the Waters of Minnetonka: (b) Lullaby (J. M. Cavanass; Thurlow Lieurance) (pf. Coenraad V. Bos)
7104 A-B-C-F   12 Jan. 1920   82189   (A)15030-1   29076

166. (a) Ave Maria (Composer not known); (b) THAIS: "Meditation" (Massenet) (w. Albert Spalding)
7126 A-B-C   21 Jan. 1920   (Rejected)

167.* Hush Little Baby, Don't You Cry (Belasco) (w. Lyric Male Qt.) (Orchestra)
7368 A-B-C   26 May 1920   82204   14887-2   29067

Discog. No.	Matrix No.	Takes	Date	Disc. Cat. No.	Cyl. Matrix No.	Cyl. Cat. No.	Re-issues
168.*	When You and I Were Young, Maggie (George W. Johnson; J. A. Butterfield) (w. Lyric Male Qt.) (Orchestra)						
	7369	A-B-C	26 May 1920	(Rejected)			
169.*	IL PENSEROSO: (L'Allegro) Sweet Bird (John Milton; G. F. Handel) (w. flute) (Orchestra)						
	7372	A-B-C	28 May 1920	[ED 725 or 726]			
170.*	THE SPRING MAID (Die Sprudelfee): Day Dreams, Visions of Bliss (H. B. and R. B. Smith; Heinrich Reinhardt) (Orchestra)						
	7390	A-B-C	7 Jun. 1920	[ED 698]			
171.	NORMA: Casta Diva (Bellini) (I) (Orchestra)						
	7712	A-B-C	31 Dec. 1920	82229			
172.	DON GIOVANNI: Non mi dir (Mozart) (I) (Orchestra)						
	7736	A-B-C	12 Jan. 1921	82229			
173.	Kom Kjyra (Norsk Fjallvisa) (Norwegian Echo Song) (Herdsman's song) (H. A. Bjerregaard?; Waldemar Thrane) (in Norwegian) (pf. Coenraad V. Bos)						
	7738	A-B-C	13 Jan. 1921	82230			
174.	Angel's Serenade (La Leggenda Vallacca) (Harrison Millard; Gaetano Braga) (vln. Spalding; pf. Robert Gayler)						
	8005	A-B-C	20 May 1921	82240			
175.	THE MERRY WIDOW: Waltz song (Adrian Ross; Franz Lehàr) (Orchestra)						
	8011	A-B-C	23 May 1921	82240			
176.	(a) The Bird Song (Der Vogel am Wald) (Taubert); (b) The Night Wind (Roland Farley) (w. flute and pf.)						
	8422	A-B-C	14 Apr. 1922	82325			
		F-G-H	5 Jun. 1924	82325			

177.* Vesper Hymn (arr. Bortniansky) (w. Lyric Male Qt.) (Orchestra)
8423 A-B-C   14 Apr. 1922   82292 |

178. (a) Ständchen (Schack; R. Strauss, Op. 17 No. 2); (b) Maria Wiegenlied (Boelitz; Reger, Op. 76 No. 52) (G) (pf.)
8442 A-B-C   5 May 1922   82269 |

179. CLARI, or THE MAID OF MILAN: Home Sweet Home (J. H. Payne; Sir Henry Bishop) (pf.)
8972 A-B-C-D   11 May 1923   82292 |

180. Elf and Fairy (John H. Densmore) (pf.)
9550 A-B-C   5 Jun. 1924   82325 |

181.* Lullaby Moon (w. flute and pf.)
10438 A-B-C   17 Jun. 1925   [ED 1666; ED 1670]

182.* On Wings of Song (Auf Flügeln des Gesanges) (Heine; Mendelssohn, Op. 34 No. 2)
18169 A-B-C   13 Jan. 1928   [ED 2437; ED 2438]

183.* On Wings of Song (Auf Flügeln des Gesanges) (Mendelssohn, Op. 34 No. 2) (pf.?)
N-105 A-B-C   13 Jan. 1928

184.* Songs My Mother Taught Me (Als die alte Mutter) (Natalia Macfarren; Dvořák, Op. 55 No. 4)
18173 A-B-C   18 Jan. 1928   [ED 2439; ED 2440]

185.* Songs My Mother Taught Me (Macfarren; Dvořák, Op. 55 No. 4)
N-106 Takes?   18 Jan. 1928   No data available

186.* Auf Flügeln des Gesanges (Mendelssohn, Op. 34 No. 2) (G) (pf. Herman Neuman)
18195 A-B-C   26 Jan. 1928   80888 |

187.* Auf Flügeln des Gesanges (Mendelssohn, Op. 34 No. 2) (G) (pf. Neuman)
N-107 A-B-C   26 Jan. 1928 |

Discog. No.	Matrix No. / Takes	Date	Disc. Cat. No.	Cyl. Matrix No.	Cyl. Cat. No.	Re-issues
188.*	Als die alte Mutter (Songs My Mother Taught Me) (Dvořák) (G) (vln. Herbert Soman; pf. Neuman)					
	18196 A-B-C	26 Jan. 1928	80888	——		
189.*	Als die alte Mutter (Songs My Mother Taught Me) (Dvořák) (G) (vln. Herbert Soman; pf. Neuman)					
	N-108 A-B-C	26 Jan. 1928	(Rejected)			
190.*	The Last Rose of Summer (Moore)					
	Exp. 185 A	11 Feb. 1929	——	——		
191.*	The Blue Danube Waltz (J. Strauss)					
	Exp. 185 A	11 Feb. 1929	——	——		

V. Deutsche Grammophon-AG (Polydor), Berlin, 1921–1922?

(All 30 cm)

Discog. No.	Matrix No.	Date	Cat. Nos.	Speed	Re-issues
192.	Peer Gynt: Solvejg's Lied (Grieg, Op.23 No. 19) (G) (Orchestra)				
	505 1/2 as	1921	043369 76417 85296	78.00	Jap. Polydor 60010; Lp
193.	La Capinera (Benedict) (I) (Orchestra)				
	513 1/2 as	1921	Unpublished		
194.	Ave Maria ("Ellens Gesang iii") (Adam Storck; Schubert, D. 839) (G) (Orchestra)				
	514as	1921	Unpublished		
195.	Ave Maria (Storck; Schubert, D. 839) (G) (Orchestra)				
	514 1/2 as	1921	Unpublished		
196.	Vespergesang, Russischer (Jubilate) (Vesper Hymn) (Trad. arr. Seidler-Winkler) (G) (w. Male Chorus) (Orchestra)				
	327av	1921	B24018 76425 85297	78.00	Lp
197.	La Capinera (Benedict) (I) (w. flute and bells) (Orchestra)				
	328 1/2 av	1921	J24002 76463 85299	78.00	Lp
198.	DINORAH: Schattentanz (Pardon de Ploërmel: Ombre légère) (Shadow song) (Meyerbeer) (G) (Orchestra)				
	333 av	1921	Unpublished?	78.00	
199.	DINORAH: Schattentanz (Pardon de Ploërmel: Ombre légère) (Shadow song) (Meyerbeer) (G) (Orchestra)				
	333 1/2 av	1921	B24017 76425 85298	78.00	Lp

Discog. No.	Matrix No.	Date	Cat. Nos.	Speed	Re-issues
200.	334av	Ständchen (Schack; R. Strauss, Op. 17 No. 2) (G) (Orchestra)			
		1921	B24038 76457 85296	78.00	Lp
201.	341av	Ave Maria (Storck; Schubert, D. 839) (G) (Orchestra)			
		1921	043370 76418 85287	78.00	Jap. Polydor 60010; Lp
202.	342av	NORMA: Casta diva! . . . Ah! bello a me ritorna (Bellini) (I) (Orchestra)			
		1921	J24001 76458 85298	78.00	Lp
203.*	758av	DON GIOVANNI: Batti, batti, o bel Masetto (Mozart) (I) (Orchestra)			
		1922?	J24006 76498 85301	78.00	Lp
204.	759av	Carnevale de Venezia (Carnival of Venice) (Pt. 1) (Benedict) (I) (Orchestra)			
		1922?	J24007 76499 85300	78.00	Lp
205.	760av	Carnevale de Venezia (Carnival of Venice) (Pt. 2) (Benedict) (I) (w. flute) (Orchestra)			
		1922?	J24008 76500 85300	78.00	Lp
206.	761av	Sapphische Ode (Hans Schmidt; Brahms, Op. 94 No. 4) (G) (pf.)			
		1922?	B24133 76501 85299	78.00	Lp
207.*	781 av	LOHENGRIN: Du Ärmste kannst wohl (Wagner) (G) (w. Felicia Kaschowska) (Orchestra)			
		1922?	B25016 —— 78543	78.00	Lp
208.*	78?av	FIGAROS HOCHZEIT: Duette (Nozze di Figaro) (Mozart) (G) (w. Kaschowska) (Orchestra)			
		1922?	Unpublished		

VI. The Gramophone Co., Ltd., Hayes and London, 1922–1924

(Bb = 10"; Cc = 12")

Discog. No.	Matrix No. -Take	Date	Cat. Nos.	Speed	Re-issues
209.*	DIE SCHÖNE MÜLLERIN: No. 2: Wohin? (Wilhelm Müller; Schubert, D. 795) (G) (pf. Clarence Raybould)				
	Bb 2009-1,-2	23 Oct. 1922	7-43043 ——	78.00	
210.*	Der Nussbaum (Mosen; Schumann, Op. 25 No. 3) (G) (pf. Raybould)				
	Bb 2010-1,-2,-3	23 Oct. 1922	Unpublished		
211.*	Auf Flügeln des Gesanges (Heine; Mendelssohn, Op. 34 No. 2) (G) (pf. Raybould)				
	Bb 2011-1,-2	23 Oct.1922	7-43044	78.00	Lp
212.*	Horch! Horch! die Lerche (Shakespeare, Von Schlegel; Schubert, D. 889) (G) (pf. Raybould)				
	Bb 2012-1,-2,-3	23 Oct. 1922	7-43045 ——	78.00	
213.*	None But the Weary Heart (Goethe; Tchaikovsky, Op. 6 No. 6) (E) (w. flute; pf. Raybould)				
	Bb 2013-1,-2,-3	24 Oct. 1922	2-3710 ——	78.00	
214.*	DIE SCHÖNE MÜLLERIN: No. 7: Ungeduld (Müller; Schubert, D. 795) (G) (pf. Raybould)				
	Bb 2014-1,-2	24 Oct. 1922	7-43046 DA 251	78.00	Lp
215.	The Night Wind (Farley) (E) (pf. Raybould)				
	Bb 2016-1,-2,-3,-4	24 Oct. 1922	2-3752 DA 634	78.00	
216.*	DIE SCHÖNE MÜLLERIN: No. 2: Wohin? (Schubert, D. 795) (G) (pf. Bos)				
	Bb 2009-3,-4	4 Jun. 1923	7-43043X DA 251; DA 634	78.00	Lp

Discog. No.	Matrix No.	-Take	Date	Cat. Nos.	Speed	Re-issues
217.	Der Nussbaum (Mosen; Schumann, Op. 25 No. 3) (G) (pf. Bos)					
	Bb 2010-4		4 Jun. 1923	Unpublished		
218.	Auf Flügeln des Gesanges (On wings of song) (Heine; Mendelssohn, Op. 34 No. 2) (G) (pf. Bos)					
	Bb 2011-3,-4		4 Jun. 1923	7-43044X DA 382	78.00	Lp
219.	Horch! Horch! die Lerche (Shakespeare, Von Schlegel; Schubert, D. 889) (G) (pf. Bos)					
	Bb 2012-4,-5		4 Jun. 1923	7-43045X DA 382	78.00	Lp
220.	None But the Weary Heart (Goethe; Tchaikovsky, Op. 6 No. 6) (E) (vln. Marjorie Hayward; pf. Bos)					
	Bb 2013-4,-5		4 Jun. 1923	2-3710X DA 205	78.00	
221.	DIE SCHÖNE MÜLLERIN: No. 7: Ungeduld (Müller; Schubert, D. 795) (G) (pf. Bos)					
	Bb 2014-3		4 Jun. 1923	Unpublished		
222.	Widmung (Du mein Seele) (Rückert; Schumann, Op. 25 No. 1) (G) (pf. Bos)					
	Bb 3040-1,-2		4 Jun. 1923	7-43049 DA 557	78.00	Lp
223.	Phillis Has Such Charming Graces (Anthony Young; words and music arr. H. Lane Wilson) (E) (pf. Bos)					
	Bb 3041-1,-2		4 Jun. 1923	2-3773 DA 205	78.00	
224.	I'd Be a Butterfly (words and music: Bayly) (E) (pf. Bos)					
	Bb 3042-1,-2		4 Jun. 1923	Unpublished		
225.	Wiegenlied (Schlafe, mein Prinzchen) (Gotter; Flies attrib. Mozart) (G) (pf. Bos)					
	Bb 3043-1,-2		4 Jun. 1923	7-43048 DA 557	78.00	
226.	Dixie ('Way Down South in Dixie) (Emmett) (E) (pf. Bos)					
	Bb 3044-1,-2		4 Jun. 1923	Unpublished		

227. JOSHUA: O! Had I Jubal's Lyre (Handel) (E) (Or. Julius Harrison)
Bb 5425-1,-2   3 Dec. 1924   2-3935   DA 676   78.00

228. Birdling, Why Sing? (Der Vogel im Wald) (Taubert) (E) (flute: John Amadio; Or. Harrison)
Cc 5426-1,-2,-3   3 Dec. 1924   03845   DB 814   78.00

229. Should He Upbraid? (Shakespeare; Bishop) (E) (flute: Amadio; Or. Harrison)
Cc 5427-1,-2   3 Dec. 1924   Unpublished

230. Should He Upbraid? (Shakespeare; Bishop) (E) (flute: Amadio; Or. Harrison)
Cc 5427-3,-4   4 Dec. 1924   03844   DB 814   78.00

231. Alleluia! (Easter Hymn) (arr. G. O'Connor Morris) (E) (w. chimes) (Or. Harrison)
Bb 5431-1,-2   4 Dec. 1924   2-3934   DA 676   78.00

232. NOZZE DI FIGARO: Voi che sapete (Mozart) (I) (Or. Harrison)
Bb 5432-1,-2   4 Dec. 1924   7-53083   DA 675   78.00

233. Vesper Hymn (Jubilate!) (Eng. words Moore; Russian air, arr. Stevenson) (E) (Or. Harrison)
Bb 5433-1,-2   4 Dec. 1924   2-3933   DA 675   78.00

VII. Electrola Gesellschaft M.B.H., Berlin, 1935

(10" electrical recordings)

Discog. No.	Matrix No. -Take	Date	Cat. Nos.	Speed	Re-issues
234.*	Auf dem Wasser zu singen (Vor. Stollberg; Schubert, D. 774) (G) (pf. Seidler-Winkler)				
	ORA1088-1,-2	Feb. 1935	Unpublished (except as dubbing from test)	78.26	IRCC-176rr; Lp
235.	Im Kahne (Mens jeg venter) (Grieg, Op. 60 No. 3) (G) (w. flute; pf. Seidler-Winkler)				
	ORA1089-1,-2	Feb. 1935	Unpublished		
236.*	Zweigesang ("A song Jenny Lind sang") (Mangold) (G) (w. flute; pf. Seidler-Winkler)				
	ORA1090-1	Feb. 1935	Unpublished (except as dubbing from test)	78.26	IRCC-176rr
237.	Kuckuck, wie alt (Franz Abt) (G) (pf. Seidler-Winkler)				
	ORA1091-1	Feb. 1935	Unpublished		

VIII. Private recordings made by RCA Victor, New York, 1936–1937

(10" electrical recordings)

Discog. No.	Matrix No.	-Take	Date	Cat. Nos.
238.	TOSCA: Vissi d'arte (Puccini) (I) (pf.) BS-013216-1		20 Aug. 1936	Unpublished
239.	(a) Parlez-moi d'amour (Jean Lenoir) (F and E) (pf.); (b) Im Prater blüh'n wieder die Bäume (Robert Stolz) (G) (pf.) BS-013500-1		7 Sep. 1937	Unpublished

IX. Radio broadcasts

240.   "Municipal Concert Hall," WNYC, New York, April and May 1943; 12 selections issued on Lp UORC 331
       1. On Wings of Song (Auf flügeln des Gesanges) (Mendelssohn, Op. 34 No. 2) (E) (pf. Celius Dougherty) (11 Apr. 1943?)
       2. Vergebliches Ständchen (Trad.; Brahms, Op. 84 No. 4) (G) (pf. Dougherty) (11 Apr. 1943?)
       3. Med en Vandlilje (To a Water Lily) (G) (Ibsen; Grieg, Op. 25 No. 4) (pf. Dougherty?) (11 April 1943?)
       4. A Bold Irish Boy (Trad.?) (E) (pf. Dougherty) (Date not confirmed)
       5. THE PINK LADY: My Beautiful Lady (C. S. McLellan; Ivan Caryll) (E) (pf. Dougherty?) (Date not confirmed)
       6. May Day Carol (arr. Taylor) (E) (pf. Celius Dougherty) (11 Apr. 1943)
       7. My Mother Bids Me Bind My Hair (Anne Hunter; Haydn) (E) (pf. Paul Meyer) (16 May 1943)
       8. Die Forelle (Schubart; Schubert, D. 550) (pf. Meyer) (16 May 1943)
       9. Wie Melodien zieht es mir (Groth; Brahms, Op. 105 No. 1) (pf. Meyer) (16 May 1943)
       10. Parlez-moi d'amour (Lenoir) (F and E) (pf. Meyer?) (May 1943)
       11. At Parting (Peterson; Rogers) (E) (pf. Meyer) (16 May 1943)
       12. Serenade ("Good Night! Goodnight, Beloved") (Longfellow; Nevin) (E) (pf. Meyer) (16 May 1943)

X. Hempel on (selected) microgroove (Lp)

Reference numbers refer to preceeding 78 rpm Discography when sources are known.

1. Die Goldene Stimme: "Frieda Hempel" (Odeon E 83,397)
   48; 80; 86; 88; 91; 94; 98; 108; 110; 218; 219.

2. Court Opera Classics: "Frieda Hempel" (CO 302)
   12; 15; 16; 17; 18; 19; 20; 21; 22; 28; 31; 32; 34; 35; 66; 71.

3. Court Opera Classics: "Frieda Hempel II" (CO 349)
   120; 121; 192; 196; 197; 199; 200; 201; 202; 203; 204; 205; 206; 207.

4. Court Opera Classics: "Franz Naval" (CO 394)
   23; 24.

5. Court Opera Classics: "Frieda Hempel; Hermann Jadlowker Duets" (CO 395)
   41; 42; 43; 44; 45; 46; 47; 48; 49; 56; 57; 58; 59; 60.

6. Club 99: "Frieda Hempel; Hermann Jadlowker Duets" (CL 99-2)
   Same content as No. 5, above.

7. Rococo (Ross, Court and Co.) "Famous Voices of the Past" (R-8)
   35; 49; 51; 52; 53; 54; 67; 80; 110; 116; 117; 127.

8. Vocal Excerpts from "Les Huguenots" (Eterna ELP 458)
   21; 22; 46; 47.

9. "Golden Age Ensembles" (RCA Victor LCT 1003 [WCT 4])
   129.

10. "One Hundred Years of Great Artists at the Met: The Gatti-Casazza Years I" (Met. Opera Guild, MET 402)
    119; 128.

11. "The Record of Singing" Vol. 1 (EMI RLS 724); "A Record of Singers" Vol. 1 (RLS 7706)
17; 18.

12. "Schubert Lieder on Record, 1898–1952" (EMI RLS 766) (See notes 214 and 216)
214; 216.

13. "Schumann and Brahms Lieder on Record, 1901–1952" (EMI RLS 1547003)
222.

14. "Coloratura Gems" (Scala 865)
109.

15. "Christmas from a Golden Age" (Legendary Recordings LR 212)
161.

16. "Twenty Great Sopranos/20 Arias" (TAP T-306)
97.

17. "The Fabulous Edison Cylinder" (Odyssey 32-16-0207)
147.

18. "Souvenirs of Opera" (First Series) (IRCC L-7011)
53; 54.

19. "Souvenirs of Opera" (Fifth Series) (IRCC L-7015)
29; 30

20. "Souvenirs of Opera and Song" (Sixth Series) (IRCC L-7016)
234.

21. "Souvenirs from Meyerbeer Operas" (IRCC L-7036)
153.

Notes

Reference numbers are Discography Numbers marked in text with an asterisk (*).

5. Reported title but not verified from an actual copy.

6. There was some confusion here in the Odeon plant: A copy of the record with xB 1508-2 clearly marked also has a marked-over "xB 2269"; also note the catalog number, 50247, which suggests this take was actually made at the next (early 1907) session. On the other hand, the playing speed is 73.00, whereas the speeds of the early 1907 session appear to be uniformly 72.00.

29 and 30. These selections are from a "complete" recording of *Cavalleria rusticana* on 11 double-sided 27 cm discs, recorded in Berlin in 1908. It was conducted by Friedrich Kark on matrix numbers between xB 4348 and xB 4369. Hempel sang the small role of Lola, the American soprano Frances Rose was Santuzza, and Franz Naval was Turiddu. Number 29 continues with Naval's "Trinklied" (Brindisi).

49. Speed suggested for key of G minor (normal score pitch) is 85.00. As this is out of line for speeds in general use, it is possible that the duet was recorded one tone below score pitch.

51. Recording begins in key of F at 78 rpm but drops to about 70 at end.

52. Key of B-flat throughout, but speed drops from about 80 to 71 rpm.

53 and 54. Cadenza written especially for Frieda Hempel by Camille Saint-Saëns. Rapid speed change in 54 from opening at 78.00 to the ending at 73.00.

60.^ Appears to be a maverick recording which probably should not have been published, as it was cut to about 1½" of the spindle hole. It was apparently soon replaced by xxB 5914 (Discography No. 66), which is sung one full tone lower.

61. (and other 1912 recordings). The conductor, Eduard Künneke (27 Jan. 1885– 29 Oct. 1953), was a popular composer of some 34 operas, operettas, and musical plays. He was the successor to Friedrich Kark as Odeon house conductor for a time.

72. Bruno Seidler-Winkler was the house conductor in Berlin for The Gramophone Co., and though not always stated in existing files, it is probable that he conducted all Hempel's Berlin Gramophone Co. recordings.

80. Victor imported this recording for Hempel's Metropolitan debut, and it remained in the catalogs into double faced lists. Victor (as did the Gramophone Co.) titled it "Variations on a theme from Donizetti's Daughter of the Regiment."

82. A note in the Gramophone Co. files indicates that at some time they substituted the Victor recording of "Il Bacio" (C-14362-1) for their Berlin version. Thus some pressings of DB 298 can be found with Berlin matrix 543m; others with Victor C-14362-1.

90. At some point, the Gramophone Co. substituted the Victor recording (C-16041-3) for their Berlin version. Thus some pressings of DB 296 can be found with Berlin matrix 2229c; others with the Victor recording (C-16041-3). Victor initially published (in November 1912) the Berlin version under cat-

alog 88383; they later substituted their own C-16041-3, so that both the Berlin and the Victor versions may be found with Victor catalog number 88383.

102. Victor assigned catalog number 88446 to this recording, but it was never used. The German double faced number is 85132. (The Victor version includes the cabaletta; the Gramophone version ends with the conclusion of the aria). The German double faced on 85132 is backed by Geraldine Farrar.

108. Some German pressings have a large letter A before the matrix number. This was usually used to denote an American (i.e., Victor) recording, but this is not true in this particular case, where its meaning is not known.

111. In 1955, George T. Keating, then of Los Altos, California, issued as a Christmas gift 100 copies of a dubbing of this recording made from a test pressing obtained from Mme Hempel. On the reverse of this same 12" disc were a dubbing of (a) G&T 43630 (805e) 1904 Vienna recording by Anna von Bahr Mildenburg of *Oberon: Ozean, du Ungeheuer!* and (b) the Chor der Staatsoper und Domchor (dir. Hugo Rudel) singing "Stille Nacht" (CW 230-1, 21 Aug. 1926).

119. "Creator's record" for Berlin and New York. Some pressings have a large A before the matrix number. This was usually used to denote an American (i.e., Victor) recording, but this is not true in this particular case, where its meaning is not known.

120 and 121. Recording sheets have been destroyed; thus the exact dates of recording are not known.

122. The Victor recording (C-14362-1) replaced the Berlin (543m) at some point on HMV DB 298; thus copies can be found with either version.

125. Take 2 has a defective final note and was on public sale for a very short time in the U.S. only before being replaced by take 3. All copies of take 3 bear a tiny R indicating a substitute for the originally issued take.

136. Victor originally issued the Gramophone Co. Berlin recording (2229c) as 88383 for U.S. sale in 1912, then replaced the Berlin recording with C-16041-3 (also as 88383) in mid-1915. See note 90, above.

146. Both takes for "Elfenlied" were approved, and a catalog number assigned, indicating that Victor was holding this for later publication. However, when the singer switched to Edison, she committed the ultimate sin as far as Victor was concerned. A note in the books says that both takes were destroyed on 28 Feb. 1921.

147 to 191. Edison Recordings. All sung in English unless otherwise noted. Takes boldfaced and underlined are those that were either shown as released in Edison files or those reported from existing copies of the records by several collectors who were kind enough to inform me of their holdings. Other issued takes may well exist. Each cylinder selection (dubbed from original discs) was assigned its own unique matrix number. Various horn connections were used, with the best being given a suffix number as shown which follows the cylinder matrix number. Some cylinders may have been made from otherwise unused disc takes, so some may be otherwise unpublished versions. Numbers 147 through 181 are vertical cut acoustical recordings; 182 through 191 are electrical recordings. The numbers prefixed ED (i.e., Nos. 181–184) are arbitrary numbers assigned to locate special test pressings made after the company

closed the recording business in 1929. There are said to be nearly 3000 of these at the Edison National Historic Site. Matrix numbers beginning with N (i.e., Nos. 183, 185, 187, and 189) are lateral (needle cut), as are ("Experimental") Nos. 190 and 191.

148, 150, 152, and 154. The Criterion Quartet was made up of John Young, Horatio Rench, George W. Reardon, and Donald Chalmers.

155. Chorus (called the Old Home Singers) in June 1918 was Betsy Lane Sheppard, Amy Ellerman, John Young, Horatio Rench, and Donald Chalmers. In September 1919 the singers were Elizabeth Lennox, Marion E. Cox, John Young, Horatio Rench, George W. Reardon, and Donald Chalmers.

157. Chorus was Gladys Rice, Amy Ellerman, Charles Hart, and Wilfrid Glenn.

161 and 163. The number of takes reflects the need for mold replacement: it was less expensive to make new takes than to replace the molds.

164, 167, and 168. The Lyric Male Quartet was composed of Charles Hart, Lewis James, Frederick Wheeler, and Charles F. Robinson.

169. Test of take C exists on special pressing.

170. Test of take A exists on special pressing.

177. The Lyric Male Quartet was composed of Charles Hart, Lewis James, Frederick Wheeler, and Charles F. Robinson.

181 and 182. Tests of all three takes of both exist on special pressings.

183. Note in files reads, "Lateral cut better than vertical." Tests exist, takes unknown.

184. Tests of all three takes exist on special pressings.

185 and 186. Lateral cut unpublished. Vertical cut of 186 (18195-A) received regular publication.

187. Lateral cut. Takes A and C marked "OK." Tests exist.

188 and 189. The vertical cut (18196-A) received regular publication; the lateral cut was rejected.

190 and 191. Special experimental recordings made from Thomas A. Edison birthday radio broadcast 11 Feb. 1929 on "The Edison Hour," originating from WJZ, New York. Note reads, "12" wax, 300 feed, .00379 stylus, 30 r.p.m." A story detailing the program can be found in *The New York Times* of 12 Feb. 1929, page 4, column 4. Charles Edison spoke from New York; Thomas Edison from Florida. In addition to Hempel, Moriz Rosenthal, the Edison Concert Band, Billy Murray, and the B. A. Rolfe Orchestra took part in the program.

203. Catalog No. 85301 also shown on the coupling (Selma Kurz).

207. Coupled with Olszewska, etc.

208. Reported in earlier discography by Barbara Stone, possibly from an unpublished recording owned by George Keating.

209. Bb 2009-2 was issued as 7-43043 but "cancelled" in 1923 and replaced by Bb 2009-4, then issued as 7-43043X.

210. See Discography No. 217.

211. Bb 2011-2 was issued as 7-43044 but "cancelled" in 1924 and replaced by Bb 2011-4, then issued as 7-43033X.

212. Bb 2012-1 was issued as 7-43045 but "cancelled" in 1924 and replaced by Bb 2012-4, then issued as 7-43045X.

213. Bb 2013-2 was issued as 2-32710 but "cancelled" 7 Apr. 1924 and replaced by Bb 2013-5, then issued as 2-3710X.
214. Bb 2014-2 was issued in EMI Lp set RLS 766, but the recording date is incorrectly given (p. 16) in the booklet issued with that set. The correct recording date is 24 Oct. 1922.
216. Bb 2009-4 was issued in EMI Lp set RLS 766, but the 78 rpm catalog number and the recording date given in the booklet with that set (p. 16) are in error and belong to Elena Gerhardt. The Hempel recording is used in the set, but the data should be corrected to read Bb 2009-4, HMV DA 251 and DA 634, and the date changed to 4 Jun. 1923.
234 and 236. Only releases are dubbings made from a test pressing.

Acknowledgments

Many hands have been involved in the preparation of this discography. I was originally asked to prepare it for the German edition of the Hempel *Mein Leben dem Gesang*, but my work took me overseas before I could complete much more than an outline. At her request, my notes were turned over to Barbara F. Stone of New York City, who had, unfortunately, to depend on some rather unenlightened reporting from a major Hempel collector. With what she had at hand, she did a yeoman's job which was published in *The Record Collector* (Vol. X, No. 3, 1955). This was the same issue that also reported Mme Hempel's death and the publication of her German-language autobiography. Stone's work, of course, formed the starting point for the present work, and should receive due credit.

I was immensely fortunate to have the help of one of the grandfathers of discography, Horst Wahl of Freiburg, who, as a Berlin employee of Odeon in the 1920s and '30s had made copies of many data sheets before the originals were lost during the war.

Alan Kelly of Sheffield generously supplied information he had collected from the files of The Gramophone Co. at Hayes, both with respect to Hempel's Berlin recordings made before the disruption caused by the war, and those she made in Hayes from 1922 to 1924.

For fundamental facts and information from the Edison company files, we are beholden as always to Raymond R. Wile of Flushing, New York, who has made much of his Edison research available through publication and is always generous in supplying new details.

Victor data is from the author's files compiled (with the late Ted Fagan) for The Victor Project, which are slowly being issued in volumes of *The Encyclopedic Discography of Victor Recordings*.

In addition to the above listed basic sources, I have had the excellent cooperation of four sterling editors who have labored with this manuscript. Lawrence F. Holdridge (Amityville, New York) was able to suggest playing speeds for a number of the early Odeon recordings which are missing from my own collection. William Shaman (Bemidji, Minnesota) and James B. McPherson (Rexdale, Ontario) vied with each other to turn up bits of esoteric information and attempt to make spelling and entries consistent. Reinhard G. Pauly, General Editor of Amadeus Press, has tried to ensure that the author's attempts to conform to the rules of "the awful German language" (as Mark Twain called it) did not go too far astray. To one and all my thanks.

Notes

KEY TO REFERENCES

MA	*Musical America*
MC	*Musical Courier*
NYHT	*New York Herald Tribune*
NYP	*New York Post*
NYS	*New York Sun*
NYT	*New York Times*
NYTr	*New York Tribune*
NYW	*New York World*
NYWT	*New York World Telegram*

Foreword

1. Freeman Dyson 1979, *Disturbing the Universe* (New York: Harper & Row), ix.
2. Mark Twain to William Dean Howells, quoted by Charles Neider in his 1959 edition of *The Autobiography of Mark Twain* (New York: Harper & Bros.)

Postscript

AN INFORMAL AND SELECTED CHRONOLOGY

1. MC (19 July 1905).
2. MA 17 (18 January 1913): 5.

3. MA 12 (9 July 1910): 14; Tuggle 1983, 113.
4. MA 6 (8 June 1907): 15.
5. MA 6 (23 November 1907): 17.
6. MA 12 (3 September 1910): 27.
7. MA 7 (2 May 1908): 11.
8. MA 9 (24 April 1909): 15.
9. MA 10 (6 October 1909): 62.
10. Hammelmann 1961, 115, 117, 132.
11. MA 11 (26 March 1910): 12.
12. MA 11 (9 April 1910): 11.
13. MA 12 (28 May 1910): 8.
14. MA 12 (20 August 1910): 11.
15. MC 61 (28 December 1910): 10.
16. MC 62 (21 June 1911); MC 62 (28 Jun 1911): 7.
17. MA 11 (13 November 1909): 24; MA 14 (27 May 1911): 1.
18. MA 16 (8 June 1912): 36.
19. MA 16 (19 October 1912): 1.
20. MA 17 (18 January 1913): 5.
21. MA 18 (31 May 1913): 40.
22. MA 18 (4 October 1913): 8.
23. MA 19 (15 November 1913): 40.
24. MA 19 (29 November 1913): 5.
25. NYS, 23 November 1913.
26. MA 19 (6 December 1913): 5.
27. MA 19 (13 December 1913): 2.
28. NYT 10 December 1913.
29. MA 19 (17 January 1914): 45; see also Davis 1966.
30. MA 19 (7 February 1914): 29.
31. MA 21 (19 December 1914): 2.
32. MA 20 (30 May 1914): 26.
33. MA 20 (13 June 1914) 33.
34. MA 20 (14 July 1914): 17
35. MC (24 June 1914): 42; MA 20 (20 June 1914): 31; MA 20 (27 June 1914): 29.
36. MA 20 (27 June 1914): 29.
37. MA 20 (11 July 1914): 14.
38. MA 20 (22 August 1914): 9.
39. MA 21(26 December 1914): 6.
40. MA 21 (9 January 1915): 5.
41. MA 21 (17 April 1915): 32; MA 24 (29 May 1915): 43.
42. MA 22 (17 July 1915): 6.
43. MA 22 (16 October 1915): 10.
44. MA 23 (6 November 1915): 11.
45. MA 23 (18 December 1915): 3.
46. MC (24 February 1916): 31; MA 23 (19 February 1916): 53, 54.
47. NYT 17 February 1916.
48. MA 23 (18 March 1916): 57.

49. MA 24 (20 May 1916): 3.
50. MA 24 (3 June 1916): 28.
51. MA 24 (10 June 1916): 5.
52. MA 24 (15 July 1916): 29.
53. MA 24 (28 October 1916): 4.
54. MA 25 (18 November 1916): 3.
55. MA 25 (27 January 1917): 4.
56. NYTr 25 January 1917.
57. MA 25 (3 February 1917): 4.
58. MA 25 (24 February 1917): 8.
59. MA 26 (9 June 1917): 3.
60. NYT 8 March 1918.
61. MA 27 (22 December 1917): 2.
62. MA 27 (29 December 1917): 7; MA 32 (28 August 1920): 2.
63. MA 28 (4 May 1918): 6.
64. Armstrong 1922, 155.
65. Contract and correspondence Edison National Historic Site, West Orange, NJ.
66. MA 27 (16 March 1918): 11, 18.
67. NYT 5 May 1918.
68. MA 28 (11 May 1918).
69. Edison Laboratory files, Edison National Historic Site.
70. NYT 9 June 1918, 16.
71. MA 28 (22 June 1918): 6.
72. MA 28 (19 October 1918): 18.
73. MA 29 (23 November 1918): 7.
74. MC 78 (23 January 1919): 38.
75. MA 29 (25 January 1919): 6.
76. MC (6 February 1919): 8; MA 29 (8 February 1919): 3, 18 (adv.).
77. MA 29 (22 February 1919): 24.
78. MC 78 (27 March 1919): 5.
79. MA 29 (16 April 1919): 29.
80. MA 30 (7 June 1919): 7, 8.
81. MA 30 (18 October 1919): 15.
82. MA 30 (27 September 1919): 8.
83. MA 31 (13 March 1920): 49.
84. MA 32 (29 May 1920): 2.
85. MA 32 (28 August 1920): 2.
86. MA 32 (25 September 1920): 37.
87. MA 32 (16 October 1920): 4.
88. MA 33 (11 January 1921): 39
89. MA 33 (26 February 1921): 6.
90. MA 33 (5 March 1921): 4; see also NYT 27 February 1921.
91. MA 34 (30 April 1921): 3; MA 34 (4 June 1921): 8.
92. MA 34 (28 May 1921): 17.
93. MA 34 (10 September 1921): 25; MA 35 (29 October 1921): 22.
94. MA 34 (22 October 1921): 26 (adv.).

95. NYT 6 September 1921, 2.
96. NYT 14 January 1922, 9.
97. MA 35 (11 February 1922): 56; MC 84 (16 February 1922): 40.
98. MC 84 (18 February 1922): 29.
99. NYT 22 March 1922, 14.
100. MA 36 (12 August 1922): 7; MA 36 (19 August 1922): 4.
101. MA 37 (4 November 1922): 12; MA 37 (18 November 1922): 36.
102. NYT 29 November 1922, 20; MA 37 (9 December 1922): 7.
103. NYT 7 December 1922, 21; MA 37 (16 December 1922): 48.
104. MA 37 (6 January 1923): 7.
105. NYT 23 April 1923, 18; MA 38 (2 May 1923): 21.
106. MA 38 (2 June, 1923): 40.
107. MA 38 (21 July 1923): 9.
108. MA 39 (10 November 1923): 39.
109. NYT 28 November 1923, 15.
110. NYT 13 February 1924, 17.
111. MA 40 (7 June 1924): 35; MA 40 (12 July 1924): 6.
112. MA 40 (13 September 1924): 11.
113. MA 41 (1 November 1924): 2.
114. MA 41 (27 December 1924): 2.
115. MA 41 (29 November 1924): 24–25 (adv.).
116. NYT 11 February 1925, 19.
117. NYT 25 March 1925, 24 (adv.).
118. MA 42 (9 June 1925): 23.
119. NYT 10 February 1926, 16.
120. *Singing* 1 (February 1926), 16, 37.
121. MA 44 (1 April 1926).
122. NYT 14 May 1926, 21.
123. NYT 26 June 1926, 13.
124. NYT 18 July 1926, 1; MA 44 (14 July 1926): 2.
125. NYT 6 October 1926, 22; NYT 6 November 1926, 15.
126. MC 94 (14 April 1927): 24.
127. NYT 12 June 1927, 24.
128. MA 46 (8 October 1927): 21; MC 95 (3 November 1927): 14.
129. NYT 23 November 1927, 3.
130. NYT 27 November 1927, ix.
131. MC 96 (5 January 1928): 9.
132. MA 47 (3 December 1927): 31.
133. MA vol.48 (19 May 1928): 20.
134. MA 48 (18 August 1928): 6.
135. MA 48 (29 September 1928): 19; MC 97 (18 October 1928): 16.
136. MA 48 (27 October 1928): 8.
137. MA 48 (17 November 1928): 3.
138. MA 48 (22 December 1928): 34.
139. MC 99 (14 September 1929): 10.
140. MC 100 (7 February 1930): 29.
141. MC 100 (15 March 1930): 39.

142. MC 101 (19 July 1930): 24.
143. MC 101 (25 October 1930): 40.
144. MC 101 (27 December 1930): 5.
145. MC 102 (31 January 1931): 16.
146. MC 102 (28 February 1931): 16.
147. MC 102 (4 April 1931): 14.
148. MC 103 (26 December 1931): 17.
149. Prentice-Hall 1947, *Tax Court Memorandum Decisions, No. 47183. Frieda Hempel: Docket No. 7993; 6-23-47. Years 1937, 1938. Sections 47-662–47-672.* Englewood Cliffs: N.J: Prentice-Hall, Inc. It should be noted that the figures given in this publication for Gross Receipts and Expenses for the years 1931 though 1942 are from what the tax report calls Hempel's "alleged profession," i.e., income received and expenses related to her singing career. They do not reflect income from other sources.
150. NYT 18 January 1932, 19.
151. MC 104 (23 January 1932): 13, 32; MC 104 (13 February 1932): 37.
152. Hempel to Gatti-Casazza, 13 May 1932, in Italian. Gatti-Casazza to Hempel, 16 May 1932. Courtesy Robert Tuggle, Metropolitan Opera Archives.
153. Prentice-Hall 1947.
154. Ibid.
155. NYT 5 February 1934; see also MA 54 (10 February 1934): 108.
156. NYT 29 June 1934, 16.
157. Hempel to Gatti-Casazza, 18 December 1934, in Italian. Courtesy Robert Tuggle, Metropolitan Opera Archives.
158. Prentice-Hall 1947.
159. MA 55(25 November 1935): 21.
160. MC 111 (30 November 1935): 2, 28.
161. Prentice-Hall 1947.
162. MC 113 (11 April 1936): 12.
163. MC 112 (2 May 1936): 8.
164. Prentice-Hall 1947.
165. NYT 30 February 1937, 9.
166. MC 115 (20 February 1937): 7.
167. MC 116 (1 August 1937): 21.
168. Prentice-Hall 1947.
169. NYS, 31 December 1938.
170. Prentice-Hall 1947.
171. MC 119 (4 February 1939): 10.
172. NYT 7 January 1939, 7.
173. MA 59 (13 August 1939): 12.
174. Gama Gilbert in NYT 7 October 1939, 21.
175. Prentice-Hall 1947.
176. Ibid.
177. Noel Straus in NYT 31 March 1941, 10.
178. Prentice-Hall 1947.
179. NYWT 6 February 1942, 6; NYHT, 3 December 1942, 20.
180. Prentice-Hall 1947.

181. MA 63 (10 January 1943): 16
182. MC 128 (August 1943): 9.
183. NYT 11 October 1943, 24.
184. Jerome D. Bohm in NYHT, 11 October 1943.
185. NYT 27 March 1944, 16.
186. Noel Straus in NYT 26 March 1945.
187. M. A. S. in NYT 20 January 1946.
188. Noel Straus in NYT 2 December 1946, 32.
189. R. S. in NYT 8 November 1951.
190. NYT 8 October 1955.

HEMPEL AND THE LAWYERS

1. MA 12 (4 June 1910): 3.
2. MC 64 (14 February 1912): 20.
3. MA 17 (21 December 1912): 25; see also MA 17 (28 December 1912): 24.
4. MA 19 (22 November 1913): 29.
5. NYT 14 May 1926, 2.
6. NYT 26 June 1926, 13.
7. NYT 18 July 1926, 1.
8. NYT 15 September 1927, 31.
9. NYT 10 June 1928, 15.
10. NYT 5 February 1929, 37.
11. NYT 8 February 1929, 10.
12. NYT 17 April 1930.
13. NYT 6 January 1931.
14. MC 102 (6 June 1931): 25.
15. NYT 3 June 1934, 27.
16. Prentice-Hall 1947.
17. NYT 21 April 1928.
18. Undated and unidentified clipping copyright 1943 King Features Syndicate, Inc.
19. Prentice-Hall 1947.
20. NYHT 2 April 1943.
21. Robert Tuggle 1983, *The Golden Age of Opera* (New York: Holt, Rinehart & Winston), 113–115
22. Prentice-Hall 1947.
23. Oral and written personal communications, various dates, GTK to WRM.

GEORGE T. KEATING

1. Keating 1929, vii.
2. Garden City, New York: Doubleday Doran Company, Inc.
3. John Archer Gee, "The Conrad Memorial Library of Mr. George T. Keating" in "Addresses Delivered at the Opening of the Exhibition of Mr. George T. Keating's Conrad Collection in the Sterling Memorial Library, 20 April 1938, with a Checklist of Conrad Items," Yale University, *Library Gazette*, July 1938, 1–28.
4. NYT 7 August 1941, 13.

Select Bibliography

Armstrong, William. 1922. "Frieda Hempel." Chapter 9 in *The Romantic World of Music*. New York: E. P. Dutton & Company.

Barnum, P. T. 1882. *Struggles and Triumphs; or Forty Years' Recollections*. Author's edition, revised. New York: The Courier Company.

Brower, Harriette. 1920. "Frieda Hempel." Chapter 21 in *Vocal Mastery: Talks with Master Singers and Teachers*. New York: Frederick A. Stokes Co.

Caruso, Enrico, Jr., and Andrew Farkas. 1990. *Enrico Caruso: My Father and My Family*. Portland, OR: Amadeus Press.

Davis, Ronald L. 1966. *Opera in Chicago: A Social and Cultural History, 1950–1965*. New York: Appleton Century.

Eaton, Quaintance. 1965. *The Boston Opera Company: The Story of a Unique Musical Institution*. New York: Appleton-Century.

Eaton, Quaintance. 1968. *The Miracle of the Met: An Informal History of the Metropolitan Opera, 1883–1967*. New York: Meredith Press.

Fassett, Stephen. 1939. "A Broadcast with Frieda Hempel and Some Notes on Her Records." *The Gramophone* 17 (December)

Fitzgerald, Gerald, ed. 1989. *Annals of the Metropolitan Opera: The Complete Chronicle of Performances and Artists*. Hempel performances in vol. 2, *Tables 1883–1985*. New York: The Metropolitan Opera Guild, Inc.; Boston: G. K. Hall Co.

Hammelmann, Hans. 1961. *A Working Friendship: The Correspondence between Richard Strauss and Hugo von Hofmannsthal*. Translated by Ewald Osers. New York: Random House.

Harvey, Hugh. 1955. "Frieda Hempel." *The Gramophone* 33 (December).

Hempel, Frieda. 1917. "Thoroughness in Vocal Preparation." In James Francis Cooke. 1921. *Great Singers on the Art of Singing*. Philadelphia, PA: Theo. Presser Co. Originally published in *Etude* (1917).

Hempel, Frieda (as told to Stephen Fassett). 1940. "Tetrazzini." *The American Music Lover* 6 (2): 43–47.

Hempel, Frieda. 1944. "On Creating Strauss Roles." *Musical Courier* (June): 5.

———. 1955. *Mein Leben dem Gesang: Erinnerungen.* Berlin: Argon Verlag.

Keating, George T. 1929. *A Conrad Memorial Library.* Garden City, NY: Doubleday, Doran & Co.

Kelly, Alan. 1994. *His Master's Voice/ Die Stimme Seines Herrn: The German Catalogue.* Westport, CT: Greenwood Press.

Klein, Herman. 1990. *Herman Klein and The Gramophone.* Edited by William R. Moran. Portland, OR: Amadeus Press.

Kolodin, Irving. 1953. *The Story of the Metropolitan Opera, 1883–1950.* New York: Alfred A. Knopf.

Lane, Kenneth. 1956. "Memories of Frieda Hempel." *Opera News* 20 (13 February): 10.

Martens, Frederick H. 1923. "Frieda Hempel." In *The Art of the Prima Donna and Concert Singer.* New York: D. Appleton and Company.

Moore, Gerald. 1962. *Am I Too Loud? Memories of an Accompanist.* London: Hamish Hamilton.

Prentice-Hall. 1947. *Tax Court Memorandum Decisions, No. 47183. Frieda Hempel: Docket No. 7993; 6-23-47. Years 1937, 1938. Sections 47-662–47-672.* Englewood Cliffs, NJ: Prentice-Hall, Inc.

Reed, Peter Hugh. 1955. "The Recorded Art of Frieda Hempel." *The Record Collector* 10 (3): 53–60.

Sanborn, Pitts. 1940. "Frieda Hempel Recalls Tetrazzini's Golden Hours." *New York World-Telegram,* 4 May 18.

Scott, Michael. 1977. *The Record of Singing.* London: Gerald Duckworth & Co. Ltd.

Seltsam, William H. 1947. *Metropolitan Opera Annals.* New York: H. W. Wilson Company and The Metropolitan Opera Guild.

Steane, J. B. 1974; 1993. *The Grand Tradition: Seventy Years of Singing on Record.* Second edition, Portland, OR: Amadeus Press.

Stone, Barbara F. 1955. "Frieda Hempel's Recorded Art." *The Record Collector* 10 (3): 53–71.

Tuggle, Robert. 1983. "Frieda Hempel." In *The Golden Age of Opera.* New York: Holt, Rinehart & Winston.

van Patten, Nathan. 1950. *A Memorial Library of Music at Stanford University.*

Wayner, Robert J., ed. 1976. *What Did They Sing at the Met?* 2d ed. New York: Wayner Publications.

Wile, Raymond R. 1971. "The Edison Discs of Frieda Hempel." *ARSC Journal* (Association for Recorded Sound Collections) 3 (Fall): 47–52.

Wile, Raymond R. 1978. *Edison Disc Recordings.* Philadelphia, PA: Eastern National Park and Monument Association, Historic Site.

Wile, Raymond R., comp., and Ronald Dethlefson, ed. 1985. *Edison Disc Artists & Records, 1910–1929.* 2d ed. Brooklyn, NY: APM Press.

Index of Names

Bold references indicate page numbers of illustrations.

Contributors

ELIZABETH JOHNSTON, literary executor of Frieda Hempel's estate and her secretary and companion from 1951 to 1955, trained extensively as a singer, composer, and musicologist. After receiving her Master's degree in music and composition at the University of California at Berkeley in 1937, she studied voice with Emmy Krüger in Munich and with Esther Mazzoleni in Siena and Palermo, and composition with Alfredo Casella in Siena. She received her diploma in voice at the Conservatory of Music in Florence before the war intervened in 1941. She returned to New York and then to Berkeley, singing in the San Francisco Bay area from 1942 to 1947 under the conductor Otto Schulman. In 1947 she returned to U.C. Berkeley as lecturer in music, resuming her work in composition as well. Her string quartet of 1937 has been recorded. In 1951, after Hempel's last New York recital, Johnston began to study with her, soon becoming her colleague and companion. She accompanied Hempel to Berlin in 1955 and remained with her until her death. Johnston returned to Berlin in 1961 and served as head of the translation department of the German Foundation for Development Aid until her retirement in 1980. She resides in Berlin.

WILLIAM R. MORAN, former vice president of exploration for Molycorp, a subsidiary of the Union Oil Company of California, is founder and honorary curator of the Stanford Archive of Recorded Sound. He is the author of *Melba: A Contemporary Review* (Greenwood Press, 1985); co-compiler of *The Encyclopedic Discography of Victor Recordings* (Greenwood Press, 1983–), an ongoing series; editor of *Herman Klein and The Gramophone* (Amadeus

Press, 1990); and author of *The Recordings of Lillian Nordica* as well as articles, reviews, and discographies published in *The Record Collector*, *The Opera Quarterly*, *Recorded Sound*, *Record News*, *High Fidelity*, and other journals. He is the producer for RCA Australia of *Nellie Melba: The American Recordings, 1907–1916* and is responsible for the transfers of historical discs used in the Grammy Award–winning *RCA MET: 100 Singers/100 Years*. He is a principal contributor to *Opera and Concert Singers* (Garland, 1985), associate editor of the Opera Biographies reprint series for Arno Press, and the author of more than twenty-five singers' discographies. He has been associate editor of the American Association of Petroleum Geologists' *Bulletin* since 1959 and has contributed many articles, reviews, and biographies to technical and scientific journals.